Nelson and Napoleon

Also by Christopher Lee

Non Fiction

A History of the English-speaking Peoples (ed.)
Seychelles – Political Castaways
From the Sea End
Nicely Nurdled Sir
War in Space
Through the Covers (ed.)
The Final Decade
This Sceptred Isle
This Sceptred Isle – The 20th Century
This Sceptred Isle – The Dynasties
Eight Bells and Top Masts
1603

Fiction

The Madrigal
The Bath Detective
The Killing of Sally Keemer
The Killing of Cinderella
The House

Nelson and Napoleon

The Long Haul to Trafalgar

Christopher Lee

First published in 2005
by HEADLINE BOOK PUBLISHING

1

Cataloguing in Publication Data is available from the British Library

Typeset in BellMT and Frutiger 57Cn by Avon DataSet Ltd,
Bidford-on-Avon, Warwickshire

Text design by Avon DataSet Ltd
Picture section by Ben Cracknell Studios
Charts by ML Design

Printed and bound in Great Britain by
Clays Ltd, St Ives plc

ISBN 0 7553 1041 1

HEADLINE BOOK PUBLISHING
A division of Hodder Headline
338 Euston Road
London NW1 3BH

www.headline.co.uk

For
Master George

Contents

Chronology

Date	Major World Events	Nelson	Napoleon	Other Events
1757	Robert Clive conquers Bengal			
1758		Horatio Nelson born in Burnham Thorpe Rectory, Norfolk		Reappearance of Halley's comet
1759	Victory against the French at Quebec and death of General James Wolfe			Josiah Wedgwood starts Burslem Pottery
1760	George III succeeds to the throne			James Brindley designs the Worsley-Manchester canal, the first man-made canal in Britain
1762				Rousseau's *Social Contract* and *Émile* published
1763	End of the Seven Years War			Dr Johnson and Boswell meet
1764				Spinning Jenny invented by James Hargreaves

1766		Oliver Goldsmith's *Vicar of Wakefield* published
1767		First publication of the *National Almanac*, an important navigational aid
1768		The Royal Academy of Arts is founded
1769		Captain James Cook lands on Tahiti before discovering New South Wales a year later
		Napoleon Bonaparte born in Ajaccio, Corsica
1770	In North America, the 'Boston Massacre'	
	Nelson joins the British navy	
1773	The Boston Tea Party	Richard Arkwright builds his first spinning mill (factory)
		Captain Cook killed in Hawaii
1775	American War of Independence (to 1783)	
1777	British surrender at Saratoga	

Date	Major World Events	Nelson	Napoleon	Other Events
1778	France joins the American war against Britain, sending troops and ships			
1779	Franco-Spanish siege of Gibraltar (raised finally in 1783)	Nelson promoted post-captain	Bonaparte sent to military academy at Brienne	
1780	Armed neutrality of maritime nations to restrain British interference with shipping			The first Epsom Derby
1781	British surrender at Yorktown			
1783	Pitt the Younger becomes prime minister			First flights in hot air (Montgolfier) and hydrogen (Charles) balloons
1784		Nelson marries Frances Nisbet, widow of a Nevis doctor	Napoleon Bonaparte commissioned second lieutenant of Artillery	Death of Samuel Johnson
1785		Nelson 'retired' on shore pay for the next five years and lives with his wife at Burnham Thorpe, all the while agitating for a ship		Edmund Cartwright invents the power loom

Year			
1786	Britain takes over the spice trade centre of Penang, Malaysia		
1787	The Regency Crisis following the apparent insanity of George III		
1788			The *Daily Universal Register* (from 1788, *The Times*) is published
1789	The French Revolution (lasts until 1799) Washington becomes first president of the USA		*Decline and Fall of the Roman Empire* published by Gibbon
1790			First steam-powered iron-rolling mill built in Britain
1792	French Revolutionary War starts		
1793	Britain joins war against France Execution of Louis XVI Reign of Terror (to 1794)	Nelson meets Sir William and Emma Hamilton	Bonaparte commands artillery at the Siege of Toulon
1794	US navy founded	Nelson loses right eye at Calvi from flying stone fragment, left eye damaged	In France, the semaphore system is invented
1795	Vice Admiral Sir John Jervis appointed commander-in-chief of the Mediterranean fleet		Bonaparte disperses Paris mob

Date	Major World Events	Nelson	Napoleon	Other Events
1796		Nelson promoted to commodore and commands the *Captain*	Bonaparte is appointed commander of the army in Italy Bonaparte marries Josephine	Edward Jenner pioneers vaccination against smallpox
1797	Battle of Cape St Vincent Mutinies at Spithead and the Nore	Nelson promoted to rear admiral and created Knight of the Bath Nelson loses his right arm at Santa Cruz, Tenerife, while trying to capture a bullion ship	Bonaparte advances towards Austria Bonaparte begins to plan an invasion of Britain	Pound notes, the first paper currency, are issued
1798	Battle of the Nile	Nelson created Baron Nelson of the Nile	Bonaparte goes to Egypt	
1799		Nelson created Duke of Brontë	Bonaparte lands secretly in France and becomes First Consul	Discovery of the Rosetta stone in Egypt
1800	Parliamentary Union of Great Britain and Ireland	Nelson takes seat in House of Lords	Plot to assassinate Napoleon fails in Paris	Co-operative reformer builds an 'ideal' community in New Lanark, Scotland
1801	Treaty of Luréville Pitt the Younger resigns to be replaced by Addington Act of Union	Separated from Frances who remains Lady Nelson Horatia, daughter of Nelson and Emma born		

1802	Treaty of Amiens West India Docks opened in London	Nelson buys Merton Place in Surrey Nelson twice unsuccessfully attacks Boulogne Nelson's father dies		*Charlotte Dundas*, first practical steam ship, built on the Clyde
1803	Treaty of Amiens collapses and Napoleonic War begins Insurrection in Ireland under Robert Emmett In the USA, the Louisiana purchase from France almost doubles the size of USA territory	William Hamilton dies Nelson appointed commander-in-chief of the Mediterranean fleet		Beethoven composes Symphony no. 3, 'Eroica'
1804	Addington resigns, Pitt the Younger again prime minister Spain joins war on the side of France		Napoleon crowned Emperor by the Pope	
1805	Villeneuve escapes to the West Indies, eventually followed by Nelson. Calder fights Villeneuve's fleet off Cape Finisterre, but disengages and Villeneuve escapes	Nelson returns to England in August and the Combined Fleet reaches Cadiz Nelson leaves Portsmouth in the *Victory* in September	Napoleon enters Vienna and defeats the Austrians and Russians at Austerlitz	

Date	Major World Events	Nelson	Napoleon	Other Events
1805	Battle of Trafalgar, 21 October Austria surrenders to Napoleon Britain and the USA quarrel over trade in the Caribbean			
1806	Death of Pitt the Younger	State funeral for Nelson in St Paul's		
1807				Abolition of the slave trade in the British Empire
1812			Napoleon's retreat from Moscow	
1814			Abdication of Napoleon	
1815		Emma Hamilton dies	Napoleon escapes from Elba Napoleon defeated at Waterloo and goes into exile	
1820	Death of George III			
1821			Death of Napoleon on St Helena	

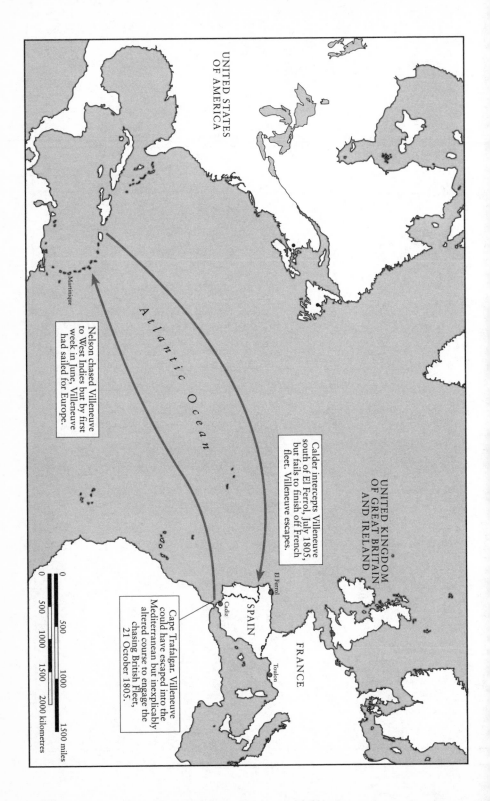

UNITED STATES
OF AMERICA

UNITED KINGDOM
OF GREAT BRITAIN
AND IRELAND

SPAIN

FRANCE

Atlantic Ocean

Martinique

El Ferrol

Cadiz

Toulon

Nelson chased Villeneuve
to West Indies but by first
week in June, Villeneuve
had sailed for Europe.

Calder intercepts Villeneuve
south of El Ferrol, July 1805,
but fails to finish off French
fleet. Villeneuve escapes.

Cape Trafalgar. Villeneuve
could have escaped into the
Mediterranean but inexplicably
altered course to engage the
chasing British Fleet,
21 October 1805.

0   500   1000   1500   2000 kilometres

0   500   1000   1500 miles

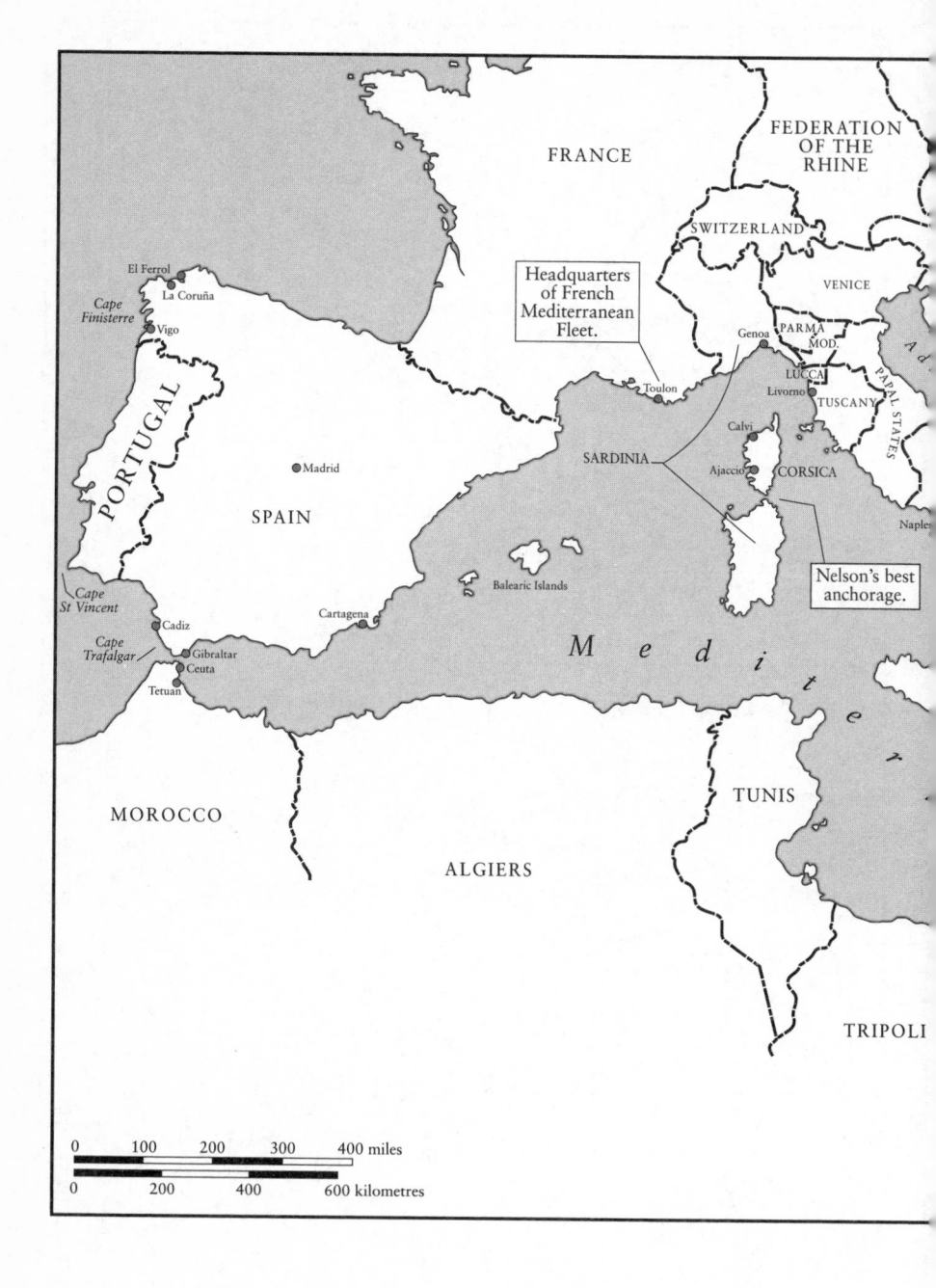

FRANCE

FEDERATION OF THE RHINE

SWITZERLAND

VENICE

El Ferrol
La Coruña
Cape Finisterre
Vigo

Genoa
PARMA
MOD.
LUCCA
Livorno
TUSCANY
PAPAL STATES

Toulon

Headquarters of French Mediterranean Fleet.

Calvi
Ajaccio
CORSICA

SARDINIA

Naples

Madrid

SPAIN

PORTUGAL

Cape St Vincent

Cadiz

Balearic Islands

Cartagena

Cape Trafalgar
Gibraltar
Ceuta
Tetuan

Nelson's best anchorage.

M e d i t e r . . .

MOROCCO

ALGIERS

TUNIS

TRIPOLI

| 0 | 100 | 200 | 300 | 400 miles |
| 0 | 200 | 400 | 600 kilometres |

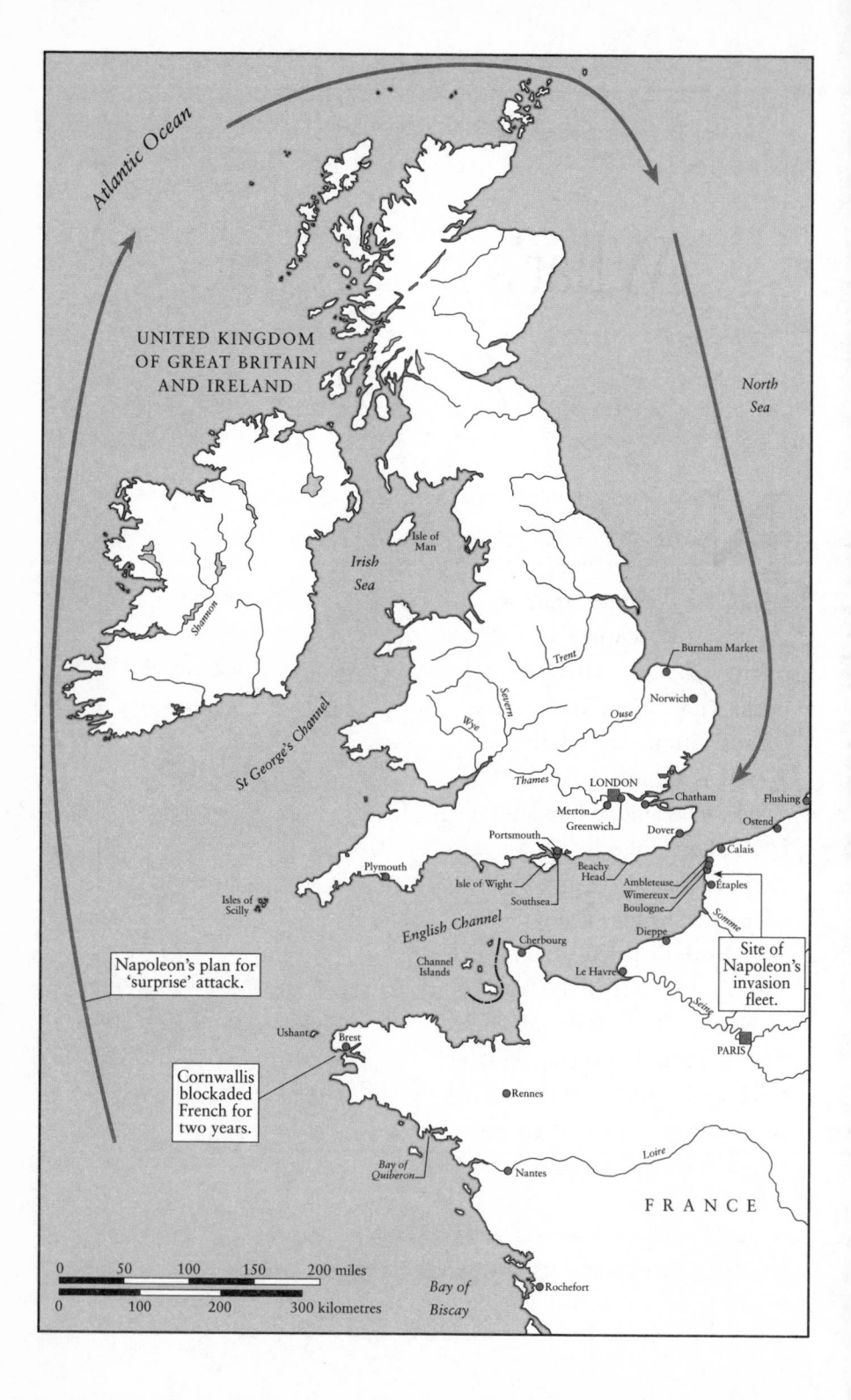

CHAPTER ONE

What's in a Name?

NELSON IS REMEMBERED FOR THE BATTLE OF TRAFALGAR. THE BATTLE itself was important to the British for two reasons. First, it by and large limited Napoleon's ambitions to continental Europe. Second, as a result of it Britain dominated the world's oceans, guaranteeing that the century to follow would be the most profitable in the country's history. After 1805 the British were never seriously challenged in the vital supply lines – known as the sea lanes – connecting these islands with the rest of the world. So Trafalgar was an economic victory as well as a military one.

Nelson became famous and synonymous with Trafalgar because he was killed there. The battle was also cited as a supreme example of his tactical genius. In reality, his famous new plan of attack was not new, was anticipated by the enemy, the French, and – for reasons the admiral could not have anticipated – did not work.

As a naval victory, the Battle of Copenhagen was a far better example of Nelson's tactical daring and showed his planning to far better effect. The fact that Trafalgar might well have gone the other way had one of the French admirals not deserted the fight out of contempt for his own commander-in-chief might rate as one of the more interesting 'What If?' discussions of naval history. The Nelson legend was created long before Trafalgar.

Once that battle was over and the nation held unlimited control of the sea lanes, Britain and its politicians no longer needed Nelson. Still his legend lives on. He had, after all, challenged the gods.

There is a British assumption that Nelson is the only story of Trafalgar – an assumption that is far from correct. However, there is no reason to tear down the vice admiral's monument, the highest ever raised to an Englishman. For Nelson is certainly a worthy hero for the British. His remarkable abilities and the use he made of his own particular talent for manipulating naval warfare to his fleet's advantage are second to none to the present day.

His ability to inspire his ships' companies to achieve successes which, under a lesser officer, might have turned to catastrophe, has rarely been underestimated.

In the early twentieth century, there were Fisher,[1] Jellicoe (the latter good at convoys and at governing New Zealand)[2] and Beatty[3]. Then, with the second great war of the century, Cunningham[4] and Pound[5]. Later, Le Fanu and Lewin[6]. None was a Nelson for none had the times. Naval warfare was hardly fashionable. The dashing officer was often regarded as a risk. Mountbatten saw himself as something special, and his men thought him so. Naval historians knew better.[7]

Moreover, by the time of the naval conflicts of the twentieth century (there were few major engagements after 1812) there were steel and steam at sea, bringing with them range, manipulation and manoeuvrability. Yet even in 1916 a government at war longed for a Trafalgar, a famous victory. Jutland was grand enough, but did not satisfy the masters ashore for it was not considered decisive. The nation could easily be persuaded to send its hurrahs to the British tars, but there was no Nelson to bring home in a barrel of drink. No admiral towered over the masses. None since Nelson is remembered today with public affection

---

[1] John (Jackie) Arbuthnot Fisher, first Baron Fisher of Kilverstone (1841–1920).
[2] John Rushworth Jellicoe, first Earl Jellicoe (1859–1935).
[3] David Beatty, first Earl Admiral of the Fleet and First Sea Lord (1871–1937).
[4] Andrew Browne Cunningham, first Viscount Cunningham of Hyndhope (1883–1963).
[5] Sir Dudley Pickman Rogers Pound, Admiral of the Fleet and First Sea Lord (1877–1943).
[6] Sir Michael Le Fanu, Admiral of the Fleet (1913–1970); Sir Terence Lewin (1920–1999), Admiral of the Fleet, later Baron Lewin of Greenwich.
[7] Louis Francis Albert Victor Nicholas Mountbatten, first Earl Mountbatten of Burma (1900–1979).

or even admiration. Indeed, many public heroes of the Great War are now among the least known, all but anonymous, remembered as those who fell amid a hail of crass decisions. It is the poets who are the named heroes. And in the Second World War? Only Montgomery's image lives on – but probably not for much longer. No admiral's does.[8]

So why do the events of 21 October 1805 stir such pride and emotion? First, the battle was conclusive. Second, because Trafalgar is now, and was then to those who waited in England, totally imaginable. Perhaps only five military events since Trafalgar have captured the imaginations of generations of British people who nonetheless never understood their consequences – Waterloo, the Charge of the Light Brigade, the Battle of Britain, El Alamein and Dunkirk. A victory has to have what the British understand by spirit, particularly in the face of near defeat. When that spirit is abroad an immortal memory is created. Trafalgar fulfilled the criterion of an inspired national occasion. Today, in the twenty-first century, only sportsmen and women can do that.

Furthermore, Trafalgar was a victory because it ended in a surrender, albeit that of a fool. It destroyed the heart of the French fleet and therefore England's only serious maritime enemy. It ignored the brilliant and brave seamanship of the Spanish contingent. (It would take another decade before Bonaparte, too, succumbed to sense.) It told the British that they had indeed obeyed God's command – as expressed in the words of James Thomson's 'Rule, Britannia', to rule the waves – and that they would do so well into the following century.[9]

Most of all, in Nelson the British had someone who was to be the most long-lasting military hero in their history since the mythical Arthur. Not even the names of Marlborough[10] or Wellington[11] would conjure up such a potent image for so many for so long. Only Churchill's, in modern times, might do that.[12] Nelson was a perfect hero: brilliant, anti-

---

[8] Bernard Law Montgomery, Viscount of Alamein (1887–1976).

[9] James Thomson (1700–1748), Edinburgh-educated writer who in 1740 wrote the words of 'Rule Britannia' for his and David Mallet's (1705–1765) masque, *Alfred*.

[10] John Churchill, first Duke of Marlborough (1650–1722).

[11] Arthur Wellesley, first Duke of Wellington (1769–1852).

[12] Sir Winston Leonard Spencer Churchill (1874–1965), British prime minister who led the country to victory in the Second World War.

establishment, romantic and – above all – victorious, especially in death. Here, then, was a figure whose deeds would earn him a place among the greatest in our history.

Then why was Trafalgar not all about Nelson? And how was it that another admiral, Cornwallis,[13] who deserved as many laurels as Nelson, came to be largely forgotten, except by naval historians, and was not even invited to Nelson's funeral? Why did that now-celebrated admiral, Collingwood, pointedly ignore his superior's final command with such terrible consequences hours after the battle?[14] Moreover, why was the most foolish genius of Europe, the Emperor Napoleon, such a powerful influence on the defeat of the Franco-Spanish fleet that late afternoon in October?

The answers to all these questions rest in the fact that the Battle of Trafalgar was partly a chance conclusion to a series of events which had started not early that autumn day just north of Gibraltar but four years before in Paris and London – particularly in Paris.

Horatio Nelson was born on 29 September 1758 at Burnham Thorpe in Norfolk. Later he preferred to call himself Horace. He was a sickly child. Many infants were sickly in those days. His mother, Catherine, the wife of Edmund Nelson, rector of Burnham Thorpe, was delivered of eleven children,[15] three of whom died shortly after birth. In the eighteenth century, a child-mortality rate of 30 per cent or more raised few eyebrows.[16] Another sailor, Rear Admiral Jeffrey Baron de Raigersfeld (of the Holy Roman Empire), born in the early spring of 1771, noted that his earliest memory was '. . . of my twin sisters, both of whom died whilst cutting their teeth . . .'[17]

[13] Sir William Cornwallis (1744–1819), commander, English Channel Fleet during the blockade of Brest prior to the Battle of Trafalgar and during Bonaparte's efforts to build an invasion fleet.

[14] Baron Cuthbert Collingwood (1750–1810), Nelson's deputy at Trafalgar.

[15] Edmund Nelson (1722–1802); Catherine Nelson (1725–1767).

[16] There is no census figure until 1801. The combined population of England and Wales at the time of Nelson's birth was about 6.6 million. The population growth rate was fewer than 600,000 a year. By the end of the century, the growth rate was more than a million, due in no small measure to a reduction in child deaths. For some limited figures see, Tranter, T., *Population since the Industrial Revolution: the case of England and Wales* (London: Croom Helm, 1973).

[17] Jeffrey Raigersfeld (1771–1844), son of an Austrian diplomat he spent sixty-three years in England, retiring as a Rear Admiral.

Nelson was born during the year of the return of Halley's comet, although that could hardly have been the only omen of conflict, let alone glory, abroad that year. Britain was at war and had been for two years. The so-called Seven Years War (1756–1763) was but a moment in the seemingly continuous conflict tearing continental Europe apart. On one side were Britain, Prussia and Hanover (Britain was ruled by a Hanoverian, the seventy-five-year-old George II) and on the other France, Austria, Russia, Sweden, Saxony and Spain.[18] The war started when Frederick the Great of Prussia[19] invaded Saxony in a bid for supremacy over that region. Britain became involved because France was. Although the commercial instincts of both French and British colonists would have led them to avoid such a conflict, the animosities and jealousies between these two nations in India and North America made fighting between them inevitable. This was the war in which Clive[20] of India and General Wolfe[21] are particularly remembered on the British side and Dupleix[22] and Montcalm[23] on the French.

The great events did not pass without remark in the rectory at Burnham Thorpe. Norfolk sent its sailors to the fleets and its soldier sons to the regiments. The church bells rang a few times and tolled a few others. Moreover, the Nelson family had parsons aplenty – going back three generations – and each took a serious view of the affairs of state, if little part in them. Two of Nelson's brothers were parsons, as had been their paternal and maternal grandfathers. The latter was the distinguished prebendary Dr Maurice Suckling of Westminster. Two great-uncles and eight first cousins were in holy orders. It was Nelson's mother, Catherine, who claimed the more distinguished quarterings. Her great-aunt had been a Walpole and – even more important to the Nelson social register – the sister of Sir Robert Walpole,[24] England's

---

[18] George II (1683–1760), reigned 1727–1760.

[19] Frederick the Great (1712–1786).

[20] Robert Clive, first Baron Clive of Plassey (1725–1774) played a key role in the development of the East India Company.

[21] James Wolfe (1727–1759) died during their successful battle against the French at the Heights of Abraham, Quebec.

[22] Joseph François Dupleix (1697–1763).

[23] Lieutenant-General Louis Montcalm, Marquis de Montcalm (1712–1759).

[24] Sir Robert Walpole (1676–1745) Britain's first prime minister (1721–1742).

first prime minister. He was created Earl of Orford, with a splendid family seat at Houghton Hall, hardly a morning's ride from Burnham Thorpe. There is no record of the Nelsons ever visiting the Hall. There is, however, evidence that they were invited to the home of the lesser Walpole, Lord Walpole of Wolterton. Here was an agreeable member of the gentry, though of little help to his cousin's husband, the overburdened Reverend Nelson. The test of family came in 1767, when Catherine Nelson died.

The family had little money and, it would seem, the rector little fortitude. Horatio Nelson was nine. He had received some education as a boarder at the Royal Grammar School, Norwich, but he had few prospects. The Walpole cousins did not come to the rescue, but Catherine Nelson's brothers did. One of the five sons, Maurice, was found a post in the Customs and Navy Office where his uncle, William Suckling, held a senior appointment.[25] However, even Uncle William could only find a place for one customs clerk, and so the rector's hopes lodged with his other brother-in-law, Captain Maurice Suckling, Royal Navy. Maurice Suckling was rather grand in the family's terms. He had had a good war against the French, gained a comfortable inheritance from his late father and made a suitable marriage to Lord Walpole's daughter, Mary. Between them the couple were related to most of the Norfolk families who mattered in regional society and also to quite a few with broader connections and influences. Through this web of close and not-so-close relatives, Nelson would have been able, at a push and through a distant seventeenth-century line, to trace family to the Earl of St Albans, Henry Jermyn, after whom Jermyn Street in London's St James's is named. Edmund Nelson, in dubious health himself, was more interested in the present for his immediate family.

The eldest daughter, Susannah, who had come into a bit of money through a legacy, was to be married off to a rich merchant and settled comfortably at Wells-next-the-Sea. Her sister, Anne, would not fare so well. The father of her illegitimate child abandoned her, and she died

---

[25] His position must have brought him a good income for he was said to have lived in some style in Kentish Town, in those days in the countryside away from London.

young. The third daughter, Catherine, still a small child, remained happy enough and was of no immediate concern to Captain Suckling. Then there were the sons.

The eldest, Maurice, apparently not such a good clerk, got into debt. William was sent into the Church – always a good proposition with the Nelsons. Edmund went to work for Susannah's husband. The youngest lad, baptized Suckling, became a wastrel and so was sent up to Christ's College, Cambridge and thence into the Church. He was never preferred. This left Horatio – named after the celebrated Walpoles. He chose to call himself Horace, like the famous literary figure of that family, also baptized Horatio.[26]

Horatio was removed from Norwich and sent to the Sir William Paston's School at North Walsham run by John Price Jones, a Welsh preacher known for sound classics teaching and regular floggings. None of this dampened the boy's initiative. When he spotted in the *Norfolk Chronicle* that his uncle, Maurice Suckling, was to command the former French ship *Raisonnable*, Horatio pestered his elder brother to write to their father, then taking a cure at Bath, telling him his son wanted to go to sea with Suckling. The captain, a good-natured fellow, agreed to take Nelson as a midshipman as well as an obvious weakling. He is often quoted as remarking that '... the first time we go into action a cannon-ball may knock off his head and provide for him at once ...' The comment has appeared consistently in the Nelson folk-story since it first appeared four years after his death, and may contain some truth. It matters not. A shot quite smaller than a cannonball would eventually do for him, but not before Nelson had made a lasting name for himself.

On a bitter Chatham day in January 1771, the twelve-year-old Nelson joined his first ship as midshipman – a sort of cadet officer. Here was Suckling's valuable act of nepotism. Many would-be officers appeared in the ship's articles lower down the social and naval scale, as able seaman or captain's servant – a recognized rank that was one step towards gaining a commission. Nelson's appointment gave him

---

[26] Horace Walpole (1717–1797), Sir Robert's fourth son and fourth Earl of Orford, although he never took his seat in the Lords. Author of the then popular novel *The Castle of Otranto*.

immediate seniority, in contravention of the naval regulations.[27]

In theory, none should be signed on as a midshipman unless he had been three years at sea. There were, however, ways of circumventing this regulation. The simplest was to have a relative who was captain of a ship enter a lad in the vessel's articles for three years before he actually joined. An example would be Tom Cochrane[28] who, from the age of five, had been entered in the ship's company by his uncle. Cochrane joined the navy in his teens and immediately assumed senior rank. The opportunity was not wasted on him, and he rose to command the North American and West Indies station, though not before being cashiered for fraud in 1814 and commanding both the Chilean (1817–1822) and Brazilian (1823–1825) navies.

Even though Nelson did sign on as a captain's servant in his next ship, the *Triumph*, and as able seaman in the *Seahorse*, he on both occasions reverted to midshipman. Not all midshipmen were promoted. We have an image of pink-faced youngsters, not yet teenagers, in grown-up uniforms and with dirks at their waists, but some of them were still midshipmen in their thirties and forties. There are recorded cases where midshipmen had barely time to be promoted before retiring. The six years' sea time necessary before trying for a lieutenant's examination did not mean midshipmen would pass. Equally, there were many occasions when a young man who had been successful, even promoted, would be unable to find a berth. There was nothing new in this. In fact, even in more modern times with the decline in, for example, the American merchant fleet, there were many occasions when someone captaining a ship one year might find himself sailing as an able seaman the next because there were so few seafaring jobs to be had.

In a modern warship there might be a couple of midshipmen. In the *Victory*, a three-decker, there could have been as many as twenty. They would have been expected to arrive on board with everything they needed. The navy provided neither uniforms nor instruments. The midshipmen berthed together, in cramped conditions, but had the advantage of the

---

[27] See Admiralty papers, 6 Series, National Archives (formerly Public Records Office).
[28] Tom Cochrane (1775–1860). Later Admiral Lord Thomas Cochrane.

freedom of the quarterdeck to take air and exercise. This was the only recognition of their status on board. Any one of them, however, stepping too far out of line would be reminded that he could be publicly punished, including a flogging. The midshipman, whatever his ambition, never forgot his place in maritime society.

So what were the sailors like in the navy Nelson had joined? If we know that, we shall get a much better idea of what it would have been like for him on that long haul to Trafalgar.

CHAPTER TWO

Of Ships, Men and Mutiny

THE MANPOWER STRUCTURE OF THE ROYAL NAVY IN THE LATE
eighteenth century would be recognizable to the modern sailor.
The ranks and rates[1] are more or less the same as they are today,
although such appointments as captain's servant, purser and master have
disappeared.[2] At the bottom of the naval pile were the seamen, those
with some experience, and landmen, those with none. The most junior
rates were those of the boys, recognized by the navy since 1794 and
given certain grades. Boys third class were seamen under the age of
fifteen. (The grade of boy seaman survived into the second half of the
twentieth century and included some individuals of a similar age.) The
fifteen- to eighteen-year-olds were known as boys second class and the
men under training to be sea officers as boys first class. The landman
(after the late 1790s usually called a landsman) was someone with
absolutely no experience. He had come straight from the land, maybe
attracted by a bounty for joining, yet his like often made up at least a
third of the ship's company. The bounty had, by 1805, risen to thirty
shillings (approximately £77 today). However, a local community such
as a city with seafaring connections might also offer a bounty of as

---

[1] From the practice of having the first lieutenant, the 'works manager' of a shop,
rate a non-officer sailor by his age, experience and capability.
[2] The purser is now called supply officer and known informally as the pusser.
The term purser has continued in the merchant navy and is the officer responsible
for victualling, rationing, stewards and all domestic arrangements, from laundry
to money-changing in larger vessels.

much as ten, often twenty times that amount. Entry into the navy was very attractive at these rates, although what kind of value the landman offered is difficult to judge. Naturally, his lack of sea time made him unpopular with regular sailors, who sometimes regarded landmen as rogues and thieves.

There were also, aboard ships, the quota men. These took their name from the 1795 Quota Act whereby civic leaders had to produce a certain quota of sailors. For example, the seaport of Bristol was ordered to fetch the navy 666 men. In 1795, London had a quota of 5,704, which it apparently met. The Cinque Port of Rye had one of ninety and Falmouth of twenty-one. The word in the ships was that many of these quota men were the drunks and dregs of the towns and cities who had been turned out by the magistrates and sent to sea. No wonder many officers believed that the 1797 mutineers had been organized by quota men.

Then came the ordinary seaman. He was an unskilled but useful sailor who was able to learn. The next in line was the able seaman, who, as the title suggests, was more than useful and able to carry out most ordinary duties. Up to this level it is very likely that the assessment of the ship's general manager, the first lieutenant, was reasonably impartial. Most of the new recruits would have been strangers, and the first lieutenant needed to know exactly who could do what and how well. There was little room for favouritism at a hundred feet above deck, handing in a sail that weighed literally a ton, with the ship heeling into a force-nine gale. Above the level of able seaman there was an element of patriotism, capriciousness and luck – both good and bad. An able seaman might become a mate – that is, deputy – to a petty officer (literally, 'small officer', from the French *petit*). This group included, for example, the boatswain's mate and the quartermaster's mate or quarter gunners as the gunners' mates were known. Petty officers were the most junior of the non-commissioned officers. A leading seaman (often known as a killick from his badge of rank, the small anchor of that name) was the equivalent of a corporal in the army. The petty officer was of similar rank to an army sergeant. However, there was no guarantee that a man would remain a petty officer. Apart from the obvious reason for being de-rated – for a misdemeanour – he might be transferred to another ship only to find himself lowly rated by the first lieutenant, and not always because of his

degree of competence. There might not be a berth for his rate. Off to
another ship, and the erstwhile able seaman might become a petty officer's
mate. The most senior of the non-commissioned officers were the warrant
officers, the chief cooks, the masters-at-arms (the ship's policemen), the
gunners and, above them all, the boatswains (bosuns) and sailing masters.

There is a further anomaly to be remembered. Though the ratings
were in the navy and subject to naval discipline, they had been recruited
not by the navy but by the vessel. Unlike the officers, the ratings
belonged not to the navy as a whole but only to the ship. They were
included among the ship's company in the muster book but were not
listed in Admiralty records.

Officers, on the other hand, were very much employees of the navy and
were trained by the navy, albeit almost exclusively at sea. There was but
one naval college – Portsmouth. For this reason the naval officers of
Nelson's time were usually referred to as sea officers. The most junior
officer of command, the lieutenant, was required to have spent a minimum
of six years at sea under training before he could even be considered for
an appointment. Sea-time qualification did not mean promotion. Thus
the surest route to a commission was either as a captain's servant or,
more likely – like Nelson – as a midshipman. An officer's son could join as
early as eleven, but others had to wait until they were thirteen, which led
many to falsify their records of service. If these seem early ages, it might
be remembered that well into the second half of the twentieth century
the Royal Navy enrolled cadets at its Dartmouth training college,
Britannia, at four and a half.

There has long been a joke about the navy having more admirals than
ships. In Nelson's time there were certainly more flag ranks than any other
kind of officer. For example, there were nine different levels
of admiral but only three commissioned ranks below that: captain,
commander and, the most junior, lieutenant. Although England had had a
navy for centuries before Trafalgar, the system of awarding ranks to officers
in a constructive way dated only from the mid-1600s. The expansion of
the navy had led to the splitting of the fleet into a system of threes, rather
in the way that the army has three companies to a battalion, three battalions
to a regiment and so on. In the mid seventeenth century the navy had been
formed into three divisions with each one consisting of three squadrons.

Each division was given a colour, that of the most senior being red, that of the next white and that of the least senior blue. Thus we read of an officer being admiral of the red, he who would have been senior to an admiral of the white or of the blue. At sea, the degree of seniority was easily recognizable from the ensign flown by a particular division. Thus the senior ships would fly the red command flag at top mast.[3] There was also a red ensign. This was a red flag with the Union flag appearing in the top left-hand corner that came to be flown at the stern. Although the composition of the Union flag has changed, this is exactly the same red ensign that is flown by British-registered merchant vessels today. Junior admirals flew either white or blue command flags. Today, the blue ensign is flown by vessels of the navy's Royal Fleet Auxiliary and any commanded by a warrant holder of the Royal Naval Sailing Association while the white ensign, a white flag with a St George's Cross and the union emblem in the top left-hand corner, is now flown by Royal Navy vessels and other vessels commanded by a member of the Royal Yacht Squadron.

The flag system was a bit antiquated, having been useful in the mid seventeenth century but proving less so in the closing days of the eighteenth. There were plenty of admirals to fly flags of almost any hue. There were nine different types, thanks to the colour system. The most senior of them all was the Admiral of the Fleet. (This rank or appointment existed until the end of the twentieth century.) There were then about sixty full admirals, that is, twenty each of the red, white and blue. Beneath them were about the same number of vice admirals, and beneath those officers the same number of rear admirals. Not all the admirals had seagoing jobs or even important posts of any kind. Many would go on half pay and could still be promoted, even as they lay dying of old age. Not a few spent their times ashore in this way, never expecting to be called for sea duties for the rest of their lives but still expecting promotion. Though it may seem bizarre, an admiral could be recalled to sea in his seventies.

---

[3] When two admirals of similar seniority were in the fleet, the commander-in-chief would order one to fly a different colour. This was largely to distinguish the ships in battle. It was really an out-of-date system which had never been changed – and should have been.

Below these flag officers (the term came from their ensigns) were the captains and the superficially more senior commodores. Commodores were temporary appointments, the office holder being a senior captain in command of a squadron of ships. This appointment to commodore continues to the present time, when a commodore may have to revert to captain although he may eventually be promoted to the substantive rank of rear admiral. In Nelson's day the number of captains and commodores might have been anything between 650 and 800. Beneath these officers there were 500–600 commanders and, finally – the most numerous of all the commissioned officers – more than 3,000 lieutenants.

The permanent ranks were the sea officers, the only sailors to hold the monarch's commission – hence the term commissioned officer. Others, almost exclusively junior officers such as masters and surgeons, held warrants – hence warrant officers – from the Navy Board.

Warrant officers included the sailing masters, surgeons, pursers, boatswains, carpenters, gunners, instructor officers (schoolmasters or 'schoolies') and chaplains. The last were beginning to enjoy an improved status by the time of Trafalgar. Until almost the end of the eighteenth century chaplains were seen as no-hopers with little knowledge of theology and not much learning. Their lot did not improve dramatically until well after 1805. There is some evidence to suggest that this view of clergymen was not confined to ships' parsons. It was not until later in the century that a proper clerical profession began to emerge.

Nelson literally grew up between the ages of twelve and twenty in some of the harshest conditions that could be set before a youth brought up in the relative comfort of Burnham Thorpe rectory. The draughts and strict rector's rules must have been as nothing compared to the hardships he would now face in his uncle's ship, with worse to follow.

To paraphrase the cynical Dr Johnson,[*] to be in a late-eighteenth-century man of war was to be in jail with the added chance of drowning. Many sailors shared Johnson's view of the navy but, unlike him, had no choice in the matter. They were, of course, victims of the press gangs, the impress service. The navy was forever concerned about the manning

---

[*] Samuel Johnson (1709–1784) whose *Dictionary of the English Language* was published in 1755.

of ships, particularly in wartime. There was always a supply of officers. In peacetime, many of those could be, and were, sent ashore on so-called half pay (which was always less than that). With few exceptions they longed for war to be declared in order to get back to sea. This offered them their only chance of promotion and financial reward – mostly through taking ships and sharing the prize money involved.

Capturing enemy ships and sharing in the value of their cargoes, even of the vessels themselves, had for some time been a formal part of warfare. Towards the end of the sixteenth century the English had set up an Admiralty court, part of its function being to judge whether a prize was lawful and had been lawfully taken. At the beginning of that century, English statements of law had been quite clear. No prize ships should be seized unless their capture was legally justified. A distinction was drawn between capturing a ship, its crew and its cargo in peacetime and doing so in wartime. It might now seem obvious that if Britain had, for example, been at war with Spain, it would have been fine for a British warship to capture a Spanish merchant vessel, especially one with supplies destined for its country's war effort. But what if a ship belonging to a neutral country and heading for an enemy port were to be intercepted by the Royal Navy? Would it have been lawful for that neutral ship to be confiscated, along with its crew and cargoes? Furthermore, it was not until the 1600s that what we would call a proper navy started to appear. Until that century, navies were quite often a collection of opportunists, mercenaries (we might call them pirates or corsairs) and assorted individuals who happened to join up with ships commissioned by the monarch. It was quite normal for a fleet to go into a battle with as many as 70 per cent of the ships on its side having private interests. Anything such vessels captured was theirs.

It is easy to see how the formality of war introduced the idea of prize-taking. Apart from the money – sometimes a lot of it – to both officers and men the tactical and strategic value of that kind of action could be overwhelming. An enemy garrison holding out for want of food supplies or a harbour-bound fleet needing bullion to pay for its stores and cannonballs could easily be thrown into a desperate situation if the supply ship – even from a neutral country like America – was intercepted. The formal and legal aspects of a case were not neglected. The judge of the

High Court of Admiralty during Nelson's time was William, Lord Stowell.[5] He was a Middle Temple judge. Stowell was adamant that the legalities surrounding the capture of ships should not be flouted. There was, for example, a document consisting thirty-two questions to be answered, known as the standing interrogatories. When a naval captain captured a merchant ship, each of the questions had to be put to her master and officers. An important point was to establish the master's sympathies. For example, if a captain was American but had lived for twenty years in Spain, he might be suspect. So the first question to be put to the master was 'Where were you born?' Then came 'Where have you lived for these seven years last past?' and 'Where do you now live? How long have you lived in that place?' followed by 'To what prince or state, or to whom are you, or have you ever been, a subject and of what cities or towns have you been admitted a burgher or freeman?' This was only part of the first of the thirty-two questions.

Also, the agent of the prize ship could contest an Admiralty ruling. After all, there was so much at stake. Acts of Parliament were passed to define the legal strength of a prize-ship gain. There was so much opportunity for corruption in the handing out of the proceeds and so many interdepartmental jealousies that around the time of Trafalgar new law was continually being drafted and redrafted. It was certainly the case that any money from a ship would go to the government and its agents, to lawyers of course, and to the captain and ship's company of the vessel that had captured it (which was why, even in battle, a captain might be seen strapping his vessel to a prize ship for fear of losing a small fortune). However, some of the money – a little over 1½ per cent – would be paid to the treasurer of Greenwich Hospital, and in the Act of 1806 there was an order that 3⅓ per cent should go to the charity administered by Greenwich Hospital, known as the Chatham Chest, so that it could extend and increase allowances to 'Persons maimed or hurt, or otherwise disabled in the Service of their Country'. The implications of these legalities and restrictions were not lost on the sailors at sea.

Even in 1805, when Nelson was planning what he hoped to be the

---

[4] William Scott Stowell (1745–1836).

downfall of Villeneuve,[6] he was sometimes to be found frantically writing letters to the Admiralty in support of claims within his squadrons for the distribution of prize money. A captain might capture a merchant ship, but, as Nelson pointed out, if he did so while being a subordinate commander to an admiral, might not the admiral benefit from the prize? We should not think that such matters were above the heads of the ratings on deck. They, too, would raise a bigger cheer when a prize ship was captured as opposed to a warship. Indeed, it was one of the incentives for joining the service. It was understandable that a seaman, who could hardly have enjoyed living in the wretched conditions on board ship, should have hoped for a share in a taken merchantman. Equally, this was not likely to appear in the pamphlets of the press gang, although the prospect of prizes certainly appeared in leaflets posted by individual captains desperate to attract crews.

Ratings were always harder to find, especially in wartime. The obvious source of extra sailors was the fishing fleets – though these were needed – and the merchant navy. The latter group was just as professional in seafaring terms. The Royal Navy was, on balance, a better place to serve in peacetime, despite the fact that a sailor could be trapped in a ship and not get home for years. The pay was marginally higher, although it rarely came through when it was due. There was a slightly better prospect of promotion, so pay rises were more likely – even though the money was often held back. Work was less onerous because there were more sailors in a warship than in a merchantman of a similar size. At the same time, it was a stricter environment, although this is not to detract from the merchant skipper's talents for brutality. So it should not seem surprising that the harsh naval discipline was often no great deterrent to the eighteenth-century seafarer. Moreover, there was always that hope of prize money. The British sailor has always been an optimist. There was a further reason for not wanting to join the navy: the prospect of being killed.

Not surprisingly, the navy was never able to maintain its wartime manning figures from peacetime complements. Therefore, unlike the

---

[6] Pierre Charles Jean-Baptiste Silvestre de Villeneuve (1763–1806). Commander of the Franco-Spanish Combined Fleet at Trafalgar, he was in awe of Nelson and considered him unbeatable in battle.

army, it would send out the press gangs to bring back sailors physically.
If this sounds unspeakably offensive to all social mores, the press
gang might be seen in the light of the wars of the twentieth century.
During both world wars there were similar manpower shortages, which
led the government to conscript as many civilians as possible. The
eighteenth-and nineteenth-century press gangs did not possess these
twentieth-century powers. In fact, there is something of a myth
surrounding the power of the press gang.

The role of the gang was not, as is popularly supposed, to nobble any
likely lad, ply him with drink and the king's shilling and make sure that
when he awoke it was on the lower deck of one of His Majesty's 74-gun
ships of the line. The press were entitled only to take sailors, not civilians.
The navy could only use the gangs to capture naval deserters – men who
were sailors anyway – and to seek volunteers, whether seamen or civilians.
It is this last role that has created the notion than none was safe from the
naval recruiter loitering by the inns of England. However, even the
legitimate role of taking sailors for the duration of a war was not always
clear-cut. After all, how did a press-gang lieutenant know who was and
who was not an ex-sailor? Moreover, what was a sailor when he was ashore
and had been for some years? Was he still a sailor and therefore a legitimate
quarry? One opinion in 1800, seems to clarify the matter. Or does it?

in every case of pressing, every man must be very sorry for the act,
and for the necessity which gives rise to it. It ought, therefore, to be
exercised with great moderation and only upon the most cogent
necessity. And though it be a legal power, it may, like many others,
be abused in the exercise of it . . . Persons liable must come purely
within the description of . . . seafaring men etc. He therefore who is
not within the description, does not come within this usage.[7]

That seemed very clear, although there were those who argued that it
was wrong that a man who had long ago given up a life at sea should have
to return. Some were clearly exempt: for example, an indentured craft
apprentice would be safe from the impressment. So, too, was a man who

---

[7] H. Cowper, Cases of King's Bench, 1800, II.

had a particular type of employment, perhaps on the rivers and estuaries, in the pay of Trinity House, an institution which, since the sixteenth century, had been responsible for the laying and keeping of lights and the buoyage system.[8]

Ironically, by an Act passed in the reign of Elizabeth I,[9] Trinity House was also charged with increasing the numbers of men in the navy. Dockyard mateys, the essential workers in the royal yards responsible for building and maintaining warships, were also exempt. However, a question could easily arise as to what really was a dockyard job and what was not. Could a casual worker be pressed? Certainly a man who owned a freehold could not be – but might his freehold be as bogus as the American citizenship that could be bought in the eighteenth century for a dollar a time? These doubts and readings of the law meant that anyone who claimed exemption would do well to apply for a certificate from the Commissioners of the Admiralty. That certificate, which would include a physical description of the civilian in question, would be shown to the press gang and, with luck, would allow him to pass by. Forged versions could, of course, be had cheaply. The lieutenant in charge of the press had therefore to exercise good judgement when at work. He would know full well that the law would not always stand by his actions if they seemed unreasonable, particularly as there was no strong legal – and certainly no public – support for the press gang. This last point was so relevant to the work of the press that it could be difficult, sometimes impossible, to get the local magistrate to sign a warrant. Furthermore, it was not unusual for an officer of the press gang to be prosecuted for assault. Test cases never proved the press illegal, but that did not mean the gangs were free to act as they wished.

A further weakness in the system was that the lieutenant was often on some form of productivity bonus. This encouraged him to produce quantity rather than quality. The latter being in the best of circumstances difficult to come by, the system was often corrupt, rarely achieved its aims and was usually controversial.

---

[8] Trinity House, founded by Sir Thomas Spert in 1514, was given its charter by Henry VIII to protect shipping by laying and maintaining charted lights and buoys and, until recently, to supply most ship's pilots.

[9] Elizabeth I (1533–1603) who reigned from 1558 until her death.

In truth, the press gang made good legend and fine cartoons, but rarely economic recruiting officers. It proved more successful in its secondary role, which was that of officially sanctioned piracy. A press-gang boat would intercept a merchantman, board her and take off all crew other than master, mates and apprentice boys (trainee mates). A skeleton crew would then be put aboard to bring the stripped ship into port. It was not always an easy business because some of the sailors aboard merchantmen were likely to be armed and to fire upon the navy's impress boat, usually a small vessel. Not a few naval ratings were killed, and many merchant sailors escaped.

The subject of press gangs was clearly an embarrassment to the eighteenth-century authorities and as controversial as the call-up has proved in more recent times. Certainly, impressment was regarded as legal and few who would have challenged that opinion had the resources to take the subject to law. The foundation of the precedent in common law was laid down in the fourteenth century, and was invoked in legal opinion – such was the sensitive nature of impressment. The Crown, it was successfully argued, had the right within precedent and parliamentary Act to impress men to go to sea in the monarch's name. The legality of the press gang was balanced in the warrant issued by the Admiralty Commissioners. During the early 1740s the Admiralty was forced to check and re-check its legal standing. The opinion was that impressment was defined as legal under common law; certainly no emergency powers were invoked to enforce the practice. There was also concern within Admiralty circles that a pressed man might never be a loyal sailor.

Britain was not alone in the difficulty of finding enough ships, and men to man them, during wartime. On balance, the British were more successful in getting almost enough of both. This was partly a surprise, because the nation's traditional enemy, France, appeared to have a more structured and a more easily enforced system for arranging these matters. The *Inscription Maritime* set out the concept of a register of sailors and maritime workers. However, it was never workable because the French people rejected it, and in the seventeenth century the monarchy had no means of establishing such a record without the assistance of its subjects. The idea was nonetheless a sound one. There were plenty of names on the register. But barely more than a quarter of those listed ever reported for duty, even though the system was a compulsory one. The French have always demonstrated a resistance to bureaucracy, at whatever level and in whatever century. It took a revolution and a Napoleonic resolve to make a form of conscription work in the French navy. Even then, the pressure had to be intense for men and ships to put to sea on the scale demanded by the emperor. These sailors did not always fight well. They sometimes had little stomach for the event, as we shall see to have been the case with the French commander at Trafalgar, Vice Admiral Pierre Charles de Villeneuve, who should never have been at Trafalgar nor even a seagoing admiral.

The events leading to the war between Britain and France and subsequently the Battle of Trafalgar gave ample warning of what was to come and of how many sailors were needed to man the navy. The fighting started because the rest of Europe, Britain included, believed that Bonaparte could – and probably would – export the French Revolution.

On 1 February 1793, France declared war. In August of that year, Admiral Hood[10] commanded combined British squadrons off Toulon, the French Mediterranean naval base. In 1794, Jervis[11] commanded the West Indies station against French possessions and the French fleet. In the same year, Howe[12] achieved a spectacular victory against a French fleet of twenty-six vessels off Ushant in the English Channel. The battle became known as the Glorious First of June, for an obvious reason. In 1797, as well as recovering from the Spithead and Nore mutinies, the navy had celebrated victories, namely Jervis's off Cape St Vincent and Duncan's[13] off Camperdown. The latter, against the Dutch fleet, effectively put paid to Irish hopes of rebellion which, until that point, had been real enough. In August 1798, Nelson was at the Nile. Copenhagen, in 1801, and Trafalgar were still to come. The navy was busy. Many of its ships were at sea for two or three years. From this alone we can see why Britain was in need of ships and – above all – sailors to man them.

---

[10] Samuel Hood, first Viscount Hood (1724–1816).
[11] John Jervis, Earl St Vincent (1735–1823).
[12] Richard Howe, fourth Viscount and Earl (1726–1799).
[13] Adam Duncan, Viscount Duncan of Camperdown (1731–1804).

In 1793 the British navy had 69,868 men and boys on its pay book, 50,000 more than in the previous year. By the time of Trafalgar in 1805, there were 109,205 'born for pay'. We should be wary of giving exact figures for this period. Often the numbers of ships and men did not tally with official and semi-official reports. Moreover, to gather the significance of numbers of ships and numbers of men we have to question the sources of this accounting. For one thing, there was no census in Britain until 1801, so we cannot possibly know with any accuracy the percentage of able-bodied men serving in the navy. Port authorities could not be relied upon to maintain an analysis of the numbers of ships for the Register General of Shipping, which was only established in 1786. More specifically, the Admiralty, while having a good record of its own ships together with their officers, did not always keep a check on the ships' companies. When an officer went ashore on leave, his name would still be somewhere on the books. However, once a rating was able to do the same he was discharged with no record of him necessarily being kept, for – remember – he had been recruited by the ship, not by the navy.

Furthermore, the fact that Parliament might vote so many thousand sailors did not mean that there *were* that many sailors. For example, a ship might be voted a crew of 800, the number generally recognized as being required to man that size and type of vessel, yet the muster book, the document containing the names and rates of the members of the ship's company, would often show far fewer. In fact, at the Battle of Trafalgar, some of Nelson's vessels, including his own flagship, the *Victory*, were seriously undermanned. Some had only 60 per cent of their required ship's company.

When a new sailor, whether Midshipman Nelson or Ordinary Seaman Whoever, arrived on board, nothing was arranged in quite the sure nautical Bristol fashion we might imagine. Even in the twentieth century it was common for a vessel calling at, say, Port Said to be boarded by bumboatmen with all sorts of wares and goods to sell to the crew. So no surprises, then, when we find that before Nelson's ship sailed it too would have resembled a veritable street market of touts and traders. Wives and whores would be tending to the cares of the off-duty sailors – and here we have the origin of the cry 'Show a leg!' First thing in the forenoon the bosun's mate, with his rope's end, would turn to the hands in port with that call. A leg would be displayed over the side of the hammock. A sharp bosun would be able to tell a matelot's from a doxy's, or even a powder monkey. Powder monkeys were boys who carried the powder from the lower stores to the guns and whose age would rarely have reached double figures. Many women were also known to sail with ships.

Old sores do not heal hardships. Robert Southey, in his biography of Nelson published in 1813, noted: 'The sea-boy has to endure physical hardship, and the privation of every comfort, even sleep. Nelson had a feeble body and an affectionate heart, and he remembered through his life his first days of wretchedness in the service'.

It is tempting to remark that times were different and that people then were used to terrible conditions, whatever their walk of life. However, conditions afloat were horrendous by whatever standard we choose. Flogging was an everyday form of punishment for apparently small misdemeanours. It took place ashore – even more severely in the army – and publicly. All punishments, whether minor or capital, were carried out in public. Deprivation was nothing unusual. Vagabonds and yeomen, sluts and maidens all struggled with poor diets, often pernicious laws and frequently ill health. A ship was a small town and its population a cross-section of all the characters to be found close by any tavern or pew. The captain was the squire, often the laird, while the able hand was at best the yeoman but often something worse. Rules and laws designed to protect villagers were often set aside by the personal intervention of the local authority and magistrate. Aboard ship, the captain was authority. The bosuns and, later, the masters-at-arms, kept order, or did their level best to do so. A ship was a contained society in which the ferment of unrest could spread like a small plague. Thus there could not be any slackening of discipline. The captain's word was law, and often above the written law. Admiralty regulations and the forerunner of the Naval Discipline Act laid down clear rules as to how men should behave and the punishment they might expect if these were ignored. A captain who had difficulty in maintaining order would frequently exceed the punishment tables. For example, the regulations insisted that no more than twelve lashes could be ordered as a summary punishment. There were many backs bared for thrice that amount.

At the time of Nelson – say, the late 1790s – sailors lived under the

1749 Naval Discipline Act (NDA) which included the thirty-six Articles
of War. This was not all about discipline and what happened if it were
infringed. It provided for the welfare of the officers and ratings, even if
the captain did become a dictator once the vessel had put to sea. Most
severely, the Act stipulated capital punishment for anyone who mutinied,
deserted, resorted to cowardice or failed to press home the function of
ship and weapons against the enemy. No one, however senior, was immune
to the consequences of contravening the NDA. For example, six years
after the Act went on to the statute book Admiral John Byng[14] was shot
for having failed to attack the French when sent to relieve the British
garrison at Minorca. Ratings could be flogged on the quarterdeck. Senior
rates, that is, non-commissioned officers and commissioned officers, would
not suffer summary punishment but would be sentenced by court martial.
As in Byng's case, the court or quarterdeck could mete out punishments
that were just as severe, including that of being flogged alongside every
ship in the entire fleet. As the prisoner was brought alongside, the bosun's
mate of the ship in question went into the boat and flogged him. The
boat would then move on to the next ship, where that vessel's bosun's
mate waited. Few if any of the prisoners flogged around the fleet ever
recovered fully from the ordeal. They were, literally, broken men.

   Fire and a breakdown in discipline were feared even more than the
French fleet. Once discipline was lost, then so was the ship. A ship's
society was tough in an even tougher environment. A further complication
was the number of ratings pressed into service from among the roughest
classes. The only way to control such additions to the ship's company was
through the strictest enforcement of discipline. Today we would use the
term zero tolerance. However, not all officers had the brilliance of a
Collingwood, a St Vincent, a Nelson or a Cornwallis when it came to
man management. The lesser officers, among them some very young
midshipmen, imposed terrible penalties either to counterbalance their
own inadequacies or simply because they enjoyed the power of being able

---

[14] John Byng (1704–1757), son of Lord Torrington (1663–1733), sometime
Admiral of the Fleet and First Lord of the Admiralty. Voltaire (1694–1778) in
Candide (1759) commented on Byng's execution: '*Il est bon de tuer de temps en
temps un amiral pour encourage les autres.*'

to deal harshly with 'men under punishment'. A whole watch of men might be flogged simply because another vessel had outperformed their ship in some sailing manoeuvre. If this appears bizarre, it might be remembered that the navy actually had a reputation for being a juster and less brutal service than the army. Even so, there were numerous cases of men ignoring the potentially dreadful consequences of stepping out of line to complain and even to petition a higher authority about the brutalities of their officers. Mutinies were sometimes provoked by brutality, but mainly they arose from a desire for better conditions.

Among the mutineers' demands was that of a living wage. Naval pay had not risen since Charles ll's[15] time, 140 years earlier. An able seaman earned about £14 a year (£720 at today's values), assuming he remained at sea throughout that period. From that amount would be deducted donations to the Chatham Chest and to the running of Greenwich Hospital.[16]

Sometimes ratings were refused their pay. A sailor could transfer to another ship while still being owed wages from his last one. The idea was that a man would not leave the navy if he were owed money. This worked, to some extent. There were also cases where a sailor claimed he was owed money from a number of ships when he was not. The navy also had an excuse for poor payment. In those days before banking facilities a ship had to pay sailors in cash. This meant that the purser (later known as the pusser) was required to have cash and all the books balanced, which they rarely were. It was not uncommon for a sailor not to have been paid for a couple of years, in a few cases for a decade, because the vessels had not returned home, the only source of English money. Nelson, for example, had been at sea for more or less two years before Trafalgar.

If the pay system was less than adequate, so then was the food supply. Victualling regulations were older than pay scales. Although times had changed, views on how to fill a sailor's stomach had not. There was no shortage of food, but what was available was simply in an appalling state, and the dishonesty of the chandlers who supplied it hardly helped.

---

[15] Charles II (1630–1685) who reigned from 1660.
[16] Greenwich Hospital can be seen today opposite the National Maritime Museum in the grounds of what was formerly Greenwich Naval College (now part of the University of Greenwich).

Keeping foodstuffs in a reasonably edible condition was an enormous task and one many ships failed to get to grips with. Even the names given to shipboard food hardly stirred appetites. The staple diet was burgoo (sometimes known as loblolly) a porridge to which almost anything might be added. The weakened, cheaper, version of this, with maybe some meat dropped into it, was called skilly. Another version, a sort of drink, was called skillygalee. Some sailors actually liked it. The best hope for food improvements came through ships' surgeons who needed nourishment for their patients. However, major improvements came with inventions. So the navy had to wait for nearly a decade after Trafalgar before the appearance of canning and tinned foods, including vegetables and, most famously, beef. This was named after the French dish, *boeuf bouilli*, and so became bully beef.[17]

It is little wonder that sailors mutinied for better pay and conditions. However, despite the two particularly significant mutinous occasions which had long-term repercussions, it might be noted that between the early 1790s and the end of the Napoleonic wars in 1815 hundreds of uprisings took place. They were like earthquakes; some were catastrophic, while others hardly registered on the scale of naval discipline, often being no more than insurrections on the part of a handful of men or even an individual. A terrible beating or an occasional hanging was all that followed.

Among the more extreme cases was the mutiny best known to us today, mutiny on the *Bounty* in 1789. More important to the navy were the two uprisings of the spring of 1797 that became known as the Great Mutinies: those at Spithead and the Nore. These were followed in the autumn by a third, when the captain of the *Hermione* was murdered by the ship's company and the vessel handed to the Spanish.

In April 1797 – the year, incidentally, Nelson lost his right arm at Santa Cruz – the Channel fleet had been at its Spithead moorings off Portsmouth, sixteen big ships and some others commanded by Admiral Lord Bridport (Admiral Hood)[18] flying his flag in the *Queen Charlotte*.

---

[17] Incidentally, here is the origin of the expression 'sweet Fanny Adams'. She was a murdered whore whose remains – so rumour had it – were canned into ships' bully beef.

[18] Alexander Hood, first Viscount Bridport (1727–1814).

On the fifteenth of the month, at the unlikely signal of cheering from the sailors, the fleet mutinied. This was the fleet designated as guardian in the event of an attack from France. The incident was no small matter. The sailors had a list of complaints: better conditions, better wages, better food and, importantly, better treatment for sailors when they fell ill and particularly when they were wounded. This last point is not without considerable significance. The sailors' lot was not a happy one.

Very quickly the Admiralty agreed to most – though not all – of their demands. The sailors received a pardon for their actions, which showed how seriously the naval authorities took their grievances, and also more wages – the first rise in the navy for 144 years. That might have been that, except that HMS *London* now found herself with sailors who wanted every single demand met. Perhaps emboldened by the ease with which major demands had been granted, they pressed their case, receiving a salvo from marine muskets for their pains and seeing five of their number killed. This merely incensed the sailors, who seized control of the ship. It was only the persuasive powers of Lord Howe – by now an ancient admiral and naval hero – that calmed the situation. The Admiralty gave in. Perhaps it was this apparently weak action that inspired the Nore fleet to mutiny. They had less good fortune.

On 20 May, the sailors at the Nore demanded more shore leave (which the navy thought a ploy to escape their ships), better wages and more regular payment of them, better officers and less brutality. This time, the navy could not afford to give in. Though the sailors held out for a month, they eventually ran out of support and courage. Richard Parker, their ringleader, was hanged along with his close supporters.

Lessons from these two mutinies and the conditions they made public were understood by the Admiralty Board. This did not prevent mutinies from occurring in individual vessels. One, the *Hermione*, was such an unhappy ship that the sailors took command. It happened at the start of the third week in September 1797, in the vicinity of Puerto Rico. *Hermione* was in pursuit of a privateer. The captain of the British ship was a martinet, who, when he felt the sailors aloft were not looking sharp, ordered that the last two down from the upper yards should be flogged. In the scurry to get below two fell to their deaths and were, on the captain's orders, thrown over the side. That night, the lower deck mutinied. The captain and eight of his officers were murdered. The sailors then sailed her into Puerto Rico and handed the ship over to the Spanish. The mutineers never escaped. The vessel was later recaptured and most of those who had survived with her were hanged. All this makes the late-eighteenth-century sailor appear utterly ruthless. Hard he most certainly was, and often most uncompromising in what he thought right. Not surprising, then, that a ship's captain was frequently a single-minded dictator who used whatever means he thought necessary to get his ship to the highest standard as a fighting platform. Equally, conditions were never good. Pressed men were rarely happy with their lot, or they would not otherwise have rebelled; after all, they well knew the penalty. So nervous were captains that ratings might desert that shore leave was often banned and a sailor might go for years – certainly, two was common – without getting a run ashore because the navy feared he would do just that – run.[19]

Even when crew members were let on dry land, they were never all permitted to go at once. A further aspect of keeping men aboard was that women were often allowed in ships – wives as well as prostitutes. On this subject records are sometimes confusing. A wife was not always a wife. When whores came aboard, usually selected from among a boatload, each would pair off with the sailor who had paid for her. The whore would then refer to that sailor as her husband. It was quite possible that a ship in port would have as many women on board as sailors. Such women were almost invariably the saddest form of dockside prostitutes. The men did not seem to mind, and it might be said that conditions ashore were not much better for some of the girls. In the ships, privacy was never considered. Cleanliness, even less so.

Admiral Sir James Hawkins,[20] in a pamphlet published in 1822, described the almost unspeakably horrid conditions that existed in a large ship, perhaps a 74-gun ship of the line.

the dirt, filth, and stench; the disgusting conversation; the indecent beastly conduct and horrible scenes; the blasphemy and swearing; the riots, quarrels, and fighting, which often takes place, where

---

[19] Run was at that time the naval term for desertion.
[20] Admiral Sir James Hawkins (1762–1849).

hundreds of men and *women* [author's italics] are huddled together in one room . . . and where . . . they must be witness of each others' actions . . . Let those who have never seen a ship of war picture to themselves a very large low room with 500 men and probably 300 or 400 women of the vilest description shut up in it, and giving way to every excess of debauchery that the grossest passions of human nature can lead them to[21]

In theory, the women had to be ashore by the time the vessel slipped her mooring. Nevertheless wives and 'wives' did go to sea, and so would even be present in battle, and were known to have carried gunpowder to the cannons. Famously, in 1798 a wife gave birth aboard ship during the ferocious battle of Aboukir Bay, later known as the Battle of the Nile (see chapter 14), and there was at least one woman at Trafalgar (see chapter 28).

The Nile was a furious battle. The French admiral directed the battle from a chair as both his legs had been blown away. There are many other accounts of brutal actions and terrible deaths and injuries. Yet, more sailors died of disease in ships than enemy action.

During the period of our story, the end of the 1790s and the early years of the 1800s, fewer than 7 per cent of naval fatalities occurred in battle. More than 80 per cent died as a result of accidents or disease. It is true also that captains were reluctant to let sick men be sent ashore for hospital treatment. It was easier to desert from a shore hospital than from a ship's sick bay. Besides, there were few hospitals in Britain apart from the newish teaching hospitals, such as St Bartholomew's in London, and many of those were built for the services.

If a sailor fell to disease or cannon, he would be treated by the ship's surgeon. This might not be a comforting moment for the patient. Medicine was rudimentary, surgery crude and the practitioner not always a trained doctor. There were cases where the surgeon, a social and professional failure ashore, was on board in spite of his formal interview. Hacking off the remains of a leg shattered in battle was never a task for the squeamish. Yet it was a job for the medical craftsman. Often that

---

[21] *Statement of Certain Immoral Practices in H.M. Ships*, 1822.

talent was missing, with terrible consequences for the patient. Trauma surgery and recovery was not a known branch of medicine. By Trafalgar the navy had about 700 surgeons, each of whom was ranked as a warrant officer not a commissioned officer. An applicant for the post might not have a medical degree, because the normal training was through an apprenticeship. A London examining board of surgeons would interview the candidate, who would not be tested in practical surgery. If successful, he would be given his warrant. He would then be appointed to a ship as surgeon's mate or – after 1805 – assistant surgeon. That was the year in which, for the first time, surgeons were allowed to wear a uniform. A young man might have received a sound training in anatomy, have some knowledge of invasive medicine, and of perhaps trauma treatment. Yet the fine schools of Edinburgh and London could not hope to prepare a man for battle surgery. He would have to learn – quickly – to work far below in a dank, cramped space, treading decks scattered with sand to make him surer-footed in the blood, while the ship heaved in a sickening swell, all the while being struck by cannonballs and crashing spars. To this operating theatre, just above the ship's keel, would be sent a sure stream of casualties. A man without the skill to quickly, and without fuss, cut off a wrecked arm or leg or close off scattered organs and a gaping stomach was not much good in a ship of the line. It was also to be hoped that he did not suffer from seasickness. Yet in the late eighteenth and early nineteenth centuries such men were indeed among the surgeons who prepared their instruments when the ship closed up for action stations.

Also at action stations were the marines. It is often forgotten that the navy took its own army to sea. Many of the story books and paintings show Jack Tars, cutlasses in hand, engaging the enemy with grappling irons and fierce cuts and thrusts, but there were, too, the navy's trained marksmen and fighters, her marines. They performed the same role at sea as they did ashore and provided a captain with the added assurance of a police force aboard. Today, the Royal Marines will claim to be the smartest people in any military service. Certainly in the late eighteenth, even nineteenth centuries they were very definitely the best turned-out individuals in a ship apart from the officers. The sailors had not yet been dressed uniformly and many were very casually clothed. Not so the marines. Their uniforms were braided tunics and even then they sported a uniform cap, a soft headdress. So from the earliest times, the marines, by then mostly volunteers, not pressed men,[22] stood out as exceptional additions to a ship's company. Their smartness was matched by performance.

The marines had their origins in the time the navy first took soldiers to sea as fighters rather than as passengers, in troop transporters. In 1664, the Duke of York and Albany's Maritime Regiment of Foot was raised, although it was only employed during a war and had no peacetime role or structure. There was no continuous marine establishment until the mid eighteenth century. In 1755, a corps was raised when the Seven Years War (see chapter 1) appeared inevitable. Records show that wherever there was a sea battle involving the navy the marines were in the thick of it. Their value was recognized by the Admiralty, who took over their running and did not stand them down at the end of the conflict, instructing them to assume the role of guard force for naval ships and establishments, thus guaranteeing them an unbroken history to the present day.

It was not until 1802 that the marines became 'Royal'. This was largely the work of Admiral the Earl St Vincent, or John Jervis as he was known for much of his career. Jervis was one of the heroic British naval commanders of the eighteenth century. He had served with General Wolfe's Quebec expedition, recaptured Gibraltar on three occasions, and in 1794 took the French islands of Guadeloupe and Martinique. His most famous victory came in 1797 with his defeat of the much larger Spanish fleet off Cape St Vincent, on Portugal's south-west coast, from whence came his earldom. It was also a victory many have attributed to one of Jervis's subordinate commanders, Horatio Nelson.

There was a Spanish fleet of twenty-seven ships 'round the corner' from Gibraltar. Sir John Jervis had a fleet of fifteen. Jervis was the perfect naval planner. He plotted the course of the Spanish vessels. His intelligence was carefully analysed – gathered, in those pre-satellite times, from nothing more than speedy, darting frigates and schooners set to

---

[22] As marines were soldiers, they were safe from the press gangs. Only men who were wanted as sailors could be whisked away for the king's shilling.

shadow and run on a good wind to the loitering British fleet. The planning done, the wind perhaps a shade shifting to the north-west, Jervis launched his offensive to engage the enemy. It was admirable planning, but every commander needs something else – luck, perhaps. Jervis had that in one of his junior officers, Horatio Nelson. It was Nelson who singlehandedly engaged six Spanish ships and decided the outcome of the battle in Jervis's favour. Oh, how they cheered him in London and even the shires! The people had waited too long for a famous victory. Now they had a hero too.

St Vincent, as Jervis then became, in many senses Nelson's champion, turned somewhat sour towards him in later years. It is possible that he would have preferred a seagoing command to the considerable distinction of being appointed First Lord of the Admiralty, a post he held between the important military years 1801 and 1804.

Whatever St Vincent's faults or sometimes grumpy disposition, the Royal Marines honoured him, and still do. For they owe him their title. He had used them wisely in his seagoing commands, especially in the Mediterranean. Jervis had experienced a few difficulties with mutineers or would-be rebels. On one occasion he had brought a ship's company to heel when he forced the sailors to hang one of their own whom he believed guilty of extreme insubordination amounting to mutiny. St Vincent valued the marines' contribution and held their service in high regard.

He relied on his seagoing infantry to protect his ship from insurrection should it become necessary. He was a hard man and perhaps used the marine detachments better than most, given that they were not always the loyal ships' marshals he claimed them to be. Their place in some vessels was, on occasion, difficult to maintain. They were isolated inasmuch as they were neither sailors nor officers, and to protect them captains often had them messing separately rather than with the hands. St Vincent, however, never had the slightest doubts about their value. In J. S. Tucker's account of Jervis, the admiral in retirement remarked on their loyalty and right to the highest degree of recognition. 'I never knew an appeal to them for honour, courage or loyalty that they did not realise more than my highest expectations. If ever the hour of real danger should come to England, they will be found the country's sheet anchor.'

However, the marines had a larger role than that of shipboard policemen and skirmishers. Today, in the twenty-first century, the Royal Marines are seen as forces best used in amphibious operations, capable with their own craft and techniques of operating swiftly in beach landings and especially in tasks demanding surprise. This was exactly the job for which they were beginning to be properly trained a decade before Trafalgar. It was most likely that a small vessel would have to put together a landing party very quickly. The task could be either something as simple as a guard duty or a more complex and often opportunistic one such as an assault on a harbour. The marines were trained for just this purpose.

None of this should obscure the fact that getting hold of marines, particularly of the right sort, was no easy task for the recruiters. As a result a newly enlisted man might well have a past as colourful as his uniform. In the ten years leading up to Trafalgar, the marine corps numbers doubled from 15,000 to 30,000. In wartime, there are always manpower shortages. A well-tried system of augmenting the soldiering part of the ship involved getting infantry from the army. This brought with it obvious problems. Infantrymen remained in the army and outside the jurisdiction of naval discipline. They also had privileges such as, in certain circumstances, that of being able to be accompanied by their wives – part of the military tradition of camp followers. The simplest answer was to persuade soldiers to transfer to the marines. They were offered bonuses to do so, and many took the bait. As there were still not enough of them for large marine contingents to be drafted into ships, officers were deployed to prison hulks to fish out likely candidates. It could be that Johnson's observation, referred to earlier, was not entirely whimsical. Whatever the ploys involved, together they worked. Regular volunteers were joined by ex-soldiers. Foreigners, taken at some time as prisoners of war, were enlisted for the duration of hostilities. A few freed black workers from the West Indies also signed on. Moreover, in 1804, the enlistment age was lowered, thus ensuring that a lad would be getting a man's wage by the age of fifteen.

Today, anyone aboard a warship knows that Royal Marines, while very much admired, are never quite part of the ship's company, for the reason that sailors and marines see themselves as quite different social and

professional animals. So it was in Nelson's ships. The marines, messed –
that is, lived – separately from the sailors. Equally, when battle stations
were called, a marine fought as hard as any matelot, including when it
came to being part of the gun crews. This meant that marines and
ratings exercised battle stations alongside one another but during normal
sailing hours, and when the hands were stood down the marines tended
to keep their own company. This was encouraged by captains and by the
Admiralty. Sailors found it only too easy to regard the marines as a group
not entirely on their side. When there were grievances, the marines were
not to be counted on. After all, part of their function was to police the
ship and protect the captain and officers in difficult circumstances,
especially mutinous ones, of which there were many. This distinction
between sailors and marines was not confined to the lower decks. Even
officers, especially the junior ones, tended to think that marine officers
had special privileges. They certainly had all the advantages of the army,
including status. One important marine rank, however, was reserved for
a distinguished naval officer in a fleet. The colonel of marines was a
naval officer and, in time of battle, the marines were placed firmly under
the navy's command.

Here, then, was the ship's company. A close-knit community. So close
that we can imagine what the atmosphere must have been like when
probably five hundred sailors were expected to sling their hammocks
within not much more than a foot of one another and, on a lower deck,
with barely six feet headroom. The hammocks were precious. The ship
gave the man his hammock, but he had to provide the bedding that went
in it. He kept it close. Should he die at sea (other than in battle, when he
would be tossed over the side) he was sewn into it before being committed
to the deep.

CHAPTER THREE

Spankers and Gallants

S O MUCH FOR THE MEN. WHAT ABOUT THE SHIPS? AGAIN, WE NEED TO know about these things because we shall then be able to appreciate the size of the vessels referred to in this story, how difficult they were to manoeuvre and what it took in terms of skill, manpower and supplies to sail them as fighting vessels.

The first thing to note is that in those days the 'ship' was not just a general term used to refer to a boat on the sea. The word had a particular definition. It told us something of the vessel's appearance.

A ship had three masts and a bowsprit. The front mast was known as the foremast and was slightly shorter than the middle mast, more properly the mainmast. At the back (stern), of the vessel, was the shortest of the three masts, the mizen. The definition of *ship* literally hangs on those masts because a ship was a three-masted vessel with square sails on at least the mainmast and the foremast. Square sails were of the sort of galleon shape most of us will be familiar with.

The second clue to the ranking of a vessel was the number of guns, mostly cannons, in a ship.[1] The number of cannons carried decided the rating, that is, the importance of a ship. There were six ratings of warship.

First rates carried a hundred or more guns on three decks, second rates between ninety and ninety-eight, also on three decks, while third rates had between sixty-four and eighty on two decks. Nelson's first ship, *Raisonnable*, was a 64-gun ship. She was also classified as a ship of the

---

[1] In the Royal Navy, sailors talk of being in a ship rather than on a ship.

line. A line-of-battle ship was exactly what the name suggests: a ship designed to form the main battle line at sea against the enemy. The fourth, fifth and sixth rates were below-the-line or second-line-of-attack vessels. These ships mostly had only one gun deck.

The number of guns also gives the maritime detective a clue that others may miss. Each cannon stuck out from gun ports (square holes, usually with flaps) in the ship's side. There had to be about eight feet between each gun port to enable the crews to work the weapons. There was also at least five feet between gun decks. Maurice Suckling's command carried sixty-four guns on two decks. Therefore there would be sixteen cannons on each deck on the port (left) side and sixteen on each deck on the starboard (right) side. The need for a distance of eight feet between the guns meant that the gun decks alone would have had to have been 120 feet, probably 136 feet, long. If we add on the combined length of the poop deck (the raised deck at the stern) and the forecastle (fo'c'sle), the deck at the front (bow), say twenty-four or twenty-five feet, we can work out that the *Raisonnable* was about 160 feet long.

So we have an image of the sort of vessels we shall come across in the story of Trafalgar. Three masts, square sails which billow, two and three rows of flat flaps – the gun ports – on either side and the ship quite chunky in appearance. A big ship, a first-rate with a hundred guns like the *Victory*, would have needed 850 men to sail her, keep her going and fight. Even *Raisonnable* would have carried as many as 500.

To give a further idea of the size and strength of these ships, we might note that it would take as many as 2,000 trees to build a ship the size of the *Raisonnable*. The hull was built from oak with elm for the keel. The best oak was English, the second choice was Baltic or – after the War of American Independence – Canadian. These were, however, second-class regions for such timbers although there was nothing wrong with their good, straight, brine-soaked mast firs.

These were cumbersome vessels with lines that would not have surprised Drake or Ralegh, although their overall length and beam might have impressed them.[2] The seamanship necessary to sail and fight[3] them was, when executed properly, of an extremely high standard,

---

[2] Sir Francis Drake, (c. 1540–1596); Sir Walter Ralegh (c. 1552–1618).

particularly when again we remember that a vessel relied entirely on wind and currents for power. If, for example, the wind were to be dead ahead – that is coming straight at the ship – there was nothing, other than altering course, that a sailing master could do to make his vessel move.

In big ships, such as the *Royal Sovereign* or the *Victory*, the array of sails may well appear rather confusing to most people living in the present century. Yet from day one, even the most wimpish lad in the Nelsonian navy could have been sent aloft 100 feet and more to hand in wet sails that could weigh close to a ton, to break out grommets holding great canvases, to scramble up ratlines and across yardarms, to raise and lower topmasts, to heave, belay and make fast. Confusion was not an option. The names of the sails were not nearly as confusing as they appear at a first reading or as they sound. Topgallants, royals, staysails, mizens and courses, each had a place in the carefully balanced design enabling a ship to manoeuvre and sail in most directions according to the strength of the prevailing wind and the way it was blowing. A brief look at names of sails will go a long way to demystify the age of canvas.

Let us take a fairly big ship. Imagine three masts, the one in the middle being the tallest, the one at the back (the stern) being the shortest. Imagine also a bowsprit, the long wooden boom sticking straight ahead from the bow and, finally, a shorter boom projecting from the stern. We would see square sails, triangular sails and oblong sails with their tops cut off at an angle. In general terms, the square sails (actually trapezium-shaped, with the top side shorter than that at the base) were on the masts and stuck out on either side of the ship. The others were set either between the masts or between the front mast (the foremast) and the bowsprit and more or less on a line from stem to stern. These were the staysails (stays'ls).

The square sails of the bottom row were called courses. So the bottom square sail on the foremast was, naturally, called the forecourse, the bottom one on the middle mast (mainmast) the maincourse and the

---

[3] Fighting a ship does not mean attacking or defending against another vessel. Fighting a ship is a term used to express how the sailor manoeuvres his own ship during battle and employs his weapons.

bottom one on the after mast (mizen) the mizen course. The next row up (and there might certainly be four rows) was the topsail (tops'l) and had the same tag as those below. So, there was a foretops'l, maintops'l and mizen tops'l. The next, the third row up, were called the topgallants. 'Gallant' comes from the word 'garland', usually a rope ring around the topmast used to reduce chafing between the rigging and the wooden mast. By the same system as before these were known as the foretopgallant, the maintopgallant and the mizen topgallant. Should there have been a fourth row – a daunting prospect for a young deckhand – these would be the royals. So there would have been a foreroyal, a mainroyal and a mizen royal.

Some ships would also carry squaresails 'hanging' beneath the bowsprit. The furthest out would also be the highest because the bowsprit pointed slightly upwards. That furthest sail was the spritsail topsail and the nearest sail simply the spritsail (sprits'l).

Now to the triangular and irregular oblongs, the fore and aft staysails. Starting at the bow (front), there were perhaps four triangular sails from the point of the bowsprit running back to the foremast. These were jib sails (and are still called that in modern-day dinghies and yachts). Starting with the furthest away, these would be called the flying jib, the outer jib, the inner jib and, finally – the smallest triangle and the closest to the mast – the fore topmast staysail.

Between the foremast and the mainmast four more sails hung out. The top three were oblongs with the tops sliced off at an angle, and the bottom one another triangle known as the main staysail. The first oblong up, the biggest of the irregular shapes, was the main topmast staysail. The next one up was smaller and called the middle staysail. The top one was the main topgallant staysail.

Between the mizen (the back) mast and the mainmast (the middle) there might be just three irregular-shaped fore and after sails. These were, from the bottom up: the mizen staysail, the mizen topmast staysail and the mizen topmast gallant staysail.

The sail furthest after was big. It was fixed to a long boom at the bottom which stretched from the mizen mast to over the stern. It then ran at an angle upwards to another boom (the gaff), also attached to the mizen. This was the spanker or, sometimes, the driver.

That was the extent of what appears at first glance as a complicated arrangement of canvas which, if sewn together, could cover a couple of acres and maybe weigh as much as ten tons – when dry.

Why have differently shaped and rigged sails? Square sails helped the ship when the wind was blowing from behind. They were apparently not much help when the wind was blowing at the ship from ahead. However much the square sails might be angled, a sailing master using this type of sail alone could only point his ship slightly towards the wind, so if the wind was blowing from, say, the north and the sailing master wanted to go north, he was unable to do so. About the very best he could hope for with square sails was to sail east north-east, that is, more than sixty degrees off course.

Fore and aft sails meant the ship would point closer to the wind, but often no better than forty-five degrees off course. This meant that to achieve its direction the ship had to tack, that is, zigzag. However, in a big ship, fore and after sails were much harder to coordinate. They were good in a small vessel, such as a cutter. As a result a combination of both types of sail was carried, with the emphasis being on the square ones.

Today, even keen yachtsmen and women often find the different rigs and sail plans confusing and remarkably inefficient. We talk of the glamorous days of brilliant craftsmanship of the wrights and riggers of yards such as Buckler's Hard on the Beaulieu (where Nelson's much admired *Agamemnon* was built). We marvel at the seamanship that sailed these vessels across every ocean. Yet we should not forget that not all ships were well designed and built. Not every Royal Naval vessel had the best-quality sails and the finest running rigging. The same cautious note should be in our minds when we judge the worth of not only the British navy, but also those of other nations, especially those of the French and the Spanish. After the Battle of Trafalgar, what the French and Spanish most admired about the British ships was the way they were so well officered and that this expertise had stood them well not only in battle but also during the treacherous weather that immediately followed.

CHAPTER FOUR

The Duel

T HIS IS THE BACKGROUND TO THE ROYAL NAVY, THE BRITISH NAVY. However, we need to remember that there were three navies at Trafalgar, those of Britain, France and Spain. In sporting terms, the summary might read: the French fought badly, the Spanish bravely, the British won.

The British fleet was governed by the diktat of the Admiralty Board. The prime minister, Pitt the Younger, more or less allowed his minister (at the time we are particularly interested in this was Lord Melville)[1] to get on with building and running the navy. The French navy was not the brainchild of Napoleon Bonaparte. He knew little of naval affairs and cared less for his admirals. At the same time, nothing was either created or attempted without the emperor's approval. The Spanish navy was altogether different. There is a British view that Spanish naval power had declined with its empire. The weakness of this notion lies in the fact that, contrary to this persistent belief, the Spanish Empire had by no means collapsed by the end of the previous century and its fleet was both efficiently run and commanded at sea, consisting of well-constructed and often enviably manned vessels. The biggest warship built in the eighteenth century, the *Santísima Trinidad*, was Spanish and was at Trafalgar. So why the illusion about Spanish decline? Perhaps it had something to do with the eighteenth-century arrogance of the eighteenth-century British, who believed above all in the divine gift of their Protestantism. All those

---

[1] Henry Dundas Melville, first Viscount (1742–1811).

who were not Protestants were, by simple definition, second rate.
Bonaparte's idea of a secular society fitted easily into this British conceit.
The Spanish Empire actually survived until the end of the eighteenth
century. The almost thirty-year rule of King Carlos III was one of
innovation, science and its industrial sibling, technology.[2] As for the
French, they understood the power of the sea in terms of building and
maintaining possessions. None doubted French tenacity and the single-
minded ambition of Bonaparte. That his obsession was destructive may
not be doubted. However, nothing he did was underrated by the British.
They watched the frustrations emerging in Bonaparte's commanders –
especially those charged with the building and rebuilding of fleets to
protect deep-sea interests and to prepare for the invasion of Britain's
south coast. Equally, no British commander ever forgot his history lessons.
The French had to be brought to account. So a combined Spanish–French
naval engagement (the joint fleet was sometimes called the Combined
Squadron or Combined Fleet) was seen as inevitable, although the British
never doubted the outcome. Unfortunately for France, the admiral
detailed by Bonaparte to seek and destroy Nelson's fleet shared the British
view that his own country would not win – not with him in command.

For here is one of the givens of the story of Trafalgar: that Bonaparte
was determined that if his greater plan for domination as far east as the
Indian subcontinent and as far west as the Caribbean were to succeed,
he had to have command of the seas. Moreover, his immediate task once
the new war with Britain had begun in 1803 was to invade the British
Isles along its south-east coast. Without supremacy over the sea lanes,
Bonaparte knew this great plan for his grand army would come to
nothing. He believed Nelson to be the key factor in British naval
superiority but not in its supremacy. In this he was wrong. Undoubtedly
Nelson was a then unsurpassable genius of maritime warfare. Yet on at
least one occasion, earlier in 1805, another British admiral could so
easily have put paid to Bonaparte's plans. After drawing up eight plans,
Napoleon believed, as late as July 1805, that an invasion was still
possible. Had Sir Robert Calder[3] succeeded in destroying Villeneuve's

---

[2] Admiral Sir Robert Calder (1745–1818).
[3] King Carlos III (1716–1788).

Combined Fleet in that same month, as he had had a very good chance of doing, Napoleon would no longer have seen Nelson as a threat (see chapter 19). There would have been no Trafalgar and no famous column in the centre of London.

The story of Trafalgar is therefore also the story of the duel, part military, part psychological, between two men, Napoleon Bonaparte[4] and Horatio Nelson. We need to know more about our two principal characters before we go any further. The 1790s were to be the deciding years for both men. This was the period when Bonaparte abandoned his Corsican origins and Nelson achieved his supreme naval reputation – as well as losing his right eye and right arm.

Like many naval officers, Nelson spent much of his time in the West Indies and the Americas. It was in the West Indies that he married the widow of a doctor who had practised on the island of Nevis. And in 1787 he took his bride, the former Mrs Frances Nisbet, home to Burnham Thorpe.[5] For five years, he remained frustrated because he could not get a command and had to settle for the lazy life on half pay. He was quite pleased when the French revolutionary wars broke out in 1792. The following year, with attacks against the French in Toulon and the West Indies, the British entered the war against France. With the exception of the mock peace between 1802 and 1803, Britain and France would be at war until 1815 and Nelson – as he would have seen it – properly employed until his death. At the start of that war he commanded what was by most accounts his favourite ship, the *Agamemnon*, built by his favourite craftsman at Buckler's Hard at the head of the navigable part of the Beaulieu river. This ship was deployed to the Mediterranean to join Lord Hood's fleet. In 1793, the French gave up their Mediterranean naval headquarters at Toulon and Hood ordered Nelson to Naples.

It was now, in 1794, that Nelson met Emma Hamilton.[6] Emma (baptized Emily) had been mistress to a variety of London gentry including a naval captain, the baronet Charles Greville[7] and then his uncle, Sir

---

[4] Napoleon is really Napoleon I. Therefore we shall refer to him throughout the text as Bonaparte.
[5] Frances Nisbet, later Frances Nelson (1761–1831).
[6] Lady Emma Hamilton (c.1765–1815).
[7] Charles Greville (1749–1809).

William Hamilton.[8] Hamilton had become British ambassador at Naples in 1764 and was to remain there until 1800. He was also something of an archaeologist, working at the Pompeii excavations and supplying the British Museum with antiquities. When Emma was passed on to William Hamilton by his nephew Charles, Hamilton had been in Naples for over a quarter of a century. He married Emma in 1791 and thus she became a lady of considerable status. When Nelson arrived in Naples, he and Emma almost immediately became lovers.

Nelson had business at sea as well as in Emma's bedroom. The intervention of Britain against the French in the French Revolutionary War found Nelson in command of the *Agamemnon* and taking part in land as well as naval operations. This was a common business for an officer in the late eighteenth century when a fleet would often have infantry and artillery embarked and naval gunners were used in any action where they could be spared. In early April 1794, Nelson had commanded the British siege of Bastia, on the top end of the eastern seaboard of Corsica. By 23 May, his force of about 1,000 men had assured the surrender of a French contingent of about 4,000.

Interestingly, from Nelson's letters, we see that he was still writing in great detail to his wife, Fanny. His letters warned her not to imagine that he had been killed and reassured her that her son, Josiah, a midshipman, was quite safe. His concern for Fanny was evident in those letters in spite of his hopeless passion for Sir William Hamilton's wife, Emma.

From Bastia, the British decided to move against Calvi, on the western coast of the island (see chart pages xvi-xvii). They believed that if they took that citadel, they would have control of Corsica, ironically Napoleon's birthplace. This attempt at the reduction of Calvi was an altogether more difficult task than the siege of Bastia. The navy's Mediterranean commander, Admiral Samuel Hood, was old and grumpy and did not much care for the army. This meant the combined naval and military operation did not always run smoothly. Nelson became the go-between for Hood and the army commander, General the Honourable Charles Stuart.[9] The French defending fire was accurate and so was the

---

[8] Sir William Hamilton (1730–1803).
[9] General the Honourable Charles Stuart (?–1827).

local virus which was accounting for almost as many British sailors as was the firepower. Stuart and Nelson landed guns and men at Port Agro, about three miles from the high point on which Calvi sat. On 12 June, flying debris and rock chips from enemy fire cut Nelson about the face. A wound through his right eyebrow left Nelson with no sight in that eye other than light and darkness. He mentioned to Hood that he hoped he would not lose his sight, but he did. Contrary to modern impressions, the wound was not so ugly that Nelson ever needed to wear an eye-patch. Blindness did not prevent him pressing on against the French and three years later, Nelson was given flag rank.

In 1797, Nelson, under the flag of Admiral Sir John Jervis, later his patron and the Earl of St Vincent, wrecked much of the Spanish fleet off Cape St Vincent (see chapter 2) Nelson was very much responsible for the tactics employed in that action. As a result, he was promoted to rear admiral.

He was sent with a small squadron to seize a Spanish ship at Santa Cruz in Tenerife. It was in this action that he lost his right arm. One-eyed and one-armed admirals were not automatically discharged from the navy. Indeed, Nelson's most spectacular victories were yet to come. In 1798, flying his flag in the *Vanguard*, he destroyed the French fleet at the Battle of the Nile. This effectively curbed Bonaparte's ambition to make his way to the Far East.

This famous victory sealed Nelson's image in the wax of heroism. He was given a peerage with the title Baron Nelson of the Nile, and an immediate pension of £2,000 a year, a not inconsiderable sum at the end of the eighteenth century. Moreover – and to emphasize the importance of the victory at the Nile and thus the destruction of the immediate threat of Bonaparte's advance towards the East – the British East India Company gave Nelson a £10,000 gratuity. The king of Naples, no longer under immediate threat from French ambitions at sea and certainly rather taken with the popular hero, created Nelson Duke of Brontë – a Sicilian title.

By now, Nelson and Emma Hamilton were openly lovers, and their daughter, Horatia,[10] was born in 1801. A curious insight into Nelson's

---

[10] Horatia Nelson (1801–1881).

character (and presumably Emma's) can be gained from the fact that even at Horatia's baptism at Bath Abbey, where Nelson and Emma were greeted by cheering crowds, they continued with the subterfuge that the child was not their daughter but that of another sailor and that they were looking after her. This state of affairs was not to continue. Here is not the place to wonder about the relationship between Nelson and Emma. It is worth noting, however, that Nelson worried considerably about what would happen to Emma should he die. He wanted her to have a pension from the state and to be looked after at Merton, the house they had bought. Of course, he knew about her weakness of character. After all, her immediate history had hardly been hidden from him and the insecurities caused by her lowly upbringing did not make up for it. She was actually arrested for debt in 1813.

In 1801 Nelson, by now promoted to vice admiral, was appointed second-in-command to Admiral Sir Hyde Parker[11] on what was to become a famous expedition to the Baltic.

Parker's command of that fleet could not have been described as a proactive one, even when he was ordered to the Baltic to confront the coalition of the Danes, Swedes and Russians. He could hardly be stirred from London, even by Nelson's urgings, and instructed the latter to observe great caution. It was Nelson's opinion that these were the only tactics understood by his superior flag officer. When told to break off the engagement, Nelson apocryphally ignored Hyde Parker's instructions by raising his telescope to his blind eye, thus claiming he could see no signal. Perhaps Parker has been treated unfairly. True, he was not a dynamic flag officer. Yet, although he did signal for the action to be left off, he did send Nelson a message instructing him to continue if he thought success was possible. The action was indeed a success, but a costly one. Many died, and the result must have been touch and go for both sides. Nelson's action at Copenhagen was considered tactically innovative, a brilliant use of reconnaissance and a measured application of daring. The war with France then went into its uneasy truce, to re-emerge as a full-scale conflict in 1803, at which time Nelson was made commander-in-chief of the Mediterranean squadron. Toulon had clearly now been returned to

---

[11] Sir Hyde Parker (1739–1807).

French control. Nelson's view was that the destruction of that fleet would clear the seaways protecting the Mediterranean, the Iberian peninsula and the West Indies station. In other words, the navy would have a superiority, which would lead to absolute control – sea supremacy. Nelson's view – and it was not his alone – was that without an effective seagoing fleet allowed to manoeuvre at will Bonaparte had no chance of protecting the invasion force he was building. Therefore Britain would be safe.

What of Bonaparte in this decisive decade of the 1790s? He was born in Ajaccio, the capital of Corsica, in 1769 (though some say, in the previous year). That island had recently been captured by the French. The Corsicans, not native French speakers, were a fiercely independent people and continued to be so. Napoleon's father was Carlo (or Charles) Bonaparte, a minor noble, while his mother, Letitia Ramolino, though considered something of a beauty, was of no great social consequence.[12] At the age of ten he was sent to a school to learn French and then on to military academy. Among the French cadets he stood out because of his lack of money, his foreignness – and his ideas. These were the ideas of a thoughtful tactician and were clearly expressed when, in 1784, he entered a military academy in Paris. The following year he obtained his commission. It is not entirely fanciful to note that Bonaparte was a gunner, an artilleryman. Even in the eighteenth century gunners thought differently from many of their brother officers, as they still do today. To the gunner a horse was a means of transport, whereas a hussar saw his horse as part of his whole personality, a dancing partner. The gunner understood distance. The infantryman and cavalryman stood hand to hand and foot to foot with the enemy. The gunner saw range and resolution as his advantages to be exploited. The cavalryman could command late manoeuvres, hot pursuit, deft withdrawal, even retreat. The gunner would argue that he had to anticipate events, get into position, consider all aspects of his targets, have a clearer understanding of the need for logistics and the possibilities created when the enemy shifted unaccountably or overwhelmed his own side. So the gunner was

---

[12] Carlo Bonaparte (1746–1785), a lawyer, he opposed Corsican independence from France; Letitia Ramolino (1750–1786).

theoretically and instinctively the commander of the bigger picture. That great command was really the result of military brilliance and tactical awareness could not be denied, yet even the dullest gunner had to know the advantages and disadvantages of distant warfare as well as of close combat. Such talents were perhaps useful for one who would be emperor.

This approach hardly made Bonaparte a plodding, unimaginative campaigner. His early experience came from the place which, at that point, mattered most to him – Corsica. In 1789, he returned to Ajaccio and there became the leading revolutionary. He wanted Corsica back from France. He was much praised, as if he had been one of Plutarch's Heroes.[13] The first-century Greek historian would almost certainly, had he lived seventeen hundred years later, have found Bonaparte a natural subject for inclusion in his great gallery of the famous. Ironically, it was in his native Corsica that Bonaparte failed. He tried to take control of Ajaccio, but could never expect to win. And so he fled to France. There was hardly any other place he could go. Why was he not caught, executed or at least banished? Perhaps because the revolutionary Jacobins, extremists of the French Revolution, desperately needed good soldiers and even better officers. So it was that Bonaparte returned to Corsica as a new form of revolutionary: a proponent of the French experiment. His Corsican comrades spat on his name. Bonaparte abandoned his homeland for France – for ever.

He had seen the start of the French Revolution. He commanded the artillery at the siege of Toulon in 1793 and found himself a brigade general. He was also regarded, as were so many others, with suspicion by the revolutionary leadership, who needed men of brilliance, but, on finding them, not unreasonably mistrusted them. Yet these stirring times produced unusual, not simply revolutionary, events. So it was little wonder that when, in 1795, Bonaparte was faced with the counter-revolution in Paris, he acted in exceptional style. He gave the mob at the Tuileries a whiff of grapeshot. He may have settled them, but he had also settled himself along his personal road to greatness. The following year he was given command of the army in Italy. It was at this point, just before his departure for that country, that Bonaparte married *his* Emma. She was

---

[13] Plutarch (c.46–c.120).

Joséphine, widow of the then famous general the Viscomte de Beauharnais.[14] Her late husband had been a victim of the Revolution, executed during the so-called Reign of Terror.

When the world is at war, comparisons and coincidences are noted among those on opposing sides. If we remember the gratitude of the king of Naples towards Nelson, we can better understand the importance of Bonaparte's occupation in Italy. Italy was not then one country as we understand it today. Its monarchy was linked to the house of Savoy, which ruled Piedmont from the eleventh century and then Italy as a unified state from only 1861. (It was not until 1946 that Italy became an independent republic.) The Piedmontese and Austrians had joined forces when confronted by Bonaparte, who set the former to rout at Mondovi before defeating the latter at Lodei. This cleared the way for Bonaparte's entry into Milan.

He then eyed the republic of Venice, which was neutral, seizing from it Verona and Legnago. By 1797, he was apparently unhaltable. Before him lay Vienna. Nonetheless, behind him was the turmoil he had left behind in France, where there was every sign that the royalists were capable of overturning the Revolution. The legislative councils of Paris were being overinfluenced by the moderates and therefore by the royalists. Bonaparte did the obvious. He separated out part of the army he did not need, telling his commanders to return to Paris to stiffen the backs of the Directory (the revolutionary government of France between 1795 and 1799) and put down its royalist and moderate opponents. That settled, the Austrians, who could hardly have expected him to be distracted any longer, sued for peace. The October 1797 Treaty of Campoformio with Austria gave Belgium, Lombardy and the Ionian islands to France, while the Austrians received Dalmatia, Istria and Venetia. Thus more of Europe was carved up. It was at this point – in 1798 – that the ambitions of Bonaparte and Nelson clashed.

Bonaparte was unstoppable – or so he believed. The Directory was becoming nervous about the strength of his ambitions. Might it be possible that this creature whom they had, if not created, then

---

[14] Alexandre, Viscomte de Beauharnais (1760–1794), who in 1779 had married Joséphine de Tascher de la Pagerie (1763–1814).

at least let loose, would turn on them? They were right to be concerned. Bonaparte's immediate objective was Egypt. He arrived at Alexandria at the end of June 1798, having added Malta to his portfolio along the way. By July, with his troops around him, he arrived in Cairo. He was far too wise to think of speeding on to India, though that option was one he would not abandon entirely. However, his first task was simply to disrupt the lucrative trade between Britain and India. A month later, his plans came to nothing when his fleet was destroyed by Nelson at the Nile. We can see more clearly now why after that conflict the East India Company paid Nelson £10,000. We can see also why Bonaparte would have regarded Nelson, rather than anyone else, as the commander most likely to frustrate his ambitions. Yet this did not mean that he was forced to abandon those ambitions in terms of Egypt. His main opposition there consisted of the Ottoman Turks and the Mamluks.

The Austrians saw Bonaparte's wide ambitions to conquer more than his forces could hold as his weakness and hoped that their forces could take advantage of what modern military call 'overstretch'. Just as the streets of London would echo with the bells of praise for Nelson, so the towers of Paris then chimed for Bonaparte's victories. What were the members of the Directory to do? They did not want this hero back in Paris. They thought it best to give him an even greater command, the most ambitious one of all: that of the army set to face the British and to even invade England. His command was overstretched, and so were French resources. They were losing on the Rhine and in Italy. Bonaparte returned to Paris. He could not be resisted.

The outcome by 1805, Nelson dead and Bonaparte rampant across Europe for ten more years, does not tell the full story. We must now grasp the tapestry of the events that took place two years before Trafalgar and examine the details of why France and Britain were at war. We will then understand the background to the almost mesmerizing duel fought between the two most important military figures then in Europe: Bonaparte and Nelson.

The reason for Britain and France going to war lies not in the beginning of that confrontation but from an event that took place six and a half years earlier. In August 1796, the Spanish and French agreed

an unpublicized treaty, the Treaty of Ildefonso. This had nothing to
do with Bonaparte.

In August 1799, Bonaparte had returned without a fanfare to France. It
was a state, yet again, in political difficulty. He joined a small group
led by the Abbé Sieyés,[15] which, directed by himself, the Abbé and
Pierre Roger Ducos,[16] succeeded in overturning the Directory. The event
became known as the the Revolution of 1818 Brumaire, the date in the
revolutionary calendar date 9 that corresponded to November 1799. The
new constitution, an intricate document that effectively suspended
democratic principles, was the work of Sieyés. Bonaparte saw the
Abbé as a threat to his own ambitions, with the result that Sieyés was
forced out. However, he kept his head and was given a fashionable title, an
estate and a generous pension. Bonaparte regarded the expenditure as
reasonable. After all, he had got a bargain: the leadership of France. He
was now First Consul.

We should remember that Bonaparte was first of all a soldier. He went
about change in an uncompromisingly military manner. His immediate
task as First Consul was domestic reform. He established a professional
tax-collecting system, famously revised the judiciary into what became
the Code Napoléon and put into place a far more efficient form of local
government, the forerunner of the system that exists today. He would
eventually restore to the people their Church, recognizing that the lower
classes especially were devout and in need of the comfort that that
institution could give them and which the state could not. His most
famous and enduring institution was a system of honours designed to
award recognition for public service without undue expense. It was
Bonaparte who instituted the Légion d'Honneur. The First Consul and
future Emperor was a soldier, an egoist fond of uniforms and titles. He
was comfortable at war, and it was certainly ever present. In the summer
of 1800, he famously defeated the Austrians at the Battle of Marengo.
His generals were equally successful, and so was the diplomacy forced
upon Pope Pius VII[17] when he recognized Bonaparte's French republic.

---

[15] Emmanuel Joseph Comte Sieyés (1748–1836).
[16] Pierre Roger Ducos (1754–1816).
[17] Pope Pius VII (1742–1823).

Bonaparte, quietly guided by Talleyrand,[18] perhaps the most famous foreign minister in diplomatic history, pleased Pius well. Even though the Pope came to recognize the self-seeking ambition of Bonaparte, he was ever reluctant to do anything likely to put at risk the Concordat which had normalized relations between Rome and France in 1801. So it was that Pius VII crowned Bonaparte emperor shortly before Christmas 1804.

By that time, conflict between the British and the Combined fleets of Spain and France was inevitable. Napoleon, in his imperial role, saw Nelson as a worthy opponent. It was as if an emperor wanted a grand master to beat. For his part, Nelson wanted revenge for what some saw as humiliation off Boulogne, and he wanted to prove that by sweeping the Combined Fleet aside, Napoleon's ambitions would be confined to the European mainland and so become manageable for the British. Nelson was a grand strategist, not simply a tactician, for which he is mostly remembered.

Napoleon kept two busts in his state apartment. One was of Charles James Fox[19] because he believed that Fox admired him. The other was of Horatio Nelson. Nelson was the worthy opponent in the strategic duel that had been in the offing for the past two years.

---

[18] Charles Maurice de Talleyrand-Périgord, Prince of Benevento (1754–1838). Variously from 1797, French foreign minister. He abandoned his emperor in 1814. Talleyrand had such a reputedly complex and devious mind that it was reported that when he died, a minister wondered aloud, 'I wonder what he meant by that?'

[19] Charles James Fox (1749–1806). Britain's first foreign secretary, he was instrumental in speeding up the abolition of the slave trade.

CHAPTER FIVE

Invasion – The Dream

ON 27 MARCH 1802, THE BRITISH, TIRED OF WAR, SIGNED THE PEACE of Amiens. It was not a peace but merely a truce. All it did was allow a breathing space in what were to become known as the French Revolutionary and Napoleonic wars. The signatories of the treaty were Britain, France, Spain and Holland. This concord was the means by which – for the moment at least – the British kept Ceylon and Trinidad but gave up the Cape of Good Hope, Egypt and Malta. The French left Naples, and Portugal's independence was confirmed.

As it happened, Britain had second thoughts and refused to leave Malta. Here was one reason why the war would inevitably resume. Also, the peace agreed at Amiens was a flimsy one whose spirit was not helped when Bonaparte suddenly annexed the Piedmont region and sent his troops to occupy Parma.

He then immediately seized Hanover – enough to excite the minds of the British Hanoverian monarchy, which reacted by supporting the royalist attempt at a coup d'état led by Georges Cadoudal.[1] Cadoudal and the rest were guillotined. For good measure, Bonaparte also had the Duc d'Enghien shot in the moat of the castle of Vincennes, even though the young Bourbon's complicity in any revolutionary tendency was doubtful.[2] Now, in May 1804, Bonaparte took the title of emperor and looked once more across the Channel. His plans to invade England were not far enough advanced.

---

[1] Georges Cadoudal (1771–1804).
[2] Louis Antoine Henri de Bourbon, Duc d'Enghien (1772–1804).

By 1803 there were no doubts in Bonaparte's mind that his invasion would depend on three distinct components. First, he would have to personally oversee the construction of an invasion fleet, which would involve the establishment of a logistical base and harbour on the northern French coast. Second, he would need his navy to provide control of the seaway between France and southern England for some time before the invasion began and also for a considerable time after his forces had landed. Third, he understood that Britain's ability to blockade his main northern naval port of Brest and Nelson's intention to hound and destroy his high seas fleet would, if successful, negate his first two plans.

In May 1803, the basis of the British opposition to Bonaparte and his opening gambit came together. On 16 May, Vice Admiral Nelson was appointed commander-in-chief of the Mediterranean fleet. On 23 May, General Berthier[3] made his first announcement as war minister for the establishment of invasion depots along the north French coast. With that announcement none in the government of Britain should have had any doubts as to the First Consul's intentions. What they might have doubted was his ability to establish an invasion army, the complex logistical train it would need and the protective naval force without which intention and capability could not be combined in an invasion.

On 25 May, the Admiralty in London made an appointment of equivalent importance to that of Nelson. Admiral Sir William Cornwallis took command of the Channel Fleet. His terms of reference were clearly defined. He was to stop the French fleet coming out of Brest, to prevent ships (including store ships) from entering that port, and to seek and destroy all French shipping with which he came in contact. Here was the most significant obstruction to Bonaparte's plans; more significant, even, than the brilliance and determination of Nelson.

During the last week of that month Bonaparte, the supreme gunner, ordered the setting up of coastal artillery and batteries and sought and found a twenty-million-franc loan to build his invasion flotilla. This was not the fleet that Nelson would face at Trafalgar, nor was it similar to it. The invasion flotilla was, at this stage, a not always clearly

---

[3] Louis-Alexandre Berthier (1753–1815), later made a Marshal of the Empire by Bonaparte.

thought-through design consisting of shallow-drafted transport vessels capable of carrying troops, beasts, ammunition and all the seemingly continuous supplies necessary for an invasion force. It was a huge version of the flotilla raised by William, Duke of Normandy in the late summer of 1066.[4] Interestingly, in spite of French ambitions through the centuries, no one until Bonaparte had made such elaborate preparations to conquer southern England.

By early June of 1803 Berthier was ordered to raise a 60,000 coastal defence force. Bonaparte was in a hurry. The importance of the blockade of Brest – and even of the battle off Cape Trafalgar almost two and a half years on – is contained in that first burst of French military energy during the spring of 1803. This is not to suggest that the British fleet would have not been at sea, nor that Nelson and Cornwallis would have been idle. However, we do well to see the events between spring 1803 and late summer 1805 from the French perspective.

Having observed that by 1802 the British wanted a rest from war, it should be said that the French also needed to draw breath. A series of treaties and protocols had been fashioned at the turn of the century. France had agreed terms with Britain's old ally, Portugal, in June 1801. In the autumn, the French also signed a pact with the Russian court. This was not an entirely obvious agreement inasmuch as it formalized French claims in the area later to be known as Germany. The Russians regarded the Prussians as their oldest and most serious enemy. (This Russian concept haunted the corridors of *kreml* power. From the days of Ivan Susanin, the thirteenth-century hero of Russian folklore down to the second half of the twentieth century Russian leaders maintained a fear and a premonition of Prussian invasion.) The 1801 Franco-Austrian Treaty of Lunéville gave France what we now call Belgium, then known as the Austrian Netherlands. The Austrian Habsburgs ceded so much during that treaty that about 112 of the mini German states were re-structured in France's favour. Only six of the hitherto fifty-one imperial cities would survive (Augsburg, Bremen, Frankfurt-am-Main, Hamburg, Lübeck and Nürnberg). This was the beginning of the collapse of the Holy Roman Empire, which was to all intents and purposes given impetus

---

[4] William, Duke of Normandy (*c.*1028–1087). King of England 1066–1087.

by yet another treaty at the end of 1802 between Russia, France and Austria. Apart from anything else, the Holy Roman Empire lost forty-five of its fifty-one imperial cities and with it a huge amount of influence with the Roman Catholic Church. Here was the diplomatic rape of much of Europe, instigated equally by Talleyrand and Bonaparte. As all this was going on, the Treaty of Amiens was inevitable. The British negotiator, Lord Cornwallis[5] (the admiral's more famous brother) was ordered by his government to do almost anything to secure that treaty, which is why the British gave so much away. It was a domestic political concession. Pitt had gone, and Addington,[6] who replaced him as prime minister, had promised peace to the people and the return of moneymaking rather than taxation. Talleyrand had, once again, served Bonaparte well, but even he must have been bemused by the way in which the British rolled over to almost every request.

If this seems a diversion into Anglo-French relations and treaty history, then we should read it as an introduction to how Bonaparte understood the British during the period leading up to Trafalgar. Why would the British have so longed for peace? They were hardly known as an overwhelmingly peace-loving people. We should remember that Britain had been almost continuously at war during the memories of its population, who had barely recovered from the humiliation and the cost, both physical and financial, of the War of American Independence (1775–1783). Moreover, the British had from that point appeared to be either going to war or preparing to go to war with the French. The prosecution of war involved more than taxes to pay for soldiers and sailors. Money had to be raised to buy off and support so-called allies on the continent of Europe. Most of the allies came to no good, but the money had to be spent all the same. It was hardly surprising therefore that thanks to war Britain was both tired and broke. There were some – but not many – who believed the 1802 Treaty of Amiens would be long-lasting. Those same people understood that it was essential to grasp an opportunity, however

---

[5] Charles Cornwallis, first Marquess (1738–1805), the general who in 1781 surrendered Yorktown to the Americans. Later, Governor-General of India (1786–1793) and Lord Lieutenant of Ireland (1798–1801).
[6] Henry Addington, Viscount Sidmouth (1757–1844), British prime minister 1801–1804.

humiliating, to regain, at the very least, economic breath. The British could rely on no ally, even the ones they had supported financially, for these had all left the coalition of forces so hopefully established by Pitt the Younger in 1793 and again in 1798.[7] Pitt had retired to the Kentish cliffs to nurse his broken health. Soon he would be back, reluctantly, as prime minister.

However, no one imagined that the peace would last anywhere in Europe. Did not the web of treaties and pacts conform readily to Bonaparte's and – more particularly – Talleyrand's principle of signing an agreement? A treaty would be established if a majority of the following conditions applied: France would give up something she no longer wanted; France would agree to the independence of something she did not want anyone else to have; France could bargain for territory she wanted in return for territory that no longer mattered to her and which, anyway, she could retrieve at any time she was able to assign a general and his army to that task. What may seem remarkable is that Bonaparte got away with it. Yet it is not so remarkable when we consider the geographical position of France, the disposition of her armies, the absolute control of the First Consul and his almost mesmeric reputation. France under Bonaparte was the superpower of Europe. Bonaparte believed in the establishment of empire.

This was at a time when the British, having lost their first empire, were building their second. The difference between the nations was twofold: whereas France built with her armies, the British built with her counting houses and maintained the territory with her armies (although in India France had tried to build its interests on a political foundation). Second, Britain's empire was entirely remote from her borders, in the Far East, the Indian subcontinent, Australasia, sub-Saharan Africa, Canada and the Caribbean. The French may have had some West Indian possessions and toeholds in Africa, but by 1803 Bonaparte's imperial capability was influenced by what he rightly saw as ever-present dangers to France – continental European powers. Britain was only threatened in any serious way by France, even though Spain would have its finest fleet at the Battle

---

[7] William Pitt (1759–1806). Second son of the Earl of Chatham, known as Pitt the Elder (1708–1778).

of Trafalgar. Moreover, Britain had the huge advantage of being an offshore island of continental Europe. To understand the importance of this we might consider two simple points: the nations and states of continental Europe had for centuries been criss-crossed by invading or transiting armies. Borders were ever shifting. The landlords were ever changing. Britain, on the other hand, had not been invaded successfully since 1066. The second advantage for Britain is a direct consequence of the first. Neither Bonaparte, nor anyone else for that matter, could simply move soldiers, guns, horses and logistics across to British territory. The Channel was a fierce barrier. Normally, even the massing of such a force at the edges of another's territory could bring about capitulation. For an invader – as Caesar[8] and Duke William had well understood – to arrive in Britain with any realistic invasion force would mean physically constructing a dedicated army, fleet, transport system and continuing logistical train. Which is why, until the advent of air power, Britain would never be a pushover for conventional forces. Little wonder, then, that Britain loved the English Channel and regarded with a centuries-old suspicion anyone or anything on the other side.

Consequently, the scale of the French invasion project and the insatiable ambition of Bonaparte meant that no treaty in Europe was worth its signatures and seals. The British may have blustered when upbraided by the French for refusing to leave Malta, but they were just as bad as Bonaparte for not observing the letter – never mind the spirit – of the Treaty of Amiens. It was no good them pointing out that Bonaparte disregarded solemn agreements. He may have needed no excuse to do anything he wanted in Europe, but Addington's administration had little moral high ground to occupy. In March 1803, Bonaparte declared he believed the British were determined to go to war once more with France. As if to signal that his prophecy would be fulfilled, he observed that the treaties of Europe were adorned with black crêpe.

---

[8] Julius Caesar (100–44BC).

CHAPTER SIX

Invasion – The Reality

THE IDEA OF INVADING ENGLAND WAS NOT, IN 1803, A NEW ONE. The original concept had been prepared not by Bonaparte but by the old Directorate. In 1798, General Bonaparte had been given command of a punitive force of 50,000 men in preparation for an invasion. That force, the equivalent of four large divisions or six smaller ones, was not the most efficient army group that could have been commanded. Moreover, hardly any preparation had been made for the event. Again, the combination of Bonaparte's military appreciation and his instincts as an artilleryman led him to accept easily the concept of long-term planning for such a huge operation, which, anyway, did not at first gather any political momentum. By 1799 the idea had been shelved. However, when, four years later, he saw the apparent sense of reviving it, he went back to the ideas formulated earlier and combined them with the experience and powers he had amassed since then.

No matter how mighty a superpower may be, it is a military axiom that in the majority of events only one major operation can be contemplated at any one time. To some extent, Napoleon was wrong when he assumed all treaties were draped in black – doomed – at the beginning of 1803. France was able to count on relative peace in the strategically important areas of continental Europe. This meant that its armies were not stretched. The First Consul could therefore prepare to concentrate his forces and – importantly – the minds of his best military and naval personnel on the notion of creating an invasion force. There was nothing Britain could do to deter him. In the past, its government had bought lesser states as allies. It was not in the position to do that now, and anyway, just as those subsidized princes and armies had melted away in the heat of Bonaparte's forced marches, so now they were unlikely to prove reliable allies for Addington.

If the England of George III was in any doubt as to Bonaparte's intentions it had only to take note of the First Consul's message laid before the Tribunate on 23 May 1803. He told the whole French nation – and effectively therefore, the British – that he had demonstrated his ability to fulfil his promise to rule both the continent of Europe and the British Isles. His view was that France was certainly strong enough to usurp the British interests in continental Europe, which meant through traditional Hanoverian ties, the German states. Should he so choose there was no way in which he could not overwhelm Europe once the British had been neutered militarily. Moreover, he felt that the British understood this. The Tribunate was told during that same month that because Britain could see the truth of Bonaparte's claim to military supremacy on the continent it would immediately start to live in fear of what his invading forces would mean to British lives and institutions.

On 24 May 1803, Bonaparte removed all doubts. He resurrected the national career of Pierre-Alexandre-Laurent Forfait.[1] Forfait had been France's minister of the navy until, largely through impatience but partly due to his own incompetence, he had been fired by Bonaparte in 1801. Forfait's career was now revived by his appointment as Inspector General of the National Flotilla. Now, what did this mean?

The National – sometimes known as the Imperial – Flotilla was the means by which Bonaparte intended the invasion force to get to the beaches of southern England. This sounds like an urgent and decisive measure on the part of the First Consul. It also demonstrates something we need to understand about his character and the way his uncompromising belief that he alone was brilliant and the rest fools was the major cause of his failure to devise a workable policy of invading England and, indirectly, why the French (as opposed to the Spanish) fleet failed so miserably at Trafalgar more than two years later (see chapter 28).

In the business lexicon of the present day, when Bonaparte wanted

---

[1] Pierre-Alexandre-Laurent Forfait (1752–1807).

something he wanted it yesterday. Moreover, the fact that he himself had ordered something to be done meant that he believed there was no sane argument against his judgement. Anyone who directly questioned his proposition was either a fool in himself or a traitor to the cause. So it was with the instructions given to Forfait on the day of his appointment.

We should never forget that Gunner Bonaparte never quite understood the navy, how it worked and how best to use it. Forfait's first order was to implement not his but Bonaparte's instructions to build over a thousand boats, almost a third of which had to be ready by the end of that year. To build even small vessels in that quantity at such short notice was nigh on impossible. Even the design had no common blueprint. A yard could not simply take a template from its shelf and build a standard sort of vessel from it. To build 300 vessels by Christmas, let alone a further 700 by the end of the following year as per instructions, imposed impossible demands on a boatbuilding – never mind a shipbuilding – industry that was simply not geared to this kind of construction schedule. Neither did it have the capacity. What were the designs needed? How might they be changed? Who would be the designer to consult? Where were they to find a sufficient number of shipwrights, smiths and riggers? Where were the timber, cordage and pitch for such a project? France itself did not have these resources. Where were they to come from? Where were the vessels to be built, and how and where were they to be delivered? And what was to happen to all the repair and building programmes for the country's deep-sea navy? If these ocean fleets were not maintained and added to, how could Bonaparte expect his National Flotilla and thousands of soldiers to be supported and protected come invasion day? Yard foremen, safely out of reach, might shake their heads and mutter. Yard owners might rub their hands at the thought of lucrative building contracts. None would dare to systematically take apart, in front of Bonaparte himself, this ambitious plan. Bonaparte had not really thought this through. He did not understand what he was asking for. All of this was to Britain's advantage, though he, of course, did not see it this way. He saw himself as, with a few exceptions, surrounded by pygmies. He was the man with the big idea. That was obvious. That is why he and not anyone else was soon to be emperor. When an official murmured about the cost, Bonaparte gave what he saw as a simple answer: he would get each vessel sponsored. A financier or business house would put up the money for a vessel and have their name engraved on the stern. When the contractors pointed out that such a building programme would exhaust not only supplies of seasoned timber but also skilled manpower, Bonaparte alone could see the answer. He instructed his officials to go to the Belgian, Dutch and German yards and fetch workers for his project.

As if Bonaparte's plan had not been demanding enough, before May was out he changed his mind. Certainly he had not listened to the protestations of shipbuilders and ministers. Instead of 300 and more vessels to be ready by the third week in December 1803 he now demanded that the work should be completed three months earlier. The whole of France was to be energized and become a boatbuilding nation. Any large centre of population close to a navigable river was ordered to either improve or set up a boatbuilding industry. To augment the programme Bonaparte told his naval minister to be on the lookout for existing commercial vessels. We can only imagine the transformation that took place in France. Bonaparte was a huge personality in military terms – but also in terms of ideas. He may often have shown an overbearing stupidity when it came to believing his own ideas, but his genius expressed itself in the way he was firmly convinced that huge concepts could not be left in the hands of officials. The whole nation state and its acolytes along the Rhine and Maas had to be mobilized. The industrial ants of France had to scurry this way and that with timbers, copper, hawsers and hemps, adzes and bitts. From this apparent confusion – whose logic only Bonaparte understood – would emerge the means of invading southern England. For the nation and the officials of Paris, for Forfait and the naval minister Denis Decrès,[2] this was exciting enough, but Bonaparte was far from finished testing their abilities and satisfying his own vision. Decrès was to be the constant that Bonaparte needed at his elbow.

Decrès had joined the French navy in 1779, at the age of eighteen, and by the early 1790s had been promoted to captain. This was a period when the uncertainties in the French hierarchy terminated promising careers with little warning. Fortunately, Decrès was not senior enough to be politically vulnerable. Moreover, just as Bonaparte had survived political

---

[2] Denis Decrès (1761–1820).

examination because the Directorate had been desperately short of good army officers, Decrès' talents as a mariner had been equally needed. In 1799 the French Revolution, which had started in 1789, gave way to Bonaparte's coming to power. Britain was now at war with France, and two years earlier Jervis and Nelson had achieved the singular success of the Battle of Cape St Vincent (see chapter 2). The Irish were in rebellion against the British, and in that same year Decrès became part of the French expedition to aid the rebels. He was rapidly becoming a distinguished post captain, and the following year he was promoted to rear admiral. This is where Bonaparte found him when he assumed power. Decrès impressed Bonaparte who promoted him to the post of minister of the navy and colonies in 1801. Bonaparte was to cover him with honours, including the highest office of the Légion d'Honneur and a dukedom. Should any doubt the importance of this man in Bonaparte's story, let them cast an eye at the Arc de Triomphe. There they will find the name Denis Decrès. Decrès deserved his monument as did all who survived Bonaparte's tempers, changing thought processes and enthusiasms.

Bonaparte was incapable of coming up with a single plan and then pushing it through to success. All the time, he seemed to believe that those about him were either fools or being served by fools. Moreover, he gave every impression of changing his mind, not through capriciousness but because he saw everything in the grand manner. While lesser men gazed at the stars, Bonaparte watched the sun rise. A scheme that might have begun with reasonable expectations expanded in his mind so that he acted as though he were preparing a magnificent chapter in the first draft of his period of French history. Also, Bonaparte saw everything – rightly – on the wider stage of the commander-in-chief. Thus a project to invade England was never regarded by him in isolation. His map of Europe was always unfurled. At his hand was ever a crayon poised to redraw the contours of influence and territory. Moreover, while some were charged with concentrating on building a fleet for the invasion, he, Bonaparte, had forever to reassess the composition of his invasion force, the timing of the event and the distractions, either at home, in the treasury or further afield. He could do nothing on a small scale. As he spied the British coastline he heard the fast political rivers running in central and southern Europe.

When Decrès was given instructions to mobilize the resources of the boatbuilders and yards along the northern French coast, these were followed, almost immediately, by orders to do the same thing on the southern coast. Why would Bonaparte have wanted to have an invasion force building in the Mediterranean? The answer was either that he had not as yet really made up his mind what he was doing and who he was invading (Egypt was still a proposition) or he was more cunning than even his naval minister, Decrès, or his inspector general of the National Flotilla, Forfait, understood. Nelson had recently been appointed commander of the British fleet in the Mediterranean. Perhaps the southern enterprise was to fool Nelson and to keep this most formidable of Bonaparte's enemies where he wanted him – a thousand miles or more from the English Channel. The French history professor Alan Schom, who has made a careful study of Bonaparte's behaviour and motives during this period, does not accept this diversion hypothesis and suggests instead that Napoleon had a habit of coming up with ill-conceived plans which he would present as if from the back of a nineteenth-century envelope without ever considering how they might be implemented. He would then either lose all interest in a plan or – worse still – insist on its being made to work even though little thought had been given to the practicalities or consequences. This mind-changing and frustration with those who were unable to cope with his broader visions was a feature of his leadership.

Those charged with the job of making this particular scheme work were faced with the additional problem that the vessels he had ordered could hardly be guaranteed to do the job. Four types of boat were ordered by Bonaparte during 1803, their total number exceeding 1,300. The biggest, a three-masted prames, was more than 100 feet long. It was a so-called bilge keeler. Essentially a flat-bottomed vessel, it had shallow draught with a centre keel and a smaller keel on either side. The theory, to a soldier anyway, was simple: it was a relatively big ship, with a lot of guns, able to operate in shallow water. To the sailor this meant a vessel which could indeed, as Bonaparte wanted, beach stably on its three 'legs' (its keels) on the other side of the Channel without tipping up. But the slightest rough weather meant that this large vessel, top-heavy with sails and guns, would be so unstable that it probably would not get to the other side with the invasion fleet.

The next vessel, a chaloupe, was a thin eighty-footer. It could carry, in theory, 130 soldiers. Once more, the sailing masters scratched their heads. It was good for beaching, but no good for sailing. The same might have been said of the two smallest vessels, the canonnier and the péniche. The purpose of these was to take as many troops as possible and to be gun platforms once they had beached. The hypothesis was credible only in the mind of a soldier. A sailor, used to the prevailing winds of *la Manche* and the strong currents, would have preferred always to look at the underwater profile of a vessel, whereas the soldier saw it as a platform. Perhaps the more reliable part of the invasion flotilla was the section of hundreds of craft taken up from trade. These were boats already built. Most of them were fishing vessels and therefore perfectly capable of sailing in almost any weather and almost anywhere in the seaway between France and England. They could be loaded to the gunwales with an invasion force. However, they would be unable to count on much protection from the new designs and only theoretically from the large fleet that was still either bottled up in port by the British blockade or roaming deep sea to avoid Nelson. A further irony is that Bonaparte's ideas were creating disadvantages for him that had hardly existed earlier. As ship designers and builders, the French were at least as good as the British and, in many cases, much better. Many of the French ships that were to fight at Trafalgar were of superior construction to the British and sailed superbly. But then they had been designed by naval architects without a gunner, however distinguished, looking over their shoulders.

Moreover, Bonaparte could not rely on his own people – or even on himself – to know the true progress of his work. He rarely had more than half the number of ships and boats available that he thought he had. What remains particularly odd about this whole episode of mistakes and fantasy-building is that Pierre Forfait, Bonaparte's inspector general, was a naval architect. He had joined the navy as a student in engineering. Even more curious to modern eyes, it was not the French navy he had joined but the British. This is not as odd as it might seem. First, there were many cases of men serving in the forces of other nations than their own, and in 1773 – when Forfait had been a young officer – Britain was not at war with France.[3] The Seven Years War had finished in 1763, and the French did not join the American War of Independence against Britain until 1778. Forfait's pedigree as an engineer and naval gunner (he was an expert on British munitions, always a useful additional qualification when at war) endeared him to Bonaparte. Furthermore, Forfait had a well-regarded list of naval achievements and specialized in the design and construction of marine transporters and store ships. In his two years as navy minister (1799–1801) before being replaced by Decrès, Forfait redrew the logistical wiring diagram of the navy. He created a more professional service. Bonaparte, therefore, could not have chosen anyone better as inspector general, except for the fact that Forfait's forte in ship construction and stability was in the design of vessels with shallow draughts that were probably better on inshore and river passages.

By the end of 1803 Bonaparte had in place the first phase of his programme and his two most important and closest confidants to implement it. He now needed construction engineers to build him harbours, dockyards to build him ships, bankers to build him huge pots of gold to pay for it all and, of course, an admiral able to go to sea with a fleet sufficiently well trained and with the necessary fighting power to defeat any British naval attempt at interrupting the grand invasion plan.

If the structure of the naval invasion scheme was madness, the search for an admiral to do Bonaparte's bidding was maddening. An admiral was a deep-sea officer, not someone who would command only the invasion fleet. The invasion had to have continuing protection once it had landed and the vision needed to extend to a large force to do so. The invasion's logistical line from, say, Boulogne to the English south coast had to be safeguarded. On top of all these steep requirements, the commanding admiral would be required to guarantee that his fleet would remain up to speed and unmolested during the period when the invasion flotilla was being built. This could easily mean – in spite of Bonaparte's scatter-gun orders – that the admiral's seagoing fleet would be called upon

---

[3] Today, both the Royal Naval College at Dartmouth and the Royal Military Academy at Sandhurst continue to train cadets from foreign forces, fully aware of the possibility of having to face them in some post-college conflict.

to maintain its freedom of the high seas for anything up to two years. That admiral would not be able to spend his time avoiding the British navy. Bonaparte's intention would be for him to rid the sea lanes of the British from Toulon to the West Indies and back to the Western Approaches to the English Channel. In other words, he wanted his admiral to get rid of Nelson and, increasingly, Admiral William Cornwallis, commander of the Channel Fleet.

We should remember again that, although the French navy had not been quite so stripped of its senior officer class by the Revolution as the army, it had few admirals of the sort of temperament and quality likely to survive Bonaparte's scrutiny. Of those he had, he liked Admiral de Bruix[4] above all others.

De Bruix might have had an academic career instead of going to sea. He was well-educated in Paris. However, perhaps because of his childhood in the West Indies, he had developed a more than passing interest in the sea. It was as a young officer that he had seen most of his early action, in what were for him his home waters, the Caribbean. Within twenty years of joining the navy at the age of fifteen, he found himself commander-in-chief of the French fleet at Brest. It was as director of the port, and commander-in-chief, that he spectacularly ran a British blockade to re-supply the French contingent in Genoa. That he had succeeded in regaining his home port only added to his already considerable reputation. If Bonaparte had needed any proof of de Bruix's initiative, it had come in November 1799, when the admiral took part in the coup that placed his ruler in absolute power. What better credentials could any admiral have presented to the First Consul? His appointment as Admiral of the National Flotilla surprised no one.

So, on paper, the great plan looked rather good. In spite of Bonaparte's contradictory notes to Decrès about the levels of efficiency and the advanced (or not advanced) building programmes, everything seemed on course – except the money. Even Bonaparte, in the autumn of 1803, could not avoid the fact that everyone needed paying. It was impossible to simply appeal to national pride. The big contractors wanted their money to pay the middle and small contractors. The small contractors had to

---

[4] Eustace de Bruix (1759–1805).

pay carpenters and caulkers who, like the others, had families to feed. Nevertheless, patriotism played an important part in Bonaparte's fundraising, although in many cases these promissory notes were not really worth the paper they were written on. Bonaparte leaned on the Dutch and the Belgians. As president of the Italian republic he virtually ordered the Italians to give money or gifts in kind – mainly ships. None could hide from Bonaparte's demands. Prefects were pinpointed so it was up to them to get their local people to come up with the necessary funds. Soldiers were encouraged to give a day's pay – not that they were always getting it anyway. By the autumn of 1803, Bonaparte's accounts showed that twenty-four million francs had been raised. This would appear to have been enough – for the moment.

Bonaparte needed to ship 150,000 troops, together with horses, ammunition, guns and supplies, across *la Manche*. That was easy: in his imagination, anything was possible. However, there was one significant item that could not be left to chance. He had no ports for his ships. Where were as many as 3,000 shallow-draughted vessels to sail from? His answer to this difficulty was enough to convince the British that his intention to invade was very real indeed.

Bonaparte's prime requirement was for that invasion fleet to arrive quickly. Yet how, when and where that arrival would take place was an enormous piece of tactical planning. First, the craft were not all able to leave France at the same time. Second, they had not to arrive at the same time. An invasion has to be staggered. The initial forces had to be beached and then cleared into the hinterland, having overcome the first of the defences. Only when the landing area was clear could other forces have the space to arrive. Immediately, some of that space would be taken up by the logistics necessary to maintain the first landing and support the second. This leapfrogging programme would have to be virtually seamless. It would need to take into consideration, for example, the tides. A landing on a rising tide would need to be clear so that the vessels could be withdrawn on either the same tide or in the early hours of its ebb. This would mean that the follow-on forces would have to wait, perhaps up to six or eight hours, before they could reach the beaches, unless of course plans had been made for them to advance over uncertain sands and mudflats below the foreshore.

If all this sounds complicated, then it should. The troops would leave the large transport vessels for smaller ones prior to the final assault, but those bigger ships still had to rely entirely upon the weather, especially the wind directions and forces. To minimize the opportunities for disaster there had to be a reliable base-camp operation on the French coast. In 1803, the nearest established French port was Brest, hundreds of miles from where Bonaparte wanted his invasion fleet to be. Moreover, the prevailing sea state and winds – interdependent factors – were totally unfavourable to his invasion fleet. Apart from the fact that Brest was 'in the wrong place', that naval headquarters had a quite different function. It was from there that Bonaparte expected his deep-sea fleet to command the approaches to the Channel and so defend the western flank of his assault on England. No port at that time would have been able to accommodate that number of vessels and everything that went with them, to perform two roles.

By mid 1803 the British Admiralty had sufficient intelligence on the French building programme centred on Boulogne to understand that there was no point in Addington's government attempting to rescue the Treaty of Amiens. Was that intelligence accurate? Certainly, because it was very easy to gather intelligence; the British did not have to rely on hearsay. Their own people could easily go to the boatyards and the towns along the rivers and coasts and see for themselves the activities that had resulted from Bonaparte's orders. Financiers and diplomats would have been well informed of the efforts being made by the First Consul to raise the required millions of francs. Bonaparte and his associates may have created diversions to keep the British guessing, but none really believed that the main activity would remain hidden from them. There was much freedom of movement and an eagerness to exploit the coming war. Suppliers, military manufacturers and inventors approached both sides. Indeed, one inventor, Robert Fulton,[5] tried to sell his design for a submarine complete with torpedoes to both the British and French. Fulton, an American engineer, was a hundred years ahead of his time. It is quite possible that both the British and the French

---

[5] Robert Fulton (1765–1815). He built the first commercially successful steamboat – the *Clermont*, and painted miniature portraits and landscapes.

recognized his splendid application of technology. However, they hardly imagined it could have a significant effect on an invasion or a counter-invasion. In this they were probably right. For a hundred years more, sea powers would rely on old-fashioned tactics.[6]

For the moment, the Admiralty was more concerned with the French activities along the stretch of coast either side of Boulogne. They had eyewitnesses who described the visits Bonaparte was making to the cliffs and sands. These provided accurate reports of his public remarks concerning sea defences. They described in some detail the personalities involved and the orders passed between officers of the likes of Decrès, Forfait and de Bruix. They gave detailed accounts of the First Consul's review of ships and men including a report on a disaster in which more than 200 had perished because Bonaparte had insisted on them putting to sea in dreadful weather conditions. There were no secrets other than the timing of the invasion itself, and even Bonaparte did not know that date. He did know that he had to build a major seaport, at Boulogne – and quickly.

In the early summer of 1803, when Bonaparte had realistically rid himself of any hope of the British renegotiating and extending the Peace of Amiens, he gave orders for work to start on the port of Boulogne. Until then, Boulogne had not been a naval planner's dream. It was a tidal estuary with an old jetty system barely able to support a minimal import–export trade. Bonaparte did not imagine that he could put 3,000 vessels there. Even he, who never quite understood naval technology and certainly not naval tactics, knew that for an invasion to work with any degree of coordination it had to be launched from more than one port. If everything were concentrated on a single base, not only would the seaways be clogged, but the roads and supply lines to the harbour would be so too. The artillerymen understood logistics perfectly, knowing that even sailors did not consider such things unimportant. Yet Boulogne had to be the focus of Bonaparte's efforts. Work began on 1 May of that year. Once more, the casual observer, unmolested by the French and assisted

---

[6] When the submarine was first offered to the Royal Navy as a practical naval weapon, there were those at the Admiralty who rejected the invention considering this an underhand form of fighting.

by sightings from small squadrons of British vessels standing not many miles offshore, supplied the information that by mid June some 3,000 French labourers were at work in Boulogne. The mouth was dammed and a harbour was being excavated.

No one in France knew where Bonaparte was to find the money for the Boulogne project and the other proposed port developments along the coast. The First Consul had been told that his building programme was financially possible. That is all he wanted to hear. As for labour, he believed there was plenty around. A soldier who was not fighting could easily be kept in trim by digging. There is not much evidence to suggest that any of the difficulties, often reluctantly reported to Paris, would have diminished Bonaparte's enthusiasm for the project. After all, without new harbours, especially the one at Boulogne, there could be no invasion. The Admiralty in London knew this, and was hardly likely to sit at its Board table without making an effort to disrupt the French plans. Royal Navy ships could easily get within firing range of Boulogne. They did so, armed with orders to send in broadsides. The purpose was twofold: to kill as many of the labourers and engineers as possible, so disrupting the work and the enthusiasm for the task, and to destroy any work that had already been carried out. The British had heard stories that Bonaparte expected Boulogne to be completed by the autumn of 1803. Even with a little thought, this seemed an unrealistic target. Bonaparte *may* have believed that it could be achieved. Any calculations on the part of the British should have demonstrated that it could not be. However, the British were in awe of Bonaparte. They had seen the strength of his ambition in other areas. They had watched him forcing subordinates to achieve the seemingly impossible. Very few in the Admiralty were willing to dismiss his programme and timetable. Indeed, it may have been that many British people had more faith in Bonaparte's vision than some of his own subjects. Little wonder, then, that the British navy maintained a seemingly unremitting bombardment.

Decrès and Forfait faced the wrath of Bonaparte. He wanted to know how it was that the British had been able to get in so close and do so much damage. Reluctantly he was at last obliged to accept the argument which Forfait had delivered for some considerable time prior to the British attack. Forfait had pointed out that such developments could not be expected to go ahead unimpeded. He had wanted to build defences to protect these projects from a British bombardment and the very real possibility that the British might attempt a landing of their own. It is a puzzle why Bonaparte, an excellent theatre and tactical gunner, should not have readily accepted Forfait's advice. Good firepower meant that the British naval vessels could bombard and yet never be within range of the limited French shore batteries. Here was another example of the fallibility so easily uncovered in Bonaparte's reputation for military genius. It is possible to conclude from this fallibility that Bonaparte could function as a military leader only in battle conditions, when a commander's sense of logic is often focused more clearly. It may seem obvious to remark that, had it not been for conflict, Bonaparte would have remained merely an obscure Corsican.

Now, in the preparation for war, the First Consul's bullying attitude and the inability of his close subordinates to convince him that he was wrong illustrated clearly the defects in his thinking and application. The fact that he had not heeded Forfait's advice on coastal defences revealed yet another weakness in Bonaparte's unstable genius. There was, of course, a perfectly practical reason for turning down Forfait's proposition. First and foremost Bonaparte wanted to get on quickly with readying his invasion force. Second, he could not bring himself to divert resources, including money, to the building of additional artillery batteries. Like many great leaders he took a panoramic view of events. When details called his grand idea into question, Bonaparte saw these devils as obstructionist, not simply realistic contributions to the greater project.

The First Consul thought he might deter the British by installing a few medium-range cannon and mortar. These did not have much effect. The British were still able to get in close and, especially at slack tide, to anchor off, get a good fix on the new installations and, with precise firepower, damage them before they had been completed and play havoc with the construction programme. By the end of the summer Bonaparte conceded that he would have to divert resources to build more secure batteries to protect the ports. These could not simply be knocked up piecemeal by casual construction workers. They had to be built at the end of a rampart to take construction materials. First, the rampart itself had to be built. His original idea was that a fort (in fact, the concept was for three) could be quickly dropped into place to deter the British. This was nonsense. Here was evidence of even more erratic thinking and hopeless optimism on the part of Bonaparte, who was sometimes ready to listen too eagerly to those inclined to tell him what he wanted to hear.

For much of the time the British offshore squadron carried on firing, partly because they had had so much time that summer in which to establish accurate coordinates. They knew exactly where they should be to find range and direction. The trick was knowing when to fire. The unfortunate labour force, privy neither to the high-level instructions of Bonaparte nor to the mysteries of advance gunnery revealed by Cornwallis's officers, could only duck and hope – unrealistically – that things would get better and that they might even get paid. Their best chance to protect the work on Boulogne was contained in the weather. It was not an element that Bonaparte had taken into consideration. But a few good Channel gales were about the only deterrent to British bombardments. Not even Admiral Cornwallis's squadrons would be able to produce so accurate gunnery in a force-eight beam sea.

Therefore, the Boulogne project had occasional respite from British naval gunners but not Paris bankers. Money was hard to raise. Certainly, Bonaparte did not imagine that the whole of France either would or could do his bidding for nothing. Hardworking labourers on the Boulogne site were unable to live on cake alone. On occasion, workmen went unpaid for more than a month at a time. Some slacked off their labours. Others walked off the job and disappeared into the countryside.

Too often there was simply not enough money. Bonaparte and his officials had raised huge loans. The distribution of those funds and the priorities on the accounts were sometimes mismanaged. Regional officials were promised large sums. However, that money was often non-existent – a public declaration of money already promised or the method of getting it from the central treasury bound up in so much bureaucracy that it was beyond the management of local projects to retrieve it. Even when funds did arrive, there were occasions on which local managers diverted money to pay off more pressing outstanding accounts. Yet the project did not come to a standstill, not even when under attack, especially as not all British efforts were successful. Surprisingly, one of the less successful adventures was undertaken by Nelson. It cost him a bloodied nose.

CHAPTER SEVEN

Pyrotechnics

E ARLIER IN 1801, NELSON HAD, AGAINST REMARKABLE ODDS, WON THE famous Battle of Copenhagen. On 18 June, Nelson left the Baltic. He may have been returning to England to receive plaudits for the astonishing victory at Copenhagen, but he was in ill health. His first task on arrival at Yarmouth on 1 July was that of visiting the wounded who had been put ashore there. A week later he was in London. He was caught up in looking to his own medal chest and the continuation of his name. He wanted to be known as Baron Nelson of the Nile and of Hilborough, in the county of Norfolk, with the proviso that the title would not become extinct if the male line disappeared. However, he did not want anyone who succeeded him to use any of his other titles for the reason that they had been awarded for military honours. Therefore the title Duke of Brontë would, together with his award of the Order of St Ferdinand, die with him. Having sorted that dynastic concern with the prime minister, Addington, he turned his attention, again with Addington, to the French. It was Nelson's view that Bonaparte was determined to grab as much of Italy – particularly of Naples and Sicily – as possible. Sicily was of particular interest to Nelson because he recognized its strategic value, as he did that of the islands of Sardinia, Elba, Malta and Corfu. By the middle of July he had set down on paper his personal thoughts on strategy, and now he wanted to – literally – settle his stomach. The reason for his return from the Baltic was always given as the fact that he was suffering from severe stomach cramps. Towards the end of the month he was once more turning his attention to the French and, particularly, to the very real possibility of Bonaparte's invasion.

Here was something of a protocol conundrum for the navy. Nelson was to be given the command of a roving squadron. That command would extend from the Suffolk–Essex coast, round and across the Thames estuary and as far west as Beachy Head in Sussex. This passed through two important naval commands, the Nore and the Downs. His was a unique command which, he realized, could give rise to all sorts of jealousies, never mind tactical confusion. He was never one to bother about that sort of local difficulty. However, he privately acknowledged it when he wrote in July 1801 to his friend, patron and the future William IV, the Duke of Clarence.

> my command is to extend from Orford Ness to Beachy Head, on both Shores; but without interfering with either the Nore or Downs command. I assure Your Royal Highness that I feel my ability to render service, in this new sort of command, only in my zeal; in many other respects I am sensible of much deficiency and require that great allowance should be made for me

He made it clear to the two major commands, the Nore and the Downs, that he would not interfere with them. Of course, that assurance carried the codicil that he, Nelson, expected them to do as he said. Considering Britain was at war and that he had just returned from an extremely famous victory in the Baltic, it was unlikely that Channel commanders would twitch in public at his 'requests'. But in private?

Nelson had been given his squadron of frigates and brigs, together with ancillary vessels because Bonaparte was taken seriously by the Admiralty. St Vincent, First Lord of the Admiralty, made it clear in a letter to the commander-in-chief of the Downs fleet, Admiral Skeffington Lutwidge,[2] that however many doubts there were the threat had to be taken absolutely seriously. St Vincent told Lutwidge that 'a descent' was certainly intended. At this point, St Vincent approached the political and

---

[1] William IV, formerly the Duke of Clarence (1765–1837).

[2] Robert Wilfred Skeffington Lutwidge (1802–1873) was the uncle of author Lewis Carroll.

service sensitivities of Lutwidge and the Downs commanders Vice
Admiral Graeme.[3] St Vincent said that, having weighed the threat against
the resources of the navy, he had come to the conclusion that the best
way to frustrate Bonaparte's intentions was to place the whole seagoing
force under a single flag officer whose task would be confined to stopping
him. St Vincent recognized that this decision usurped the authority of
both Lutwidge and Graeme. However, as he said to Lutwidge, he had a
great deal of respect for the public and private character of his admirals
and was therefore certain that they would rub along with his, St Vincent's,
decision. It is not entirely clear that Admirals Lutwidge and Graeme
were mollified by St Vincent. Equally, they were both good sea officers
and were hardly likely to argue with him – not if they wanted to keep
their commands.

Nelson hoisted his flag in a relatively small ship, the frigate *L'Unité*, off
Sheerness on 27 July 1801. He did so having delivered to the Admiralty
a detailed plan to foil Bonaparte, which included his assessment of how
Bonaparte's commanders would act. In some part Nelson was really
saying how he would do the job. His gracious assumption that they were
as good as he was, was always, to his mind, the best way of being prepared.

He believed that the target of Bonaparte's force was likely to be London.
Also, intelligence reports suggested that troops would have to be rowed
from Boulogne. This would take forty-eight hours. Nelson could see no
possibility of this attack succeeding. The weather alone, together with
tidal conditions, would foil the attempt.

He therefore assumed that the invading force would have to come from
as far afield as Le Havre and – with typical Nelsonian foresight – Ostend
and Flushing. If the object remained London, the French would have to
land from all directions on the Sussex, Thames and Essex coasts to be
within a hundred miles' striking distance of the capital. This would
mean that not only would the sensitive Downs and Nore fleets be engaged,
but also the North Sea fleet commanded by Admiral Archibald Dickson.[4]

The Royal Navy would therefore be as stretched as the invading force.
We must remember that these were wind-powered vessels, not necessarily

---

[3] Vice Admiral Graeme of the White (?–1818).
[4] Admiral Archibald Dickinson (*c.*1740–1803).

able to manoeuvre at will or to direct themselves at an enemy at high speed. Britain's navy was as reliant on its sailing masters – in often unpredictable weather conditions – as was the French. The shortest distance from France to England might, in favourable conditions, be rowed in twelve hours. That was all the time Nelson believed his defensive force would have to engage the enemy. His hope was for relatively rough weather. In a flat calm, the rowers would have the advantage over the frigates. Thus he planned to deploy his resources in layers, starting from as close to the French coast as possible and ending with a flotilla of small vessels standing off Margate, Ramsgate, the Essex salt flats and Thames estuary to the north Kent coast off North Foreland.

The admiral had to anticipate the most disadvantageous weather conditions and the possibility of ships being becalmed. Here, the smaller vessels would come into their own. Nelson called them Thames galleys. The choice of this Roman-style muscle power seems somewhat bizarre given the popular image of Nelson stood beneath the billowing sails of a majestic 74-gun ship. Instead, in that summer of 1801, with the strong likelihood of gentle easterlies if any winds at all, this very deep-sea admiral had to assume that his special plan might eventually come to rely on techniques Caesar would have understood. If that came to pass, the British sailors and marines would be called upon to show a very special kind of gallantry. Nelson's biggest hope was that Bonaparte's commanders would get wind of the defences and remain in port. The plan in place, the vice admiral then set his vessels and gunners to deal with the main target, the twenty-four French ships anchored off Boulogne.

Nelson had lined up his forces between Dunkirk and Dieppe. He doubted if any Frenchman could put to sea without being engaged. At the beginning of August he attacked. From his then flagship, *Medusa*, on 4 August 1801, he wrote to the First Lord, St Vincent, his admirals, captains and, of course, to the prime minister, Henry Addington. To Addington he wrote:

> My Dear Sir, I think I may venture to assure you that the French Army will not embark at Boulogne for the invasion of England; they are suffering this morning from allowing a collection of Craft

to be assembled in their Port. Five Vessels of different descriptions are sunk on the outside the pier by our shells; they were all fitted with heavy guns, and full of men

It all sounded rather good. Within the month the news was not so well received.

The attack, which involved hurling his bomb-ketches into the vulnerable vessels at Boulogne, had been something of a demonstration to the French and to his own fleet of Nelson's determination to support St Vincent's observation that the French could invade England if they wished but they would not be allowed to do so by sea. In fact, a few weeks later, on 1 October 1801, the two nations agreed a ceasefire. On 27 March 1802, the Treaty of Amiens was signed. It lasted until 16 May 1803, when Britain again declared war on France.

Nelson, hero of the Nile, Copenhagen and, to a large extent, Cape St Vincent,[5] recognized that pyrotechnics alone would not decide the fate of the French force. He was – or should have been – particularly impressed by the French commander he faced across the Channel, Rear Admiral Louis de la Touche-Tréville.[6]

His inclination was to attack the French fleet at Flushing. This was, as Admiral Dickson in the North Sea could easily have explained, a risky assault. The approaches to Flushing were not sufficiently well charted and were full of sandbanks and currents that could have left even a skilled force stranded. So Nelson took another look at Boulogne.

---

[5] Battle of Cape St Vincent, 14 February 1797; Battle of the Nile at Aboukir, 1 August 1798; Battle of Copenhagen, 2 April 1801.
[6] Admiral Louis de la Touche-Tréville (1745–1804), often referred to as Latouche-Tréville.

CHAPTER EIGHT

Invasion – The Nightmare

THE PLAN AGAINST BOULOGNE IN THAT LATE AUGUST OF 1801 WAS AN audacious one, audacity being perhaps the hallmark of Nelsonian tactics in general. He was to send in fifty-seven small vessels armed with small guns and split into four groups. The idea was that some of these would go alongside the French vessels, slice through their mooring cables, land marines aboard to attack the French crews, destroy those they could not manage and take whatever vessels they could as prizes. The plan deserved an A-plus for imagination, but no more than C-minus for forethought. The timing of the attack was wrong. Nelson's commanders – and, given his close involvement in the details, he himself – should have worked out the rate of the flood tide as these were naturally powered vessels. Second, might Nelson's arrogance have obscured his regard for Touche-Tréville? The French Boulogne force had only a couple of weeks earlier been bombarded by the British. It was hardly likely that the French commander would ignore the possibility that Nelson would be back. The combination of these two mistakes spelled a minor disaster for the British.

Many of the small craft could not be controlled in the fast-flowing current and went straight past the moored Frenchmen. Moreover, why Nelson's force should have imagined it was going to slice through mooring ropes is difficult to understand. French captains had replaced their ropes with cables and chains. Also, most of the vessels had been reinforced and had posted well-armed sentries. The French retaliation was uncompromising. The British withdrew. Forty-five were killed; more than 130 sailors and marines wounded. Nelson had not led this attack.

Later he was to suggest that if he had it might have been successful. It may also have been that Nelson did not give planning enough of his attention. Why? He was not well; he was furiously busy sailing this way and that about his fleet. He was, according to his recorded correspondence, very much possessed of images of Emma Hamilton, whom he clearly missed. He was also suffering from seasickness. It was a badly thought-through operation and one that is sometimes ignored by those obsessed with Nelson's more glamorous campaign record.

Nelson of course, immediately wanted revenge. He wanted to get back at the French. His pride seems to have been damaged more than his belief in his own tactical awareness. He accepted that he had not given the attack on Boulogne his undivided attention. His confidence during the previous weeks and months of that year, 1801, seemed to have led him to believe his own publicity. Like many brilliant men he marked setbacks, especially those to his reputation. That a single failed assault, of no great consequence in military terms, should have detracted from the achievements of his great battles may seem of little importance. Also, Nelson found it difficult to deal with criticism. There were plenty, certainly in the safety of the London coffee houses, who, while not delighting in this defeat, wondered aloud at his failure to properly exercise his command. They, and others, wondered also about the influence and distraction represented by Emma Hamilton. Nelson was obsessed with her, at a time when he should have been even more obsessed with doing for the French fleet once and for all.

Two years later, with Bonaparte's plan for Boulogne under way and Cornwallis's determination that it would come to pass, the whole naval picture had changed. Nelson was now on a two-year search to destroy the French fleet at last and, just perhaps, carrying with him the stain of Boulogne. He may have left it behind, but Bonaparte's huge project had not evaporated.

The engineering difficulties encountered by the French meant that work on the command harbour for the invasion was nowhere near as rapid as their leader had imagined. Moreover, the plan to establish other harbours was fraught with technical, financial and managerial difficulties. This should not be seen in any way as incompetence on the part of those doing Bonaparte's work. Imagine in this period, say, 1803 to 1804, the intense activity required for a rapid survey of a stretch of the French coast which until that point had not been regarded as an area of outstanding French naval activity. Brest, much further to the west, was the major French port. What we now see as commercial harbours were then river estuaries with landing stages for a limited amount of coastal traffic and anchorages from which smaller craft, including barges, could offload cargoes for onward passage to the riverside towns and up the rivers. Also, a marine chart was not enough to tell an engineer what was needed to build a major embarkation point. The charts would show soundings, the content of the sea bottom, but not necessarily what was below it – rock or more sand – and tidal ranges, together with sandbanks that were covered or uncovered at various states of that tide. This was very good information for the sailing master. The engineer needed to know far more if he was to discover the extent to which he could build, with strong foundations, the various harbours, moles, sea defences and gunnery platforms (including the three forts at Boulogne) that were required within a very short space of time. Moreover, the more Cornwallis's extended squadrons intensively bombarded the French workforce, the more urgent the need for these diversionary ports became. What would happen, asked Bonaparte's staff officers, when the flotilla began arriving in stages – as it most certainly would – only to find the harbour unfinished and a lack of safe moorings for the new vessels? The answer was to slot them into adjacent creeks, inlets and rivers. This seemed a simple operation. Yet the very nature of that coastline, with its shallows and silting, meant that men desperately required to work in the main project at Boulogne were to be diverted to these secondary tasks.

There were some established berths along that coast. For example, Admiral Bruix had identified Calais as an excellent, if limited, port. On closer examination, the amount of dredging and rebuilding necessary made it a seemingly expensive project in terms of time and money. The British navy knew Calais very well.[1] It had, after all, been the last English possession in France. That may have been more than two centuries earlier, but British mariners, and certainly Cornwallis's pilots and gunners, knew every inch of the local seabed, tidal streams and anchorages. They knew

---

[1] Calais was captured by Edward III after the Battle of Crecy in 1346. The French got it back in 1558 on the eve of Elizabeth I's accession to the throne.

that anyone wishing to berth anything more than a small flotilla would have to anchor off the harbour entrance and so would be sitting ducks to the Royal Navy. This had not escaped the notice of the French. The furthest west the French navy and engineers could go was Dieppe. Most of the other so-called harbours going in an easterly direction demanded engineering projects that seemed almost hopeless, among them a need for heavy and constant dredging. The French engineers even looked at Ostend. This was a good harbour, occupied by the French but, yet again, within range of Cornwallis's gunners. Apart from Boulogne, the best chance of developing an invasion port was Flushing, then part of the Batavian republic.[2] This was the area between the Waal river and the Rhine. Its people were Germanic Netherlanders, and although occupied by the French these Batavian were hardly likely to be reliable conscripts. In short, the Dutch did not want to work with the French, despite being told by Bonaparte to provide ships and men. The Dutch, remember, had no great love for the British. Neither did they think much of the French. Decrès considered Flushing an ideal port, or as close to one as he was likely to get. It was, at the very least, possible to put many ships in there on standby for the main event. Admiral Cornwallis rather hoped that Decrès would widen the deployment. He liked the idea of the French forces being so scattered because his squadrons could cope with pockets of the French navy, largely because there was then less protection. Decrès had to ask his own navy to provide that protection. It was not easy to get. Bonaparte, in the meantime, regarded all this as mere detail. He remained interested only in the grand plan and thought his commanders should be bolder in their planning. For example, he wanted to deploy mobile artillery batteries. These, reasonably enough, he saw as counter-gunnery to the British Channel Fleet raiders and as a deterrent. He may not have understood much about the navy, but the French leader certainly recognized the military value of manoeuvres and encouraged Decrès in his insistence that the vessels then being built should be put into action. He wanted them to be got up to professional speed and any weaknesses to be quickly identified. He must have known where the problem lay because his own instincts, along with those of his

---

[2] Betuwe is the island and, for centuries, the Germanic people were known as Batavi or Batavian.

naval captains and sailing masters, told him that the main one was to be found in the ships' fundamental design. Yet, there was strength in the relentless supply of vessels and, Decrès hoped, in the ability of what by then should have been a standing naval force in the Channel, to protect that fleet. Here was what was to remain the biggest hole in the planning. The French had as yet no standing force. Decrès had to accept that Cornwallis controlled the sea lanes. This advantage of Britain's would never be countered by Bonaparte's vision of a string of coastal batteries extending along French foreshores from Flushing on the state's north-eastern area of influence as far as the Mediterranean. A grand plan was all very well, but whether or not his army minister, Alexandre Berthier, would be able to implement the scheme was another matter. Berthier needed no reminding that Bonaparte was an artilleryman. Bonaparte needed no reminding that if the batteries were not working properly it was Berthier's fault. Perhaps the firm friendship between the two men saved Berthier's job and also saved Bonaparte from losing a good man. The greater truth, however, is that yet again Bonaparte's concept displayed great imagination while its execution revealed poor resources, inter-regimental rivalries, indifferent training and, in most cases, ineffectual gunnery. The rivalry between the services had a practical effect. At some stage there had to be an overall commander apart from Admiral Decrès. When, in the summer of 1803, Admiral Bruix became commander of the National Flotilla, he also assumed command of the coastal batteries.

It will be seen that Bonaparte's plans were often poorly executed and that, in spite of the considerable financial and physical effort on the part of the French, his engineers, planners and military commanders had few of the resources and none of the time necessary to bring the grand venture to fruition. Moreover, the difficulties his navy faced, especially around Boulogne and along that stretch of coast, were made infinitely more complex by the quiet and supremely efficient understanding of his role shown by Admiral Cornwallis. It might well be argued that, if that command had been in the hands of a lesser admiral, Bonaparte's invasion plans would have been further advanced than they were by the spring of 1805. By that time Cornwallis's continual disruptions appeared to have made invasion unlikely, and because the war had turned against him elsewhere, Napoleon had lost faith in his idea.

CHAPTER NINE

Whitehall Warriors

AT THIS POINT WE SHOULD KNOW WHAT THE BRITISH WERE DOING other than having Cornwallis's ships chase up and down the Channel. The answer to that is partly the answer to why the Battle of Trafalgar took place. It most certainly was not just another confrontation with the French or, for that matter, with the Spanish.

Perhaps the first proper indication of British concern was expressed between the commander-in-chief, Admiral Lord Keith[1] of the Home fleet, and his superiors and subordinates, in the autumn of 1803. The Home fleet consisted of the flotilla and squadrons that patrolled the Kent and Sussex waters, the Nore and the Downs. At that time Keith was gathering intelligence from vessels stopped by his fleet, as well as from spies ashore, that the French and Dutch were involved in the build-up at Flushing. Intelligence gathering was, of course, a relatively simple process, but, as ever, the difficulty for commanders lay in making a sure analysis of that information. For example, Keith, like Cornwallis, seemed convinced that the main thrust of any invasion (or descent as it was sometimes termed) would come from Boulogne. Another school of naval thought made different use of the intelligence. Some officers believed it quite possible that the main thrust would eventually come from the Dutch region, particularly Flushing. Then why all the activity at Boulogne? It was seen

---

[1] George Elphinstone Keith, later Viscount Elphinstone (1746–1823). It was Elphinstone, as commander-in-chief Channel Fleet, who was responsible for sailing Napoleon to St Helena in 1815.

either as a diversion created to wrong-foot the British or as an indication that this was a secondary port. Logistics officers could appreciate why both ports might be important. For one thing, invasion traffic would not be one-way. Supplies could come from one port while the military offensive came from another. Moreover, it had to be assumed that returning ships might go elsewhere and thus maintain offensive and supply circuits. The relatively sophisticated maritime and military analysis was to be commended. However, such sophistication produced uncertainties. It is a military-intelligence rule that capabilities may be assessed, whereas intentions remain a mystery until the opening salvos.

Keith's position at the Downs station for his Home fleet made it doubly important that his analysis be correct. While Cornwallis had the major fleet of the two, his task was to tie up Brest, harass any French or Spanish vessels in the Channel and block off the Western Approaches to the Channel; Keith, therefore, represented the main naval defence of the south coast. An important reminder came from the about-to-retire First Secretary to the Admiralty, Sir Evan Nepean.[2] (The title was later altered to that of Permanent Secretary.) The pen portraits of men such as St Vincent and Nelson could be described as illustrations of public lives. It is certainly true that they get most if not all the glory, and – when it suits biographers and historians – the criticism. We again come across a case where a large part of our story was influenced by someone other than the main characters. Sir Evan Nepean was such a person. This most senior civil servant in the Admiralty was typical of his ilk, inasmuch that he had a more intriguing career and was also a greater intriguer than the apparently more glamorous fighting admirals.

By chance, Evan Nepean was not at the Admiralty at this time. Nor, also by chance, was he working directly with St Vincent. He had joined the navy as a clerk in 1776, the timing being not unimportant. The previous year, the American revolution had begun at Lexington and Concord. George Washington had become commander of the American Patriot troops, and in that year of Nepean's joining the American Declaration of Independence had appeared. It was a time when the navy needed every man afloat rather than at its desks at the Admiralty. Nepean

---

[2] Evan Nepean, from 1802 Baronet (1751–1822).

went off to enter that most precarious but potentially profitable class of warrant officers, the pursers (see chapter 2). He was assigned to an armed sloop, the *Falcon*, then on the North American station. There he was successful. The ship got its stores, which kept the men's bellies full and his captain happy. The following year he joined the *Harpy*, two years later the *Hero*, and, most importantly, on 1 April 1780, aged twenty-nine, he was appointed to a much bigger ship, the *Foudroyant*. Why was this significant? Because its captain was John Jervis. Jervis would go on to become an admiral and, after his most memorable battle, Earl St Vincent. Jervis thought rather a lot of Nepean. In 1782, with the war in America over – Yorktown had fallen the previous year – Nepean was to further his administrative education. He was appointed secretary to the important port admiral of Plymouth, Lord Shuldham.[3] Very quickly Nepean, the sometime clerk and therefore scholar of detail, learned the intricacies of the British naval dockyard system. He understood what caused civilian malingering, common theft, disruptive work patterns, failed supply schedules, rotting ships and poorly maintained repair programmes. He also learned all the good points of a dockyard and how, if properly run and managed with an approach of which Nelson would have approved, drawing all levels of personnel, from the lowest to the highest, into the confidence of the commander, that it could be the most supremely hardworking and efficient example of British industry.

It was at this time, 1782, that the prime minister, Lord North, had to resign and the Marquess of Rockingham[4] formed his Whig administration. Ironically, it was Rockingham who had been most responsible for bringing into law the Declaratory Act enforcing British sovereignty over the colonies. There was going to be a war of American independence anyway for which his predecessor, Lord North, was really to blame. Rockingham began the peace negotiations with America and set off at a cracking pace to reform the economy, as well as taking on other major issues such as Irish parliamentary independence. He had been in office for less than five months when, in July 1782, he died. North, with Charles James Fox and the new MP Pitt the Younger,

---

[3] Molyneux Shuldham, Admiral Lord (*c.*1717–1798).
[4] Charles Watson-Wentworth, second Marquess of Rockingham (1730–1782).

waited on the sidelines. A Fox-North administration was formed, but fell in months. The new prime minister was to be Shelburne,[5] who instigated a shuffle of postings in which Nepean became an under-secretary.[5] Shelburne lasted no time at all, but Nepean did. In 1795, already a commissioner of privy seal, he became secretary to the Admiralty.[6] St Vincent was well pleased to have a man he trusted above almost any other as his senior civil servant in the Admiralty. However, a slight dent was made in that admiral's confidence when, in January 1804, his favourite was appointed secretary of state for Ireland. As far as St Vincent was concerned, this was an appalling situation. Here was the navy, all that stood between England and the French invasion, losing its best possible administrator – and, for good measure or bad, a man who saw eye to eye with St Vincent, which could not have been said of many in the Whitehall bureaucracy. Within nine months St Vincent had brought Nepean back to the Admiralty as a lord commissioner. The man who was truly a friend to St Vincent – and, equally important, a close friend to Nelson – was now exactly where both admirals needed him.[7]

This potted history of Nepean should serve to emphasize that an account of the years immediately preceding Trafalgar should not focus exclusively on the time Nelson spent scurrying up and down the Mediterranean and back and forth across the Atlantic in search of what he had prophesied would be a famous victory leading to a permanent place in St Paul's.

Thus Nepean was clearly one of the two most influential figures in the Admiralty. During the autumn of 1803, he wrote to Keith. The instructions would have seemed obvious to any commander in that situation. However, Nepean couched them in language suited to addressing an admiral at war.

---

[5] William Petty, first Marquess of Lansdowne, second Earl of Shelburne (1737–1805).

[6] He succeeded the able but ageing Sir Philip Stephens (1725–1809).

[7] After Trafalgar and the death of Pitt the Younger and the consequent changes at the top, Nepean left the Admiralty. However, his career continued, and in 1812, with the guns at Moscow ringing out for a reason quite different from that of celebrating his elevation, he became governor of Bombay.

My Lord, as it appears essentially necessary that some plan should be adopted for defeating any projects the enemy may form of a descent on that part of the coast within the limits of your Lordship's command during the winter months, my Lords Commissioners of the Admiralty have deemed it advisable that I should transmit to your Lordship for your consideration a general outline of the plan which they conceive to be best adapted to that purpose . . . first, that of having an active force on the enemy's coast for the purpose of keeping a vigilant and constant look-out on their proceedings, and preventing, as far as may be practicable any considerable number of boats or craft from leaving their ports unmolested; and secondly, to fix such stations on our coast as may be best calculated to operate against the enemy in case they should elude the vigilance of our cruisers on their coast[8]

Clearly, Addington's administration took the matter of French preparations very seriously indeed. They had done, since the previous war; certainly since 1801. Most importantly, the man who took them most seriously – as indeed he had then – was the First Sea Lord, St Vincent. He was no socialite officer. He was battle-hardened, intelligent and extremely willing to speak his good mind, especially when he thought little of the minds in government. St Vincent had been Cornwallis's predecessor as commander, Channel Fleet, in charge of the most important seagoing command in the navy. In February 1801 he had come ashore to be Addington's First Lord. The arrangement was never to be a partnership. St Vincent thought most politicians fools and, sometimes, treacherous ones. Clearly he was a good sea officer but a poor Whitehall warrior. He could get the measure of French and Spanish fleets, but never, it seems, of his political and bureaucratic sailing masters. When, in 1805, he completed his brief memoir of his time at the Admiralty, its contents were so vitriolic that on his death eighteen years later all but one copy of the document were destroyed.

St Vincent's time at the Admiralty was one in which he was not alone

---

[8] Secret communication from Sir Evan Nepean to Admiral Lord Keith, Admiralty Office, 11 October 1803.

in believing that one day the French would attempt to invade England. His main task was to produce a navy that would be able to counter such an attack but also, more importantly, one so obviously impressive that it would deter Bonaparte from ever attempting such an operation.

He was able to get his best commanders – people like Nelson, Keith and Dickson – to work their squadrons up to a reasonably high state of efficiency. Above all of them he judged Cornwallis to be his best commander-in-chief. However, he had inherited a navy in which discontent on the lower decks was never far from the surface. The Spithead and Nore mutinies had taken place within recent memory (see chapter 2). Many of the arguments between sailors, marines and the Admiralty had been settled. Nevertheless, life at sea remained taxing, and even the prospect of battle and prizes did not improve morale and conditions sufficiently for him to be convinced that he had a trouble-free service. Moreover, at a time when the navy needed to build new vessels and maintain existing ships in a state of wartime readiness, the Admiralty was not certain it could always rely on the dockyard workers. Even with the threat of war and then, in 1803, its declaration, there were not always the rousing cheers and patriotic fervour that was the historical jingoism of the time.[9] In fact, the degree of patriotism in the country at large in time of war has been, throughout the centuries, remarkably exaggerated. Even in the twentieth century, munitions workers went on strike in wartime. In St Vincent's time at the Admiralty it was quite common for dockyard mateys to steal from the very ships and materials they were working on. The so-called brilliant craftsmanship in the yards was too often rather shoddy. Work was late and schedules were often unmet. Overcharging and profiteering were no less opportunistic than they had been at any time in British history. There were indeed many occasions when the militia had to be sent into the royal docks and shipbuilding yards in an attempt to put some order into a workforce that, when not stealing from under the very noses of the managers, was in open rebellion for better conditions and pay. One irony was that when employees

---

[9] Jingoism is a much later nineteenth-century expression, but its common usage makes it ideal for almost any century as it is a more boisterous word for patriotism.

complained that equipment, stores and materials had not arrived in the yard on time even though they had been paid for, it was very likely that all those things had been 'diverted' along the way and resold. The frequently corrupt workforce, commercial management and suppliers did not always see wartime as a moment to pull together but instead viewed it as an opportunity to exploit the tensions and needs of the nation.

We only have to look at the space devoted in *The Annual Register* for 1804 to what it called the 'mal-administration of the navy' to realize that the service was in a poor state and that this had become a political issue, partly, of course, because it concerned national security. The navy was in a poor state, but then so were the army and the militia. Much of the blame was placed on Addington's administration, as *The Annual Register* made clear:

> The immense pecuniary resources of the empire, and the liberality with which they were contributed for every purpose of national defence, gave the public a right to look for armies and fleets, sufficiently numerous not only to place the country in a state of indubitable security, but to give the enemy that general and effectual annoyance, which might induce him to curb his restless ambition, and restore tranquility to Europe.
>
> In the application of these great means, however, Mr. Addington's ministry were miserably deficient.
>
> To restore the reduced regular force, disposable for every purpose of defensive and offensive measures, no direct means were taken; while to raise an armed body, limited both in respect of locality and duration of service, the legislation were wearied for the great part of two sessions of parliament, in discussing and enacting bills . . . but it was the subject of the mal-administration of the navy, that Mr. Pitt chose to put forth all his strength, and to come down to parliament, towards the close of the last session, to move for an enquiry into a comparative statement of that force, during the periods of his and Mr. Addington's administrations, on which to ground an enquiry into the conduct of the earl of St. Vincent, then first lord of the Admiralty. On this point it was that government was most vulnerable.

In 1804, Pitt authorized an inquiry into the state of the Royal Navy and therefore questioned the conduct of St Vincent. Addington, later Viscount Sidmouth, had been prime minister during most of the period of this apparent maladministration. The *Annual Register* was quite clear that this debate went beyond Whitehall and that public opinion had been against Addington. Most importantly, this was not the time for an inquiry that would be public and decisive.

The general opinion was that the British had taken what was then called a lofty tone towards the French at a time when war seemed inevitable. Not unnaturally, the assumption was that a great admiral, as St Vincent clearly was, knew how to put the navy into such good order that the French would be led to fear a direct confrontation. Yet there were those who saw the navy as a disorganized service heading for ruin rather than victory. Addington was very much to blame. Corruption, inept management, arrogance and political inertia all played their part in producing a navy that was really not as powerful as some of the French admirals thought.

The Admiralty Board of Commissioners was involved in virtually suspending the proper running of the Royal Navy until any reforms had been put in place. Imagine the consequences of preparing a navy for war, only to find that ships could not be put in the necessary order because some of the best dockyard officers and craftsmen had been sacked. Moreover, the Admiralty told the Navy Board that all requisitions for stores and even armaments were to be suspended. The navy did not take this quietly. Yet the only place in which public debate could have changed the system, the House of Commons, all but ignored the dilemma until the Expenditure Bill came before it. This was probably the only thing that made Pitt aware of the seriousness of the situation. Moreover, he was reluctant to hold a public inquiry because that would surely have led to the French becoming fully aware of the extent of the Royal Navy's lack of preparedness.

At the time of the Peace of Amiens there had been much British talk of humbling the arrogance of France and thus making that nation aware that peace was to its advantage. Addington's equivalent of 'peace in our time' could only be backed by a strong military potential. Expressly, the British, more or less confined on their island, could do little about Bonaparte's ambitions with his army. They could, however, usurp those ambitions by having control of the high seas. When, for example, Nelson had decimated the French fleet in Aboukir Bay on 1 August 1798, the French plans in Egypt were more than disrupted. Thus the thinking that had brought about the downgrading of the Royal Navy was spattered with bizarre decision-making. Look, for instance, at a Nelsonian warship, and what do you see? Sails and ropes. Without the sails the ship will not move. Without the ropes the sails will not get up to the yards. Yet those in the Admiralty responsible for such decisions ordered that rope be sold off so that they would not have the expense of maintaining storage depots.

What of those who assured Parliament that all would be well because ships could be brought up to scratch within weeks and vessels built at short notice? The truth: a lack of stores and dockyard facilities, including a shortage of artificers. There was timber available but no point in sending woodsmen into the royal forests with the mistaken idea that the material to be found there would be mature enough for shipbuilding. As *The Annual Register* noted,

> it was found, that, at the awful crisis of a renewed war with France ... we had an exhausted, unrepaired, and ill-equipped fleet, and, worst of all, a system of naval management which forbad any hope of amendment or amelioration nor was the evil confined to naval equipment alone – it pervaded the whole of the service. The harsh and tyrannical measures of the Admiralty, from which they never deviated, were imitated and adopted by many officers, in the interior regulations of their ships: and the privations which the sailors endured in consequence thereof induced several to fly to foreign service, in complete disgust, rather than serve on board the king's ships

The authors of the *Annual Register* confirmed suspicions that the Admiralty was hopeless in all its decision-making. In the case of the description shown above, they were reporting accurately. However, they inadvertently fell into the trap of believing that when serious criticism is justified future criticism must also be worthwhile. Consequently, when they supported what they believed to be St Vincent's view that the blockade of Brest was a waste of time, they were actually making a fundamental strategic and tactical misjudgement.

Nevertheless, there was a general view, supported by St Vincent, of the need to get to sea and destroy the French fleet. The decision to appoint Cornwallis as commander-in-chief Channel with the task of preventing the French from sailing out of Brest was sound. Cornwallis was a determined officer, even if he was criticized for a reluctance to delegate. He was also, on more than one occasion, criticized for repairing to Torbay to escape the worst of the weather. Yet all this failed to take into account what was really just sensible seamanship. In a very harsh gale, the French were prevented from leaving westerly-facing Brest. It was thus better for the British to take shelter in the lee of Torbay, keeping their ships and men in a good condition for when the storm had slackened. The big distinction drawn between battle and containment was not merely something devised at the beginning of the nineteenth century. It was all very well for armchair critics to demand a major battle in order to be done with the French, but the best way to counter Bonaparte, especially with an ill-prepared fleet, was to bottle up the French naval capability. The only disadvantage was that Napoleon Bonaparte would continue with his ambitions to invade England, trusting that the French fleet would eventually sail from Brest and the other ports which they were being prevented from leaving.

In practice, containment was a good policy, especially as the main commanders, perhaps with the exception of Orde, always hoped that the French commanders would take their chances and make a run for it.[10] The British at sea were spoiling for a fight, and they wanted it on their own terms. Moreover, every British admiral knew that engagement often came about by chance. A simple change in the weather, or picket frigates and lookout vessels off station, could easily allow an enemy fleet to escape. St Vincent understood how easily and quickly the weather and tides could turn to the enemy's advantage. But while he could get the seagoing fleets in reasonable shape, he could not always cope with the civilian deficiencies. So when in Whitehall he was told the British workforce was the salt of the earth he naturally responded by going red in the face and expressing his anger to anyone prepared to listen.

---

[10] Sir John Orde (1751–1824).

St Vincent was appointed First Lord of the Admiralty in 1801. His huge, ruthless personality was exactly what they needed. He was required to guarantee that within weeks the country would have a well-stocked and well-fitted-out Baltic fleet. He had no doubts about his commanders, or at least about one of them – Nelson. His reaction to the recalcitrant yard workers and suppliers was as uncompromising as thunderous lightning. Once his wrath was on its way, it could not be stopped; the only means of deflecting it was compliance. By the end of March he had his way. The only weak link in his Baltic fleet was its commander-in-chief, Admiral Sir Hyde Parker.[11] This last point hardly mattered. Nelson was really in charge, and St Vincent made it clear that had it not been for him, the First Sea Lord, there would have been no famous victory at Copenhagen. It was a view he was to repeat – with some justification – after Trafalgar.

St Vincent was a troubled soul. He cared passionately about the navy and about England. He was undoubtedly a supreme naval commander. There was, theoretically, no retirement age for naval officers. By the time war resumed against the French he was well into his sixties. We might think that no age for an experienced officer. Indeed, he really wanted to get back to sea. There were those in Downing Street who solemnly wished he would. The only major command was Cornwallis's. That even St Vincent could not have again – at least not yet. However, by the spring of 1804 the pattern and direction of British politics had changed. Addington, a likeable but not always effectual individual and certainly no wartime leader, was about to depart. He had been prime minister since 1801 and for three years had held steady the English political tiller. It now needed a stronger touch. This was the moment for the ailing – indeed terminally ill – William Pitt the Younger to return to Downing Street.

---

[11] It was to Hyde Parker's (1739–1807) disengage signal to his subordinate commander that Nelson famously turned his blind eye. However, Nelson had also been instructed to press the attack if he could. The incomplete story caught more imaginations.

CHAPTER TEN

Corruption

I N 1804, PITT WAS APPROACHING HIS FORTY-FIFTH BIRTHDAY. HE WOULD be dead within two years. The second son of the esteemed but unfulfilled Pitt the Elder, Earl of Chatham, William Pitt had arrived in the Commons in 1781, famously its youngest member. Two years later he became Britain's youngest ever prime minister. Thus from 1783 to 1801 he directed the transition of Britain from its first empire to that period after the War of American Independence, which saw the rapid rise of the Industrial Revolution (a vague term but one illustrative of the changes in British life), and later directed the nation's effort in the French revolutionary war.

To better understand the times we might remember that when it took place, the French Revolution, and even its bloody consequences at the guillotine, held a certain fascination for the British.

Revolutionary Paris even became a tourist attraction for them. For the politicians and political thinkers the Revolution gave rise to deeply mixed feelings. The political and social philosophers often saw great merit in what was an uprising against the old order, the monarchical system that existed in England as well as in France. With industrial exploration came social expectation. The French may have been a traditional, even convenient, enemy, but their constitutional experiment was viewed by certain philosophers as worth repeating on these shores. After all, the French Revolution had occurred barely 150 years after England's own rebellion. The English had practised regicide long before the French, for constitutional reasons. The Hanoverian monarchy in England was never overwhelmingly popular. The first Hanoverian, George I,[1] had been unable even to speak English. The second had hardly bothered with the language, clearly thought little of his subjects and wanted to use British forces to defeat his continental enemies. George III[2] at the time we are discussing was usually seen as an amiable soul, although rumours of his illness (not a form of madness as has often been suggested) did not arouse much in the way of public sympathy. The eighteenth-century Protestant arrogance that caused the English to believe themselves superior to all other nations (largely because these were either viewed as savage or were Roman Catholic, most likely both) was probably any government's best hope of revolution not spreading to the British Isles. That could be seen as a slight exaggeration given that the Irish, and to some extent the Scots, would have encouraged such an excursion of French revolutionary thought. Therefore the question uppermost in political minds from the 1790s onwards was: would the Revolution spread to England?

The coronation of Bonaparte in 1804 as Emperor Napoleon I meant that the Revolution was over. Napoleon was determined to establish a dynasty. That did not mean the idea of revolution was dead. Political thinkers could easily be agitators. St Vincent's assault on the dockyard workers and pernicious suppliers, together with a continuing unease on the part of the military and admirals about the political allegiances of those under their command, raises two issues. If the soldiers and sailors who, admittedly by our standards, lived in sometimes horrendous conditions were not yet satisfied, they possessed the means – literally – to weaken the nation. Second, might not grumblings that had come to the surface, albeit seven years earlier, be some sort of reflection of the disquiet and disgruntlement that existed in the wider civilian society of Britain? The answer to the latter point is most surely yes. A third question arises from these two. Our impression is that the whole country would have risen up against a Napoleonic invasion. But would it have done? In the spring of 1804 there was no leader, royal, political or social, who was an inspiration to the people. Napoleon inspired France. Might he not also

---

[1] George I (1660–1727), reigned from 1714.
[2] George III (1738–1820), reigned from 1760.

have found in southern England, if not a welcome, then a less than overwhelming opposition? The only hero the British – more particularly the English – had was Nelson. He was England's Napoleon, its figurehead, though his role was utterly different, his ambition being not to conquer but to defend. His frailties were public knowledge and many of his actions famously unrealistic. He was also physically weak. Yet he, Nelson, was the people's god. In 1804 there was none other. How desperately, then, the government needed Nelson's victories.

With Bonaparte across the Channel, the English, secure within their own countryside, felt reasonably invincible as long as Nelson piled up the victories. However, Copenhagen had taken place in 1801, exactly three years earlier. The French threat had still not receded. The political leadership in Whitehall had little to commend it to the nation. Henry Addington was weak, having played his best political role between 1789 and 1801 as a competent Speaker of the House of Commons. He had succeeded Pitt the Younger as prime minister on his resignation in 1801. True, he had a breathing space that year in the form of the autumn armistice in the war with France. The following spring, the Treaty of Amiens was seen as a woeful capitulation to the French on the part of an administration in desperate search of a quiet life. Never quite sure of himself as premier, he was one of those men whose indecisions are final. So by the spring of 1804, with Britain at war and the threat of invasion real rather than imagined, the pressure on the lonely Pitt – unmarried and comparatively friendless – to return to Downing Street was proving unbearable. Truly, Pitt was in bad health and would have preferred a quiet existence living out his time at Walmer. But return he did nonetheless.

We have been heading towards the Battle of Trafalgar. In spring 1804, no one envisioned such an event. Pitt was preoccupied only with Bonaparte and that man's ambitions to rule Europe including the British Isles. As a later leader saw, a century and more on, there was no way in which a mighty enemy seized with cruel ambition could be defeated by a single nation. Britain in the twentieth century knew perfectly well that by itself it could never sustain a war in continental Europe and beyond. Even with its pattern of empire, which covered a quarter of the globe, there was no means of responding to large-scale military and ideological tyranny other than through a coalition of forces. The same was true when Pitt returned to power. For this reason he sought and found a coalition, with Austria, Russia and Sweden, that he believed might check Napoleon. In fact, this coalition failed in the year of Trafalgar when the Austrians and Russians were defeated by the French at Austerlitz.

We should not give the impression that with Pitt's return to Downing Street Britain now had the ideal political and military combination with which to defeat the enemy. Pitt's arrival showed that his anxiety did not go unshared. St Vincent could (and did) rant against the Admiralty and politicians in general. When it came to polemics, Pitt was more than the First Sea Lord's equal. Even before his return, ill and ill-tempered, to lead the Treasury bench, he had made public his contempt for both Addington and the hero St Vincent. Pitt's view was that in spite of his stomping, old salt-style rhetoric and behaviour, the admiral was not really a good servant of the Royal Navy. Pitt saw an enemy, then looked at the navy and was horrified. He believed the First Sea Lord had not cared properly for the fleets. Ships and conditions, training and efficiency were, in his view, below the standard necessary for wartime. Moreover, he had examined the naval building programme, which was very much the responsibility of St Vincent and presumably of his bureaucratic partner Nepean, and had soon come to the conclusion that in spite of their reputations and claims to be rescuing the navy they had no idea what they were doing. To Pitt the navy under St Vincent seemed to be doing what it had always done: building itself as many big ships as possible in order to go deep sea and have a mighty battle with whatever enemy it came across. Pitt looked and listened to intelligence reports, saw what was being built on the other side of the Strait of Dover, listened to alternative voices who talked about local conditions and came to the conclusion that St Vincent was building the wrong ships. The prime minister said that the navy needed smaller vessels that were easier to manoeuvre within such confined spaces and against that type of landing fleet. There was a clear need, in his opinion, for small vessels such as gunboats capable of harassing, dispersing and preferably destroying an invasion force. Pitt saw clearly that this was not simply a battle of ships versus ships. In this he was right. An invasion force goes from A to B. It has no other function or ambition, unlike a fleet which can stand off and wait while collecting itself and seeking other targets. Therefore the concept was for small vessels able to lead an assault – supported and defended by larger ships, of course – in the event of the single-minded Bonaparte's launching an attack.

We are seeing big personalities at work. Pitt was a man who had seemingly brilliantly directed Britain's effort against the French in their War of Revolution. He had been a revelation in terms of political management and had, in some respects, achieved everything his father, Pitt the Elder, had never managed. He had witnessed the uselessness and vacillation of Addington's administration. There is no real evidence that he had ever wanted to return to power, but he was forced to. As well as being ill he was probably close to personal bankruptcy. His country was at war and Bonaparte was, ostensibly, on his way. And what did he see on returning to office? The remnants of a short-lived administration that had failed to take the necessary steps to deter the enemy. Deterrence, in Pitt's mind, was even more important than looking for a victory. What was the point in fighting if you could deter the enemy from seeking you out in the first place? He was not much impressed by the Admiralty. Though there were some first-class appointments at sea, including Cornwallis, Nelson, Collingwood and, potentially, Calder, Pitt regarded the navy as an entity not a series of impressive cameos. Yet Pitt and St Vincent were not really that far apart in their thinking.

St Vincent had been working on a plan whereby it would be known that he personally had saved the navy from itself. If credit was due, the First Lord might easily attach his name to it. If there were to be discredit, he would make it clear to everyone what fools he had about him.

When St Vincent became First Lord, the first phase of the Anglo-French war was at its end. The Royal Navy needed to take a deep breath. The command system had not really forced through a new generation which would surely be needed in what was hoped to be an expanding service. It was certainly necessary to expand the fleets. Forty or fifty years earlier the navy had looked in good shape, largely thanks to the efforts of the then First Lord, Admiral Lord Anson.[3] George Anson had

---

[3] George Anson and first Baron (1697–1762) Famous for his circumnavigation of the world (1740–1744).

been the father of the Georgian navy. He was, truly, the most complete naval officer. No stay-at-home society sailor, he had earned his first major promotion, to flag rank, an account of his occasionally spectacular circumnavigation of the globe between 1740 and 1744. He was very popular with his men, partly because he was very good at capturing French and Spanish prize ships (see chapter 2). Anson accumulated more than £500,000 of Spanish bullion by the time he returned to Portsmouth in the summer of 1744. It was Anson who in 1747 picked up a further £300,000 having defeated the French at the Battle of Cape Finisterre. Four years later he began his first stint as First Lord and, after a break in 1756, he returned the following year for a five-year spell at the Admiralty. It was during this period that Anson consolidated his ideas for reforming the structure of the navy, including the way it trained its men and the style and number of vessels it built. The service had been in decline for certainly more than half a century. It was he who rescued and reformed it. Perhaps most importantly, he transformed the officer class – once a bunch of rough and ready, sometimes aristocratic, ill-disciplined sailors. He drew into the navy that stratum of society that makes it successful: a middle class. Until well into the second half of the eighteenth century many of the ships that put to sea as naval vessels were little more than privateers. Anson introduced changes which, by the time of the Nelsonian navy, had led to an increase in a discipline and formal structure. Ships were often painted in different styles. Anson thought ships should be made as easily recognizable to one another as possible. Not only was this good battle practice but it created a sense of unity and discipline necessary to the formation of a homogenous fighting fleet. Similarly he introduced a common uniform for sailors.

While admirals, and even lesser commanders such as post captains, could and were expected to put their own squadrons and ships in recognizable order, it was really the Admiralty, through its various Boards, whose role it was to find the funds, set the common standard and put into practice a building, maintenance, victualling and training programme. Nelson cursed the Admiralty Board – rightly. Pitt agreed that too little had been done to change things for the better, which was why he dismissed the grandiose claims of St Vincent. Too many members of the Admiralty lined their pockets. None of this paints a very noble picture of a navy that was supposed to be taking on the might and ambition of Bonaparte and seeing off the combined squadrons of France and Spain.

Was St Vincent really a charlatan? No, he was not. Pitt's low regard for him was unfair. That admiral had spent three years as First Lord, and in that time had made a personal audit of the yards and the systems for supplying the Royal Navy. He had got rid of between twelve and thirteen per cent of the dockyard workers, mainly, he claimed, because they had been either incompetent or employed with no work to do. Pitt saw that as reducing the royal yard capability. Pitt's judgement was poor. The main reason St Vincent had set to and done something about the practice in the royal yards was that at the time of his joining the Navy Board in 1801 no one else had done anything whatsoever. Everyone who had ever worked in a yard knew of corruption and incompetence. So why had it been allowed to continue, especially when Britain was at war? Seen from St Vincent's point of view – and probably also from Evan Nepean's – the problem lay with the state of the Navy Board itself.

The First Lord had contempt for those he saw as conspirators in the running down of the Royal Navy. Both before he was fired and certainly afterwards, St Vincent believed that the Board was morally corrupt and that it had even contrived to divert money to private interests.

Pitt's own view was a muddle of privatization policies. He said it would be much cheaper to give a private contractor set guidelines to build a ship of the line than to continue the tradition of entrusting the work to the royal docks.

He was wrong. Despite the corruption, poor materials and unreliable workforce often to be found in the royal yards, it was still less expensive to build there than to employ a commercial contractor. When a similar policy was adopted in the late twentieth century the Royal Navy expressed similar sentiments against government policy for privatization. In 1804, the difficulties involved in producing good ships on time could hardly be left to the judgement of a grumpy admiral and a reluctant prime minister.

Pitt could be as short-tempered as any admiral, especially with anyone he thought a fool. On his return to Downing Street he was certainly in no mood to tolerate the First Lord. So St Vincent departed, and would have to wait until the moment he could get his hands on Cornwallis's Channel command. That, however, would not happen until well after Nelson had cleared the high seas of any French ship worth attacking. Pitt placed in the Admiralty one of his most loyal supporters, Henry Dundas, raised to the peerage by Addington as Viscount Melville and Baron Dunira (the name of the family seat not far from Comrie in Scotland). The dejected, rejected First Lord was no longer able to contain his anger. He accused Melville of being as corrupt as any of the rogues in commerce. He insisted that certain sections of the Treasury were equally corrupt because they had known of Melville's corruption. A great deal of this was nonsense. Some of it was true. That year, with the very shores of England under threat, none of it mattered – but it would, and Melville would fall (see chapter 12).

Melville had begun his professional life as a Scottish jurist. In 1774, aged thirty-two, he entered parliament as the member for Midlothian. He became Lord Advocate the following year and then, rather grandly, in 1777, was appointed Keeper of the Signet for Scotland. Despite his success it would be hard to make a case for Melville being over-principled when it came to political allegiance. He had, for example, been an advocate of the war against America during the time Lord North was prime minister. He had slipped very easily into the Rockingham camp on North's forced resignation following the debacle of that conflict in 1781. When William Pitt the Younger came to power, Dundas – as then he was – lent him his support. There was a period in the 1790s when, to his great credit, he had a hand in some new legislation that was to improve the daily lives of a rapidly changing British electorate. When Pitt in 1801 decided to resign Dundas also resigned, but was back within the twelvemonth in the Addington administration. When, on his return to power, Pitt turned to Melville to be the First Lord of the Admiralty, this caused some difficulty for Melville, who found himself impeached for 'gross malversation and breach of duty' allegedly committed during his time as navy treasurer. St Vincent was not the only one to point accusingly at the Scottish peer. In 1806 Melville was tried by the House of Lords and honourably discharged from the accusation. By now there was no place for him in any administration – Pitt was dead – and Melville retired to spend more time at his family seat.

By late 1804, with Bonaparte, shortly to be Emperor Napoleon I, ordering full speed ahead for the invasion and the British deep-water fleet at sea, Britain had a new and clearly more dynamic leadership to continue the conflict. Melville immediately took one of the most important naval decisions of the war. He told Cornwallis to remain as commander-in-chief, Channel Fleet. This was not a local command. It extended as far south as Gibraltar. Although Cornwallis took part in the containment of the French effort around the Channel ports of Boulogne, Dieppe and the rest, his main concerns were to bottle up French fleets in port thus preventing them from providing the invasion's protection flotilla, to attack French ships wherever they might appear and to take merchant ships as prizes. Even in a modern war all these tasks would prove difficult. One can only imagine the breadth of seamanship, forward planning, knowledge of meteorology, sailing skills and stamina they would have demanded in 1804. Cornwallis may not have had Nelson's audacity, but he had the wisdom and instincts, together with what we might call management skills, that make a truly memorable commander. St Vincent had thought him the best man for the job. Whatever Pitt and Melville thought of St Vincent, they too came to rely almost totally on Cornwallis.

William Cornwallis was hardly likely to be a nation's hero. He had none of the dash necessary to excite the people. The gods did not quake at his name. He was not a famous fighting admiral, nor did he fit the navy's stereotype. The navy was, and remains, a service that draws its officers mainly from the middle classes. In those days aristocrats sent a son into the army and bought him his first commission. He then went on to buy his promotion, certainly up to the rank of colonel. Few aristocrats have ever bothered to go to sea. Maybe it was the discomfort. Certainly the life of a naval officer left only a little time for levees, county balls and fashionable London society. It was quite difficult to hold a seagoing command and hunt three days a week – not even a French frigate was a good enough substitute fox.

Yet Cornwallis came from an aristocratic family. His father was a marquess and the fifth Lord Cornwallis. His older brother was an earl and the more famous of the two, as a general – the one who surrendered at Yorktown. William Cornwallis was a countryman, another anomaly for a seagoing officer. His roots lay in his Hampshire estate just inland from Lymington. He was quiet and retiring, regarded his stables with greater interest than salons and never thought it necessary to take a wife. How was such a man able to win such a post? To begin with, Cornwallis was totally devoted to the navy. He had been at sea for half a century and contrived to spend much of that time in a ship. He had served in every theatre of war and patrol. He had sailed from the Far East to the West Indies. He had stood off the African seaboard, patrolled the Mediterranean, the Caribbean and, of course, the North America station. He had never commanded a fleet during these times, but he continued to be extremely well regarded. St Vincent thought him the most competent seagoing admiral of his day. Presumably he believed that because he himself happened to have a shore job. He certainly considered Cornwallis a better fleet commander than the nation's hero, Nelson.

Equally, Cornwallis justified this respect by being a superb sailing master, an almost instinctive weather forecaster (an extremely important accomplishment in the days of sail), a thoughtful tactician and a good judge of a ship's company. Officers liked being in his squadrons. He had a reputation for selecting the best people for appointments to his ships, causing those commanders under him to view themselves as an elite force of men. In return he expected – and usually got – 100 per cent of their attention and competence. Nelson saw him as a friend but, more importantly, thought of him as a first-class officer and an equally good commander. The two, as St Vincent observed, did not always go together.

When Cornwallis was confirmed in his appointment in May 1804, he was already sixty-one years old. His was the most demanding of all the naval commands. He was the senior commander at sea and thus someone whose decisions and actions could affect those of the secondary ones, such as Nelson in the Mediterranean and Keith off the Downs (see chapter 15). It was also, arguably, the most wretchedly uncomfortable command. He was based in an often dank and seemingly ever cramped vessel experiencing, week in and week out, some of the worst weather that could be thrown at a 200-foot sailing ship attempting to keep station in the heavy chops of the English Channel and the debilitating swells at the very edges of the Atlantic. An admiral of his age and of those times was not necessarily very fit. Cornwallis was inclined to be portly, his eyesight had deteriorated and he was not in continuous good health.

There were few who knew this. As far as Cornwallis was concerned, if he needed to be at sea for a year or two then so be it. This was the common lot of the commander in wartime.

This had been an important period in the restructuring of the government and the command and control of the Royal Navy. Yet of the three important people in that story only Pitt would survive in the historical appendices to Trafalgar – and that was because he was already established as one of the more remarkable leaders Britain had known. Melville's understanding of reform and likely future events was forgotten in the debacle of the charges that removed him from office at such a sensitive moment in war planning. His decision, which no one thought to overturn, to keep Cornwallis in place was far more important to the outcome than anyone could have then imagined and few have later acknowledged. Cornwallis's blockade of Brest would do more to frustrate Napoleon's plan of invasion than would Nelson's chasing of the combined Spanish–French fleet across the Atlantic and back. Nelson got the column; Cornwallis had hardly a footnote.

CHAPTER ELEVEN

Cat and *Souris*

I N 1804, NELSON'S TASK WAS NOW TO WATCH FOR ANY CHANCE TO DESTROY the French Mediterranean fleet. This was not simply a case of Nelson spending his whole day pacing the quarterdeck with his remaining eye peering through his spy glass at Toulon. A number of practicalities had to be taken into account when an early nineteenth-century sailing ship was in the process of keeping a station and, with it, the admiral's squadron. Even in a more southerly latitude than that of the Channel, the Mediterranean in January was not necessarily a place of balmy seas. Nelson's squadron did not simply heave to off the French port and wait for the mouse to appear. Moreover, not all of the squadron would have been assembled there. For example, some vessels would have been dispersed at anchorages short distances away. It was always a concern of Nelson that he had to protect those anchorages as well as blockading the port. At the beginning of January, Nelson wrote to one of his captains, Francis Fremantle[1], mentioning the difficulties of finding good havens for his ships while enduring the prevailing winds and at the same time maintaining a proper force outside Toulon. It would have been very good for morale and the condition of the ships to allow the men a run ashore, but, as Nelson pointed out to Fremantle, who had just joined the squadron in the *Neptune*, everyone was remaining at sea and the best that could be hoped for was a night at anchor.

---

[1] Thomas Francis Fremantle (1765–1819). He was captain of HMS *Neptune* and later a vice admiral and knight.

... I should most assuredly rejoice to have you here, but we none of us see the inside of a Port: I have twice taken shelter under the Madalena Islands on the North end of Sardinia, which form a very fine anchorage. The Village, I am told, for I have not set my foot out of the Victory, contains forty or fifty small houses. As to Malta, it is a perfectly useless place for Great Britain; and as a Naval Port to refit in, I would much sooner undertake to answer for the Toulon Fleet from St. Helens, than from Malta; I never dare venture to carry the Fleet there. I know your friends think differently from me, but they talk of what they know nothing about in that respect, and I know it from dear-bought experience. During the winter, generally speaking, I cannot get even a Frigate from Malta, the Westerly winds are so prevalent; and as they approach the Gulf of Lyons, they are blown to the South end of Sardinia. Perseverance has done much for us, but flesh and blood can hardly stand it. I have managed to get some fresh provisions from Rosas in Spain, which with onions and lemons have kept us remarkably healthy. We are longing for the French Fleet, which is to finish our hard fate. I am, &c.

　　Nelson and Brontë.[2]

From the sailing master's point of view, the important passage in Nelson's letter is his reference to the westerly winds. The sailing characteristics of his ships of the line meant it was little wonder that he was unable to get them on passage from Malta up to the support squadron standing off Toulon. Nelson says he couldn't sail 'even a frigate' against those winds. His point to Fremantle would have been well understood. The frigate was smaller, faster and better rigged to sail to windward. Here is the practical illustration of the difficulty of both navies, French and British, at that time in positioning itself, tracking and then engaging an enemy fleet. There was far more to naval warfare than a broadside from a 30-pounder.

Nelson, who was at sea in his flagship, the *Victory*, during that first week of the year, now had what he believed to be good intelligence that the

---

[2] Nelson had been created Duke of Brontë, and both proudly and grandly, always signed himself as such, including in his letters to Emma.

French based in Corsica intended to invade Sardinia. This was territorial warfare which extended to the anchorages, whose importance should not be underestimated. On 4 January 1804 Nelson wrote to Parker, captain of the *Amazon*. The ship was in an anchorage off the island and it was essential that Parker should keep his station and protect the Sardinians.

> An invasion of Sardinia is intended immediately on our departure, by the French from Corsica; it is therefore my direction that you remain at your present anchorage, and use your utmost endeavours in preventing the invasion of the French, and give every aid and assistance in your power to the Inhabitants, should it be attempted. The Cameleon will give similar orders to Captain Staines, and direct him to remain on this service till further instructions; and you will get under weigh occasionally, as you may think proper.

The *Victory* herself used the anchorage at La Madalena. It was not difficult to see why Nelson needed to protect the islands. That end of Sardinia was almost touching Corsica across the Bay of Bonifacio, and it would have been an easy task for the Corsicans to land on Sardinia. The islands had another advantage in that the Madalenas were at the top right-hand corner of Sardinia. This made them good protection against the westerlies Nelson so much disliked. Malta, to the south, was not in normal circumstances a difficult sail. Nelson and his captains must have prayed for a wind change. The admiral knew he could not find sufficient forces in his fleet to stop the Corsican French. He had asked for about a thousand soldiers to be sent from Malta in the event of an attempted invasion from Corsica. He was not simply taking seaman-like precautions to protect his harbours. The Sardinians had already been threatened with an invasion by the French if they continued to allow the British fleet to anchor among those islands.

The role of admiral was both complex and time-consuming, involving far more than sailing up and down the French coast in a threatening manner. For instance, his sailors and marines had to be fed. This was not an easy task for the purser, who was required to send a longboat ashore for fruit and vegetables. For all his glorious deeds, above Nelson's head floated a dull-witted cloud of Whitehall bureaucracy. Every penny piece of warfare had to be accounted for through the books that unimaginative clerks carefully guarded. In the heat of a campaign, an admiral could expect reams of mail from his Admiralty bosses demanding an explanation for even the smallest expenditure. Examples abound of gallant careers being pitched into courts of inquiry because after the events which had brought glory the commander in question had found himself quite unable to recall who had spent what, when and why at a time when all he had been thinking about was the execution of a campaign against the king's enemies.

So on New Year's Day 1804, Nelson was in his cabin writing to the transport agent – through whom he was obliged to deal – in Malta, asking for a store ship, a so-called transport for the shipping of food. He had then to order from yet another bureaucrat, the agent victualler on Malta, Patrick Wilkie. He even had to detail that he wanted the supplies put into one vessel so that it could be towed by one of his precious warships. He could not afford to send vessels backwards and forwards for supplies, especially as the prevailing winds made it impossible to guess the times of return. Victualling agents were assumed to be corrupt and the process corrupted, with the result that an admiral supposedly planning one of the most complex of blockades and, quite possibly, a decisive naval battle, was to be found that day worrying about his men's bread ration.

> Madalena Islands, 1st January 1804.
> Sir,
> I am to desire you will immediately cause to be shipped on board the largest of the Transports named in the margin [*Ellice* and *Eliza*], a proportion of bread for 5600 men for two months, with every other species of provisions to six weeks, except wine, of which none is wanted; and should there not be a sufficient quantity of sugar in store for the above purpose, you are not to purchase, but send what remains. And as it is of great consequence to have all the provisions in one Transport, in order that the Vessel of War which convoys her may take her in tow, you will endeavour to have the provisions all put into one Transport; and, therefore, if it cannot be stowed in such Victualler, you will only send a month's beef and pork, instead of six weeks', as our little supplies of fresh beef will, in some measure, make up the deficiency. You will send me an

account of the provisions which you may ship, as before directed, by the first opportunity, as well as a regular account of the remains of every species in store, by any of his Majesty's Ships joining me from Malta, that I may on all occasions know what supplies can be drawn from the stores under your charge. I am, &c.

Nelson and Brontë

Thus the detail of a two-year naval campaign that would never be depicted in the Painted Hall.

At first glance, the deployment of the navy appeared to protect British interests at every major point. When St Vincent left the Admiralty, the Royal Navy had about 400 ships, excluding the auxiliaries. This did not mean all these vessels were at sea. We might, for instance, have found that Cornwallis had about 50 vessels under his command, including 33 ships of the line. However, he could never expect to have all those ships in one area or even at sea at any one time. Some might be temporarily transferred to reinforce another command. Others may have been damaged, not by battle but by the weather. A further group would be in a continuous rotation for repairs, either alongside for short 'assisted maintenance periods' or in dock for expensive and time-consuming refits. There was also the chance that some of the fleet would not be where it was supposed to be, simply, again, because of the weather. It was quite common for a weather front to be severe enough to blow a ship right off course, and for the vessel to be hundreds of miles from where it was supposed to be by the time her captain had regained control. For example, a square-rigged craft close to the French coast when a westerly storm blew up would risk being blown on to what sailors would call a lee shore. So the captain would have to sail as best he could away from that shore and, probably, away from the weather. This could easily take a vessel two days' sailing off station, and it might take days, sometimes weeks, before a squadron was usefully reunited. Thus the weather, the limits of sailing rigs and the utter difficulty of finding another vessel meant that although the Admiralty was nominally in charge of the sea war against Napoleon, the local admiral often had no option but to act without consulting his Whitehall masters. In Nelson's view, this was an adequate arrangement.

CHAPTER TWELVE

The Melville Affair

A MAIN CAUSE FOR CONCERN AMONG THE SEAGOING ADMIRALS WAS THE fact that the navy lacked both the quantity and range of vessels necessary to the formation of a well-balanced fleet. The 1801–1804 building programme was not particularly impressive, resulting in the addition of only five large ships. One was a refitted French vessel while the others came from British yards. Big ships may have been the glamorous vessels, but the smaller frigates, capable of being adapted for so many uses in addition to being faster and more manoeuvrable, had been in continuous short supply. Melville, St Vincent's replacement, and William Marsden,[1] who replaced Nepean, now had the task of bringing the navy up to speed to the satisfaction of Cornwallis, Nelson and Keith as well as the uncompromising Pitt. Melville was the driving political force, while Marsden managed the bureaucracy. It was not an unsuccessful partnership. The fleets may have been short of men, stores and certain vessels, but during 1804–1805 the vast majority of them were kept at sea. The main blot on the Admiralty horizon was the welter of accusations about to be levelled at Melville for alleged corruption and maladministration.

If the admirals thought they were having a hard time, it might have been due partly to the realization that despite the competence of the three chief protagonists, Pitt, Melville and Marsden, the political and administrative functioning of the war, particularly with regard to the navy, was unsatisfactory.

---

[1] William Marsden (1754–1836); and First Secretary (1804–1805).

Pitt had never wanted to return to office, being in almost constant pain despite his relative youth – he was only in his mid-forties. His political anguish had as much to do with his relations with other leading politicians and with George III (which were never cordial), as with the preparations for war. In the House of Commons, Pitt had trouble raising a majority when it came to military measures. He did, briefly, manage to bring Addington back into his Cabinet, an ineffectual appointment that barely lasted until the summer. Yet he pressed on amid opposition, intrigue, incompetence and, needless to say, the Melville affair. It would have been easier if Melville had either ignored or been ignorant of the affairs of the naval paymaster, Alexander Trotter.[2] Trotter had diverted public money to his own investment schemes, although he had repaid these sums. Melville should have known about this because for nearly twenty years he had been Treasurer to the Navy. He had, at the same time, been a number of other things in the Cabinet. He professed ignorance of the misdemeanors. How could he, he complained, have been expected to know what Trotter was up to? Pitt and Melville had spent much time trying to discredit St Vincent, and now it was St Vincent's own inquiry into the administration of the navy that was throwing up the connection between Trotter and Melville. Almost inevitably, the inquiry concluded that Melville was far from being the overworked minister unaware of Trotter's business arrangements that he claimed to be. According to St Vincent, Melville had had a part in it. Melville might have been treated differently had it not emerged that Trotter had given him a loan.

It may be that Melville was entirely innocent of any wrongdoing. History provides innumerable examples of self-proclaimed innocence being rejected by a suspicious public and an opportunistic political opposition. Imagine Pitt's position. In April 1805, his whole strategy was to go into battle against the Franco-Spanish fleet. Bonaparte, by now Napoleon I, was still intent on invasion. Instead of being able to concentrate on these matters Pitt found his key minister, Melville, faced with a censure resolution in the House of Commons. The mover of the motion and resolutions against Melville was Samuel

---

[2] Alexander Trotter (?–1834) was the Navy's paymaster.

Whitbread,[3] a scion of the brewery family. This censure must have angered and hurt Pitt. After all, Whitbread had been an ally. The House was divided over Melville, as were the leading politicians of the day.

Britain was at war with France and its admirals were at their wits' end watching their politicians at Westminster at war with one another. In April 1805, the House was called upon to vote on a censure motion against Melville. It was equally divided. All eyes now turned to the Commons Speaker, Charles Abbot.[4] Abbot is remembered as the man who brought in the parliamentary Act that established the census in Britain. Pitt would remember him to his dying day – then not far off – for having cast his Speaker's vote against Melville.

This was, in effect, a censure motion on Pitt's administration. With Charles Abbot's vote, there were 217 against the government and 216 for. Worse was to come. Whitbread felt a political head of steam rising in his favour. He moved an impeachment motion against Melville. Eventually it got through. Melville would not go on trial until the following year. By that time, Pitt would be dead and so would Nelson. For the moment, and on the brink of two of the most decisive naval engagements in British history, the navy had lost its First Lord of the Admiralty. Moreover, there was more to come – and what was to become of St Vincent?

It would have been quite easy to bring Cornwallis ashore and have St Vincent return to a seagoing job as commander-in-chief Channel. Certainly, the latter had not become an office wallah. He gave up his sea command in 1799, through ill health, not for higher office. He would eventually replace Cornwallis when, in 1806, he once again took command of the Channel Fleet. However, just as Melville and St Vincent had agreed that Cornwallis was the best man for the job (about the only thing on which they did agree) it was decided to leave the aristocratic admiral where he was. In time of war with, for the moment, the navy being the more important of the two services, it seemed obvious that what was needed was a senior admiral who was also a good administrative and political warrior. The area of naval confrontation was now well defined.

---

[3] Samuel Whitbread (1758–1815) the son of the founder of the brewery, became MP for Bedford in 1790.
[4] Charles Abbot, (1757–1829). Baron Colchester, 1817. Speaker 1802–1817.

Thus, it seemed a straightforward decision to acquire for the post someone who had experience of commanding in those waters. Pitt often failed to do the obvious. Instead, he dug out of virtual retirement a man who was in his eightieth year and whose last days at sea no one could remember. In fact, many of the commanders and certain post captains had not even been born during his time at sea. True, he had flag rank. But as long as an officer had reached a seagoing appointment – for example, as captain – he could be promoted simply on the death of someone senior to him. So it was with Sir Charles Middleton.[5] Most people knew nothing more about him other than he was a practising Methodist. Curiously, he was a relative of Melville.

Across the Channel, Bonaparte and his commanders could only marvel at the goings-on in the British parliament. Napoleon was an enthusiastic public-relations man. He immediately ordered publicity to be given to the Melville affair. He ordered a special pamphlet to be printed which was to be given the widest circulation. The pamphlet would show the whole of France what a corrupt nomenklatura ruled Britain. Only he, Napoleon, was able to command the moral high ground.

Government in these times was often a family affair. Patronage, the more traditional form of what we now call cronyism, was a centuries-old practice. It was not such a poor way of filling vacancies as we might think. Even as late as the beginning of the nineteenth century there were very limited ways of getting the education and experience necessary to take a man into the higher levels of administration and politics. Pitt the Younger was an anomaly inasmuch that he was a loner without the intricate matrix of kinsmen that so often had a half a dozen families scattered in influential positions either in government or on its important fringes. The ruling class was a small society of relatives mostly drawn from the aristocracy at a time when parliamentary seats were bought, sold and owned by that same aristocracy. This is why certain aristocrats popped up in all sorts of government jobs. In a long-running administration, it was common for a middling aristocrat to be a little like influenza. As was noted, once he had been in close contact, almost every prime minister would catch him in his cabinet. So it was little wonder

---

[5] Sir Charles Middleton, Lord Barham (1726–1813).

that there were all kinds of social candidates for the job of First Lord of the Admiralty. It had been quite common for an individual to hold more than one job. There was certainly more than one for each one.

We can imagine the topics of the day discussed from parlours to clubs. Why on earth had Middleton been given such a crucial job? The fact that Pitt had told George III that he was to raise Middleton to the peerage as Lord Barham was irrelevant. Had not Pitt granted his own banker, Robert Smith, an Irish and then an English peerage?[6] For goodness' sake, bankers were, at the end of the eighteenth and the beginning of the nineteenth century, considered as trade. From that point onwards anything was possible. The main subject under discussion was Pitt's health. There were those, especially his political enemies like Addington, who wondered whether his physical state had affected his mental health. Was his political judgement therefore unreliable?

Such questioning of the physical and mental state of perhaps the most important political leader of his age was pertinent because Pitt was also a wartime leader. He would not have been prime minister had there not been a war with France. We can imagine also the mood of Bonaparte, who had enormous regard for Pitt as a leader. He saw Nelson and Pitt as formidable adversaries. It was clear – or so Napoleon thought, along with many in the clubs of St James's – that Pitt had made a poor judgement. Was this really the case?

Middleton may have been an old duffer who had forgotten his port from his starboard, but he was not entirely a slouch in the department where Pitt most needed him. The prime minister did not need a swashbuckler and fighting admiral at his side. He wanted those sorts of officers at sea. By the spring of 1805 he was racked with pain and political intrigue. He therefore needed an excellent administrator. He wanted someone who was supportive of the navy but also a good manager and bookkeeper. Therefore the new First Lord had to know how to work with the Treasury and the comptroller of the Admiralty to obtain the money

---

[6] Robert Smith (1752–1832) was created the first Baron Smith, an Irish peerage, in 1796. Later the family name was changed from Smith to Carrington, thus beginning the line of Carrington peers, which has included the Marquis of Lincolnshire and Margaret Thatcher's first foreign secretary, the sixth Lord Carrington.

and resources necessary to keep ships, men and guns at sea in the best fighting trim. Middleton was probably a better man for the job than Melville had been and was most certainly a vast improvement on St Vincent. The navy's cause under the dull Middleton would be in good hands. Pitt may have been losing his fight for life, but he had not yet lost his powers of judgement.

Pitt certainly needed what remained of his powers. His administration, which had always been a cobbled-together affair, was in a terrible state. That summer of 1805, Addington, by now Lord Sidmouth, resigned. Addington's reputation is that of a vacillator. There seems to have been hardly a celebrated moment in his career. His resignation upset the king, who already thought little of Pitt. Pitt needed to shuffle his Cabinet. He had to have a new secretary for war and at least a new President of the Council, Addington's old job title. His biggest concern was that his entire government could collapse. This was not the anxiety of an ailing man. The possibility was a real probability. Imagine the concern of Pitt and his remaining allies. They had not the slightest idea in that late spring and early summer of 1805 that Bonaparte was being forced to reconsider his invasion plan. They could not have known that an invasion of some sort would not occur at any moment. Napoleon was a man of erratic judgement. Even on the eve of being forced to abandon the Boulogne adventure, he was quite capable of launching a punitive raid across the Channel. Moreover, Pitt could not be certain that the populace would remain loyal to their own country.

Pitt needed his friends and true supporters in his Cabinet. The monarch was still an authority in the land and the prime minister most certainly could not appoint ministers without George III's approval. The King refused to consider those he either disliked or whose motives he questioned. Why, he thought, should Pitt, in the middle of a war, be so concerned? It was all a matter of parliamentary votes. There was an absolute necessity for Parliament to accept his wartime budget proposals. He was certainly not going to get 412 votes, but he wanted a proper majority. He needed those people who could either swing votes or use their own votes to push through the most important of the money Bills. George III, who had gone to take the summer airs of Weymouth, waved Pitt away. His had been an administration without proper authority. It hardly helped Pitt's cause, nor the country's, that the Royal Navy was losing one of its best chances of bringing the war at sea to an end. Calder engaged the enemy, but not closely enough. Had he done so, there would never have been a Battle of Trafalgar (see chapter 19). There were moments in the final year of Pitt's life when he must have felt that none of his efforts would come to anything. Yet he was presiding over the government of Britain in a year – 1805 – that was to become one of the most significant dates in the nations's history. None would suggest that Trafalgar was a historic turning point comparable to, say, the Norman invasion, the execution of Charles I or the beginning of the First World War. The year 1805 was important because it saw Britain rise to the position of supreme maritime nation, which enabled her Empire to develop into an entity of remarkable power and profitability. It was also the year in which Napoleon abandoned his attempt to invade England. We cannot lightly dismiss this latter event. Preparations had gone far enough for those who governed Britain to understand the consequences of Napoleon's getting even a toehold, never mind anything firmer, on English shores. In practice, it could have happened. The need for Napoleon to divert his forces, together with the inordinately long time it had taken him to prepare the invasion, meant that modern historians in both Britain and continental Europe were left merely to speculate about what might have been a very different turn of events.

CHAPTER THIRTEEN

Alliances and Empires

I N January 1805, Napoleon believed that the war he was fighting, predominately against the British, would become a much bigger event. Pitt's arrangement with the Russians and Austrians was, on first examination, not much more than he intended it to be: a way of relieving pressure on his own resources.

It is quite likely that one of the consequences of the great preparation for the invasion of England was a confirmation of Napoleon's wider belief that he really could one day have the whole of Europe under his command. He may have felt confident of becoming emperor not merely of France but of the entire continent. When a pope uttered warnings, he may have thought it reasonable to dismiss them with a simple question – 'How many divisions does he have?' – as did another dictator in the next century.[1] No one questioned the military authority – and most certainly not the ambition – of Napoleon.

To his commanders and those whose task it was to do his bidding, Napoleon was erratic. It was never possible to know whether his orders of the day were those to be obeyed or that others would follow to countermand them, or even that they would be abandoned without further instruction. His vision was a broad one. Where one of his generals or – in the invasion plans particularly – one of his admirals would be so hard pressed as never to take his eye off the target displayed by his emperor, Napoleon himself might easily see a plan as a piece of dough which, as it

---

[1] Joseph Stalin (1879–1953): 'The Pope? How many divisions does he have?'

took shape, suggested another use. For example, the gathering of forces necessary for an invasion could suggest, to a far-sighted commander, alternative plans. Napoleon did not want to arouse suspicions in the rest of continental Europe (apart from the Italians, who were perfectly aware of his capabilities) that he might have the intention of controlling the whole region.

By 1805, all Europe knew about Boulogne, the manpower, materials and calls on the bankers. But supposing, while they all watched to see when the invasion would occur and its consequences, Napoleon sensed that this was a moment for historic subterfuge? The emperor knew that the other European powers were obscuring his preparations and therefore saw – or thought they saw – a breathing space for themselves. All Napoleon's efforts were directed towards his cross-Channel project. But was he not, on the quiet, examining the huge force he was assembling, weighing the huge obstacle yet to be overcome and asking himself why he was not simply turning that force to the east and towards the defences of the continental powers? There is a record of him suggesting as much to the Conseil d'État in January 1805. Had Napoleon already decided to head east? None of the effort would be wasted. His armies were in a state of high alert and in training. New naval squadrons had either been built or, in some cases, were near completion. Moreover, he had more or less financed and had under construction a major port that was not only close to the Sussex and Kent coastlines but also provided him with a logistical and assault headquarters for the southern North Sea coast of continental Europe. Boulogne would join Toulon and Brest as a major headquarters.

Even this conjecture puts into perspective the state of British uncertainty and urgency during that period of late 1804 and almost the whole of 1805. It supports entirely the military conundrum that regardless of how much a commander may know about an enemy's strengths and the composition, even deployment, of all his forces, that commander can never be certain of what the enemy intends to do with those forces and nor, in frequent cases, can the enemy. The defending commander may know the size of enemy guns, but he will not know for certain if they are to be fired, and he most definitely will not know when. The British Admiralty were not only chasing their tails; they were chasing the French intentions, too. The one was as elusive as the other. Nelson was sure of a single point: if the French navy were destroyed, the uncertainty over intentions would be resolved.

Much has been made of the alliance sought by Pitt with Austria and Russia to counter Napoleon. Less has been said about that arranged with Spain by France. When the truce of Amiens, to which Spain was a signatory, was abandoned in May 1803, Spain was supposedly a neutral state. In the spring of 1803, the French army had been working on the invasion plan in terms of where to deploy troops prior to the assault, how to have them coming from more than one direction at a time and how to situate them so that each group of forces could be supplied and re-supplied without getting in the way of another and be inserted into the invasion at the right time to avoid bunching and confusion. That deployment was more than a logistics exercise. With it went the need to make sure that, while the main operation looked north to the Channel and then to England, care should be taken to prevent France from being attacked from behind when, militarily, it was looking the other way.

While it is possible that Napoleon may have decided (and was eventually forced) to make a sudden right turn and head inwards to the continent, the army commanders were made very much aware that France would be vulnerable while it concentrated on putting such a huge force across the Channel. In truth, it was unlikely that anyone would want to attack France. The instincts, motives and capabilities of other continental countries precluded this threat. Yet no commander was stupid enough to suppose the possibility did not exist. Therefore, after much mind-changing on the part of Napoleon, the group deployment of soldiers having varied between four and six garrisons, he agreed that there should be three major military districts. One would be based at Bruges, another at St Omer and the third at Montreuil. This, effectively, was the establishment of three corps under the command of General – later Marshal of the Empire – Soult.[2] Soult, a dynamic and humorous thirty-four-year-old, had been given command of the whole invasion force. Napoleon saw in him a quick-witted officer who tended to think military manoeuvres were possible to execute – rather than near impossible to contemplate, a trait of many soldiers at the time. One of the reasons it

---

[2] Nicolas Jean de Dieu Soult (1769–1851).

had taken from the spring of 1803 to the autumn of that year to settle
the deployment was the fact that Napoleon had concerns about Spain.

At one time, there were six military areas to be established, one of
them being at Bayonne. This was to be the rearguard against the Spanish.
That the Spanish might go to war with France was always a possibility.
A large deployment at Bayonne was intended as a deterrent. The
best holding operation against a potential threat is some formal, even
informal accord. So Napoleon and his foreign minister, Talleyrand, made
agreements with two key countries, Holland and Spain. Why would they
have signed such agreements? Not to protect France, but to protect
themselves from France. This, however reluctantly those two countries
felt about the agreement, meant that in theory the treaties protected
France while Napoleon's mind was on the grand scheme. Furthermore,
as a guarantee of good faith, both the Dutch and Spanish were expected
to make a contribution to Napoleon's plan.

In June 1803, the Dutch – seemingly quite against their better
judgement (but they were physically and militarily in no position to
resist) – agreed to side with France, and to supply ships to the Boulogne
expedition and, more immediately, between 15,000 and 16,000 troops. In
October of that year, the French pulled off a most important agreement.
Napoleon, during the summer, had got the very secret agreement of the
Spanish royal family to an alliance. It gave him great confidence and also
– what was more important to him at the time – the promise of money.

So in equal secrecy, on 19 October 1803, and with as much reluctance as
the Dutch had displayed, the Spanish prime minister, Godoy,[3] ironically
known as the prince of peace, signed up Spain to France's side. There
would be no Spanish soldiery in France's army, but the navy would form
with that of France a Combined Fleet. Of more immediate importance
to Napoleon, the Spanish signed a standing order of between five and six
million francs a month for the war effort. Such is the price as well as the
benefit of an alliance.

Part of that Franco-Spanish arrangement allowed the French to use
Spain as a highway and refuge. If, for example, a French ship needed
emergency repairs and was unable to make it home to Brest or Toulon, she

---

[3] Manuel de Godoy, Duke of Alcudia (1767–1851).

could now put into a Spanish port such as El Ferrol or Cartagena. If she happened to be a troop transporter, she could wait alongside, say, Cadiz while French soldiers marched through Spain to the dock. Consequently, with such maritime and military movement both through and to Spain, the agreement could hardly remain a secret. At first sight, it seems odd that the Spanish should have got involved in this conflict. It was costing them a great deal of money even though they did not always pay as much as they had promised. The agreement was also placing Spain in considerable danger. Once it was clear that they had signed up with France, the Spanish were, as far as the British were concerned, at war. So their ships became legitimate targets and could be taken as prizes. This also applied to merchant ships. The only explanation for the Spanish agreement to an alliance was that they really believed the French would invade them unless they signed. The French corps based around Bayonne certainly concentrated the Spanish diplomatic mind. Within months of the October 1803 Franco-Spanish protocol, the Spanish realized that their signature had meant that the French would not stick to the simple terms of the agreement but would regard Spain and all its facilities as part of Bonaparte's war effort. The Spanish were in and unable to get out. A further consequence was that once Pitt had returned to lead the government, he agreed with his admirals that Spanish ports should be blockaded and Spain's vessels at sea regarded as fair game of war. The pretence of Spanish neutrality was, certainly by the autumn of 1804, abandoned.

Bonaparte was rather pleased at the Spanish embarrassment and pique. Talleyrand was brilliantly Talleyrandish. Far from protesting about Spain's attitude, he immediately became full of commiseration. He now observed that Britain seemed to have started a war with Spain and that the French must therefore make every effort to protect their continental cousins. Rejecting the charade of a secret treaty, Talleyrand felt an urgent need to help Spain which, he said, could only be achieved through a new and very public alliance which would unite Spain with France against a common enemy. The Spanish could not escape from Talleyrand's masterful grip. France, with Spain now on board, was part of a very public coalition: equal sides against a common enemy. Tacitly, everyone knew that this so-called equal partnership was run by the French and that only they had a proper say as to what happened and when.

It is at this point that the British, and particularly the Admiralty, began to take greater note of Don Federico Carlos Gravina.[4] Gravina was the most talented of the Spanish admirals. It was he who would lead the Spanish Navy into the Combined Fleet under the hapless Villeneuve. Admiral Gravina was not a Spaniard but a Sicilian from Palermo. The Spanish connection was through King Carlos III, whom most accepted as Federico Gravina's real father. It was through King Carlos that Gravina had joined the Spanish navy as a cadet. At this time it was common for sailors and soldiers to be in the service of nations other than their own. Equally usual was the presence of young military and naval officers in the academies of other countries.

It is, then, no surprise to learn that Gravina had been a student, in Britain, of British naval tactics. The British considered him a more than all-round sailor. He was thought to be an exceptional naval tactician. The Royal Navy's judgement was sound, as Gravina went on to demonstrate on a number of occasions. Equally sound was his family connection. It was the king, by now Carlos IV,[5] who had sent him as his personal representative to the coronation in December 1804 of Napoleon Bonaparte. Gravina was more than an admiral now; he was Spain's ambassador in Paris. Thus he met everyone that mattered, in particular the French naval minister, Denis Decrès, who the previous year had been given command of the invasion plans. Watching Gravina's movements will give us some idea of the progress of Napoleon's invasion operation.

Gravina was clearly pro-French, had a Spanish admiral's traditional regard for the British and was therefore all for seeking any opportunity to take as many British vessels as prizes as he could. At the beginning of 1805, with ships under Cornwallis's overall command attacking Spanish vessels, King Carlos was in no position to doubt that war against England was now a reality rather than a diplomatic subterfuge on the part of the French. It remains likely that the Spanish would have preferred neutrality. It was a luxury which Napoleon and Talleyrand refused them. Gravina, as we have seen, knew the British, appreciated the Royal Navy's brilliance and knew its weaknesses. He saw a combined Spanish and French

---

[4] Gravina, Federico Carlos (1758–1806).
[5] Carlos IV (1748–1819).

confrontation with the Royal Navy as inevitable. If he had any doubt, it was probably about the capability of Villeneuve, whom he had met on a number of occasions. They were quite different characters. Gravina was a sturdy Sicilian with bastard royal blood and a reputation as a fine naval commander. Villeneuve was very much part of the surviving French aristocracy. He had an aristocratic profile and mannerisms and even the style of a dilettante.

For the moment, Gravina could dismiss Villeneuve from his thoughts. His first role as an admiral, but also as his monarch's ambassador, was to make sure that the need for an alliance was put in stronger terms than ever before. He did not see any advantage in Spain being a subservient partner. Gravina looked at the arrangement from the point of view of a practised military mind. It was a waste of time simply to have a document that tied Spain to France's war – almost to be told when to come to the war and what to do. Gravina believed, rightly, that such an arrangement would leave the Spanish without any influence whatsoever as to the rehearsal of that conflict. He and Denis Decrès were at one with this concept. Decrès understood the need for the major part of Spain's deep-sea fleet to have far more than the support of just the Spanish navy. The fleet needed to be a combined one in the best of senses. It had to be as one. Furthermore, it seems very likely that Decrès saw Gravina as a superior commander to Villeneuve. It seemed as though Villeneuve had been appointed to command the French fleet because France had run out of seagoing admirals. Gravina was a much better tactician than Villeneuve, with a better understanding of the British navy and a degree of professionalism which the French admiral could never have displayed. However, Gravina was not French. It would therefore have to be arranged for him to become the fleet's deputy commander, and certainly, given the composition of that force, such an appointment was unquestionable.

On 4 January 1805, Gravina completed the first part of his role. As ambassador, it was he who signed for Spain on behalf of the king the treaty with France that formally brought into being the Combined Fleet of the two nation states. This was now a force far greater than that which would fight at Trafalgar. This French and Spanish combination could, in the view of Decrès and therefore presumably of Napoleon, be deployed from Toulon in the south to the Caribbean in the west and the Channel and southern North Sea in the east. This was a grand fleet, potentially bigger than Britain's. To Spain it represented a certain extra layer of protection from the British. Equally, they had to accept that British attacks since October 1804 had, by this agreement, been legitimized. Spanish possessions and interests, from Cadiz to Latin and Central America, were now regarded by Britain as fair and legal game. Considering the differing natures and maritime concepts of the two navies, the speed with which the French and Spanish fleets came together was encouraging to Decrès and Gravina. Certainly by the spring of 1805 the vessels were operating in company. Tactical appreciation of any potential engagement was always constrained by the size and deployment of vessels and, above all, by the weather conditions of the time. It was, however, possible to reduce the chances of failure by improving two important aspects of potential war at sea.

There had to be a common signalling procedure in order that every captain and sailing master, whatever the size of his vessel, could recognize what was expected of him and his ship. If this seems obvious, we have only to study the naval engagements of even one national fleet to realize that the fog of war is not a recent phenomenon. Signals could not be seen at night. Unless there was a prearranged plan with a unique signal to start it, or the action of the lead vessel made intentions obvious, most signalling and communication was carried out by means of a series of flags. These had to be run up signal halyards and then within proper spyglass range; otherwise they were meaningless. Needless to say, when the time came for engagement it was a case of each ship, broadside and boarding party for itself. Even if a flag officer wished to signal other vessels, it was very likely that rigging and spars would be so badly disrupted or even destroyed that few signals could be flown and, even if they were flown, not much could be done about them. However, flag officers still signalled in battle, although the results were often uncertain.

Battle at sea at the beginning of the nineteenth century was rather like a performance of a Birtwistle[6] symphony – to the uninitiated, it was impenetrable and, once started, best left to be played out to the last bar.[7]

---

[6] Sir Harrison Birtwistle (1934–).
[7] With apologies to students of certain kinds of twentieth-century music.

Once the guns had fired, the engagement had to run its bloody – often chaotic – course. Indeed, chaos could often be the saving of lives. A further weakness in naval warfare was the lack of common tactical procedures. Some examples may seem obvious, yet it was true also that many of the officers were unprofessional. There were no closely adhered-to battle-operating plans other than two lines of ships firing at each other. Engaging an enemy was first and foremost reliant on the skill of the commander of the fleet, flotilla or squadron and his perceptiveness and ability. He had to understand the depth of responsibility and capability of each ship in his group. That meant he had to know the degree of seamanship and gunnery in each of those vessels, especially the bigger ones, which would be first in the line of battle. Consequently, the admiral would or should know the level of competence of his captains – not as a group but, again, as individuals. If we imagine that all this should be taken as read, we underestimate the levels of incompetence that existed among early nineteenth-century commanders.

Commanding a sailing vessel, whether a 12-foot scow or a 74-gun three-decker, is rather like horsemanship. Once a person takes command of a vessel or a beast, there can be no doubt about their level of competence. A ship at sea, under sail and under the stresses and influences of tides, winds and sea states, has nowhere to hide. An individual's ability to manoeuvre that ship in all conditions and to work up the crew, whether it be two in a dinghy or 800 in a three-master, is there for everyone to witness. A ship's company is always willing and usually proud to sing the praises of a good skipper. Equally, the fleet soon knows when a skipper is not up to the job. One of the first signs is that he blames his tools, the ship's company.

At the time of Nelson's and Villeneuve's navies there were fine seamen and naval officers. The means of promotion and the amount of time spent in one ship – often years – generally led to a good level of competence. It was the sailing master who made the ship work, more precisely in the direction that the captain wanted it to go. But it was the captain who was required to have a full understanding of his admiral's instructions and train his ship's company to carry them out. This was where the weakness sometimes lay. A quarterdeck of indifferently led officers could so easily result in a lower deck of less than competent hands. It was certainly not enough to rely on the discipline of scrubbing decks until they were bare-bone white. Nor was the warning that unless the ship's company were well trained they would be blown out of the water by the enemy – a simple enough challenge to improve a ship. Sailors are craftsmen. Like the best craftsmen, sailors can make proper judgements about other vessels. In the early nineteenth century there was a general understanding, even among ratings, that if a ship looked right then she probably was. An experienced bosun or first lieutenant in the Royal Navy could eye the scantlings and lines of a French ship and know how she was built, what her strong points were and whether or not she could sail and manoeuvre better than their own vessel, and would know, just by looking at her, whether she was well turned out and ready for war as opposed to merely ceremonial duties. Many of the men, of course, knew a lot about French and Spanish vessels. They were quite often serving in them, because when a ship was captured it was usually put into service, sometimes without changing the name.[8]

If we consider all these differences of view and competence, we begin to understand how important routine and improvements to that routine would have been for an individual ship and for the fleet commander. Nelson's navy had no sure way, other than by estimation and the rudimentary use of horizontal-angle geometry, of assessing the range of an enemy vessel for its gunners. Even with luck and accuracy, the other vessel was on the move. It was easy to bombard a shore target because, as the navy demonstrated when attacking Boulogne, they could, by taking three bearings of known landmarks, fix with absolute certainty the position of the gun deck in relation to that target. The navy was so confident of ranges and vulnerabilities that they could, in the gently shelving seabed off the north French coast, anchor and thus have guaranteed positions from which to fire.

At sea in a force-six wind with an adverse sea swell, gunnery could at first sight be literally a hit-and-miss affair. The craft of the gunnery officer was properly practised by only the best. Added to the mathematics and geometry of that craft was the sheer competence of the ship's

---

[8] It is not always clear why the name was so rarely changed, although there is the maritime superstition that it is unlucky to change the name of a ship.

company, from the eleven-year-old doing his best to scamper with the gunpowder and shot to the aimers and gun crews working as teams just eight feet apart in seemingly the most chaotic conditions, knowing that they were literally in the front line and objects of the enemy gunners. Their only protection lay in the skill of their captain and their own competence to do unto the enemy what he would have done unto them. A gun that could not be fired, recoiled, reloaded and ready to fire again in a minute and almost nothing at all, was incompetent. A captain who failed to work his ship up to that level of competence threatened the lives of his own men and – worse still – the entire operational command of his admiral.

A single-nation navy was likely to have procedures and established ways of working. Admirals would have time to get to know both their captains and also, most importantly, the capability of a particular vessel to respond to even well-thought-through commands and to keep the sea, that is, to sail well even in adverse conditions. Just as Nelson thought the *Agamemnon* the best ship in which he had ever served, so he knew the characteristics of almost every vessel in his fleet. He knew how the hull shape affected a vessel's sailing characteristics and whether or not she would go well to windward or wallow when running before the wind. He knew if a vessel sailed well with her existing rig. He knew if she was difficult to sail, whatever the competence of the captain. That was part of the advantage of having a single fleet commander. We should, then, admire the way the French and Spanish succeeded in working together. It is true that, given the limitations of ship construction and stability, together with the gun systems, there were few differences to sort out. It is true, also, that the Spanish element of the Combined Fleet, especially under Admiral Gravina, was keen to demonstrate to the French that it was superior. The Spanish had an advantage inasmuch as they had great respect for their admiral – unlike the French seamen, who did not have that same level of regard for Villeneuve.

The Spanish fleet could not immediately join the French. The first task was that of officially appointing Gravina, through King Carlos, commander-in-chief of the Spanish fleet. At that stage, Gravina was still in the ambassadorial trappings of his Paris appointment. But, as with many coalitions, there was very much a senior partner. As diplomatically as possible the French ordered him back to Madrid to get on with the very real task – by January 1805 more urgent than ever – of organizing Spanish ships and men to join the French fleet.

At that stage, the Spanish expected to be able to put together some thirty ships of the line. For the moment they would be based at three ports: Cadiz, home of the main fleet, Cartagena and El Ferrol. The energy of Gravina and the effort he inspired in others meant that his was a whirlwind existence. Orders were sent from his naval headquarters at Cadiz and positive responses were returned there. The task at first seemed overwhelming. The Spanish could count their own ships and knew in theory how many would be ready at the three ports by the beginning of spring – that far south, probably the end of March. There is more to putting a fleet to sea than counting ships. The most difficult task for Gravina was one that was common in the French navy and also in the British: to find a sufficient number of sailors. The Spanish were no less reluctant than other nationalities to sign up for the navy. The average British matelot would have been able to think of much better ways of spending his life than expending it in an uncompromising battle with a French fleet. While the Spanish showed an equal reluctance to join the ranks of those who had had their heads blown off by a cannonball, a distant noise of battle did not entirely explain Spain's difficulty in raising enough men for its ships. Just as the British commanders were often genuinely appalled at the physical state of recruits from English ports, so the Spanish captains were equally distressed at the state of some of their potential able seamen and, more particularly, frustrated by the numbers who had died from diseases during epidemics in the ports.

Napoleon, of course, believed everything was possible. All he had to do was insist. He had produced yet another plan of action. It does seem that at this stage Napoleon's list of cunning plans was growing by the month, with each one simply replacing the previous plan. The emperor had two objectives. The first and most constant objective until later in 1805 was that of invading England, even though it must have crossed his mind that the force he was gathering was either ill-prepared or would have been better deployed to the east (see chapter 19). The second target was the line of British possessions in the Caribbean.

CHAPTER FOURTEEN

Yet Another Plan

THE BRITISH HAD BEEN IN THE CARIBBEAN SINCE THE EARLY seventeenth century. The Spanish, of course, had been there two centuries earlier. For Britain, its island possessions in the West Indies were not merely territorial possessions of some strategic value. They also had enormous economic significance. There were really two British Empires, the second being the one that existed – or was being consolidated – in the nineteenth century. It would reach its apogee by the end of that century and be helped in doing so by Britain's victory at Trafalgar. The first British Empire, which had included the tenuous occupation of the eastern seaboard of North America, had made possible the overwhelming imperial adventure that would lead eventually to Britain ruling a quarter of the world's inhabitants. That first empire had been created on purely economic terms between the latter part of the 1500s and the early part of the 1700s. This series of settlements and colonies, and therefore the whole history of British imperialism (in its most benign as well as its sometimes more abrasive sense) would not have existed had it not been a good business. Britain – founded by the English and often run by the Scots – had gone into the empire business at a very late stage compared with the other major European maritime nations. The nature of that empire was also different. Where, for example, the Spanish had searched successfully for treasure, the British, while hoping for gold, had had to be content with sugar and spices. These condiments proved in the long term a better investment and the key to Britain's imperial success. The English East India Company, established by royal charter in 1600, returned from the East Indies with spices. It was the fighting with the French during the Seven Years War (1756–1763) that removed the final obstacle to the construction of the British Empire.

By the time of Nelson the celebrated (by some) days of Clive of India had come and gone. Clive's legacy and Protestant values had impressed themselves on the hearts of a large number of the eighteenth-century population.

Much later, India would become the jewel in the often tarnished crown of British imperialism, the greatest of British possessions. However, the economic catalyst for the successful establishment of empire and economy lay on the other side of the world, in the Caribbean.

The British interest in the West Indies had started memorably with Sir Francis Drake. It was there that he died in 1596 while on an expedition with Britain's most infamous slave trader, Sir John Hawkins.[1] The British had got into those islands partly because the Spanish were no longer interested in them. To them Britain had imported slaves from West Africa and then, from England, indentured labour – most of whom were virtually slaves. With that labour force they grew and harvested sugar cane, which became the seed corn of the British Empire. Britain relied on its Caribbean possessions for both economic and strategic reasons. No wonder Napoleon saw them as not just valuable but *vulnerable* targets.

He saw three good reasons for attempting to bombard the British West Indies. One was that he could order his forces to capture Trinidad, an island the Spanish regarded as their own. What a splendid thank-you letter would the deeds to Trinidad – delivered to Madrid – have made. Second, attacking and disrupting the West Indian stations of colonial Britain would allow the French to re-establish a strategic grip on that region. Third, and for a very practical and immediate reason, an attack on those settlements would necessarily draw British vessels across the Atlantic to defend them.

There were already ships on the West Indian station. More would be sent. This was not simply a British stamp collection, it was an economic

---

[1] Sir John Hawkins (1532–1595), a vice admiral in the fight against the Spanish Armada in 1588.

and strategic holding of enormous importance. To force the British to divert naval assets across the ocean would make Napoleon's proposed invasion fleet less vulnerable to British attack. That, anyway, was a reasonable assumption.

But how – or, more importantly, who – would make that assault on the islands? Napoleon thought the answer very simple: Admiral Villeneuve. However, Villeneuve did not quite see it that way. His first very good reason to doubt his master's voice was that he himself, together with his fleet, was stuck in Toulon harbour, all victims of the British Mediterranean blockade. Napoleon was a very persuasive ruler. For all his reluctance, Villeneuve was given his sailing orders and told to hop across the Atlantic. Easier said than done – but surely it would have to be done.

While Nelson, sent to the Mediterranean, was busy with red tape, Napoleon was, as he thought, redesigning his mental empire. Bonaparte had always tossed aside most objections to details of his planning as weak thinking. He had been to Boulogne for three days at the end of June 1803 and again for almost two weeks in the November of that year. He had been back again in January 1804. The significance of these visits was twofold. Certainly by the end of June 1803, Bonaparte knew how far behind schedule his plan was. The First Consul at that stage appears to have thought the lack of progress due largely to incompetence, to individuals not carrying out his orders, and perhaps – only perhaps – to the burden as well as the inspiration presented by his scheme. As that summer cooled into autumn, tens of thousands of artisans and labourers were occupied in constructing barracks for the force. Things looked good, but they were not. By then Bonaparte had understood that the soldiers he was putting into this force would have to get used to being afloat. They were the invasion force. They had to be agile on the water. There was no point in him sending even his finest soldiers across the Channel if half of them were to end up seasick and unable to help man the vessels, never mind leap ashore to fight.

Bonaparte was effectively turning even his celebrated guards into a form of marines. He insisted that his commanders train the invasion soldiers in basic boat handling and seamanship. He was determined to leave nothing to chance. The French were used to their leader talking in grand terms. In November 1803, he told General (shortly to be Marshal of the Empire) Augereau[2] that he thought his plan would succeed and that he was determined it would, because invading England was effectively an act of vengeance. He believed there was a thousand years of history to put right. Napoleon Bonaparte may have got his arithmetic wrong – but not his sentiments.

Bonaparte's November visit to Boulogne turned into far more than a military inspection. Having ordered the construction workers to produce a new barracks and arsenal, he then revised the training programmes. He had his Guards and other regiments exercised at night. He made it clear that a force intended to travel across the Channel could not expect a beach picnic on the other side, followed by rest and recuperation. From the moment they formed up to join their vessels, Bonaparte made it clear that they would need to be prepared to fight in any circumstances, including darkness, for long hours – perhaps days – before resting. The romantic notion, drawn from Arthurian legend, of the noise of battle rolling about through day and night, was usually just that: a literary vision. The set-piece attacks and skirmishes, hindered by the difficulty of commanding by line of sight, often meant battle was day work. So Napoleon personally commanded his troops at Boulogne on their first night manoeuvres.

His confidence, expressed through short letters to ministers and commanders elsewhere, cannot be taken as a sign that he was satisfied. Sitting in their ministries in Paris, Bonaparte's most senior advisers must have thought all was well. He had praised the craftsmen, the troops and their combined dedication. Hardly any of his correspondence refers to the vessels designed to carry out his ambition. The date of that fortnight's visit is important. Bonaparte was there in the second half of November. Even allowing for fair spells, there was no Indian summer. Bonaparte himself referred to being soaked to the skin day after day. What, therefore, he saw was that his great plan for flat-bottom boats had been ill-conceived. He saw also that the chances of getting what was, by any standards,

---

[2] Pierre-Francis-Charles Augereau (1757–1816). Augereau had his army at Bayonne during the all-important negotiations with Spain and before moving to command at Brest prior to the planned invasion.

an enormous force across to England were slim if it put to sea after late September to early October. The weather conditions and thus the sea state simply could not be guaranteed. It was one thing planning to go in, say, May and then waiting for a weather opportunity. It was quite another to still be there by the end of September, by which time the likelihood of a fair weather condition would have diminished. Moreover – as the Romans and the Spanish Armada had known – the later in the year, the more horrendous the short, sharp seas and funnelled gales could be across that stretch of water we call the Dover Strait. He also recognized that even if he did manage to land his army into southern England, the wintry conditions, including rains and mud, would represent a meteorological division sometimes harder to overcome than the brigades of the English defenders.

Bonaparte had always wondered about the construction of the vessels and their design and had never really understood ships and sailors. Ideally, it might be supposed, he had hoped for a warm summer invasion with little or no wind. This would have allowed his bell-bottomed boats to be rowed across the Channel and for the English fleet to have become becalmed and less able to challenge the invasion. This was another reason why there were those in the Admiralty who, like Nelson, favoured the idea of using smaller vessels as a protection force on the Downs and Nore stations. Anything more than a millpond would prove an enormous obstacle to Bonaparte's fleet. Bonaparte observed the captains of these smaller vessels and flotillas during November 1803. From them he learned how incapable the vessels were unless operated in the best conditions. Yet he could hardly change the whole construction programme. Furthermore, it was clear to him that in spite of the work that had gone on from Boulogne to Wimereux, none of the coastal ports was of the right size or location to provide a safe haven for the vessels while they waited for the weather. The ships most certainly could not be anchored offshore. Bringing them into harbour would clog up the beginning of the operation. Even under the most ideal sailing conditions, with every soldier and piece of equipment on board, the commanders still had to face a simple fact of marine life: tides. These ports could only be dredged harbours. There was not the marine engineering to dredge protected fairways. Therefore only a few vessels at a time could escape the harbour a couple of hours at the most either side of high water. Consequently, there could be no steady line of invasion. If, on the other hand, they were mustered beyond the ports at anchor, they were vulnerable to a sudden south-west gale which, at the very least, would sweep them into the North Sea and raise the real possibility of a pitched battle with the British fleet. Bonaparte's commanders needed one of three things to happen. That the whole exercise should be called off, which was unlikely; that the the French fleet could be brought up Channel and overwhelm British vessels, which was at that stage equally unlikely; or that the British fleet could be diverted so as to be nowhere near the invasion force. That last was possible – hence the Caribbean plan.

Bonaparte relied on his instincts and perhaps on too many subordinates who knew only too well that they would be sacked if they actively opposed him. One person he did listen to was Admiral Honoré Ganteaume.[3] Ganteaume had figured in Bonaparte's thoughts a great deal. It was Ganteaume who had escorted Bonaparte on his secret return from Egypt in 1799. By the late autumn of 1803, Ganteaume was prefect in Toulon. By the spring of the following year he would command the fleet at Brest, Bonaparte having finally lost patience with Vice Admiral Laurent Truguet[4] and dismissed him. Before he did so, Bonaparte had returned to Ganteaume for his opinion on the Boulogne fleet. Was it big enough to carry 100,000 Frenchmen to battle and victory against Albion? Equally important, was it the right structure to be armed with the gunnery he insisted was necessary? Was it the right fleet, in the right place, that would be protected at the right time? Ganteaume penned his thoughts as a sailor and a tactician. As a tactician he judged the entire invasion to be doomed to failure, at the very least risky, unless fate really did intervene on the side of France. As a sailor he knew the chances were slim of getting protective squadrons past Cornwallis's Channel Fleet in the absence of any particular weather advantage, such as rough seas, that would make it difficult for the British fleet to attack. Knowing the prevailing winds came from the south-west, Ganteaume thought the only hope of getting a defensive flotilla up to Boulogne was to rely on

---

[3] Honoré Ganteaume (1755–1818).
[4] Laurent-Jean Truguet (1752–1839).

those following winds and run before them well to the north of Cornwallis's station. Of course, there was an alternative. It was possible to take the westerlies and Gulf Stream round the north of the British Isles and then, relying on uncertain conditions down the North Sea, make it into the Dover Strait (see chart page xiv). Where would such a fleet come from? The answer was Toulon. However, there had to be an enormous deception if it were to succeed – quite apart from a victory over all the weather patterns, of course. Ideally, the Toulon squadron would break out into the Mediterranean and then, either by sowing false information which would be picked up by spies or by generally setting vessels in an easterly direction, Nelson would be given the impression that the Toulon-based vessels were heading for Egypt. The idea was that Nelson would then divert his flotilla, with himself in his flagship, in the general direction of the Nile. Meanwhile, the main French fleet would head west into the Atlantic and up towards the approaches to the English Channel. Those ships would, of course, need support.

The reinforcement for that deception would have to come from the squadron based on Rochefort, part of the Brest command. There was one small difficulty facing the French navy. Cornwallis was blockading the Brest fleet and Nelson was doing the same in the Mediterranean with the Toulon squadron.

The plan was that the squadron from Toulon would break out in mid-January 1804. The Rochefort squadron would also break out and the two would meet. After the rendezvous, the combined squadron would split into two parts. The fastest and most manoeuvrable vessels would make all speed for the Channel. The others, if seen, would simply confuse the British. So, unlikely as it may seem, Toulon – at the further end of France and in totally different waters and conditions – was the key to the success of an invasion from Boulogne and adjacent ports. If we examine charts, the prevailing winds and likely weather conditions between, say, January and spring, the whole concept may appear nonsensical. Bonaparte was really running out of people to believe. Ganteaume was a good tactician. Bonaparte understood big tactics that verged on becoming strategies. Ganteaume had endorsed what was effectively Bonaparte's plan. Thus, if for no other reason than that, Ganteaume's judgement was, according to the First Consul, sound.

If everything relied on the breakout of the Toulon squadron and the elaborate deception of Nelson with the phoney excursion to Egypt, Napoleon judged that the Toulon fleet commander had to be a man of exceptional talent. At the end of 1803, Vice Admiral Latouche-Tréville became commander-in-chief of the French Mediterranean squadron. Bonaparte may have thought it one of his inspired appointments. It had a drawback. By the spring, poor old Latouche-Tréville was dead. His successor was to be one of the most unfortunate yet most celebrated naval appointments made by Bonaparte.

Latouche-Tréville came from a respectable rather than an elevated military family. His father had, prior to the Revolution, been the equivalent of something between a rear and a vice admiral. His father's brother had been a general. The man's reputation was that of a thoughtful and particularly gallant officer. Bonaparte had perhaps three really first-class admirals: Ganteaume, shortly to become the fleet commander at Brest, Eustace de Bruix, commander of the invasion flotilla, whose exceptional career had begun during the American War of Independence and who had spent a year as naval minister, and Latouche-Tréville himself. Bonaparte's reputation for sacking admirals and generals who did not perform is often given as evidence of his impatience and poor judgement in blaming others for failing to carry out his impossible commands. Many of those commands were simply unworkable. Admirals of the quality of Ganteaume had the knack of being able to plant an alternative plan in Bonaparte's mind with such skill that the First Consul naturally assumed he had thought of it himself. He was able to trust their judgement because they were men of the first rank.

Latouche-Tréville was quite admired by the Royal Navy, including Nelson. Bonaparte knew this. It had been Latouche-Tréville, then a local commander, who had caused Nelson so much of a scare when he had thought himself able to attack the Boulogne fleet in August 1801. Nelson's high regard for him led him to refer to the French admiral in his letters. Though it was not an obsession, the Englishman referred to wanting an opportunity to meet up once more with Latouche-Tréville in order to get his own back. Now that Nelson was commanding the Mediterranean fleet, the Frenchman was just as eager to get at the British admiral. Consequently, it is not difficult to understand why Bonaparte hoped for so much from his new commander of the Toulon squadron.

In January 1804, Latouche-Tréville had instructions to review his fleet and put to sea. Bonaparte clearly believed that the admiral's new command was seaworthy. It is not at all clear that Latouche-Tréville shared the First Consul's enthusiasm. There were thirteen ships in Toulon. They were manned by officers and men who were hardly an advertisement for the navy, let alone a navy that was the keystone of Bonaparte's maritime plan. Nelson, through his shoreside spies, must have been well informed of the state and competence of the new command and observed without any hint of contempt the way Latouche-Tréville had begun knocking into shape his – till then ineffectual – fleet.

He was well aware that even among his own people there was some admiration for the French admiral. Whether or not he really had something to prove to the commander of the Toulon squadron does not really matter. It is what was thought at the time and what he thought too. So did Latouche-Tréville.

The captains of the French squadron at Toulon had plenty of time in which to raise their ships to a more warlike standard. They practised improving on the time it took to bring the watches to battle stations. They worked on up-anchor times, which included setting topsails, in order to be able to put to sea as speedily as possible at the shortest possible notice. They ran out their guns so many times that they were able to be ready for firing sooner than they had ever been before in that squadron. Along the Mediterranean coast, Nelson watched and waited. He could see ships weighing anchor, sails being set and speedy departures being made, only for those same vessels to turn about before coming in range. His captains timed these procedures. Every time they carried out this exercise, the French seemed to be getting better.

Nelson gave an order that he wanted to know when the Toulon squadron was making ready to sail. The French admiral's instructions had been to get his squadron into a state of efficiency that would allow him to put to sea and, if necessary, to engage the British enemy, certainly by the end of the third week of January 1804. In fact, despite improvements, his squadron was not ready. That hardly mattered because the preparations at Boulogne were far from complete. Moreover, the other part of the great naval operation of Bonaparte, the essential rendezvous with the Rochefort squadron, was impossible in the present circumstances, as with so many of Bonaparte's schemes.

The ships at Rochefort and Brest were either unready for sea or unable to find enough manpower, or both. The blockade by the Royal Navy was working. The so-called invasion fleet was hardly a fleet. There were not enough ships, and many that had been built were unable to put to sea, partly because they were still trapped in their river moorings. Matters were made worse for France's navy because its army was indeed ready. At least, that was the impression given by the ever-optimistic generals, particularly the commander of the Montreuil corps, General Ney.[5] There were few dissenters and those whose acts were considered treasonable (as indeed some were) were used as target practice for the firing squads. Bonaparte refused to entertain the merest whiff of counter-revolution. When the royalists thought it time, at the beginning of 1804, to set themselves against Napoleon, their leaders, Georges Cadoudal and Charles Pichegru,[6] were dispatched without ceremony.

It is at this point, in the early spring of 1804, when it is difficult to understand whether Bonaparte's thinking was muddled or whether he had taken lessons from Talleyrand. Here he was, getting his Toulon commander into a position to put to sea, to join up with a second squadron which was, as he well knew, entrapped, but at the same time knowing that he had insufficient ships, and a naval plan which relied far more on hope and optimism than it did on intelligence. He had another difficulty if he expected the Rochefort squadron to perform as ordered. It was commanded by Villeneuve.

As we shall see, Villeneuve was and has remained something of a naval puzzle. His reputation, even allowing for the wasting of many of the old naval officers, was high in Paris. Yet he was partly responsible for one of the most dreadful debacles in French naval history. The Battle of the Nile in August 1798 had blocked any plans Bonaparte had for a proper Egyptian campaign and therefore his interest in pressing forward and eastwards. One of the reasons for Nelson's success was the fact that he

---

[5] Michel Ney, Marshal of the Empire (1769–1815).
[6] Charles Pichegru (1761–1804). His death was curious: he was strangled in his bed in the Temple Prison.

had caught the French fleet not on the high seas but in the suicidal confines of their anchorage at Aboukir Bay. Admiral Brueys, the French commander – who, incidentally, perished in that battle, along with his infant son – took the decision to stand rather than sail and fight, partly – perhaps mostly – because he was urged to do so by his three main commanders. These three officers became the key naval characters in the French part of our story, the long haul to Trafalgar. They were Ganteaume, then Brueys' chief of staff, Denis Decrès, who commanded his light squadron, and the officer commanding Brueys' rearguard squadron, Villeneuve.

The luxury of hindsight fails to take into account both the conditions which would not allow the French fleet to get to sea so easily and the poor French judgement that Nelson's fleet would have a hopeless task because it would be unable to manoeuvre safely within the confines of the anchorage. The rights and wrongs of the tactics on both sides at the Battle of the Nile are for another place. What should be mentioned here is the fact that the three officers who advised, apparently strongly, on the French tactic were now Napoleon's prized admirals. Decrès was now his trusted minister, Ganteaume his confidant and future commander-in-chief at Brest, and Villeneuve the sad figure who was to be the most remembered French admiral in British naval history. Villeneuve in particular gave no good account of himself at the Battle of the Nile. He even failed to make proper use of his command to intervene against Nelson's fleet in order to help his commander-in-chief. Yet these were the three stars of Napoleon's fleet. Ganteaume was undoubtedly gallant and a better tactician than his Egyptian record suggested. Decrès was a good at political matters. Yet it is hard to make a case for commending Villeneuve other than to say that he was possibly a last resort.

Ganteaume's experience of the Nile could, in theory, have explained why he so wanted the Brest command. Apart from the obvious desire for promotion, which this was, the Brest appointment was in no way within the theatre of naval war in which Nelson now operated. As for Villeneuve, there is every reason to believe that he feared Nelson. To come out of Rochefort, where he was, for the moment, squadron commander, and join with Latouche-Tréville's Toulon fleet heading north was one thing; to come face to face with Nelson's squadron quite another. Moreover, much of the plan relied on the new Brest commander, Ganteaume, being able to break out and interrupt and disperse Cornwallis. If that could be done, then, again in theory, Latouche-Trèville and Villeneuve would have a clear run into la Manche. Meanwhile, the former was still trapped in Toulon. His standby sailing orders had been for 21 January 1804, but by the summer he was still there. Even at this stage there has to be some doubt about Napoleon's plan of invasion. He had recognized that the French fleet was too small. The Spanish would not be added until early the following year, and even then the Combined Fleet would not be big enough for the mastery of the seas that Bonaparte – quite rightly – understood to be absolutely necessary.

There is evidence that in the spring of 1804 Bonaparte was already planning a fleet of some 100 ships of the line, that is, front-line vessels. Even with his determination, he had come to accept that the 100-strong big-ship fleet he wanted could not be ready until perhaps 1809 or even the following year.[7] He expected then to dominate global sea lanes. That ambition would not resolve his immediate problem. This is not, of course, to suggest that Bonaparte had written off the concept of an invasion. However, it is one indicator that he was, surprisingly, not totally confident that an invasion would be a success under the present scheme. He was working on yet another final plan for the invasion and its support.

The erratic nature of the planning may be exaggerated. The scheme had to be a flexible one. The resources involved dictated constant change. Equally, it was true that Bonaparte would order one grand scheme to be implemented without delay and then produce another equally grand one, sometimes without countermanding the previous one. This is often a sign of megalomania and common enough among political leaders who have enjoyed rapid success and come to believe that, on the whole, they are surrounded by much lesser mortals. Bonaparte displayed almost constant megalomania. Equally, the enormity of his overall plan against England should not be allowed to disguise the fact that the shores of southern Britain were not his only targets. Bonaparte had Europe to conquer. After Europe, anything would be possible – if his army and

---

[7] Letters from Napoleon to Decrès, 21 April and 28 April 1804 (a paper in the London Library).

navy were capable of holding on to conquests. For all this naked ambition there was, too, the complexity of the planning. Although the concept had not altered, the means of fulfilment was ever-changing in his mind. The numbers of men, horses and guns, quantities of ammunition supplies, food stocks, big ships and small ships were all estimates of what was needed.

There were no certainties when it came to an invasion of this sort. When it came to invading, say, the Netherlands, Italy or Austria, the issues involved were relatively simple. A general moved up his troops, got them into position, judged the military opposition, the fortitude of the political opponent and then, if the weather was reasonably favourable, marched in on the principle that however determined the opposition, a big army should always crack a small one. This principle could not be applied to a Channel invasion. These were, literally, untested waters. Sending an invasion force by sea was always hazardous. The British reinforcement of North America during the War of American Independence had proved unsuccessful. The part played by the French in that war had been an opportunistic support operation. The maritime logistics and amphibious forces simply did not exist to sustain a mass invasion against well-defended territory.

So what the maritime tacticians would have called the circle of certainty should really have been rewritten as the circle of possibility – not even of probability. It was therefore totally reasonable, no matter how unreasonable we may imagine Bonaparte to have been, for him to have come up with changing plans and, even, totally new ones. It is quite remarkable that there were not more of them. Much of the time he considered everything possible as long as it had come from his thinking. He was beginning to understand the frailties of amphibious warfare which, particularly then, before the age of steam, relied so much on weather conditions. However, he still displayed a disbelief, to the point of anger, that those he had raised to such high positions were unable to overcome nature in the name of the First Consul – and by December 1804 – the crowned Emperor, Napoleon I.

On 19 July 1804, there was a perfect example of Bonaparte's insistence that whatever the conditions his will should be done. By that time, the French along the north coast had, at four jumping-off points (Ambleteuse,

Wimereaux, Étaples and Boulogne), 1,800 boats of different sizes, together with troop and supply barges. Thus his fleet invasion commander, Bruix, had in theory an operational flotilla. With 120,000 men waiting to board the boats, Bonaparte was in buoyant mood, despite the fact that he could not have expected the protection fleet to be ready. On 2 July he had written to Admiral Latouche-Tréville. He reminded the good admiral that although he respected the way in which he was the only commander to have put Nelson on the run, he, Bonaparte, had raised Latouche-Tréville to high office and so expected high returns. He even gave the admiral his tactics. He told him where he believed the British ships of Cornwallis lay, saying that they would be decoyed by vessels in the French squadron at Brest. Latouche-Tréville was told to mislead Nelson into thinking that the French were heading from Toulon to Egypt. He was then to execute the earlier plan. This was to rendezvous with the Rochefort squadron and proceed with it either up the west coast of Ireland, across the Scottish seaway and down through the North Sea or, by cutting close into the English southern coast, to make all speed for Boulogne (see chart page xiv). The First Consul believed that all the French fleet had to do in Brest was to keep every activity going that would lead Cornwallis to believe it wanted to put to sea. Thus Cornwallis would order his blockading fleet close into Brest in order to stop them. Having done that, Cornwallis would in effect be leaving the seaway behind him open for Latouche-Tréville to sneak through. He did not expect the admiral to arrive off Boulogne much before the end of September. But Bonaparte imagined that it might still be soon enough and that the invasion could take place during an Indian summer. Yet another cunning plan.

And so to 19 July 1804. This was the day Bonaparte, by all accounts at the time, arrived in Boulogne to review his sailing fleet. The weather was wretched. Bonaparte thought it no obstacle. Admiral Bruix told him that he only had to look out to sea and understand the anticipated gale force winds to know that this was not a time to review his fleet. Bonaparte told him to get on with it and, according to some witnesses, the two almost came to blows. Bruix, his old comrade and friend, refused to give the fleet review order. Bonaparte had never been put off by sound advice and, almost never, openly contradicted. He ignored Admiral Bruix and turned instead to one of the commander's senior flotilla officers, Charles Magon.[8] It was Rear Admiral Magon who, confronted by his emperor, gave the fleet order that his own senior officer refused. Magon did not last long at Boulogne. He returned to sea duties, which pleased him no end. However, he was not there for long. He was killed at Trafalgar.

Bruix had been absolutely right. They had hardly begun to put into open waters for Bonaparte's chest-pouting review before the storm arrived. It hit the flotilla creating chaos and tragedy, and continued to do so until the early hours of 21 July. How many men lost their lives remains uncertain. The official figure was of some fifty casualties. Local people said four times as many had perished. In London, the gossip was of hundreds dead. A report in *The Annual Register* of 1804 observed that Bonaparte needed to understand that there was an even greater enemy than English soldiers and sailors that would deal with his fleet, and that he had had a lesson from which he ought to learn.

Bonaparte seemed to think that he had been witness not to disaster but to some heroic dream. He spoke of the poor wretches perishing, but seemed to experience the whole disastrous occasion as a curious suspension of his spirit. Nor did he slink away. He remained at Boulogne, reviewing troops, building works and deployments. He could not have been encouraged by what he saw and by the reports that he read that came from as far afield as Ostend, Brest and Toulon in the south. As ever, his most encouraging news had come from the Mediterranean. Latouche-Tréville had once more given Nelson's fleet – or certainly part of it – a bloody nose. Perhaps only the British pride bled. That did not prevent the French press, always equal to any British propaganda, from claiming that their admiral had forced the British one to make a run for it. Nelson kept the report and vowed that one day he would make Latouche-Tréville eat those words.

Bonaparte was particularly cheered by all these stories and, not unnaturally, believed the publicity which, like all good spin, was based on truth. This could have put Latouche-Tréville under considerable pressure to break out, as his instructions had been in the original plan. He was saved from his emperor's enthusiasm by the fact that the invasion flotilla

---

[8] Charles-René Magon de Médcine (1763–1805).

was still not in position and unlikely to be so for some weeks. In fact, it would never get into the right order and the right numbers. Bonaparte, via his minister, Denis Decrès, told his admiral that he had another month. It was almost as if the instructions were tactical rather than springing from a necessity. Bonaparte had come to the conclusion that the autumn would be a good time to invade (just as Duke William of Normandy had thought seven centuries earlier) and so, in the middle of August, feeling in need of celebration, Bonaparte handed out insignia of the Légion d'Honneur, the order he himself had instituted.

That month had, until the beginning of the third week, found Bonaparte in a buoyant mood. The emperor – he had been declared so earlier in the year, although his coronation would have to wait until December – was at last seeing his invasion force beginning to take on a threatening form. This was extremely good news given the difficulties which had followed the storm during his visit to Boulogne in July. Moreover, the news from his eastern front was not nearly so disturbing as he had imagined it might have been. He remained concerned about what might be needed to counter a Russian and Austrian alliance that was forming with Britain. On his immediate flank, the Rhineland seemed in French control and, even where it was not, was no direct threat. Furthermore, his inspired selection of Vice Admiral Latouche-Tréville seemed more than justified as the admiral in the southern command was making sure that his ships, though blockaded by Nelson, were occasionally able to harass the British fleet. Any small squadron beyond the main flotilla might be vulnerable. Bonaparte was particularly pleased at the news of yet another nose-bloodying of the English flotilla in the Channel. A Royal Navy squadron had once again attacked Boulogne, only to find its French defenders more than a match for them. The first report suggested that at least six dozen British sailors had been killed and their captains forced to withdraw, or, more correctly, retreat as the French version would have it.

The only gloomy note thus far that August was a report that had reached Decrès in Paris that Latouche-Tréville was not at all well. Like many sailors and civilians appointed to the West Indian station, the admiral had picked up some bug which had turned to fever and which, annoyingly, kept returning. At the beginning of the second week in August the admiral was aboard his ship of the line, the *Bucentaure*, not at sea but at the Toulon anchorage. At that time, high summer in the south of France, that was the most comfortable place. Also, with Nelson's fleet apparently feeling the stress of its long blockade of the southern naval headquarters, Latouche-Tréville had judged that it was then about time to make a run for the Atlantic. The fever reoccurred, and he took to his bunk. He never got up again. On 20 August he died. What was Bonaparte to do?

The first thing he did was once again prove that he regarded the control of information as an essential element in his grip on France and also on his military planning. He gave orders immediately that to announce Latouche-Tréville's death would be to give comfort to the British.

Latouche-Tréville had been more than a key player in Napoleon's drama. It was this admiral who had angered and distracted Nelson, something no other French commander had been able to do. This was the admiral whom Nelson had promised would eat his words. Also, it was hardly the case that Bonaparte had a whole barge of admirals eagerly waiting for such an important command or – more importantly – in any way capable of competently filling a senior seagoing appointment. In spite of the stream of promotions that had been posted earlier in that year when Bonaparte had been declared emperor, few officers were capable of coming up to the standard necessary to fulfil his battle plan. In that summer of 1804, it seems unlikely that the emperor would have had a choice of more than three or possibly four officers.

Latouche-Tréville's obvious successor was Eustace de Bruix, who had been the fleet commander at Rochefort until 1803 when Bonaparte moved him to be the commander-in-chief of the invasion flotilla. Bruix was hardly the fittest man in the navy anyway. Bonaparte had suggested to Decrès that he might consider the option of Bruix, but he was never particularly enthusiastic about the idea, as Bruix knew perfectly well. Bruix believed that since his public objection to Bonaparte's demand for a fleet review in such inclement weather he had lost the confidence of the emperor. He also believed the emperor had utterly ignored his achievements and had instead picked on those tasks that remained to be completed. Bruix knew that the job at Boulogne was making him seriously ill. He seemed to have a fascination with the possibility that he was dying and that the only thing keeping him alive was the need to complete the invasion preparation. Thus he was hardly the person to send to Toulon with orders to either avoid or obliterate Nelson's fleet, join up at an as yet uncertain rendezvous with the Rochefort squadron, avoid Cornwallis's squadrons centred on Brest and finally sweep either round the north coast of the British Isles or, in the case of a westerly, speed up the northern side of the Channel, eventually arriving at Boulogne to support an invasion flotilla which he, Bruix, as its current commander, knew to be not ready in any case.

Even if Bruix had been suitable, shifting him to Toulon would mean finding another commander for the invasion. It was as well that he was not selected for the seagoing command as he died the following March. The most obvious man for the invasion appointment in place of Bruix would have been the relatively inexperienced junior admiral Jean-Baptiste Lacrosse.[9] Furthermore, as Bruix's deputy, Lacrosse was totally aware of the plan and the capabilities of the forces available to execute it. Accordingly, apart from his junior rating as a seagoing commander, Lacrosse could not really be spared from Boulogne. The next person on the list would have been Admiral Rosily-Mesros.[10] Rosily was a perfect example of how first the Revolution and then the system that replaced it had disrupted the natural progression of good senior officers to flag rank. A number of nondescripts had survived. Even with the rise of Bonaparte and the effective end of the Revolution, flag officers with recent experience were rare. Rosily was one of these officers, who had been coasting along since 1790. He was not at all the admiral to fill Latouche-Tréville's place. The fourth option was, in truth, the only candidate. The job had to be given to Pierre de Villeneuve.

Shifting Villeneuve from his present command of the Rochefort squadron was no simple matter. First and foremost, he was in post and therefore presumably had his ships and men trained as best as he could for the combined operation with the Toulon squadron. Furthermore, when a flag officer is sent to another post an appointment has to be made to replace him. The Rochefort squadron was hardly a backwater in terms of Bonaparte's naval plan. If the Toulon squadron

---

[9] Jean-Baptiste Raymond Lacrosse (1765–1829).
[10] François Étienne Rosily-Mesros (1748–1832).

ever managed to escape the Mediterranean, it was totally useless unless the ships from Rochefort made the rendezvous. So, far from shifting a reasonably good admiral, as Bonaparte still believed (from Decrès) Villeneuve to be, he and Decrès had also to find a first-class replacement. The deputy commander at Brest was Edouard Missiessy.[11] That was the easy part.

Villeneuve had nearly a quarter of a century's experience when he was appointed to what would become one of the most historic squadrons in French naval history. Apart from a glitch early in his career when he had been dropped a rank simply because he was a nobleman and this was the beginning of the Revolution, there had been little to suggest that he was anything but the best of naval officers. He was lucky – a quality which all sailors and soldiers hoped for in their commanders. There is safety in luck, as warfare demonstrates more than most pastimes. Villeneuve was also supposedly gallant and, again like a good naval officer, a seeker after glory and medals as long as nothing might be done that would hazard his ship and therefore his men and reputation. So far so good, for Bonaparte's plan. Villeneuve reported to Paris and the office of his friend, the naval minister, Decrès. He was instructed in what was expected of him and of the urgency of putting to sea the Toulon squadron. Decrès told Bonaparte that Villeneuve listened attentively, in fact coldly, to the instructions. There is a sense that Villeneuve wanted reassurance that Napoleon's plans were feasible before accepting the appointment – a bizarre reaction. Missiessy, on the other hand, was reported as being somewhat dejected on not being given the Toulon appointment. Worse still, he had not been promoted from rear admiral. Together, the initial reactions of Vice Admiral Villeneuve and Rear Admiral Missiessy, if truthfully reflected by Decrès, seemed to suggest a disposition among Napoleon's senior naval officers that would be hard to imagine today. However, in both the British and French navies of that period ruthless politicking and self-promotion were never far below the surface demeanour of any naval officer, young or old.

According to Decrès, Villeneuve had questioned the operation only because he wanted to demonstrate his bravery and show that he

---

[11] Edouard Thomas de Burgues Missiessy (1756–1837).

could succeed even in the most adverse circumstances. There was something much deeper in Villeneuve's character that was perhaps not understood by Decrès and certainly not by Bonaparte. Villeneuve had no distinguished career, as found in any search of naval history. It was not until his seemingly incomprehensible lack of spirit, even cowardice, at the Battle of the Nile that we begin to gather his career details rather than just a list of dates and appointments. According to his portraits he resembled a caricature of a dandified hussar rather than a straightforward naval officer. Moreover, he seems to have come into his own only when promoted to vice admiral towards the end of 1796. It was as if Villeneuve had started to play the part of commander-in-chief because of the uniform he wore. This is not a notion to be dismissed. It is common enough for senior officers, content with the trappings of their new appointments, to display elements in their character that had until then been disguised.

Villeneuve was hardly liked by brother officers, but then these were curious times from revolution to emperor. Moreover, not many survived close scrutiny at the Battle of the Nile. Decrès was also there and 'escaped'. The siege of Malta that followed gave them both opportunity to regain some self-respect, and each indeed restored enough reputation to go on with their careers. So Decrès understood Villeneuve, to the extent that he saw the better side of his character. He was probably one of the few who did not brand Villeneuve a coward for his conduct at the Nile – conduct which might easily have put an end to his career. So when Decrès reassured Bonaparte that Villeneuve had thought through the possibilities of the emperor's plan and then quietly accepted his command, it was probably from a perspective which few others would have understood. The important factor is that Bonaparte believed it. Or did he? For all his enthusiasms, he was aware of Villeneuve's record. He also knew about the connection with Decrès. Furthermore, Bonaparte only believed anything he was told if it came from one of the few he trusted (and Decrès was not always one of those, but Ganteaume – not a Villeneuve fan – certainly was) or if that information or advice either coincided with his own view or he decided to accept it as his own scheme.

Most of all, Bonaparte knew that in losing Latouche-Tréville he had lost by far the best seagoing admiral in his fleet. The vice admiral's death must have made Napoleon wonder if his overall plan was not holed beneath the waterline. There are two pieces of evidence for this, and they are important if only to further demonstrate the possibility that even before the year of Trafalgar the emperor was considering postponing the invasion. As early as September 1804 he had warned Decrès that it might be necessary to mark time on the northern preparations. This did not mean that he was calling off the invasion. It did mean that he believed the opportunity of a late September, or early October assault on England was unrealistic given the amount of time left. The reason for this was only partly because of uncertainties in the invasion flotilla. The main and obvious cause of his questioning its autumn feasibility was Napoleon's realization that Latouche-Tréville could not be replaced at the drop of a tricorn. The fleet could not go to sea quickly enough, could not liaise with the Rochefort fleet, and so there is evidence to suggest that he had dismissed invasion that year as a possibility. The more the invasion programme became bogged down, the more Bonaparte knew his precious military resources would be needed elsewhere.

There is a particular disappointment here. It is perfectly possible that Bonaparte desperately wanted the invasion to be carried out that autumn and for him to have overwhelmed England by, at the very latest, the end of November. Why should this have been so? The answer is simple: because he was going to be crowned Emperor Napoleon at Versailles at the beginning of December by the Pope. What a spectacular triumph that coronation would have been to the whole of Europe for Napoleon to have proclaimed himself Emperor of France and Great Britain. The fact that Bonaparte was already seeing the invasion not as an expeditionary force but as a means of establishing a regime adds to this hypothesis.

Instead of the hope of a glorious coronation – which would be sumptuous and as regal as any seen in France – Bonaparte had to accept Decrès' assurance that they had a superb admiral in Villeneuve. Bonaparte could not have believed that Decrès meant anything more than that they had the best immediately available. An example of Napoleon's uncertainty appeared at the end of September, when he came up with yet another plan. He had to. Neither Villeneuve nor Missiessy were ready and the wind was hardly set fair for England.

His new scheme differed from the previous one inasmuch as the

Boulogne invasion effort was not the main thrust of his tactic. The reason was simple enough. With the moment for an invasion passing, the need now was to look at the wider naval operation. There were four parts to Bonaparte's plan, none involving the invasion of England. Remember, this was autumn 1804. The arrangement with Spain for a Combined Fleet was not yet in place and would not be until January 1805.

The first part of the plan instructed Villeneuve to sail from Toulon, avoid Nelson's ships and then complete an Atlantic triangle. Part of his force based at Toulon would head south to West Africa. This African voyage was to attack English settlements. Having covered that force, Villeneuve, who would have had soldiers and marines in his squadron, was to sail for St Helena and take it. The irony of that ambition would not become apparent until after 1815. With St Helena under a French flag, Villeneuve was then to head for the Caribbean. We can see why, in part two of Napoleon's thinking.

By now, Missiessy was in command of the squadron at Rochefort. He, too, would have a brigade of soldiers and marines. Missiessy had orders to break out from Rochefort and head for the Caribbean. Some of the soldiers would be used to protect the French interests at Martinique and Guadeloupe. Missiessy and Villeneuve would then rendezvous under the command of the latter and their first task would be to counter-attack the English on Dutch Guiana, then in British hands.

The third part followed the first and second. It was now that the attention would re-focus on Europe and the possible invasion. The combined Villeneuve–Missiessy flotilla would return, to be based at Rochefort, having first attacked the English blockade on the Spanish port of El Ferrol.

The fourth and final part of the plan was partly a diversion but was eventually to be the key deep-water protection that an invasion would require. Ganteaume was still in command of the squadron at Brest and thus blockaded effectively by Cornwallis's squadrons. It was anticipated by Napoleon that the actions of Villeneuve's squadron and Missiessy's – in Africa and the Caribbean – would do two things: eventually draw Nelson into the Atlantic, but on a westward rather than a northward course and divert the attention of Cornwallis from his main task, the blockade of the most important French naval port, Brest. If this strategy succeeded, Bonaparte surmised, almost all the efforts of the main English striking fleet would be concentrated on Villeneuve and Missiessy. In fact, for this plan to work, this had to be the case, because six weeks after Villeneuve left Toulon Bonaparte wanted Ganteaume to quit Brest. If he was right and the British were looking across the Atlantic, Ganteaume's task would not be impossible. Ganteaume was ordered to take on board at least three brigades of soldiery. This was for the invasion not of southern England, but of Ireland.

Certainly since the sixteenth century, the French had known that Ireland was a very good base from which to threaten the English. The English also knew this. Thus the mere presence of 18,000 French soldiers landed in Ireland would divert British resources to Wales and the western coast of England to defend the country from an invasion from across the Irish Sea. This would weaken the British army and its ability to counter an invasion in the south-east because the army would then be split. The French, and indeed the Spanish, had tried this tactic before. However, Ganteaume was not expected to stay off the coast of Kinsale once troops were ashore. He most certainly had other tasks to perform. Instead, the command of the French expeditionary force in Ireland would be under Augereau, whom Bonaparte had created a marshal of the empire that year. The movement of Augereau and the 18,000 troops suggested a definite tactic rather than a possible diversion. Augereau had commanded the army at Bayonne, the main defence against a possible Spanish attack on France. To even suggest that the marshal should now be moved to Ireland could only be made if the memorandum of understanding between France and Spain was in place and had the absolute support of King Carlos. This was clearly the position in October 1804.

Ganteaume was instructed that once the army had landed in Ireland he was to sail for the Channel and stand off Cherbourg for orders. The route to the Channel could well be expected to be around the northern tip of the British Isles. In that case, Ganteaume was to join up with a flotilla of Dutch ships and transporters at Texel, off Holland. That Franco-Dutch force amounted to some 25,000 men. The orders were to act as convoy escort of that force and get it to Ireland. With more than 40,000 troops in Ireland Napoleon could certainly see conquest of that place, but – more importantly – future triumph over England. He assumed there would be no difficulty from the Scottish or British troops based there. They, after all, would have enough on their hands policing the North Britons.

The timing of this operation shows quite convincingly that Napoleon had abandoned the idea of an 1804 invasion. Villeneuve was not leaving Toulon until 12 October and did not expect to join with Missiessy until towards the end of November. Part of the credibility of this scheme was that Villeneuve and Missiessy would be on far more than a pillaging operation in the West Indies. Their actions to draw off station Nelson's squadron and, more importantly, large elements from Cornwallis's command, would take weeks to achieve. Therefore Ganteaume could not even think about attempting his escape from Brest with a large squadron – 18,000 troops took up many ships – until Christmas of that year. Even in his enthusiasm, Bonaparte could not see Ganteaume putting to sea until 22 December. So this plan, which crossed the Atlantic, zigzagged back, and part of which moved the equivalent of two corps of soldiers, could not possibly come to anything until April or even May 1805.

Was Bonaparte really to believe the British were so simple as to fall in with his plans? French historians of the period seem to think that he was confident much of this operation would succeed. And yet Decrès must have advised him that an admiral of Cornwallis's experience, not to mention his tenacity, would never dream of abandoning the Channel blockade thus letting Ganteaume through from the west into Cherbourg and would certainly not allow a 25,000 troop invasion force to move in full sail down the Channel from Texel. Was Bonaparte simply working the Royal Navy to a frazzle, chasing plans that no longer mattered? Certainly, his fleet was keeping every good flag officer of the Royal Navy at sea for months – and in some cases years – on end. Would any of this work? The answer is no. Although other plans were put in place, the function of this exercise was, first, to confuse the enemy and, second, to get the French ships to sea, having released them from the impossible situation of being port bound. The function of a navy is to stop an enemy's navy from doing its job. For the preceding few months, through a few exceptional skirmishes, the Royal Navy had succeeded in this by bottling up the French squadrons in the main ports of Brest, Rochefort, El Ferrol and – in the Mediterranean, – Toulon. Inevitably, all Bonaparte's plans slipped. There was no sailing by Villeneuve in October. By Christmas, instead of the whole fleet from Toulon to Brest being at sea and drawing away British ships from their proper positions, not one of them had moved.

CHAPTER FIFTEEN

Imagined Victories

I N December 1804, Napoleon had his coronation. Pope Pius VII, perhaps marvelling at the arrogance of Napoleonic power, had crowned the emperor and then made his way quietly back across the Alps and so to the Vatican. The Royal Navy, Britain's overriding strength and the deciding factor in so many of the nation's overseas exploits throughout two centuries, remained in charge of the sea lanes. And no matter how many new plans Napoleon dreamed up, not one of them seemed to be bringing him any closer to his goal of conquering not just England but the English.

By seizing command of England Napoleon would have control of all British possessions around the the globe. He intended to do far more than invade Kent and Sussex. That would be merely the first step. On marching into London he would gain the entire British Empire. He knew that until every flag officer's ensign was struck he could not even begin to believe he had succeeded. There was a further agitation in his mind, and particularly among his staff.

The emperor was able to rally opinion and effort through the sheer force of his personality and his almost superhuman self-confidence, yet – as every commander understands – you can only keep troops at fighting pitch for a short period of inaction. There quickly comes a point when soldiers lose interest in the scheme of things. As 1804 turned to 1805, his commanders were already concerned about the state of morale. These were not disciplined professional soldiers.

The troops of those days were a pretty ragged lot. A duke might one day march his soldiers to the top of the hill and march them down again, but any large-scale movement of troops devoid of a sound tactical objective would eventually lead to discontent. A degree of dissatisfaction was being felt by Napoleon's armies, as could be seen from an increase in the number of desertions.

What has all this to do with Trafalgar? It tells us the supreme confidence of Britain's enemy but also of his abject failure in terms of strategic planning. Napoleon had the grand idea of the invasion of England. He believed he could remove the country's leading admiral from the oceans, having created a naval master plan to deal with Nelson and Cornwallis. He would produce an army devoted to the invasion and an amphibious fleet bigger than anything ever seen in military history. Having done this, he would rule the whole of Europe, bringing his own peculiar form of democracy to former adversaries that would recognize his imperial authority. He would be on the verge of becoming emperor of the British Empire. However, in 1805, Napoleon was proving to all around him that often the grand idea can only succeed if the enemy has fallen in with the concept.

Napoleon's concept of France having, within four or five years, a big-ship navy to rival that of the British showed he understood that to overwhelm his enemy he would need to command the sea lanes. He would not be able to rely on a union with Spain for ever. His vision was that one day, under its great emperor, France would regain the naval power it had enjoyed in the heady days of Colbert.[1] That seventeenth-century statesman had reformed the finances of Louise XIV, vanquished much of the corrupt bureaucracy that was crippling the nation, and restructured and added to its empire. Most importantly, he had devised a means of defending that empire, building the most impressive fleet France had ever known.

Colbert had been a genius, but the people had had to pay for this. By the time of his death in 1683, he was regarded as a tax collector, not as a man of great vision who had brought stability and order to the French nation. Napoleon looked across the Channel and saw in the British a nation of shopkeepers, perhaps, but also a state that Colbert would have admired.

---

[1] Jean-Baptiste Colbert (1619–1683).

Like Colbert, Napoleon saw Britain's navy as the key to its stability and prosperity. Little wonder that he admired Nelson so much. He thought he could build a navy to rival the Nelsonian fleets, but could not. Everywhere he turned to execute his plan, the Royal Navy got in the way. At sea, the French were simply not good enough. The ingenious idea of landing perhaps 40,000 men in Ireland, 1,500 or so on St Helena and tens of thousands in the West Indies had to be abandoned.

Instructions had been sent to his three commanders. Missiessy was ready, and so too – mainly reluctantly – was Villeneuve. However, Ganteaume was not. The orders for what was Napoleon's most imaginative naval operation – stretching from Europe to Africa to the Americas – never reached that admiral because they were intercepted by the British. This was not to say that Ganteaume was entirely in the dark. Once it had become clear in Paris that the admiral was taking time to respond, he was updated on Napoleon's plan. This turned out to be a waste of time. The whole scheme was laid bare on the desk of the one person Napoleon should have feared more than Nelson – Admiral Cornwallis. Napoleon's instructions were very clear, and now that Cornwallis had them he too was clear as to what should be done. Cochrane,[2] then a rear admiral, had been watching the Spanish fleet in El Ferrol. At this stage no public agreement existed between Spain and France. Once Cochrane had formally complained to the Spanish that they were helping an enemy and were, therefore, now fair game themselves, the preparations for storing and arming their ships came to a halt. Cochrane was cruising off Ushant, already in receipt of Cornwallis's orders to intercept any French vessel trying to leave port. It was during this patrol and armed with Cornwallis's instructions that one of Cochrane's commanders, Captain Moore[3] in the *Indefatigable*, intercepted four Spanish bullion ships before they could get into Cadiz. This was the trigger, in December, for Spain's declaration of war against England. Here, yet again, was an instance of the British retaining control of the seas by keeping the enemy in port and picking off vessels at will. The

---

[2] Sir Alexander Cochrane (1758–1832).
[3] Graham Moore (1764–1843). His more famous brother was General Sir John Moore, who commanded British troops against the French in Spain.

return and interception of the treasure ships from the West Indies is worth mentioning here.

Almost until that moment, Napoleon's plans were feats of imagination. He did not have the resources. Moreover, he was still concerned that the Spanish might take advantage of his activities to harry his rearguard. This was why Gravina was such an important ally in Paris, having as he did the ear of King Carlos of Spain. It was also the reason for Napoleon having to deploy such a large garrison, of almost corps level, at Bayonne with, as we have seen, one of his most important generals in command. Cornwallis's instruction to Moore, which allowed the captain of the *Indefatigable* to intercept the Spanish vessels, turned out to be the catalyst that brought Spain into the war. It would also, of course, strengthen the French naval effort prior to the time when Gravina's fleet combined with Villeneuve's, the weakest element in Napoleon's planning. It is interesting to speculate whether or not Spain would have been able to prevaricate and avoid joining the war had that attack not taken place. Almost certainly the Franco-Spanish Combined Fleet would not have sailed in the way it did and Trafalgar would never have taken place. This order from Cornwallis to Moore was not a case of the admiral telling one of his captains to attack any shipping he came across. Spain was not at that stage at war with England. An attack could thus be seen as an act so provocative that it would lead to war.

Moore, in the *Indefatigable*, along with three other vessels, the frigates *Amphion*, *Lively* and *Medusa*, patrolled between Gibraltar and Cadiz. The engagement was hardly a warlike one, as one might imagine. It was carried out in what we may now see as the peculiar, even gentlemanly style of navies in the late eighteenth and early nineteenth centuries. It certainly began in an almost theatrical manner. The result was a gruesome one. Moore sighted four Spanish ships, tacked to come alongside them, and then stood off within hailing distance. His yeoman signalled the Spanish to shorten sail; in other words, to slow down and await instructions from the British. The Spanish commander pressed on. With that, the *Indefatigable* fired a shot across the leading vessel's bow. It had an immediate effect, and the Spanish squadron of four shortened sail. This was not simply a matter of stopping in the water. It took a considerable time to hand in and furl, before the vessels were nearly hove to. At this point, a junior officer from the *Indefatigable* was rowed across to the Spaniards. He went aboard and gave the commander the message that Moore had instructions to detain the Spanish flotilla. At first, according to Moore's report to Cornwallis, it seems he feared that his junior officer might not be able to get back. So another shot was fired across the bow. His officer then returned, only to tell Moore that the Spanish had refused to obey the British command.

The Spanish were, after all, laden with bullion, at that stage not at war and able to make a run for it as they were pretty close to Cadiz and safe haven. As if to prove there should be no doubt about their intentions, the Spanish then fired on the *Amphion* and Moore's own vessel. His reaction was predictable. The *Amphion* was already closed up at action stations. Within ten minutes, one of the Spanish ships exploded right alongside the *Amphion*. Twenty minutes later, two of the other three surrendered and the fourth vessel went about and escaped. It took a whole day's chase for HMS *Lively* to capture the Spanish ship. The commander of the Spanish frigates, Rear Admiral Don José Bustamante,[4] was taken prisoner. The British had got three of the four ships, and their treasure. However, more than a million silver dollars went to the bottom with the explosion that occurred in the fourth Spanish vessel.

Spanish vessels not at war had been attacked. Two hundred and forty Spaniards had been killed. Some of those dead were friends of Spanish royalty. War with Spain was inevitable. There was no way in which King Carlos could not go along with Napoleon's requests to join France in fighting the British. Moore was a gallant officer and an efficient one. Cornwallis was a masterful campaigner. Yet still it is worth wondering if this single action on 6 October 1804 made the events of 1805 more likely. It should not be overlooked that the British – certainly Cornwallis – perfectly understood the enormity of what had happened. Although, in September 1804, he had instructed Captain Moore to watch for two Spanish frigates (in fact there were four, as we have seen), he did not publish the formal order to do so until four months later, in January 1805. By that time, of course, Spain had declared war, which lent Cornwallis's

---

[4] Don José Bustamante (1759–1825).

order of January an authority and legitimacy that might not have stood close scrutiny four months earlier.

Considering the gravity and consequence of this event of 6 October 1804, was this engagement the result of a foolish command on the part of Cornwallis? Could it, for example, explain why the admiral was all but ignored after Trafalgar? Some have thought Cornwallis guilty of bad judgement. Yet the decision to engage the Spaniards was not his. The intelligence that Spanish ships were at sea with bullion had first reached the Admiralty. It was Melville who had sent orders to Cornwallis to detain the Spaniards. It may be that the First Lord of the Admiralty was directly attempting to provoke Spanish involvement on the side of the French. It was likely that by September the British knew of Napoleon's determination that the Spanish would come over on to his side. It was also a calculated risk that, by attacking the Spanish, the British fleet was always going to be in position to destroy or at least neutralize them. Needless to say, it could have been a plan that went wrong. Once an order to detain a vessel was given, those involved could not be expected to anticipate any violent consequences that might result from it.

Also, Melville's order could possibly be seen as a strategic determination on his part to destroy the only element of the Spaniards the British feared: her navy. We might remember that Nelson and his commanders would not have agreed with many modern historians that the Spanish navy was finished and commanded by noble amateurs. Nelson truly understood that it contained some very fine ships, some good sailors and not a few excellent commanders. Much better, therefore, for Melville to decide to get at the Spanish navy on his own terms rather than Gravina's. Whatever the reasoning, Cornwallis was obeying a higher command, not having a temperament like Nelson's which enabled him to dispense with those orders with which he least agreed.

For our purposes, there is another aspect of that engagement that makes it easier to understand the way warfare was conducted in that period. We might, for example, think it perfectly reasonable for Moore to have found the Spanish ships. By modern standards that reasoning is not difficult to accept. Yet let us think the process through. Somewhere in the Caribbean, Spanish frigates laden with bullion prepared to sail. They could have only one destination – Spain. Most likely, their port would be Cadiz. British spies and reconnaissance ships in the Caribbean thought that at first just two, as opposed to four, frigates were in the process of loading. This information was relayed back to London by fast frigate under full sail. It had two destinations, one being the Admiralty and the other Cornwallis. To get to the Admiralty the ship did not have to sail to London. It put into Plymouth, and the news arrived there within a few hours. Cornwallis had known earlier because one of his frigates had intercepted the intelligence ship.

There were at the time procedures whereby vessels might be found. For example, an admiral might have positions in the ocean where he would keep a frigate for such a rendezvous. These stations would have numbers. So, for instance, another vessel might well have instructions to meet on a certain day at Rendezvous 47. Cornwallis would get the intelligence. He would know where Moore was patrolling and send a fast vessel south with his orders to engage the Spanish ships. But how, in the vast expanse of the Atlantic Ocean, would Moore have known know where to find the Spaniards? His navigator would have known when those ships had left the West Indies. At certain times of year the currents and even the prevailing winds could be estimated. The type of ship would be described. Moore would know that the speed of that two- or even four-ship convoy would be judged by that of the slowest vessel because the group had to stick together. So, given a great deal of luck, an estimated speed, plus knowledge of the prevailing conditions and the known destination, Moore was able to deploy his four vessels in a line or perhaps a triangle not to intercept but to sight the Spanish ships. The first vessel to see them would be able to signal the others, if the weather was good enough, by line of sight. In fact it was the *Medusa* that spotted the Spaniards on 5 October. By the following afternoon the engagement was over and the course of Britain's war with France had changed. It was now almost impossible for Spain to stay out of the way; therefore Napoleon was very confident of victory.

There would be no diversions, unless we see a letter from Napoleon to George III at the beginning of 1805 as a ploy to put the British off guard. Some have regarded the letter he wrote on 2 January 1805 as an offer of peace. But was it really that?

My dear Brother,

Since I was called to the throne of France by Providence and by the suffrage of the Senate, the people, and the Army, my foremost and most earnest desire has been for peace. France and England are squandering their prosperity. Their struggle may continue for centuries. But are their governments discharging their most sacred duty? Is not their conscience troubled by such a useless effusion of blood with no real end in view? I count it no dishonour to be taking the first step in this matter. I fancy I have shown the world that I am nowise daunted by the hazards of war; indeed, war holds no terrors for me. Peace is the dearest wish of my heart, but war has never diminished my deputation. I charge Your Majesty not to reject the happy opportunity of yourself conferring peace upon the world. Let not that sweet satisfaction be left to your children! . . .

For, for all things considered, there has never been a fairer juncture or a more auspicious moment for stilling all the angry passions and listening only to the voice of humanity and reason. If the moment passes, how can this war reach an end, when all my efforts have failed to bring it to a conclusion?

In the last ten years Your Majesty has won more territory and wealth than all Europe contains. Your kingdom is on a peak of prosperity. What advantage can it hope to gain from war? To form some coalition of the continental powers? But the Continent will remain undisturbed; the only result of such a coalition would be to increase the pre-eminence and the glory of France. To revive internal conflicts? But times have changed. To ruin our finances? But a financial system founded on a basis of sound agriculture can never be ruined. To relieve France of her colonies! But for France colonies are a secondary factor: and in any case has not Your Majesty already more colonies than you can maintain?

If Your Majesty will but consider the matter personally, you will see that the war is purposeless, and can lead to no definite result. And it is a miserable prospect for two peoples to fight merely for the sake of fighting. The world is big enough for both our peoples to live in. Reason commands the means of reconciliation, given good will on both sides. In any case I have discharged a sacred duty, and one very dear to my heart.

I trust that Your Majesty will credit the sincerity of the sentiments I have expressed, and of my desire to prove them in action.

That the letter was dated 2 January 1805 is significant. Six days later, the French naval minister, Admiral Denis Decrès, and Admiral Federico Gravena, then ambassador, signed the memorandum of understanding that would lead to the Combined Franco-Spanish Fleet.

A week later, the British wrote to Napoleon that they could not possibly give any kind of unilateral response to his approach. After all, they would most certainly need to discuss his offer with the Russians and Austrians. Pitt used this alliance order to show Napoleon that he was dealing with a much larger force than the British alone. The Russians, in particular, considered they had much to lose if Napoleon was allowed to further his ambitions of expanding his empire to include the whole of Europe.

The British received Napoleon's letter with something approaching contempt. The State Papers for January 1805 reflect also a belief on the part of Britain that the emperor, determined to overwhelm the continent, had probably abandoned his invasion plan, even if he had not yet recognized this himself.[5] *The Annual Register* for 1805 stated clearly the British position on three important aspects of relations with Napoleon's France: war had been officially declared with France's new ally, Spain; the letter from Napoleon was considered a bit of nonsense; and the threat of invasion, while still prepared for, was thought less likely to occur.

On 15 January, George III opened a new session of parliament. As the *Annual Register* reported, George

proceeded to state that the conduct of the Court of Spain, under the direct influence of French councils, had been such, as to compel him to take decisive measures to guard against hostility from that quarter, at the same time that every effort had been made by him [the king] to avert the calamities of war with a country so

---

[5] State Papers, No. 605, 1805.

circumstanced. The refusal, however, of satisfactory explanations on the part of that power [Spain] had obliged the English minister to depart from Madrid, and war had since been declared by Spain against this kingdom . . .

in general conduct of the French was . . . recently marked by every species of outrage, and the most unequivocal determination of that power to violate every principle of public law or civilised usage, which impeded the career of the present ruler of France [Napoleon] towards an uncontrolled predominance in Europe, if not to universal dominion

This last point tied in with the belief that Napoleon was determined to attack British interests in the West Indies, and most certainly in India, if he could only produce a fleet and flotilla of military transport to support his projects. George III announced to parliament that he had 'lately received a communication from that Government [Napoleon] containing professions of a pacific tendency to which, however, his Majesty had been pleased to reply only in general terms'.

When Lord Elliot,[6] the leader of the Opposition in the Lords, rose to reply to the king's speech, there was no doubting the unanimity at Westminster. As the *Register* reported, Elliot

appeared to doubt the sincerity of the French Government in the late overtures for negotiation, and observed, with pride, that the presumptuous boast [Napoleon] made at the commencement of the war, that this country [England] was no longer able to cope 'single handed' with France, was now given up, and that after the enemy had brought his preparations for invasion to the highest state, he now seemed conscious of that vanity of his hopes; an affect for which he [Elliot] considered the country indebted to the excellent measures adopted for our defence to the skill and gallantry of our officers and seamen to the admirable discipline of our Army and militia, and to a new description of force, in the order of our brave and patriotic volunteers . . .

---

[6] Lord Gilbert Elliot Murray Kynnynmond, first Earl of Minto (1751–1814).

his [Napoleon's] motives in making the late overtures, might
have been to embarrass the Government, to create divisions in
Parliament, or discontent in the country...

Little of this mattered anyway, because the emperor's latest plan to get
his fleet to sea was being acted upon. The agreement between Spain and
France to combine forces boosted Napoleon's position and had an
immediate effect on his maritime planning.

France now, with Spain, had a seagoing navy of seventy major ships.
Had that agreement not been signed, it is doubtful whether by spring
1805 it could have had at sea many more than forty-seven large vessels.
Even the Combined Fleet of seventy was still less than half the size of
the British one. While numbers were important, it should also be
recognized that the role of those ships was the key to their success,
rather than an overall order of maritime battle. The British, for example,
needed many more vessels to maintain blockades than they might have
done for a striking fleet. The physical toll taken on ships and men by a
harsh winter of Atlantic gales could sap the fleet's strength. Craft were
always being sent back to England for repairs and sometimes complete
refits – a process that could keep a ship alongside or in dock for weeks on
end. Moreover, the maintenance of a blockade required a larger number
of vessels that could be scattered over considerable distances. A striking
fleet (one that attacked or had to break through enemy lines) could be
smaller because it was able to focus its energies at one point. Therefore it
was quite likely that a combined French and Spanish force, whose main
intention was to divert the Royal Navy and then go in support of the
invasion, could actually consist of a relatively small group of squadrons
– relative, that is, to the overall superiority in number of the British. The
French and Spanish had to bring that combined force swiftly up to
operational speed. Levels of seamanship, gunnery and sailing instruction,
including ship handling, had to be improved.

When the Decrès and Gravina document was signed that January,
there was not a great deal of evidence to suggest that standards in the
French contingent were high. However, the only way to improve
standards in any ship is to get it to sea.

Sailors could be trained for months on end when a ship was alongside, at anchorage or even ashore. However, a commander needed to get his ship's company to sea, up and down masts and out on to yards, loosening grommets and sail lines or handing them in when they were treble their weight from the rains of a south-west gale and the ship was plunging and heaving with a fifteen-degree list to starboard. He wanted to know how he and his men would react and when that simple sailing routine had gone on month after month with, all that time, the possibility of being surprised and then attacked by an enemy squadron. A commander cooped up in port for months on end by the British had to get his ship to sea before he could begin to know how efficiently he could close up for action stations, have the decks cleared with everything in place from dry powder to the surgeon's saw. An agreement signed on a gilt table beneath a high painted ceiling in a Parisian salon was no sure means of producing a navy capable of taking on Nelson.

Those same difficult sea conditions that would test captains and crew now came to the aid of the French. The storms and poor visibility meant that the English ships blockading the French coast had to stand well off. There were then, of course, no thumping diesels able to get a sailing ship off what is known as a lee shore. This term applies when a wind is capable of blowing a ship on to the shore – when it arises on the weather side as opposed to the leeward or shore side of the vessel. The British, keeping a healthy distance between ship and shore, gave the French an advantage. They could set sail without the British seeing them. During the second week of January 1805, this is exactly what Missiessy did. He ordered his squadron of ten ships, five of them frigates, to get ready for sea and then broke out from his anchorage off the island of Aix. The same wind that threatened the safety of the blockading British now came to his aid.

The heavy gales that had begun towards the end of the previous October had blown in from the Atlantic with hardly any respite. Collingwood's flagship, the *Dreadnought*, at one point standing off Rochefort blockading Missiessy, had taken such a battering that she was in no state to attack the French squadron. Admiral Cochrane, sailing in the same region, had hardly a single ship that could have gone to action stations. In January, the 74-gun *Illustrious* had been sent from England to reinforce his squadron. By the time she had battled her way through the gales to Cochrane's rendezvous – in itself a superb example of seamanship – she had lost two of her topmasts and was incapable of being manoeuvred during an engagement.

Some of Cornwallis's ships were so badly damaged by the weather that they could not be steered. In twelve months the navy had lost more ships to storms than it had in any engagement with the enemy. Cornwallis was now in the dreadful position of having much of his fleet either scattered out of sight by the weather or dismasted. The most efficient naval blockade in living memory was being broken up without the enemy having to fire a single shot. There was only one thing Cornwallis could do: make such signals as he could and return to Devon for repairs. There was no point in staying on station if he could not do the job. He had had some 50 ships patrolling France's western coast from Bordeaux to Brittany. By the end of January there was hardly a British ensign in the region. There was another aspect to consider. If Cornwallis's surviving fleet was battered and bruised, incapable of concentrated action, what was defending England in the Atlantic and Channel approaches? Not much except the weather. Further to the east, the Downs fleet had survived. But that was hardly a major naval task force.

Cornwallis's extraordinarily sound management of the blockade had proved successful since the spring of 1803. This had only confirmed the belief ashore that all that was necessary to contain the French was to order the Royal Navy to prevent that country's ships from leaving Brest, Rochefort and Toulon. As Missiessy would now show, and Villeneuve would pathetically attempt to demonstrate, the task was never that simple. In theory, of course, the difficulties the Royal Navy had experienced from the Atlantic gales and those in the Channel meant that the French were also at a disadvantage. It was certainly not that easy to put to sea into a prevailing wind – or indeed any wind – when it was gusting at force eight and more. The French, moreover, found themselves held back by receiving contradictory orders from Napoleon, quite apart from having a less than efficient fleet which, of course, did not really need to be at sea because there was no other fleet to link to and the command was not ready to move on to Boulogne.

If Napoleon's main task was to use his deep-sea ships to draw off squadrons of the Royal Navy while others defended the invasion fleet, the Frenchmen could easily stay alongside and at their anchorages, because the invasion was not yet ready. In the opening months of 1805, the emperor's scheme was supposedly to be set in motion. Villeneuve and Missiessy were to go to the West Indies, beat up on the British and then return in time for the autumn invasion. With the British navy scattered and much of it in port in England, at least one part of the French plan was about to get under way. On 11 January, Missiessy was set to put to sea. One squadron had been left on station by Cornwallis. It was under the command of Rear Admiral Graves,[7] flying his flag in HMS *Foudroyant*. One of his frigates, the *Felix*, sighted the French squadron on 12 January. Even at that time of year, sunset was early in the afternoon and sunrise accordingly late in the morning. The weather was inclement. It was so bad that Graves had to heave to on his station in Quiberon Bay. Here is an example of signalling that modern sailors would find most frustrating. Signals could, obviously, only be sent, within line of sight. Even then, with the elaborate letter-and-number system, information was only ever given in outline. But if a ship with the latest intelligence was unable to see his point of contact, the captain had to sail and find it, hopefully at one of the numbered rendezvous. This is what happened that January 1805. The *Felix* picked up the French squadron at sea, running down the coast and presumably about to make as much westing into the Bay of Biscay as it could. It had only just come out of Rochefort. The *Felix* had somehow to get its information to the admiral, and her captain could not be exactly sure where Graves was located. He was, in fact, still at anchor in the Bay of Quiberon, partly protected by the headland and the paradoxically named Belle Île to the north of the *Felix*. It took five days from that sighting down the coast from Rochefort to get the intelligence to Graves in his anchorage. Cornwallis's difficulty was obvious to the navy; less so to the politicians who demanded action without having a clear understanding of what that action should be. Cornwallis had not the ships that could have remained with the French squadron while the *Felix* returned with the news. Consequently no one – certainly not Cornwallis – had a clue as to the whereabouts of Missiessy. It was not

---

[7] Sir Thomas Graves (1747–1814).

until the end of February, close on seven weeks later, that Cornwallis got news of a second sighting.

Just as army intelligence-gatherers question travellers, so naval captains made alongside merchant ships. Although the Atlantic had its easterly and westerly trade routes, there were certain points at which vessels frequently passed one another going in different directions. So, not surprisingly, it was from a disinterested source, a Swedish merchant marine captain, that the Royal Navy heard that a squadron of French ships had been seen not far from Tenerife making in a generally south-westerly direction. What was Cornwallis to do? His immediate order was to Cochrane, who had been patrolling off El Ferrol in a small five-ship squadron. Cochrane was to set off on a similar course and, at the very least, track Missiessy, assuming that was who it was. This presented a further conundrum for Cornwallis. What was he to do about monitoring the naval activity in El Ferrol itself? Local intelligence picked up from the harbour suggested that a French squadron of maybe five ships had stored up and was standing by to put to sea.

Now that the Franco-Spanish concord was effective and war with Spain had been declared it was very likely that Spanish vessels in El Ferrol would sail with the French. Also, the news from Brest was that there were as many as twenty-five or perhaps even thirty French vessels, at least three of which were three-deckers, making ready to sail. Spring was on its way, and so was naval action. The irony was that although signs of hustle and bustle were apparent in the yards and in the sea lanes, no one – quite likely not even the French – really understood what it was all about. Cornwallis was guessing, the Admiralty had more theories than admirals, and the French and Spanish commanders were following orders which, in some cases, had already been countermanded and whose purpose, anyway, few if any of them understood. It would be only a slight exaggeration to say that Napoleon had a different flash of inspiration with every lunar cycle, his admirals were not entirely up to speed in terms of knowing what was expected of them and that any sailing directive they received was seen, on close examination, to contain quite obvious limitations.

The squadrons could in theory have swung north to support the Boulogne expedition, but would not do so because the Boulogne commanders were not ready. They could have put into the Mediterranean to join up with Villeneuve's Toulon fleet and take on Nelson. That would have seemed sensible. It would have meant that Missiessy and Villeneuve had more firepower than Nelson. Moreover, they knew that the British admiral had been at sea for a considerable length of time, even though he had the comfort of the Sardinian anchorages. Certainly defeating him would have boosted their own credibility, relieved them of a major naval threat and dealt a heavy blow to British morale, given that the vice admiral was Britain's most important flag waver. Alternatively, they could have headed for the West Indies. This would have enabled them to attack British positions and, if he followed them, to take on Nelson in that area, guaranteeing the correct timing for a return, all flags flying and guns blazing, to the Channel. With Missiessy sighted on a south-westerly heading, this latter hypothesis would seem most likely. All it needed was a clear assurance that Villeneuve was following the same plan. So where was Villeneuve while Missiessy was heading comfortably into the sunset and warmer climes?

CHAPTER SIXTEEN

Unhappy Christmas

A T CHRISTMAS 1804, VILLENEUVE HAD STILL BEEN IN TOULON, BUT with eighteen ships, seven of them fast frigates, standing by to cast off and weigh anchor. He had been waiting for a change in the wind direction. His sailing masters needed a northerly to get them to sea as speedily as possible and then, ideally, an easterly to get him through the Strait of Gibraltar. No one could guess what the wind direction would be by the time he cleared the Strait. He got, during the third week of January, a north-westerly. Though not exactly what he had been looking for, it was pretty close. His main concern, or that of his captains, was that the wind would not sustain them. Villeneuve needed it to hold until he was in the Atlantic. That was an impossible hope, because the properties and wind directions off the coast are quite different from those at sea, and because the Mediterranean, by the mere fact of its geography, produces more influences on the wind than could be forecast with any accuracy by an early nineteenth-century sailor. As if that were not enough, Villeneuve was having doubts about his mission.

It was becoming clear, or had always been obvious, to his officers that Villeneuve was no Latouche-Tréville. If his officers felt that, within the close-knit community of a sailing ship, then so would the ratings. Also, all servicemen since warfare began have had an instinctive knowledge of their commanders. Some they will follow anywhere, while others they will rarely trust. Villeneuve was hardly an inspiration to his men, especially given the example of his predecessor Latouche-Tréville who, if Nelson had had a beard, would have singed it.

The French were clearly aware that Nelson's squadron was never far away from Toulon. They believed there was nothing they could do that would hide their preparations for putting to sea. Port spies quickly got information to the English. The crewmen of a sloop or frigate standing off the harbour would be able to see from a telescope any preparations being made at the mastheads and know from experience what these meant.

Villeneuve himself revealed his weakness as a commander by making it clear – supposedly in confidence – to some of his officers that he felt Nelson must know of their intentions and that it would be impossible for them to sail without the English admiral knowing exactly what was going on. Furthermore, the captains themselves knew that if the right wind should come up and blow them out to sea, that same gust would allow the forward frigates of Nelson's squadron to run quickly downwind to wherever he, its commander, was waiting. The intelligence that Villeneuve's fleet had set sail could reach Nelson within hours, as the French admiral knew only too well – and he feared the consequences.

By Christmas he was writing to Denis Decrès in Paris warning him that it was impossible for the French to sail without Nelson knowing exactly what they were doing. He told Decrès also that even the number of troops he had embarked would be seen by people ashore and widely reported. After all, security in Toulon was unexceptional. In fact, Villeneuve's preparations, including the embarkation of thousands of soldiers, had been something of a spectator sport. Worse still, even if he did get away from Toulon unmolested, could he guarantee that every ship would get out at once? If they did not, when would they be able to meet up? If they were scattered, they could be picked off one by one.

So when Villeneuve at last sailed from Toulon during the morning of 18 January 1805, Nelson knew about it by teatime the following day. He had been lying at anchor off Sardinia. Exactly as had been imagined, the wind that had blown to the advantage of Villeneuve also blew for Nelson's forward observation frigates.

It should have been a simple matter for him to track Villeneuve and engage him long before he reached the Atlantic. However, the limitations of early-nineteenth-century naval warfare meant that all Nelson knew was that the French commander had sailed and, when last seen, was making a southerly course. Given the wind direction, that for the moment was very likely. What Nelson did not know was where Villeneuve intended to go on that southerly course. Might he stand on until running to a point that would allow him to alter course for Gibraltar? Was he trying to maintain it and heading for the North African coast? Nelson made the mistake of thinking the latter. He thought Villeneuve was heading for Egypt. This was exactly what Napoleon had predicted. Nelson ordered his commanders to weigh anchor and leave the comfort of the channel where they had been hiding off north-east Sardinia.

By early evening, his squadron of eleven ships of the line were clear of Sardinia. Out of the shelter of the island the squadron began to feel the first whips of a Mediterranean northerly storm. This increased to gale force and by the following day had strengthened even further to what we would generally call storm force ten or even, hurricane force. Nelson's squadron was having difficulty and, in a seamanlike manner, was hove to against the storm. Villeneuve had no success in mustering his ships. Part of his fleet found itself detached. Some vessels were dismasted. Villeneuve was in a blue funk. He gave up all hope of carrying out his orders to get into the Atlantic. He went about, and those parts of his squadron that were able to make sense of his signals saw that they had been told to run for home. By 21 January, all but four of his ships limped into Toulon. His sailors could have blamed the weather, but instead they preferred to spit on the name of their commander, who had got them into that difficulty in the first place. However, at least they were safe in Toulon. But where was Nelson?

Nelson had overestimated Villeneuve's power of command and seamanship. He assumed Villeneuve would also have ridden out the storm, which lasted for four days. Consequently, his squadron headed further south and at first put into Sicily at Palermo in an attempt to pick up any intelligence on Villeneuve. There was none to be had. Convinced that the French squadron was still at sea, Nelson firmly believed that his original judgement was correct and so ordered all sail for Egypt. The British fleet was off Alexandria by 8 February. There were no signs – not even rumours – of Villeneuve.

In Paris, the emperor and Decrès certainly had news of the man they thought was their gallant admiral. Villeneuve was full of his own praises, explaining how well he had prepared his men and ships, only to be thwarted by the most terrible weather conditions. The point was a fair one. It did not, however, say much for the seamanship of his squadron. After all, Villeneuve was back in port having mislaid at least three ships and given the local shipwrights far too much trade. He went as far as to suggest that it was because of his skill that Nelson was now lodged in Egypt. That was not the best piece of bragging. Had it not been his emperor who, in some earlier plan, had suggested that a diversion by his Toulon squadron would lead Nelson to believe it was heading back to Egypt?

It is at this stage that we can see what a poor servant of his emperor Villeneuve really was. He was a wimp and simply wanted to go home. He made it clear to Decrès that he had never really wanted the command in the first place. Worse still, he had no interest in combat, which represented a certain drawback in his career, especially as a flag officer. Villeneuve was not the sort of officer to seek glory or – worse still – to risk having it thrust upon him. Operational duties could, after all, end in the death of even a good man and an admiral who failed to achieve success was always heavily chastised. In all the services of that period, there were officers who were fond of promotion but really wanted little more than a career of – to use Villeneuve's phrase – 'usefulness'.

Ever since the nonsense of his action, or perhaps non-action, at the Battle of the Nile, Villeneuve had been haunted by comments and doubts expressed of his ability as a seagoing officer. Yet this was the man who, Decrès had assured Napoleon, had blossomed on being promoted to vice admiral and been delighted at the prospect of commanding the Toulon squadron. This was the man, again described by Decrès, who had weighed the proposition of the command with coolness and reported that his squadron was in fine fettle and ready to put to sea. Perhaps Decrès was simply telling Napoleon what his emperor wanted to hear. What Napoleon most certainly did not want to hear was that Villeneuve was running scared and wanted out. Yet that is exactly what the admiral was telling Decrès. He said that nothing would please him more than if Napoleon were to give the Toulon squadron post to another admiral. He even went so far as to tell Decrès that as far as he, Villeneuve, was concerned, the only thing that mattered was to ensure that he did not become a byword in Europe for disaster.

Villeneuve was declaring far more than his honourable resignation. He could have been utterly demoralized, foolish or simply a coward. Perhaps the characteristics of the third are combined in the first two. On 22 January 1805, he repeated something he had said before: that he had never asked for the command. He then made the bewildering statement that 'about all one can expect from a career in the French navy today is shame and confusion'. The man was a classic case of the over-promoted officer. He saw the navy as somewhere to be rather than a force giving its all to defeat the enemy. He certainly believed – and told Decrès – that anyone who thought the French navy was any good was utterly blind and incapable of straight thinking. Villeneuve's opinion was that Nelson was unbeatable. He felt it was impossible for him to defeat the British fleet, even had both sides been equal.

Villeneuve actually told Decrès that even if Nelson's squadrons were a third weaker than those of the French, still the British would win. It was his view that when safely at anchorage his squadron was rather like himself: with a little care and attention it could certainly look the part. Once at sea, however, and faced with even a modest enemy, the squadron's fabric would be stripped bare to reveal a third-rate navy lacking the stomach for a fight and in total awe – and fear – of Nelson. He was, to a considerable extent, telling the truth about his ships and men. Certainly, lying at anchor everything looked well.

However, it did not take a very practised naval eye to see that while the ships themselves may have had stout hulls they were poorly rigged and quite incapable of resisting the stress of a strong gale. This point was reinforced when the qualities of the French sailors were analysed. The men were not good at their jobs and had been poorly trained. Though they had not spent all that time locked up under blockade, these crews were inexperienced, often commanded by less than brilliant officers, and the training programmes for them, where these existed, were of a limited nature. The combination of second-rate equipment, poorly rigged and canvassed vessels and lacklustre crews meant that when a craft got into difficulties the standards of ship handling, sail handling, setting and trimming were below what were required and the ropes and other materials were also unable to withstand poor weather conditions, especially when used badly.

However, contrary to some recent assessments, the French sailors were brave and performed far from hopelessly at Trafalgar (see chapter 28). Unfortunately, their commander-in-chief did. Villeneuve, an officer who should have been left in the Paris salon, was most certainly not the inspiration his squadron needed. Apart from anything else, he did not know how to make his squadron any better.

In earlier times such an admiral would at least have been dismissed from his post, perhaps from the service, or even, *in extremis*, executed. Instead, Villeneuve, a commander who gave the impression of never wanting to see a ship again, was left where he was. There was no one of his rank to replace him. Understanding this, Decrès had no intention of informing Napoleon of Villeneuve's utterly hopeless character and his requests which almost verged on demands.

It is very likely that Napoleon would not have been at all surprised to learn of Villeneuve's whining. He never did think much of him, considering admirals, with few exceptions (Latouche-Tréville and Ganteaume among them), a hopeless waste of time. Napoleon's view was that he could never trust an admiral as he could a general. The idea that the commander of the Toulon squadron should have run into a bit of bad weather and then gone into an absolute decline probably did not surprise him at all. It certainly did not help Villeneuve's cause that Nelson had ridden the same gale and then pressed on to Alexandria, not only in one piece but still spoiling for a fight. And, as Napoleon knew full well, Nelson's squadron had been at sea, not tucked up in harbour, for twenty-one months. Perhaps if the French had also been sitting out gales in the Gulf of Lyons on and off for nearly two years, they too would have got the hang of the seamanship that was all the difference between Nelson's and Villeneuve's fleets.

As to why Villeneuve was not sacked on the spot, even before handing in his tawdry letter of hopeful resignation, it can only be repeated that, first, there was no one to replace him; second, Decrès was successfully hiding the worst aspects of the admiral's character from Napoleon or possibly Napoleon had another plan. If that were true, and it was something other than his ever-present thought of invading India and the British Empire, then at that stage nothing had been presented to Decrès and most certainly not to Villeneuve and Missiessy. The latter had escaped the British fleet. He had sailed across the Atlantic and was standing off Martinique, wondering what had happened to Villeneuve, who, according to the joint orders, was supposed to be in the West Indies. Apart from being underequipped for his original task of attacking British settlements, by escaping to carry out his orders Missiessy had actually reduced French naval power in European waters. If Napoleon had indeed changed his mind and not told Decrès – which, on the face of it, seems unlikely – this was yet another hopeless misunderstanding of the use of the navy. Effectively, Napoleon was for the moment left with a half-dismasted fleet in Toulon, a couple of ships in El Ferrol and a blockaded fleet in Brest. Not much of a navy. Moreover, because Missiessy had been the only officer to carry out Napoleon's orders the whole scheme had to be abandoned; none of the others had managed to turn up for the occasion.

For Napoleon, it was back to the drawing board. Villeneuve would eventually take command of the Combined Fleet. However, in the opening months of 1805, Napoleon did not want this to happen. He thought Villeneuve a pathetic creature. Still, the only officer Napoleon trusted – and had for some time – was Ganteaume. In admiration, Missiessy came second, with Villeneuve as a poor third in the emperor's affections. Whatever Napoleon thought of his naval officers, he had few options other than to centre his revised thinking on the fact that Missiessy, unlike the others, was not stuck in port but where he had been told to be – in the West Indies, waiting for the Toulon commander to busy himself and cross the Atlantic. Thus Napoleon quite rightly circled Missiessy's fleet, standing off Martinique, when he revised his battle plan, published on 2 March 1805.

The first order was to put the three admirals together. Accordingly, Missiessy was to remain on station at Martinique. Villeneuve had nineteen ships under his command, eleven of them ships of the line. His instructions were simple: to get out of Toulon as quickly as possible, to rendezvous with any Spanish warships that might be available and able to break the blockade off Cadiz, and to sail with good speed to Martinique.

Ganteaume was ordered also to sail from Brest. His was much the bigger fleet, which reflected the importance of the town as command-fleet headquarters. He had a double task. There was still the small squadron consisting of French, and a few Spanish, sailors in El Ferrol.

Ganteaume had about thirty ships, including two troop carriers. He first had to break out from Brest, then sail for El Ferrol, knock out the British blockade, rescue the El Ferrol squadron under the command of Rear Admiral Gourdon,[1] then sail to Martinique.

When the three fleets plus the Spanish vessels were gathered in Martinique, they were to be commanded not by Villeneuve but by Ganteaume. Some have seen this as a direct indicator of Napoleon's disdain for Villeneuve. Yet Ganteaume had seniority and commanded the largest of the three squadrons as well as having the confidence of his emperor. Whether or not any of his admirals properly understood Napoleon's intentions is uncertain. Villeneuve, for example, had been told to rendezvous with Missiessy and linger for up to six weeks until the arrival of the squadron from Brest. However, there was a real possibility that Ganteaume might not get out of Brest in that time. Therefore Villeneuve and Missiessy would have to sail for the Canaries, wait once more for Ganteaume and, if there was still no sign, set a course for Cadiz and there wait for orders. Ganteaume supposedly had the master plan. The West Indian rendezvous made sense. It allowed the three squadrons, accompanied by the Spanish, to work up to an efficient fighting force of at least forty ships. Ganteaume was given an ultimate aim of arriving off Boulogne somewhere between 10 June and 10 July. So did this mean that the British assessment that Napoleon had abandoned his invasion plan was incorrect?

The age of simple communications had not yet arrived. In the case of Ganteaume, this did not much matter because he was still ashore in Brest and so easily able to receive orders from Paris. What he did not know – and neither did Napoleon – was whether Villeneuve and Missiessy also had those orders. Napoleon, and probably Ganteaume, was hardly confident that Villeneuve would carry them out even if he did get them. His fleet, in spite of the three weeks he would have had between Toulon and Martinique, was still not in good order. As for Missiessy, he presented an entirely different difficulty for Napoleon. Missiessy was a contradiction of Napoleon's views of the navy. He was efficient. He worked Rochefort

---

[1] Adrien Louis Gourdon (1765–1833), who had been squadron commander at El Ferrol since 1804.

squadron into a proper fighting force. He did his best to carry out orders. Often, his best was good enough. On 11 January, Missiessy had escaped from Rochefort.

The British had cursed Missiessy for his good luck in escaping. In fact, he had got away in difficult circumstances. As well as ships' companies he had dispersed in his squadron more than 3,000 soldiers and was fully laden with ammunition and stores for the ships and the army. Napoleon had, on 24 December 1804, instructed the rear admiral to sail for the rendezvous with Villeneuve *and* to take some of the smaller British islands in the West Indies, in addition to landing reinforcements at Martinique and Guadeloupe. He was then to sail among British settlements, destroying as many as possible and disrupting those he could not overwhelm.

Missiessy had made careful note of his emperor's orders and was sufficiently determined and competent to carry them out. Imagine, then, his anxiety as he waited with troops aboard, stores accounted for and sails bent on at the anchorage off the Île d'Aix. He wanted to get away. The weather was varied. The winds were in the right direction to get him out into Biscay, but it was snowing, which was a mixed blessing. It meant blind pilotage but also cover against a prying British frigate. Missiessy at last got his squadron together and put to sea. Again, the weather was on his side because a gale blew up which got him inside the now dispersed British fleet. That same gale, however, dismasted his own flagship, the *Majestueux*, and four other vessels were damaged. So, far from having an easy sail under the nose of the British, Missiessy's captains had to lash their damaged vessels as best they could and had no real chance of proper repairs until they reached the West Indies. Good seamanship and command got them across the ocean.

Once there, and with his squadron repaired, Missiessy set about British settlements, although his greater success was in capturing more than thirty English merchant ships. Unprotected, the British cargo vessels were easy pickings. This was a very rich area of the British Empire and there was plenty of shipping to attack. Missiessy might have continued for some time if he had not had orders to return to Europe. His emperor, through the instructions of Decrès, was calling him home to Rochefort, or so he thought. Too keen, too quick, Missiessy – despite protestations from the governor of Guadeloupe, who feared losing his protection –

immediately ordered all sail for Europe and Napoleon's bidding. It was not what Napoleon had had in mind at all. That had been the previous month's idea.

On 1 February, a small fast brig was sent to tell Missiessy that Villeneuve had made a botch of getting out of Toulon and that he should therefore ignore the order to rendezvous. Four weeks later, another brig was sent telling Missiessy to stay where he was and there to join up with Villeneuve (Napoleon lived in hope) and Ganteaume. That would have been fine except for the fact that the second brig did not get there. So, in the belief that Villeneuve was not coming, Missiessy sailed for Rochefort. On 20 May, this super-efficient rear admiral and his ten ships arrived back in their home port. As far as Napoleon and Decrès were concerned, this first-class officer, by observing the naval dictum of always obeying the last pipe (order), had completely fouled up the emperor's plan. For efficiency, Missiessy deserved a medal. Instead, Napoleon thought him an unspeakable bodger. The emperor was already in a bad mood because on 18 March his commander-in-chief of the Boulogne invasion flotilla, Admiral Bruix, had died.

As for Missiessy, he was now a dejected figure. Reports were sent from Guadeloupe claiming that he had left them in the lurch, when all he had done was follow orders from Decrès. Napoleon was angry because Missiessy had done exactly that. On top of this, the rear admiral had driven himself tirelessly and was extremely ill and now hopelessly disillusioned. The fact that Missiessy was probably the most devoted of Napoleon's admirals was not seen as a saving grace. How different matters might have been if that second brig had caught him, either in the West Indies or on the way back to Europe.

In the Admiralty in London, all these comings and not many goings were confusing. There was a reasonably good offshore intelligence system monitoring Brest, Cadiz, El Ferrol, Rochefort and Toulon. It was anticipated that Napoleon would still try to get a fleet to Boulogne. Merely because the assessment suggested he had given up the idea of invasion did not mean that the Admiralty would call off its efforts to suppress Napoleon's master plan. The emperor was also making indiscreet noises about invading India. This was assumed to be a diversion. The Admiralty was right in this assumption. But a diversion from what?

Out of the five squadrons, only the one from Rochefort was at sea. What were the rest expected to do? It was certainly not tempting to let them out and find the answer to that question. What was needed was some indication that would tell the Admiralty if Missiessy's expedition to the West Indies had been planned or whether it was part of a bigger scheme that had backfired. The first indication of a general breakout came from Cornwallis's deputy, Vice Admiral Cotton.[2] Cornwallis had gone ashore. Lord Gardner,[3] who was to assume command in Cornwallis's absence, had not yet arrived. At the end of March, the Admiralty received a signal from Cotton that almost thirty French ships had emerged from Brest harbour and were anchored off. To Cotton there was every sign that they intended to run the blockade. Gardner immediately sailed to assume his temporary command and joined Cotton's fleet off Ushant by 3 April. He was ready for action. Clearly the French were not. They had gone back into the harbour.

Among admirals, Gardner was a good man. While very little should be said against Cornwallis, it should be noted that he had been at sea for nearly two years, often felt his age and was not always in absolute control of what was the most difficult command in the Royal Navy. There were many who thought that despite his advanced years Gardner should have been given substantive command of the Channel fleet. Among those who appeared to think so was the sometimes unapproachable but ever wise Vice Admiral Cuthbert Collingwood, who believed that in Gardner the navy had an officer who was a perfect master of fleet discipline. This certainly was needed. It was a difficult command. For one thing, it needed to be scattered to watch over the latitudes of the Atlantic blockade. Calder, who would soon fail to deal with Villeneuve's returning fleet (see chapter 19), had spent a miserable time in gales and was finding that because many of his ships were damaged he was having to report that only five larger vessels and one frigate were operational. Moreover, this deficiency occurred at a time when three times that number of French and Spanish vessels were preparing for sea in this area off El Ferrol. Gardner was therefore forced to send Calder three more major

[2] Sir Charles Cotton (1753–1812).
[3] Lord Alan Gardner (1742–1809).

warships. However, these could not be conjured from an inexhaustible supply. It meant that Gardner's immediate command was thus reduced by the same number.

By the early spring of 1805, Napoleon was into his seventh invasion plan. Number five had been sent to his commanders at the end of February that year. On 22 March, he was forced to change his mind. Ships were not in position, and it was impossible that they could be to comply with his orders. On 30 March, Villeneuve at last set sail from Toulon. Out came Napoleonic plan number six. The orders were to forget going to the West Indies and instead – yet again – set sail for the west of Ireland, across the top of Scotland and south through the North Sea, making for the Dover Strait. This seemed a long way round for the invasion protection fleet, but it had the advantage of drawing the British off station. Almost as a matter of course, the plan had a short shelf life. On 13 April, Napoleon came up with invasion scheme number seven. The West Indies were once more back on the Napoleonic chart.

As a diversionary tactic, some of the Spanish fleet were to busy themselves in and off Cadiz, thus attracting some of the already depleted British fleet. The rest of the Spanish vessels making up Gravina's short squadron – five major warships – were instructed to meet up with Villeneuve, who had seventeen ships under his command including eleven ships of the line. Villeneuve, with Gravina, was ordered to meet up with Ganteaume, wherever he was. Their game plan was to hurl the British from the Windward Islands in the Caribbean. They would then destroy the British prosperity there by wrecking estates and, if possible, seizing them, putting French soldiers into Dominica and St Lucia. In addition, they would reinforce the French garrisons at Guadeloupe, Martinique and San Domingo by leaving nearly 13,000 extra soldiers in the islands to protect French interests. It would never happen.

The seventh plan contained orders that would divert Villeneuve from the West Indies, back across the Atlantic, to deal with the British southern blockade at El Ferrol in order that the dozen or more French and Spanish ships in that anchorage could join his own reinforced fleet. That done, Villeneuve had only to go north, break the British blockade on Brest and free up ships still in port which would be under Ganteaume's command. The Combined Fleet would then sail straight up the Channel, heading for Boulogne, the invasion and for orders. All this planning was designed to allow the French to have freedom at sea for between six and seven weeks. That was the period Napoleon had estimated he needed to get the Villeneuve fleet into the Channel in support of the invasion, leaving him with, he assumed, only the British Downs fleet to deal with and the support of a diversion of Spanish ships heading for Toulon. The reason for this last expedition was supposedly to trick Nelson into believing the French were about to attack Sardinia. We have already seen from at least one of Nelson's letters that he considered this a possibility.

Why the emperor should begin to trust Villeneuve with this exercise is not clear. Yet again, the answer is: who else was there?

Villeneuve was continually writing to Decrès, saying that he foresaw that the whole thing could turn out to be a disaster. The admiral went so far as to commiserate with Decrès, assuming the latter to be in total sympathy with him. He told Decrès that he imagined that he, the naval minister, had to be under enormous pressure from Napoleon because otherwise he himself could not begin to conceive how Decrès could so often issue him insane orders. Villeneuve prayed that fortune, which he so badly needed, would smile upon him. He was, by the beginning of April, in the awful position of having to resort to wishing himself good luck.

His ships were, in theory, splendid enough. Some were 80-gunners, others 74s, and there was also a squadron of highly manoeuvrable 40-gun frigates. They looked good at anchor. Their graceful, menacing lines were let down by those on board. The French sailors were, after all this time of preparation, still poorly trained. Their sail work, ship handling and gunnery most certainly did not come up to the potential of the ships in which they served. Moreover, there were not enough of them. Few fancied their chances aboard Villeneuve's fleet, so while still in Toulon he had had to draft in soldiers. They were taken aboard and informed that a great deal was expected of them in the name of the emperor (not that he knew anything about this) and that they were about to get a head for heights. They were sent aloft and out on to the yards and told which lines to tug, which ones to bend on (tie) and which grommets to pull. They were rushed up and down the main deck and instructed in hauling away on blocks and tackles and then down to the gun decks to learn to run out cannon and fire without putting their hands over their ears. Being soldiers, it was hoped that they would make fair sailors. They may well have suspected that they could hardly make a worse job of it than the matelots already aboard. How good the instruction was remains unclear. Villeneuve saw little to inspire him with the confidence that was required for the exercise ahead.

However, on 30 March 1805 he put to sea. He had worried, rightly so, that Nelson's squadrons might hammer him as soon as he was clear of the Toulon roads. Thus far his wish was holding and fortune smiling on him. The winds were favourable enough – probably north-westerlies – for Villeneuve to keep inshore, pass between the Spanish coast and Ibiza and, on 9 April, clear the Strait of Gibraltar and sail into the Atlantic. He was supposed to have been joined before Gibraltar by the Spanish squadron at Cartagena. On average, a squadron might be six ships. That would have made a particularly useful addition to Villeneuve's fleet. He did pause at Cartagena, but turned down the offer of the Spanish squadron. Some have been tempted to point to this as yet another quirk of the admiral's complex character. That might be unfair. For some time an epidemic of a flu-like disease had been raging in Cartagena. Although the Spanish would have been confined to their ships, Villeneuve may not have wanted to risk, literally, carrying the disease in his fleet.

Second, although the Spanish squadron could be quickly readied, its commander would have had very short notice of Villeneuve's arrival. Therefore, and especially if there had been disease among the fleet, it would have taken some time to fully store up those six vessels, bring the ships' companies up to seagoing levels (perhaps replacing ill sailors) and have them fully ready to join Villeneuve's fleet. It might well be that Villeneuve, because he feared all the while that Nelson would come upon him, was unwilling to hang about the Mediterranean for an hour longer than necessary. If the Spanish squadron could get out on its own and rendezvous at some later date, then that was fine. It would not be overgenerous to observe that Villeneuve made the right decision in not accepting the reinforcements and pressing on in order to fulfil the emperor's plan as best he could.

When the French liaison officer in Cartagena reported to Paris that Villeneuve had departed and had refused the Spanish squadron, Napoleon assumed that the said liaison officer needed his mind attending to. Surely there was some mistake? Surely none would refuse reinforcements? There is always a reason, especially in battle, for the inexplicable. In spite of the evidence, Villeneuve deserves some credit for moving on. In fact when, in the evening of 9 April, he arrived at Cadiz – having evaded the rather sketchy British blockade – one of his first actions was to warn the Spanish commander, Gravina, that he was absolutely certain Nelson could not be far behind. He imagined Nelson might even be as close as the cape south of Cadiz, Trafalgar. The irony, of course, was that when Nelson did eventually catch him, it would be six months later off that very headland.

Villeneuve was certainly not happy to stay in Cadiz for a moment longer than he had to. He saw the great harbour as a welcome haven. Even so, the prospect of a conflict with Nelson in or off that place was too much for him to bear. He had arrived at 8 p.m. on 9 April, and six hours later he was gone again. Gravina was expected to go in convoy with the French admiral. The Spanish admiral may have been a splendid sea officer, but unfortunately his ability was not shared by all his sailing masters and those on the lower decks. Instead of neatly slipping moorings and weighing anchors, at 2 a.m. on 10 April, the Spanish, who had been swinging at anchor for some time, produced a farce of basic seamanship. Cables, moorings and anchors were a jumbled mess. Orders were yelled and ratings cursed. Steel hawsers are deaf to bosuns' oaths. The great Gravina and his squadron were stuck fast. Villeneuve, looking back, would have seen very little of this, even in the moonlight. He kept going. His destination yet again was the West Indies. Eventually the Spanish untangled themselves and sailed too. Just short of six weeks later, Gravina and Villeneuve met again in the comparative safety of the offshore anchorage of the French island of Martinique.

How did they get away? Had there not been specific instructions from the British Admiralty to bottle up the French fleets in Brest and Toulon and the combined squadrons in El Ferrol and Cadiz? There are two possible explanations of how Villeneuve managed to escape the blockade. Either the British Cadiz squadron did not see him or it was too frightened to attack him. Sadly, for the reputation of the Royal Navy and Nelson's temper, the squadron did see Villeneuve and left him alone.

Certainly, in the case of the squadron's commander, Vice Admiral Sir John Orde, the odds appeared to be against him. To be faced by the

Toulon fleet, by now three times the size of his own squadron, certainly gave Orde pause for thought. Nelson would have probably decided that even with just six ships it was worthwhile having a go at Villeneuve. This would not have been foolhardiness. Villeneuve was a frightened officer effectively fleeing from the British fleet. He had, as we have seen, an incompetent company of ships and men. Moreover, he had a single destination, Cadiz harbour. A combination of fright and objective meant that had he wished to avoid the British – it was unlikely that he would have chosen to attack them – Villeneuve would have been obliged to issue complicated sailing instructions and manoeuvre orders in a relatively strong south-west wind. With his fleet in its present state, it would probably have executed such an instruction with confusion.

Furthermore, Orde was close enough to be able to engage the enemy at the outset. He had the advantage of superior seamanship, room to manoeuvre and the choice of, at the very least, hacking into the stragglers of Villeneuve's fleet. He was hardly lightly armed. The six ships in his squadron included Nelson's favourite vessel, the 64-gun *Agamemnon*, commanded by Captain Sir Edward Berry[4], Captain Robert Redmill's[5] 64-gun *Polyphemus*, the large 74-gun *Defence* and his own 98-gun flagship, *Glory*. Any commander worth his gold lace should have been able to disable if not destroy a good part of Villeneuve's fleet. It is quite possible, even with those odds, that action by Orde would have foiled yet another plan of Napoleon's because it would have brought about the final humiliation of Villeneuve and bottled up both him and Gravina in Cadiz harbour for the foreseeable future, certainly until Nelson's arrival.

However, Orde was an unexceptional officer. Moreover, he was jealous of Nelson. In 1798, also off Cadiz, Orde, then a rear admiral, had been one of St Vincent's commanders. When St Vincent put Nelson, in theory not a senior officer to Orde, in command of the Mediterranean fleet, Orde had made his objections very clear. He was so obviously jealous and unreasonable that he was sacked from his flagship by St Vincent. In 1805, he had only recently been given a new command as a flag officer. There

---

[4] Sir Edward Berry (1768–1831). He was still in command of the Agamemnon when she fought at Trafalgar.
[5] Captain Robert Redmill (?–1819). Also fought at Trafalgar.

he was, at the beginning of April, standing off Cadiz – for him, a sea area devoid of happy memories – with specific instructions: he was to keep the Spanish in port and to report any other ships' movements, particularly the appearance of Villeneuve's Toulon fleet, to the man he most detested – Nelson. He did not send a fast vessel to inform Nelson that Villeneuve had escaped the Mediterranean.

Did Orde know what was going on? Most certainly. That evening of 9 April 1805, Orde was standing so close to Cadiz that he clearly saw the arrival of Villeneuve's fleet and the bunting at every signal mast to welcome it. Furthermore, he had reasonably accurate intelligence regarding the numbers of Spanish vessels under Gravina that were ready to join Villeneuve. Instead of engaging the enemy closely, which would have been Nelson's instructions to him, Orde judged it best to play safe and keep out of the way. He claimed not to have told Nelson because he had not known where his brother officer was. Anyone even slightly sympathetic to Orde in his predicament would have pointed out that by the time he had managed to get a message to Nelson both Villeneuve and Gravina would have been sailing westward for many days. Perhaps that was even more reason for threatening Villeneuve's fleet in the first place.

Nelson had naturally assumed that Villeneuve would break out from Toulon. He was also willing to believe that the French admiral would stay in the Mediterranean when he did so. Nelson had been cruising the waters between Sicily and Sardinia, the latter being his fleet's safest anchorage in the region. Villeneuve had gone on 30 March 1805. It was not until the early morning of 4 April that news of the French escape reached the *Victory*. Nelson's instinct was to search the waters off Sicily for the French ships, or at least to intercept merchant vessels on the local trade route, which might have given him intelligence of the whereabouts of the French fleet. Napoleon, as we have seen, hoped that Nelson would go as far as Egypt believing that to be Villeneuve's destination in support of another French attack on the North African coast. In fact, Nelson was at a loss to explain the manoeuvrings of Villeneuve, and more than a week elapsed between the Frenchman's leaving Cadiz for the West Indies and Nelson finding out that the Toulon fleet was no longer in the Mediterranean.

In theory, Villeneuve was now nothing whatsoever to do with Nelson.

Nelson was, after all, commander of the Mediterranean fleet. He had no business leaving the Mediterranean unless instructed to do so by the First Lord of the Admiralty, Lord Melville. It was nothing to do with Nelson that Villeneuve was in the Atlantic, apart from the fact that he had failed to keep him in port and, worse still, having let him out, had failed to destroy him. Villeneuve, hardly a model of ruthless navy efficiency, was now rightly considered a threat to British maritime interests, to West Indian concessions and perhaps also to the British defence against an assumed future invasion. Nelson was at fault. On 19 April 1805, he was lying to the west of Sardinia in the *Victory*. All the time Villeneuve had been either in port or in Mediterranean waters his British adversary had been very much in the thick of the Napoleonic war. With Villeneuve gone, Nelson had either to hope that he had been forced back into the Mediterranean or even to expect to see some of the ships in his squadron removed to reinforce those running up the Iberian peninsula to Brest. He wrote to the First Lord of the Admiralty that day telling him that he was going to pursue Villeneuve. Once more we see the difficulty of getting accurate intelligence at short notice.

We now know that Villeneuve was heading for the West Indies. Orde's report at the time suggested a westerly escape. A later piece of intelligence from Vice Admiral Calder confirmed other reports and impressions that the squadrons from Cadiz were heading west. The Admiralty appears to have believed this to be so. In fact they believed so strongly that the Toulon and Cadiz blockades had been blown that they could no longer see any use for the clearly ineffectual Sir John Orde. If Villeneuve and Gravina had escaped to the west, Orde could return to England. He was ordered home to strike his flag. We need no longer bother ourselves with the career of this not very good officer. Orde had never liked Nelson, and Nelson felt bitter towards Orde. Nelson, like so many dashing national figures, needed medals and money in either order, and the best way to get money was to capture enemy ships. Orde was about to start living off the proceeds from captured Spanish galleons that should have been Nelson's prizes. That had been Melville's decision, and so, in his darker moments, Nelson was not sorry to see the back of either man. However, his immediate concern was the whereabouts of his official enemies.

CHAPTER SEVENTEEN

The Chase Begins

HAD HE BEEN A MODERN COMMANDER, NELSON WOULD HAVE HAD satellite intelligence buzzing into his operations room aboard his ship. As it was, in 1805 he did not always know, what was happening at sea, but, being Nelson, believed that he most certainly did. In Nelson's opinion, any suggestion that Villeneuve and Gravina were heading to the Caribbean was quite clearly nonsense. He felt certain that he knew exactly what was going on and told Marsden, the naval secretary, that Villeneuve was in fact heading north to sail round Ireland and the northern tip of the British Isles.

Victory, April 19th, 1805; 10 leagues West from Toro. Wind N.W.

Sir,

The Enemy's Fleet having so very long ago passed the Straits, and formed a junction with some Spanish Ships from Cadiz, I think it my duty, which must be satisfactory to their Lordships, to know exactly my intentions. I have detached the *Amazon* to Lisbon for information, and I am proceeding off Cape St. Vincent as expeditiously as possible; and I hope the *Amazon* will join me there, or that I shall obtain some positive information of the destination of the Enemy. The circumstance of their having taken the Spanish Ships which were for sea, from Cadiz, satisfies my mind that they are not bound to the West Indies, (nor probably the Brazils); but intend forming a junction with the Squadron at Ferrol, and pushing direct for Ireland or Brest, as I believe the French have Troops on board; therefore, if I receive no intelligence to do away my present belief, I shall proceed from Cape St. Vincent, and take my position fifty leagues West from Scilly, approaching that Island slowly, that I may not miss any Vessels sent in search of the Squadron with orders. My reason for this position is, that it is equally easy to get to either the Fleet off Brest, or to go to Ireland, should the Fleet be wanted at either station. I trust this plan will meet their Lordships' approbation; and I have the pleasure to say, that I shall bring with me eleven as fine Ships of War, as ably commanded, and in as perfect order, and in health, as ever went to sea. I have the honour, &c.,

Nelson and Brontë.

I shall send to both Ireland and the Channel Fleet, an extract of this letter, acquainting the Commander-in-Chief where to find me.

In spite of the fact that what intelligence there was could, metaphorically, still see the wake of Villeneuve's squadron steering west-south-west, Nelson knew better. He said so, adding that he would abandon his instructions to police the Mediterranean and head out into the Atlantic, turn north and go and get Villeneuve. He ordered his fleet to set sail for the Strait of Gibraltar with a last formal line to Melville, trusting that his intention would meet 'their Lordships' approbation'.

Nelson – rather like Napoleon – thoroughly believed in himself and in the foolishness of others. Like Napoleon, he had few reservations about changing his mind, especially for tactical reasons. In the stuffiness of the drawing room, this quality, even habit, might be dismissed as inconsistency. In a warfare planning office, only a fool remains committed to his original tactical appreciation. To be on the safe side he sent Melville a private note declaring that wherever Villeneuve went he, Nelson, would pursue him, whether to Brest, to Ireland or even to the 'East or West Indies'. He was making a very bold statement. He was telling the First Lord of the Admiralty that he would decide for himself what was to be done.

There should be a footnote to this boldness that bordered on insubordination. Nelson was unwell. His fleet's senior physician had felt sufficiently strongly about Nelson's health to write a formal letter to his admiral instructing him not to stay in the southern latitudes during the summer and to return to England for his own sake. It is not always easy to judge the seriousness of Nelson's health. He had been at sea for close on two years. He suffered continuously from seasickness. His general constitution had never much improved from that of the sickly child he had once been. Yet his stamina was not much questioned. Ill health among commanders as well as ratings was not unusual. A ship was not the ideal healthy environment. Whether or not Nelson's metabolism affected his judgement is a matter to be considered elsewhere.

By then, of course, though Nelson did not know it, he was really writing to the wrong person. As we have seen, Viscount Melville was being investigated. On 30 April 1805, he was forced to resign from the Admiralty. He was succeeded by Barham (see chapter 12).

On the same day as he wrote to Marsden, 19 April, Nelson wrote to Lord Gardner telling him he was sure that if Villeneuve and Gravina were heading for Ireland, then his own ships would be 'no unacceptable sight' to the commander-in-chief. He added that if Gardner did not want his help all he had to do was say so. Nelson knew full well that no commander-in-chief ever refused assistance unless he wished to deploy that aid in another theatre. So certain was Nelson that Villeneuve was heading north that, although he had marked the French admiral for his own gain, he expressed a hope that Gardner would annihilate the Franco–Spanish ships.

At sea, the weather knows how to temper the ambitions of men – even famous admirals. What was to be the start of one of the most fatal yet famous chases in naval history got off to something of a slow start. Nelson had the wind against him. For a fortnight his fleet beat against westerlies. On 26 April, Nelson wrote to the Gibraltar commissioner, Otway.[1] He said that from 9 April, fifteen days earlier, he had been trying

---

[1] Sir Robert Otway (1770–1846). It was Otway who was sent by Hyde Parker to Nelson in Copenhagen at the height of the battle, with a confidential instruction to hang on as long as possible, thus suggesting that the famous story about Nelson turning a blind eye to Hyde Parker's signal to disengage has been exaggerated in Nelson's favour.

to get to Gibraltar. It was not until 26 April that the wind shifted to the east.

Even when Nelson got to Gibraltar, he was still no wiser as to Villeneuve's whereabouts or intentions. We might also remember that, as we have in seen at the beginning of the year, Nelson was also having to deal with the practicalities of his command. If we are really to understand the detail of this huge adventure we need to remind ourselves of the logistical effort of it all.

On 5 May 1805, Nelson would have been found writing to Keats,[2] captain of the *Superb*, with instructions about taking on drinking water, confirming that Keats would load up with bullocks for the fleet and telling the agent-victualler not to pay for anything not delivered on board. Another note refers to wine. Yet another instruction had to be sent to the naval secretary, Marsden, concerning the discharge of sailors and the seemingly boring procedure of the weekly account books. On 26 April 1805, a date when we might imagine him to have been totally preoccupied with the image of a disappearing Villeneuve, we find him having to argue the case for the petty officers' wages to be paid.

Even in the most demanding circumstances, the vice admiral refused to ignore the rights and requests of his sailors. The navy had a habit of avoiding payment of wages. Nelson refused to condone this. And so, in a letter to William Marsden, he wrote that the petty officers were 'very justly entitled to their wages' and that they had to request that Marsden would be 'pleased to move the Lords Commissioners of the Admiralty, to give the necessary directions to the Navy Board for this purpose, as it would be a very great hardship that the said men . . . should be deprived of the wages . . .' When he did get to Gibraltar, as well as eagerly seeking news of Villeneuve, he found himself having to intervene on the behalf of a bosun called Joseph King. Men were paid according to their duties as well as to their rating. For example, a bosun of the sheer hulk was involved in moving ships in the harbour, but was not as senior as a bosun of the yard. Joseph King was a bosun of the yard – the most senior rate in a dockyard. He had not been paid since 1802 as boatswain of the yard, but only as boatswain of the sheer hulk. Moreover, in the sheer hulk he

---

[2] Richard Goodwin Keats (1757–1834).

would need accommodation. When King went ashore to be boatswain of the yard, he should therefore have been granted a rental allowance for his house. Furthermore he had additional duties. Imagine Nelson, again, concerned about the state of his ships and the storing of them and being beside himself with anxiety as to why he could find no intelligence on Villeneuve's whereabouts, having to sit down in *Victory's* Great Cabin to pen a plea for justice for the bosun. These apparent irrelevancies are important points if we are to understand more deeply the character of Nelson and the procedures which, even at the height of war, had to be observed. However, on 7 May, *Victory* was back at sea, stocked with more food, wine, water – and disappointment.

Nelson had hoped that Orde would have dispatched one or two of his frigates – the intelligence-gatherers of the Nelsonian navy – to meet him in Gibraltar. These fast vessels were often quite capable of standing off an enemy fleet to leeward in safety. The reason for standing off to leeward was that it would then be much easier to escape by running downwind and then altering course when out of sight should an enemy commander detach a couple of his vessels to deal with the snooper. Nelson had expected Orde to have a frigate or two tailing Villeneuve and Gravina. The task would have been to send one of them back to Gibraltar with the vital information of Villeneuve's sailing direction, even though there was no reason why the Franco-Spanish fleet should not have altered course once out of sight, just as an evasive frigate might have done. However, Orde had not sent one of his frigates to Gibraltar.

Consequently, the end of the first week in May 1805 found *Victory* cruising off Portugal's Cape St Vincent. This area was one of the predetermined rendezvous of the Royal Navy. Nelson hoped that if Orde had not sent a frigate to Gibraltar, he would have sent one to Cape St Vincent. It would have had orders to loiter there because Orde must have known that once Nelson or any other Royal Naval vessel was out of the Mediterranean it would make for the official station in order to pick up news. For the moment, partly thanks to Orde, Nelson had no intelligence other than rumour. He was anxious to take up the chase. So, in another letter to Marsden, we find him repeating his determination to track Villeneuve. He wrote that he had heard rumours that the Frenchman might not be sailing north after all but to the West Indies. Nelson said it was his duty to follow the French fleet, even if it went south to the Antipodes. In fact what he did not tell Marsden was that he was inclined even then, on 7 May 1805, to break off from his Iberian station and head west to the West Indies. Why should Nelson have begun to believe the rumours about the westerly course of Villeneuve when just a few weeks earlier he had been utterly convinced that the Combined Fleet was heading north? The answer may be as simple as the logical assumption that if Villeneuve's fleet had been heading north, as he thought, it would have by now been sighted, if not intercepted, by Cornwallis's relief, Gardner, or one of the outer squadrons. For example, the *Amazon* was cruising off Lisbon. Moreover, the greater fleet stationed in a line from Brest would surely by then have spotted Villeneuve, and Gardner would not have kept the French admiral's position to himself.

By the second week of May Nelson knew that he had to sail for the West Indies (see chart page xv). He did not know for certain that Villeneuve had gone there. He was not convinced by the general opinion that Villeneuve and Gravina had sailed west and stood on that course. Yet where else could they be? He told the Admiralty that his ships would be taking on enough supplies to be away for five months. He would go to the West Indies and search for Villeneuve. He was already a month behind the Frenchman, who was by then in the Caribbean. The best Nelson could hope for was to meet in mid-Atlantic a merchantman or even a naval frigate that had in recent days sighted the French and Spanish ships. Once in the islands, he would hope for better intelligence. He had also to accept that even if Villeneuve had sailed to the West Indies, by the time he himself reached those islands, the Frenchman could be back again in European waters. We should remember the basic style of pilotage and navigation of those voyages. The idea would be to cross from east to west on trade winds and from west to east with the aid of the Gulf Stream. Therefore there was a slight possibility that a westbound ship could meet an eastbound one. Nelson and Villeneuve could cross the same line of longitude going in opposite directions, and one would never know the direction of the other. So if Nelson got to the islands and could not find Villeneuve, what was he to do? He told Marsden at the Admiralty that he would then return to Cape St Vincent. Here again is a moment when Nelson, supposedly acting on the instructions of his superiors, issued himself his own orders. Whatever he did, it would be, as he put it, 'according to the best of my judgement'. This was not entirely a case of Nelson going his own way. The navy in 1805, and indeed well into the twentieth century, had often to rely on the squadron commander to use his initiative because in the vast theatre of the oceans, before the days of electronic signalling, airborne patrolling and satellites, the Admiralty rarely knew more than the local man.

In his letter to Marsden is a reminder of the importance of that area off Cadiz. Apart from being a sailing rendezvous, it was the point at which a squadron could either put into the Mediterranean or prevent an enemy from getting in and out. It was also the southern area in the chain of naval command; in army terms, the southern flank. It was the jumping-off point of a transatlantic voyage and a natural point of return. Nelson's letter to Marsden also tells us – although he could not have known this – of the very real possibility of the future confrontation that coming October – in this very area.

Three days later, in another letter to Marsden at the Admiralty, Nelson once more committed himself to the West Indian voyage, mentioning the possibility of returning to the waters off Cadiz and then of following his doctor's orders and returning to England, although all that turned out to be so much nonsense. He spent the time in Whitehall. But it is the period when he last saw Emma and explains why he was not at sea and then made the now famous departure from Southsea and then south to Trafalgar.

The letter to Marsden is therefore of more than passing interest.

Victory, May 14th, 1805. 38 leagues from Madeira.

My dear Sir,
Under the most serious consideration which I can give from all I hear, I rather think that the West Indies must be the destination of the Combined Squadrons. A trip to England would have been far more agreeable, and more necessary for my state of health; but I put self out of the question upon these occasions. And, although it may be said I am unlucky, it never shall be said that I am inactive, or sparing of myself; and surely it will not be fancied I am on a party

of pleasure, running after eighteen Sail of the Line with ten, and that to the West Indies. However, I know that patience and perseverance will do much; and if they are not there, the Squadron will be again off Cadiz by the end of June – in short, before the Enemy can know where I am gone to; and then I shall proceed immediately to England, leaving such a force as the Service requires; and as the Board will know where the Enemy are, I shall hope to receive their orders off Cape St. Vincent, should I return, from their not being in the West Indies. I shall trouble you with a few letters, and be assured that I am, my dear Sir, your most faithful and obliged, humble servant,

Nelson and Brontë.

And so on 12 May 1805, having picked up his convoy of ships, Nelson gave the order to bear away to the West Indies. So much for the doctor's orders. He was on his own admission, in a letter dated 10 May to his friend Rear Admiral George Campbell,[3] worn to a skeleton by disappointment. That was an understatement. As he told Campbell, 'I am, in good truth, very, very far from well'. Campbell, though a rear admiral, was in the Portuguese naval service. It was he who gave Nelson the best assessment, the one that almost convinced him that the French had sailed west. Nelson was grateful. The Portuguese were not. Shortly before the Battle of Trafalgar, Nelson heard that the fact that Campbell had gone aboard the *Victory* that May had cost him his Mediterranean command. The importance of this lies not so much in the hard-luck story of Campbell as in the reminder that just as soldiers could be found commanding the regiments and brigades of continental armies, so a naval officer might be found employed in a foreign fleet. It was sometimes the case that this was the only job available. Thanks to Campbell's advice, Nelson's first stop would be Barbados, not Ushant.

Nelson was no hypochondriac. He did, however, let it be known that he was ill. Among the bundle of letters he wrote from *Victory* off Cape St Vincent that May before departure, was one to Addington, Viscount Sidmouth. It speaks of his personal condition but, more importantly, of

---

[3] Rear Admiral George Campbell (*c.*1762–1821).

his determination not to relinquish his desire to send Villeneuve and the French to the bottom of whichever ocean he found them in.

> My dear Lord
> ... not withstanding my very, very indifferent state of health ... and my leave of absence to go to England, I cannot forego the desire of getting, if possible, at the Enemy; and, therefore, I this day steer for the West Indies. My lot seems to have been hard, and the Enemy most fortunate; but it may turn, – patience and perseverance will do much ...
> ... I shall see you very soon, and, I hope, a Victor; that it shall be so, nothing shall be wanting on the part of, my dear Lord, your most faithful friend,
> Nelson and Brontë.

Even here, with his focus apparently to the west, we have another instance of the commander having to think broadly about his own fleet and those left behind.

Some ships and convoys of transports were remaining in the area. A junior admiral, Knight, was moving on to Gibraltar. Nelson was immediately concerned that the flag officer should be up to speed with his own thinking on the pilotage into Gibraltar and also on the danger of being picked off by pirates. So, on 11 May, *Victory*, shortly after breakfast, was weighing anchor under her staysails and jib. To give some idea of the time all these sail settings took in relatively calm conditions, it was not until nearly one and a half hours later that the topsails and foresails could be set and not until noon that the squadron of Nelson's ships were able to form up in company. That afternoon at about four o'clock, Rear Admiral Knight, in his flagship *Queen*, saluted the departing squadron. Nelson made sure that his letter to Knight was taken across to the *Queen* at that point. He told him not to go too close to the land along the stretch between Cadiz and Cape Trafalgar, but to go wide before turning on a run into the Strait of Gibraltar. Most importantly, he had to keep in the middle of the Strait – known as the Gut – until Gibraltar was bearing north-north-west. The reason for keeping in the middle of the Gut was that Nelson knew that privateers standing just offshore would try to attack the transport ships. He took it further, pointing out that Knight and his warships should act as proper shepherds for those transports. None of them was as manoeuvrable or capable as the warships. Therefore Nelson told Knight in his letter that he should not let any of his vessels anchor safely in Gibraltar until he knew for certain that all the transports were safely in harbour. Any stragglers would be easily attacked, boarded and plundered. The fact that Nelson, with everything else that was going on in his mind, should have taken the time to warn Knight tells us two things: first the enormous attention to detail and concern he gave every aspect of his command and those on its fringe and, second, that he perhaps knew Knight was not that familiar with the waters and the procedures. Nelson left nothing to chance in spite of the fact that so many of his armchair critics – and not a few at sea – believed he took too many chances.

CHAPTER EIGHTEEN

Wrong Signals

THE MAJORITY OF THOSE WARY OF NELSON'S PLANS TO FOLLOW Villeneuve did not even know he had gone. Fortunately, there was no great incident that would rebound on Nelson. The Atlantic crossing was uneventful and Nelson sailed into Carlisle Bay, Barbados on 4 June, little more than three weeks after leaving Cape St Vincent. Not until the day before he arrived did he receive news confirming that the Combined Fleet of Gravina and Villeneuve was indeed sailing in West Indian waters. One of his vessels, HMS *Amphion*, intercepted a merchantman who claimed to have seen the French. The use of intercepts was one of the most reliable forms of intelligence-gathering for a commander. Local information might be gathered in a port. However, this could often be inaccurate and sometimes deliberately misleading. Meeting a merchant ship was useful because often the master felt an incentive to tell what he knew and could be quizzed intelligently. A merchant skipper might well judge it best to hand on information rather than to risk retaliation, either then or at a later date. Furthermore, one of Nelson's captains would speak the same language as the merchant master. The merchant skipper would be able to tell him not only where he had seen the French but also when.

A merchant seaman's eye would have been able to judge the direction the French and Spanish were taking. He would have known the speed they were making. Because he could tell his interrogator the numbers of ships and their different sizes, the naval officer might judge if the flagship was keeping a course and speed for the benefit of the slowest vessel. The merchantman would also have known what sails had been set, what condition those sails were in, and what the weather conditions were at the time. This would have told the naval officer something about the state of the enemy fleet and its efficiency, and by judging the sails set and the weather he might have hazarded a guess as to whether the enemy was cruising, making an easy passage or making all speed. The merchant vessel might well have observed the fleet for some hours and thus gained a reasonable idea of whether it had been standing on its course. As long as the naval officer had been able to establish where the cargo ship had been when the enemy was seen, he would probably have been able to use his knowledge of the tides and wind conditions at the time to make a reasonable guess at the enemy's destination. So from this we can see that from a simple questioning of a passing vessel a good deal of intelligence could be gathered and even a battle plan drawn up. Also, if Nelson knew that Villeneuve had left with seventeen ships under his command and that the merchantman had counted more or less the same number, he would then know the whole fleet was on the move. If, however, the merchant master counted, say, nine vessels and all of them French, Nelson and his officers would conclude that the fleet had split. The reason for doing so could not be assumed. However, it would only take a second merchant skipper to say that he had seen, let us say, eight other French and Spanish ships elsewhere for a pattern to emerge. Moreover, Nelson knew which islands were friendly to the French and Spanish, and so by noting the course, speed and weather plus when the ships were seen might even have allowed him to pinpoint or at least narrow down the likely destination.

Equally, Villeneuve's ships were also interrogating merchant vessels. It is quite possible that within a couple of days of *Victory* arriving in the West Indies the French admiral or his agents would have known of the event. Thus for Nelson, that first sighting by *Amphion* at just after eight in the morning of 3 June 1805 must have been the most important piece of intelligence of all. He knew that the French were in the West Indies. They possibly did not know he was there, although he had to make the assumption that they knew he was on the way.

By 4 June 1805, Nelson had met up with HMS *Northumberland,* the flagship of Rear Admiral Cochrane. Cochrane and his squadron had, since the previous spring, been patrolling the waters off El Ferrol and La Coruña. A few weeks earlier, he had been ordered to Jamaica. Cochrane also had information from British officials in the islands. His general impression, put together with Nelson's outline intelligence, suggested that the French were sailing for Trinidad and Tobago. While still in Carlisle Bay, Nelson embarked 2,000 British troops, nominally under the commander-in-chief in the Leeward Islands, Lieutenant General Sir William Myers.[1] Myers was not to see the summer out. He died in July 1805.

Yet again, we have an occasion when Nelson is either obliged or chooses to get involved with the apparently minute detail of domestic arrangements within his fleet. He definitely wanted the 2,000 troops Myers was offering. But what did the captains of his ships do with that number of troops? Where could they put them? Who, for example, was going to pay for their food? Should they have less food than the sailors? If so, where was that food going to come from? If there was less food for a soldier, what would be missing and who should decide? This was petty bureaucracy at work. The consequences could easily be enormous. Nelson understood immediately that instructions had to come from the top. He, Nelson, was the top. He immediately, on 5 June, sent a signal to Captain Hardy,[2] the captain of his own ship the *Victory*, and to the captains of the other vessels involved, *Belleisle, Canopus, Conqueror, Donegal, Leviathan, Spartiate, Spencer, Superb, Swiftsure* and *Tigre*. They were instructed, but not without first receiving an explanation. Nelson always took his captains into his confidence. They would rarely have a signal to do something without him telling them why. He told the captains – being perhaps sensitive to their feelings towards the army – that the reason 2,000 soldiers were coming on board was to frustrate the French intentions of plundering the British Leeward Islands. He then told them that the soldiers had been given very short marching orders, were tired and were embarking on a dangerous mission. Therefore it was up to the navy to make them as comfortable as possible and give them the same food and conditions as the sailors. This was not simply good command. Nelson

---

[1] Lieutenant General Sir William Myers (?–1803).
[2] Captain Thomas Masterman Hardy (1769–1839).

knew the frustrations of the pursers on board and that they would need to enter that kind of high authority in their records in order to account for the extra expenditure to a distant victualling agent and the Admiralty. In Nelson's mind, attention to detail and consideration towards those expected to fight alongside made victory more likely.

Having dealt with the matter of the feeding and the watering of 2,000 extra men, Nelson and his captains started their search of the islands for Villeneuve. From Carlisle Bay his squadron sailed south, fetching off Tobago in the early evening of 6 June. That same evening, the *Victory* picked up intelligence from a schooner which suggested the Combined Fleet of French and Spanish was at Trinidad. It might be remembered that part of Villeneuve's orders was to wreak havoc among the British possessions.

The schooner had got its signals mixed up, but at that stage Nelson did not know this. Moreover, on that same day, 6 June, the master of an American brig told one of Nelson's boarding parties that he had been intercepted by the French fleet off Grenada and that the fleet was on course for Bocaz da Trinidada. Excited by this news, Nelson's squadron headed for Trinidad and the Bay of Paria. There was no enemy. A further confusion was that information coming from St Lucia that the combined squadron of French and Spanish had been sighted to windward was also likely to be misinformation. Also, it was necessary to distinguish between the major Franco-Spanish fleet and another squadron. Such was the difficulty in assessing whether or not intelligence was accurate. If this seems unlikely, it might be remembered that, no matter how sophisticated the intelligence sources, assessment remained – and remains – the most difficult part of producing a proper picture. We have only to look at one signal sent by Nelson to William Marsden to understand the frustration behind the former's search. He told Marsden, in a letter dated 11 June 1805, that off Tobago he had learned about the American brig supposedly being boarded by a French boat crew from the Combined Fleet. More accurately, the boarding had taken place off St Vincent Island. That would have been on 3 June 1805. According to the master of the brig, the French were heading south.

The second piece of confusing information came that evening. A signal from a schooner suggested that the French were at Trinidada.

On 8 June, Nelson had information from one of the West Indies-based captains, J. W. Maurice, that the French were planning to attack Grenada and Dominica.

The following noon, 9 June, Nelson arrived in St George's Bay, Grenada. The governor of that island was Lieutenant General the Honourable Sir Thomas Maitland.[3] He told Nelson that the French had most certainly not been there. He believed his island to be safe along with the islands of St Vincent and St Lucia. In fact, he believed, the French were still in Martinique.

An hour later on the same day, one of his fast 'messenger' ships, the *Jason*, arrived with the apparent news that eighteen ships of the line, six frigates and three brigs and schooners had been spotted flying the French and Spanish flags, heading northwards. What was Nelson to think? He did not have a clue. Most likely, if the latter report were true, the French were heading to attack Antigua or St Kitts. Equally, such a course would have been made by a squadron planning to pick up the Gulf Stream to go home to Europe.

On the morning of 12 June, the *Victory* anchored off St John's, Antigua. No French. No Spanish. There was a report that the French had been seen heading for Antigua. They did not get there. The best information was that the French had passed by Antigua, heading northwards. This chasing of the stern light of Villeneuve's squadron may have seemed, on the face of it, a fruitless expedition. It was not. The very presence of Nelson's fleet made Villeneuve even more jumpy than usual and he was never able to fulfil his emperor's instructions to plunder British possessions. This was no unimportant factor. Simply by being there Nelson had probably saved dozens (he thought, more than 200) of Britain-bound ships laden with their precious cargo of sugar.[4]

---

[3] Lieutenant General Sir Thomas Maitland (1761–1824).

[4] The First British Empire in the Americas and the West Indies was established because the original planters from the late seventeenth century onwards had established sugar plantations there. The enormous demand in Europe for refined cane sugar became a cornerstone of the financial returns that paid for the early decade of the Empire. In 1805, long after the American colonies had gone, the British sugar islands' produce was still a crucial part of the corporate profits within the Empire, especially at a time when Pitt was desperate to find funds for the Napoleonic War.

Imagine Nelson's frustration. From the time of his arrival in the West Indies, he was never much more than a day's sail from Villeneuve's fleet. He needed to find the French admiral to justify being there. Nelson had sailed out of the Mediterranean, all but defying his masters in London to tell him to stay put. What he needed, therefore, was a big battle. He needed another Nile, and was probably never much more than eighteen to twenty-four hours away from creating one. Nelson had worked out that had he not been given false information, either through deliberate misleading or a wrong assessment by his own people, he would probably have met up with Villeneuve off Dominica, ironically in the waters where his hero, Rodney,[5] had beaten the French in 1782 (see chapter 22).

While we can commiserate with those whose task it was to provide information from such sketchy and quickly moving pictures, we might also commiserate with Nelson because he could not always trust those who should have known better. One such person was the commander of the island of St Lucia, Brigadier General Robert Brereton.[6]

It was Brereton who had told Nelson that he had sighted the French off his island. However, he had added the crucial piece of misinformation that Villeneuve had been sailing south to Trinidad when in fact he had been going north to Martinique. Nelson had no reason to doubt Brereton. After all, they were on the same side and he was an experienced officer. It was Nelson's view that it would have been better if Brereton's lookout had been looking the other way and had missed the French fleet. It may, of course, have been that the general was being slightly misleading because he wanted to keep Nelson and his fleet in the West Indies as protection. In fact, when it came to making the decision to leave, there were many islanders, especially governors like Brereton and the settlers, who were not at all happy. They felt vulnerable. Indeed, Nelson, in his reports to London, made a great deal of the fact that he had waited in the West Indies until the passage of sugar ships seemed free. Nevertheless, he believed Brereton had denied him the opportunity for a victory on 6 June 1805, that had he trusted his own instincts rather than Brereton's

---

[5] George Brydges Rodney, first Baron (1719–1792).
[6] Robert Brereton (?–1818).

report victory would have been his. Nelson was to write to Emma that he would hate the name Brereton for as long as he lived.[7]

Villeneuve certainly had orders as to what he should be doing in the West Indies. Yet in his actions there seemed little purpose other than to avoid Nelson. What he most wanted was the arrival in the West Indies of the whole of the Brest fleet of twenty-one ships to add to his own squadrons. With those sort of odds, Villeneuve felt more confident, especially as he might then be able to hand over command and – as he had done at the Battle of the Nile – keep out the way. Vice Admiral Villeneuve never did see much point in soiling his linen with the anxieties of naval warfare.

So he waited for the arrival of Ganteaume and his squadrons. Villeneuve had arrived in the harbour at Martinique on 16 May 1805. He felt reasonably comfortable in the natural harbour defences, with the French artillery batteries ranged on shore and pointing out to sea. Equally, Villeneuve was mindful of the circumstances of the Battles of Copenhagen and the Nile, when the defending fleets had also felt reassured by their surroundings, only to be destroyed by Nelson's tactical appreciation and execution.

Villeneuve was formally very welcome in Martinique, a French possession. The captain general of the Island was a distinctly grumpy French vice admiral with the rather contradictory name of Villaret de Joyeuse.[8] Although only in his late fifties, Villaret de Joyeuse had something of the stompy old sea dog about him and thought the new generation of Napoleon's admirals fools for the most part and inept for the other. He could not for the life of him understand why Villeneuve should not have been sailing with supplies for other French garrisons and, when that was done, attacking British shoreside stations. He never did suspect that, instead of doing the captain general's wishes, Villeneuve was writing letters of desperation to Decrès in Paris asking for news of Ganteaume. Villeneuve was caught between his orders to wait for Ganteaume until 22 June before returning to Europe and dodging the

---

[7] For more on this, see the Lady Llangattock Collection in the Nelson Museum at Monmouth.
[8] Louis Villaret de Joyeuse (1748–1812).

exhortations of Villaret de Joyeuse. Of course, when he arrived in May, Villeneuve was still acting under the orders he had received two months earlier. In that plan, Napoleon had said: go to the West Indies, wait for Ganteaume and do nothing else. But Napoleon had had one of his frequent mind changes. He decided that Villeneuve should do exactly what the captain general of Martinique wanted him to do. He had issued the new orders to Villeneuve at the end of the second week in April. Villeneuve had then been at sea. It was not until six weeks later, on 30 May, that Napoleon's new orders caught up with the admiral. Here was the instruction to reinforce the French garrisons, attack British settlements and – on the assumption that Ganteaume had not reached him in time – sail for El Ferrol, pick up reinforcements of at least fifteen vessels, sail north to Brest, rendezvous with Ganteaume, who would assume overall command, and then proceed to the invasion fleet rendezvous off Boulogne and stand by to bash the British.

Vice Admiral Villeneuve wanted to go home. However, under the direction of Captain General Villaret de Joyeuse, he became quite military and attacked a rock. In fact, the rock contained a British force. It was called locally Diamond Rock and, by the Royal Navy, HMS *Diamond*. The significance of HMS *Diamond* was that it was a geophysical accident sitting just off the main harbour, Fort Royal, of Martinique, inside which Villeneuve's fleet was sheltering. For three days the 128 British sailors who manned the rock HMS *Diamond* fought against the clearly overwhelming odds under Villeneuve's command. Villeneuve and Villaret de Joyeuse felt rather pleased about this victory, which was, sadly, a terrible surrender on the part of the commander of the rock, Captain J. W. Maurice. When, on 6 June, Nelson heard about the surrender that had taken place four days earlier, he immediately realized the need to praise Maurice and his men, rather than to castigate them. He wrote personally to Maurice and copied his letter to the Admiralty, saying that he perfectly understood the circumstances, that he was in no doubt that Maurice and his men had acted in the highest tradition of the service and that Maurice should be personally congratulated for having been able to hold out for such a long time and, particularly, with so few casualties.

Villeneuve, realizing how bad a commander he probably looked because of his previous inactivity, now made certain that Decrès in Paris understood that he was full of enthusiasm, especially as the best intelligence from home suggested that Nelson was still wandering somewhere off Egypt and that only an inferior squadron of Cochrane's was in Villeneuve's area. So Villeneuve did not immediately know of Nelson's arrival in the islands.

Villeneuve also committed to paper remarks that amounted to a typical act of ineffectual duplicity. He had been quite happy under the protection of the Fort Royal guns. His nervousness, which the captain general put down partly to his need to get on with the war, had in fact more to do with the possible arrival of Nelson. Now that Villeneuve had his orders to attack the British in specific island locations as well as wherever he found them, it might have been expected that he would use that nervous energy to good effect. Not so. Villeneuve wrote to Decrès saying that all the time he had been sitting in the safety of the harbour in Martinique he had felt frustrated at being unable to go into action. Those in Paris could have no idea of how much he, Villeneuve, such a splendid officer, wanted to get among those British. Now he had new orders. He was absolutely delighted to learn that between getting those orders and the three weeks he was obliged to wait for Ganteaume's arrival, he could go into action. However, he was sure that Decrès understood that it would take ages to get the right stores on board and the right supplies positioned before he could actually manoeuvre his ships into enemy range. In other words, there was no way Villeneuve was going to run out any guns in anger other than for his own defence. The capitulation of Diamond Rock was, then, about his level.

Rear Admiral Magon arrived on 4 June with two big ships of the line to reinforce Villeneuve. Villeneuve now had twenty ships of the line. So, three weeks after arriving in Fort Royal (or Fort de France, as the French had renamed it), Villeneuve's fleet weighed anchor for Guadeloupe to pick up extra soldiers, bringing his total complement of troops to more than 14,500. He picked up 700 more in Guadeloupe and then headed north to Antigua, which was British. It is still a mystery why he took that northerly route. He said it was because he wanted to land soldiers in the islands between Antigua and Montserrat. His voyage was interrupted by a lucrative prize. A convoy of more than a dozen British merchantmen, carrying coffee and rum for England, were easy pickings for this

'The Hero of the Nile' –
a caricature of Nelson.

The Battle of Copenhagen, 1801,
during which Nelson is supposed
to have raised his telescope to his
blind eye.

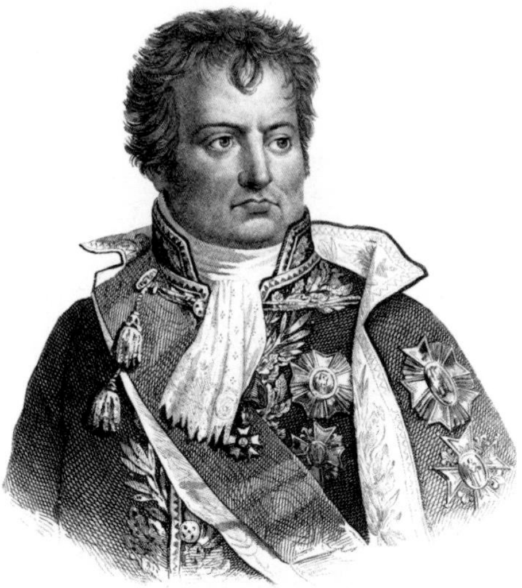

Denis Decrès – Napoleon's navy minister and Villeneuve's last friend.

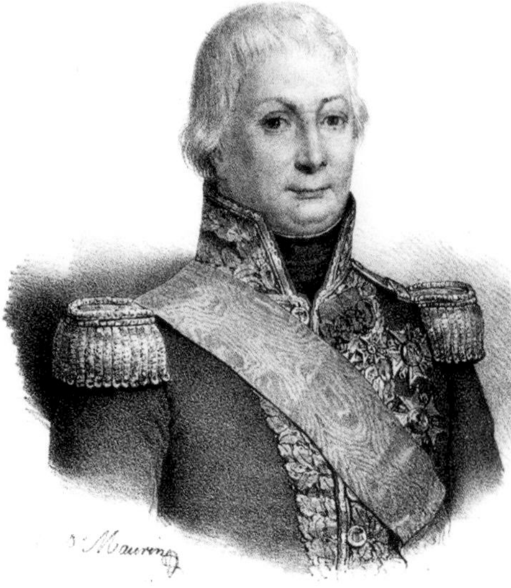

Admiral Honoré Ganteaume, a fine French admiral who commanded the Brest fleet 1804–1805.

Napoleon reviews progress of Boulogne invasion harbour, 1804.

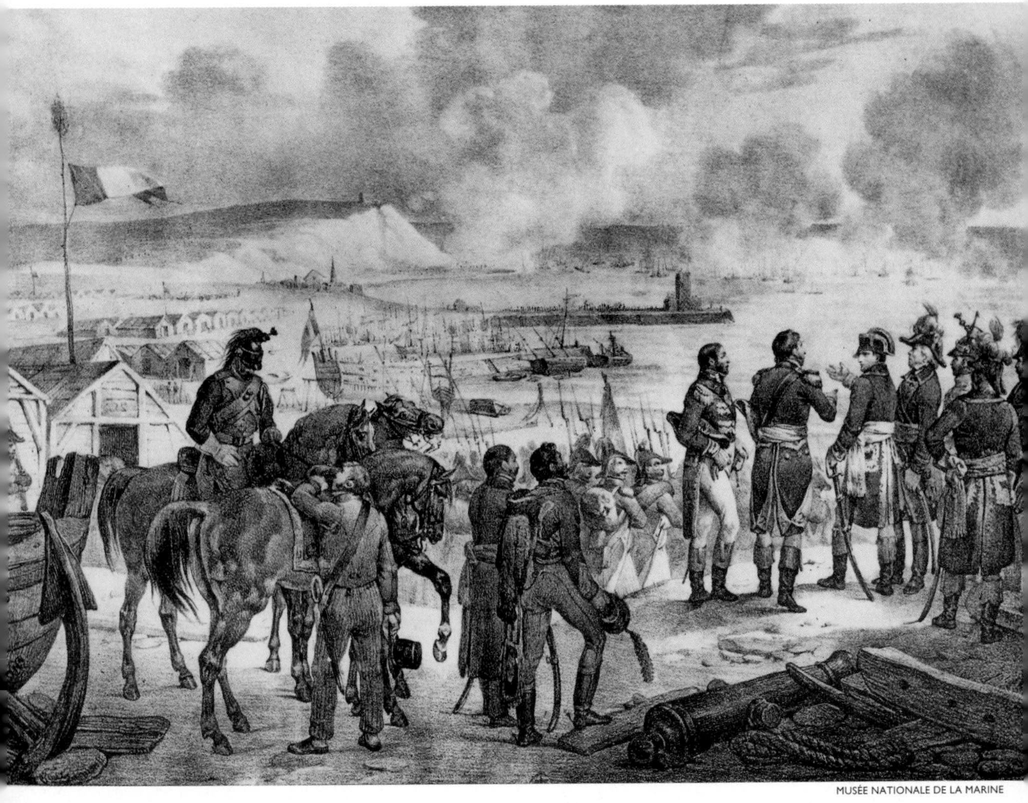

MUSÉE NATIONALE DE LA MARINE

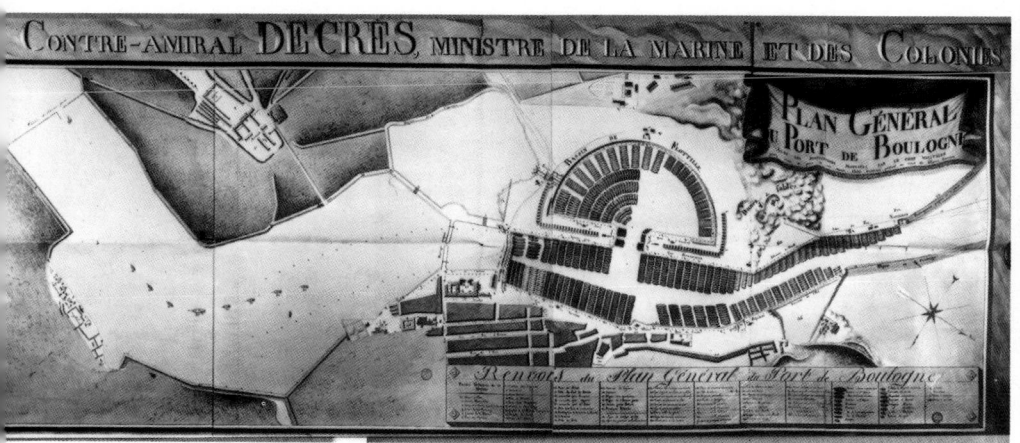

Plan of Napoleon's invasion harbour at Boulogne in 1804. Before this, Boulogne was a silted fishing port.

Designs for the French invasion fleet based at Boulogne. The instructions were Napoleon's. They were ill conceived because he had no knowledge of vessels.

MUSÉE NATIONALE DE LA MARINE

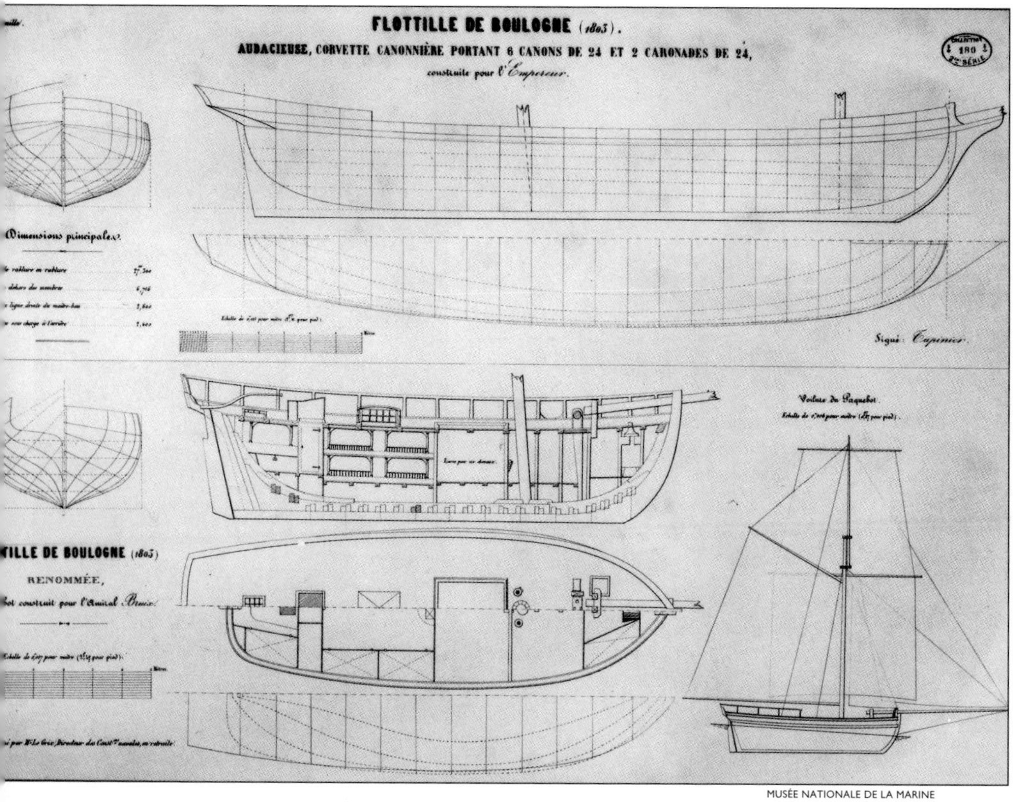

John Jervis, Earl of St Vincent, the scratchy First Sea Lord and the man who restructured the navy. An admirer of Nelson, but also a critic.

Vice-Admiral Sir Robert Calder who failed to finish Villeneuve's fleet in July 1805. Had he done so, there would never have been a Battle of Trafalgar.

Admiral Sir William Cornwallis whose ships blockaded the French fleet in Brest for two years. His heroic and determined seamanship – and not Nelson's – was the biggest single reason for Napoleon abandoning his invasion plan.

Sir Robert Calder.

ADMIRAL CORNWALLIS

Henry Dundas, 1st Viscount Melville. Melville was First Lord of the Admiralty for eleven months until April 1805 when he was accused of 'gross malversation' during his previous job as treasurer.

William Pitt the Younger returned as prime minister to fight the war in 1804. He died in 1806.

NATIONAL MARITIME MUSEUM

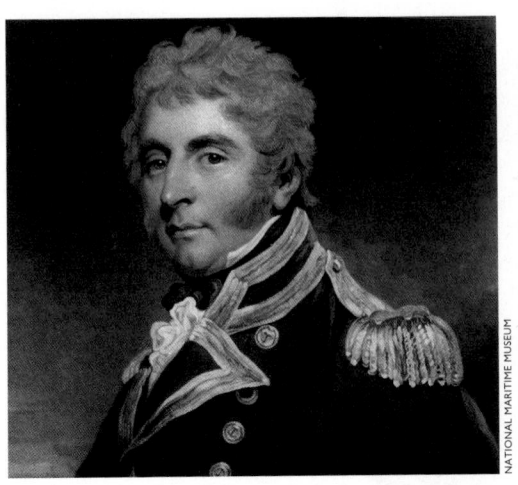

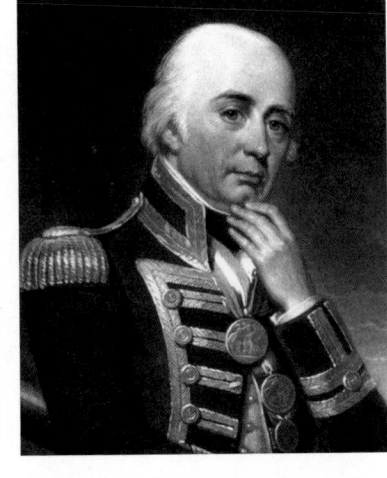

Captain Henry Blackwood of the *Euryalus*, one of Nelson's best captains, who failed to persuade his admiral to move to a smaller vessel and out of danger.

NATIONAL MARITIME MUSEUM

Vice-Admiral Lord Collingwood took over command after Nelson's death.

Trafalgar. It started around noon. It finished by 5.45 pm with the explosion aboard the French ship *Achilles*.

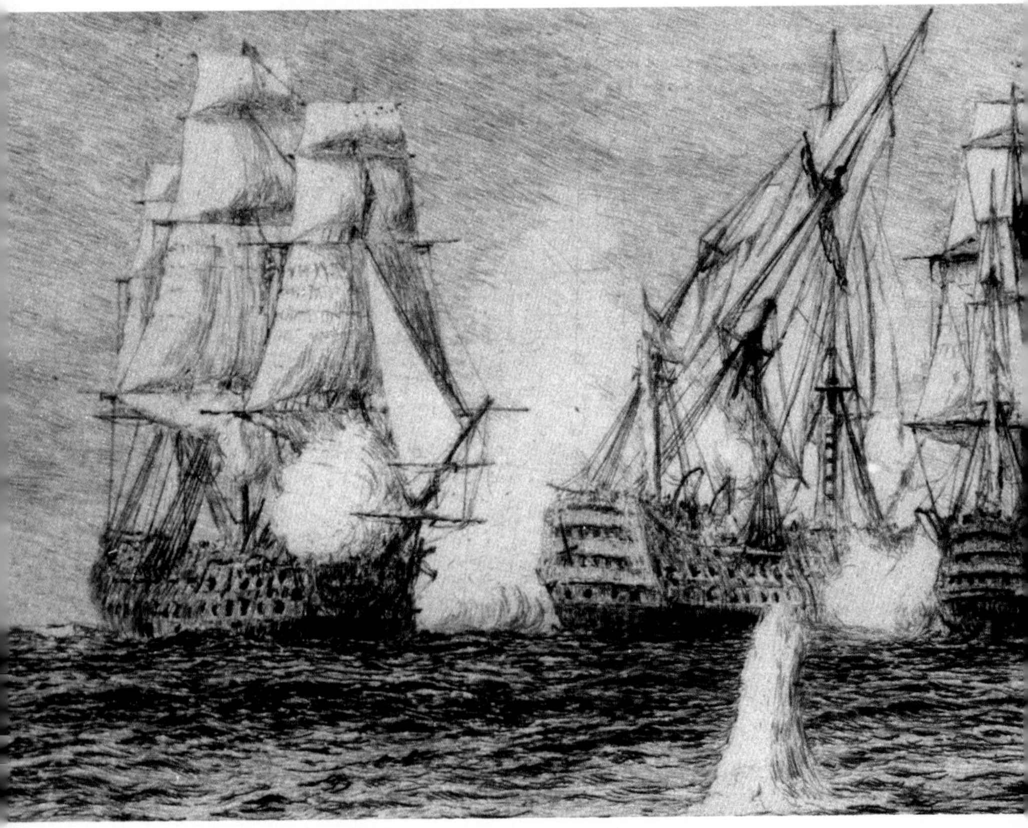

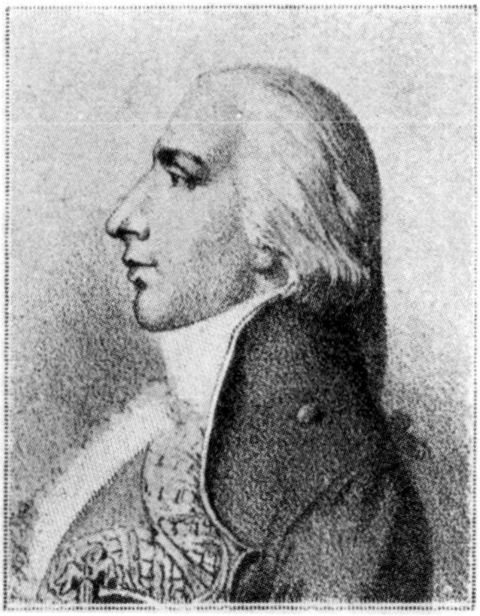

MUSÉE NATIONALE DE LA MARINE

Admiral Federico Gravina, deputy commander of the combined French and Spanish fleet and a much better naval officer than Villeneuve. He died of his wounds.

RÉUNION DES MUSÉES NATIONAUX

Charles René Magon criticised Villeneuve for running away from Nelson. He was killed aboard his flagship during the Battle of Trafalgar.

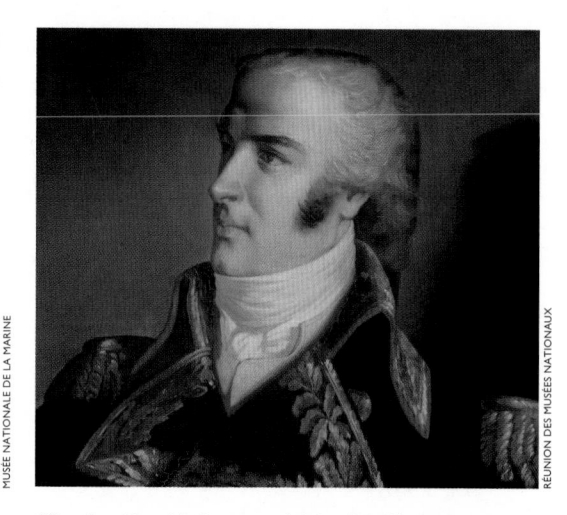

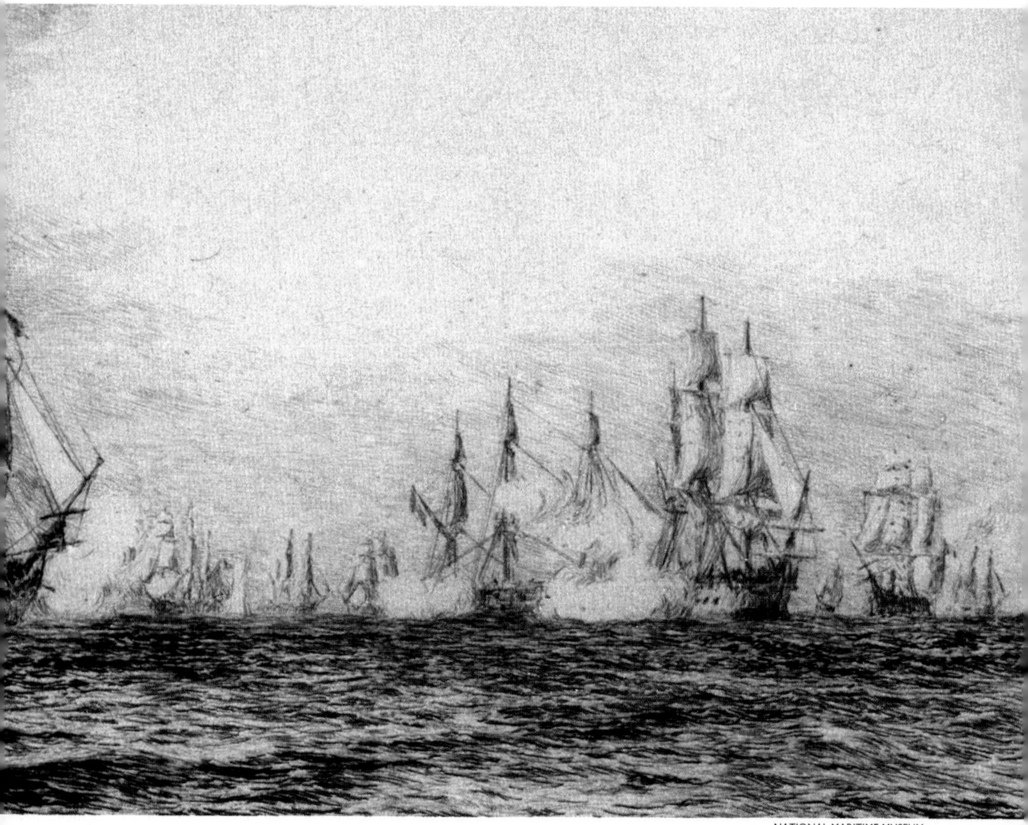

NATIONAL MARITIME MUSEUM

RÉUNION DES MUSÉES NATIONAUX

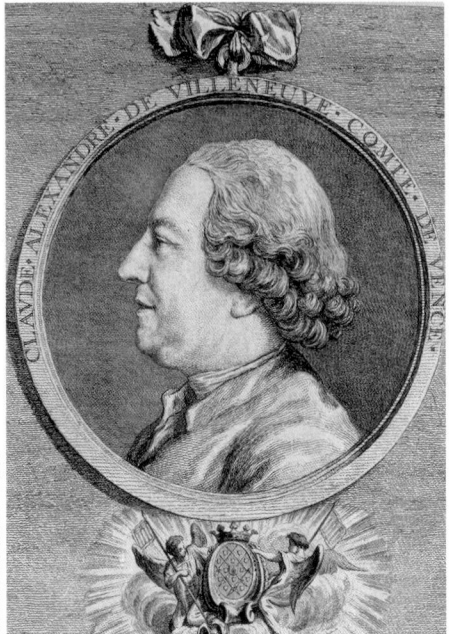

Admiral Villeneuve never wanted to be a fighting admiral. Found stabbed to death in 1806, some said he was assassinated, others said it was suicide.

The funeral flotilla off Greenwich, where Nelson's body had lain before being taken to St Paul's.

ROYAL NAVAL MUSEUM

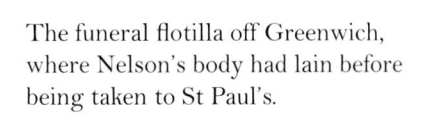

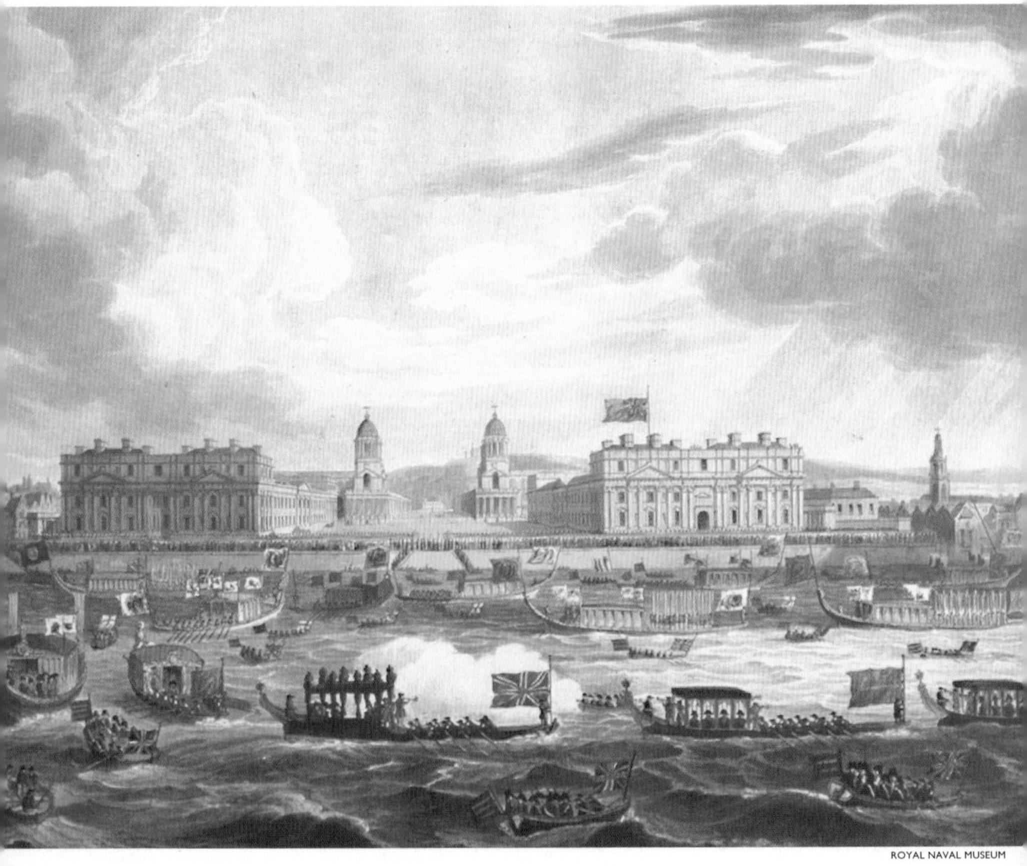

Combined Fleet. The cargoes were worth millions of francs. He got more than coffee and rum.

The British merchant sailors told him that Nelson was in Barbados and that Cochrane's squadron had joined him. Villeneuve – to be kind to his reputation for a moment – was faced with a dilemma. We might say that it was one Nelson would have relished. Villeneuve's best guess, considering the easterly winds, meant that if he tried to return to Martinique it would certainly take him more than a week to get there. It could even be two weeks. Apart from his sailors, he had soldiers on board, which he saw as a burden. The ships were in poor health and so were his men, which is puzzling considering the time they had spent in the harbour at Martinique until just a few days earlier. It is also doubtful what he would be able to do by returning, which was an instinct to be followed because, first and foremost, it was a good refuge and had shore artillery and, secondly, because it was the area in which he was to wait for Ganteaume. It is doubtful, however, that the facilities at Fort de France were good enough to supply the increased fleet and extra soldiers Villeneuve had picked up on his short cruise. A further dilemma for him, about which he was quite open, was that by going back to Martinique he could well find himself engaged by Nelson.

Within a couple of days, with the word spreading that Nelson was in the West Indies, Villeneuve decided to go. He had sailed all the way from Europe with more than 12,400 soldiers on board. He was bringing them with orders to land them as a guard force for the French possessions. So desperate was he to quit the same longitude as Nelson that he decided not to land the troops because sailing close to the islands might well mean that he would be spotted by either Nelson or his frigate lookouts.

Nelson was determined to have Villeneuve. Villeneuve knew this. Napoleon had told his admiral to stay in the West Indies for thirty-five days and to meet up with Ganteaume. However huge a figure Napoleon was in the mind of Villeneuve, he was far more afraid of Nelson than he was of his emperor. He had no confidence in his own ability as an admiral. He had little confidence in his fleet. He had every confidence that the one-armed Nelson would be able to beat him with one eye closed. So what did Villeneuve do? He piled on as much sail as his spars could carry and made a run for it across the Atlantic to what he idiotically thought of as safety. If the British admiral, Calder, had been worth his flag, that should have been the end of Villeneuve as he approached the coastline of continental Europe. Calder had let him off the hook.

Nelson, once convinced that Villeneuve had skipped the West Indies, set sail after him. He actually believed that he could probably catch him in the Atlantic. What Nelson did not know was that Villeneuve was on the more northerly course while he was heading in the direction of the southern European coastline. On 12 June, he wrote to his friend the Duke of Clarence, the future William IV, that he was heading back. It was to Clarence that Nelson expressed his anguish at not finding Villeneuve. His heart, he wrote, was 'almost broke'. He was also partly referring to his medical condition. Nelson was utterly exhausted. So was his fleet. Since leaving, it had sailed about 3,500 miles. Except for brief moments, none of his men had been ashore. They had never stayed anywhere long enough to store up, as any other ship – certainly a fleet – would have done on an Atlantic crossing. None in the fleet had slept much more than a couple of hours at a time.

Nelson had mixed feelings about missing Villeneuve. It would appear from letters and also briefings to his captains that he felt instinctively that it would have been far better had he found the French admiral and destroyed his Combined Fleet. Even given the state of Nelson's ships and men, which had been under considerable stress for months, it is unlikely that the French and Spanish would have been successful in battle against him; after all, they too were far from fighting fettle. However, a second thought running through Nelson's mind was that he had effectively driven Villeneuve from the West Indies. In doing so he had done the British West Indies possessions a considerable favour. He had removed from the area a very real threat to the settlers and their economic survival. His reference to some 200 sugar ships gives some indication of the volume of trade in and out of the archipelago on a monthly basis. For the empire to survive it had to be economically successful. For Pitt's war effort to survive it had to be able to draw on finances resulting from that economic success.

It is not unusual to come across a politician making a speech to one audience while addressing its content to another. So it was in 1805. Nelson was able to bemoan the loss of the opportunity of getting to grips with Villeneuve and thus being applauded for his heroism while at the same time defending the ability of his captains and ships' companies. This last point is not insignificant. To keep ships at sea for a couple of years, with the men living in difficult circumstances and the officers itching for prizes and some glory that would advance their careers, needed constant pep talks from Nelson, and keeping ships and men at peak battle fitness was a big problem. His letters to senior officials, the future king and the First Sea Lord had most certainly to show that he had been very close to coming face to face with Villeneuve. His other letters, saying what a good thing it was that he had chased Villeneuve from the West Indies, thus protecting that bit of the empire, were also aimed at those in authority over him. He still needed to justify that lengthy voyage and also to further demonstrate to his own men that the operation could be construed as successful.

The weakness in this argument (which Nelson did not touch upon) was that he may have driven Villeneuve from the West Indies, but the Frenchman was now approaching the one place Nelson was not – European waters. Supposing Villeneuve and Gravina attempted a quick, decisive action against an unsuspecting British fleet in those waters? The reinforcements from the western Mediterranean that a senior admiral would normally expect to call upon were not there. They were just leaving the West Indies, with their admiral putting the blame on a soldier called Brereton for having fouled things up.

As it happened, Villeneuve was about to engage the British, or at least be engaged by them. Nelson could not be blamed for the fact that Villeneuve had got away from the British. He might, however, take some of the blame for Villeneuve's having got that far. If he were stage-managing his own glorious end in the coming October, he could not have written a better script than that which was played out between April, when Villeneuve escaped from the Mediterranean, and July, when he escaped from Calder, and September and October when, once again, Villeneuve was sighted in a battle formation.

Nelson had reached, on 8 July 1805, the Atlantic rendezvous off southern Spain. It was here that he met up with Collingwood. Two days later, Nelson was in Gibraltar and preparing to return to England. He was exhausted, and it was at this point that he wrote the rather sad letter to

Marsden remarking that he was as miserable as his greatest enemy could wish him to be. He sailed across to what today is Spanish Ceuta, and it was there that he heard the latest on Villeneuve. The news that the Frenchman had been seen on a northerly course to Europe only now reached him. The scent of a quarry makes for good adrenalin. Nelson once more put to sea, turning west to get into the Atlantic and north to get at Villeneuve. The winds once more frustrated his ambition. They were for days on end the most infuriating for all sailors: they were light and variable. He could have done with a good south-easterly. Instead, his sailing masters were confronted with flappers from every direction which left the vessels becalmed or totally reliant on currents once through the Strait.

Nelson had already written to Cornwallis, who was back at sea saying that he had heard Villeneuve was on the move and that he hoped desperately that he could get north in time to engage him. He did not say so but, even with his sense of disappointment, he could not bring himself to believe that anybody but he would have the right – not even the fortune, but the right – to force Villeneuve to strike his colours.

Once more, through all the excitements, disappointments and determination of his own spirit and of his men we find Nelson having also to concern himself with details. On 21 July 1805 he was writing to the shore admiral asking for transport for 3,000 pounds of onions. Otherwise there would be no onion soup for the sailors. Nelson even had to bother himself about who was going to pay and how much. He mentioned in a formal letter that he had heard that for the amount of onions in question the pursers would need two pence halfpenny a pound. To another captain, Henry Bayntun[9] (who would be the captain of the *Leviathan* at Trafalgar), he wrote on 21 July requesting him to get some bullocks for the ships. The next day he was dealing with the paperwork connected with the recent capture of two American cargo ships. The ships' masters had lodged a formal complaint. Even in 1805 reports had to be written, cases made and reams of documents forwarded to the Admiralty, including these formal complaints from the Americans. On that very day, 22 July, if he had known what was going on further north, Nelson would not have been interested in bureaucracy. Calder had spotted Villeneuve.

---

[9] Henry William Bayntun (1766–1840).

CHAPTER NINETEEN

The Victory That Never Was

NAPOLEON HAD MANY FLAWS. HIGHLY POLISHED BOOTS, PRECISELY honed cutlasses and a field marshal's baton in a knapsack easily turned an observer's attention from the fact that the bearer of such trappings is often far less than the sum of his reputation and acquired admiration. Napoleon had many weaknesses. All commanders, including generals, are vulnerable to events which, even though they may have been anticipated, disrupt the finer points of planning. At the start of the nineteenth century, for example, an epidemic passing through a regiment can ruin the most meticulous planning of an army corps. A stumbling horse may lose a general one of his best regimental colonels. Napoleon was as vulnerable as any other commander. His inflated reputation has allowed his record keepers and biographers to sometimes overlook the fact that often he was a poor emperor and an equally poor commander-in-chief. As mentioned elsewhere, his inability to understand naval warfare was an obvious failing. He might be excused for having no faith in his navy because by the early nineteenth century some of his best officers had been cleared out. He was left with the likes of Villeneuve. But when a dictator expects something to happen because he has decreed it will, this might be fine if it is a matter of ordering a good breakfast but not if it concerns the deployment of a poor admiral across 3,000 miles of uncertain ocean in unpredictable weather. Napoleon had said that he expected Villeneuve to be off El Ferrol between 20 July and 29 July. He expected him to be in Boulogne within ten days of 8 August 1805. This

was not unreasonable planning – at first sight. However, when we then
see Napoleon telling Decrès that the Rochefort squadron would sail off
the Irish coast between 4 and 9 July and then stand off El Ferrol for four
days from 29 July, we see a weakness that, surprisingly, remained in
Napoleon's planning. Given the emperor's by now considerable
experience, he should have known that it was impossible to stick to such
a tight timetable given all that could go wrong at sea.

In fact, Villeneuve had had a good voyage across from the West Indies.
He had left the islands north of Guadeloupe around 5 June and, sailing
on a northern track, was off the Azores by 1 July. His crossing had not
gone unnoticed by the British. Again, it was impossible for news to travel
faster than a well-rigged sloop.

The mail ship that had been detached from Nelson's fleet had made out
the Combined Fleet on its starboard horizon. Its captain had the choice
of finding and seeking out Nelson to tell him what he had seen or – as
the navy would have put it – of obeying the last pipe and proceeding
as quickly as possible to Plymouth. The captain decided to obey that last
pipe. On 7 July he arrived in Plymouth Sound, having been driven across
the Atlantic on a brisk westerly. By the early morning of the following
day, the Admiralty had the news from Plymouth that Villeneuve appeared
to be heading on that northerly track and therefore not for Cadiz, but
probably for El Ferrol.

Shortly after lunch on 8 July, a fast ship was speeding to Cornwallis's
blockade with instructions for him and his two junior admirals, Stirling[1]
and Calder. Stirling commanded Cornwallis's Rochefort squadron and
Calder that of El Ferrol. Their instructions now were to put these two
squadrons together under Calder's command. By 15 July, Stirling had
linked up with Calder on the latter's station off El Ferrol. Calder then
ordered a course for a point 100 miles due west of Cape Finisterre.
This was judged to be the likely intercept point should Villeneuve proceed
on his expected course and should the weather conditions remain as
they were.

Small frigates were posted on picket duty in advance of Calder's flotilla
and other smaller vessels between those pickets and Calder. Here, then,

---

[1] Rear Admiral Charles Stirling (1760–1833).

was a line-of-sight signalling system that, in reasonable conditions, could relay news of the enemy in less than an hour. By 16 July, little more than a week after the arrival in Plymouth of Nelson's mail ship, the Royal Navy had assessed the intelligence. The Admiralty sent that assessment with instructions through to the admiral and his commanders. Fifteen ships of the line under Calder were added to Cornwallis's eighteen big-gun ships off Brest. In addition, there were the small squadrons of Collingwood and Bickerton covering Cadiz and the escape route into the Mediterranean and Cartagena.

Also, Villeneuve's rear was not covered but was cut off by Nelson, even though he was totally unaware of what was going on and, anyway, sailing a southern course. The fact that he was also becalmed for much of the crossing did not help his mood. The Admiralty and Cornwallis more or less disregarded Nelson's position. The argument about whether he should have been where he was in the first place was set aside for the moment. Inadvertently, the fact that he had left his post in the Mediterranean to chase Villeneuve across the Atlantic but failed to find him had, as it turned out, worked in favour of the British. If Calder had been a sharper man, the Royal Navy would have had game, set and match over the French fleets – and any thought of invasion – by the third week in July. Without knowing it, Nelson had driven Villeneuve into Calder's arms. However, a wet hog takes some holding.

Napoleon was in the dark. He could not see what Villeneuve was doing and, for the moment, was working on poor information. For example, he had been told that Nelson had arrived in the West Indies on 20 June. This was in fact more than two weeks after Nelson had got there. Napoleon thought Villeneuve would be acting under his earlier orders. It then dawned on him that, in spite of his determination to have precise planning, even he had to accept the eccentricities of naval passage and intelligence-gathering and dispersal. So as late as 16 July, Napoleon was sending instructions to El Ferrol to await Villeneuve's arrival. He was to link up with Gourdon, who commanded the El Ferrol squadron, and then gather to him the Rochefort squadron and, hopefully, ships from Brest, sail up the outside of Ireland, across the top of Scotland, down the North Sea and 'gain command of the Straits of Dover' (see chart page xiv). If all else failed, Napoleon recognized that Villeneuve might go to Cadiz.

Why go to Cadiz? The only logical reason would be failure to gather the Brest squadron and that would make the defence of the Boulogne operation well-nigh impossible. If he had not done so beforehand, Napoleon decided to abandon what he called the final eclipse of Britain and therefore have his second most important squadron for the moment in Cadiz. For anything else Napoleon had in mind for the French Navy, an action off the Spanish coast would seem most likely. He needed the Combined Fleet with Spain, as almost all the British fleets were either in the Atlantic or the Channel. The Mediterranean squadron was down to a handful of ships and either Decrès or Napoleon, or both, estimated that the possibility of an engagement with a combined and reinforced Cadiz squadron would bring the British ships out of the Middle Sea. In this they were right.

The weather conditions in the Atlantic had changed. The winds that had blown the *Curieux*, Nelson's mail ship, at a good speed had been followed by a depression. The winds had backed and then veered, making headway difficult and, sometimes, altogether impossible when the wind dropped entirely. We might imagine the state of Villeneuve's fleet at this point because it makes Calder's action even more of a missed opportunity.

If we go back, let us say, four months, we find Villeneuve with a motley crew, ill-trained, poorly officered, trying to get out of the Mediterranean. Villeneuve himself wanted to be an admiral – but not this admiral. As he wrote to Napoleon, he would certainly like to be useful, but unfortunately did not see himself as very warlike. Every single person in the fleet knew this. Finally, Villeneuve felt encouraged to write positively to Decrès. Decrès, by then, knew exactly what sort of person they had in command and also understood the highs and lows of that personality. Villeneuve's fleet then made it through the Strait of Gibraltar and round to Cadiz. A small triumph. Yet on 9 April we saw Villeneuve not daring to linger in case Nelson caught up with him, and so fleeing across the Atlantic as fast as the wind would carry him, leaving Gravina – a much better sailor, a better commander and with a better squadron – to catch him up. Once in the West Indies, Villeneuve continued to display a tendency to fear Nelson's arrival. The local French general thought his behaviour odd. When just one report came from captured merchantmen that Nelson was in the islands, what did Villeneuve do? He piled on as much sail as possible to get back to Europe. He even failed to see to the disembarkation of the soldiers he had brought across the Atlantic for the defence of French settlements in the West Indies. Did he think he was safer in European waters? Certainly, Villeneuve knew he would not be safe per se. However, any pride was better faced than Nelson's pack. Now we come back to 22 July 1805. Disillusioned, tired, inept and led by a frightened man who – to be kind – could be described as a realist, the Combined Franco-Spanish Fleet was making little headway towards the imagined safety off El Ferrol when its guard ships reported ahead, late that morning, Calder's reinforced squadron.

The importance of this part of the story is fog or, at least, a July Atlantic mist from the cold sea and a sun which had yet to burn off the haze. This was not quite naval blind man's bluff. There was no indication around noon that day that Villeneuve behaved anything else but correctly. The fact that neither fleet could see the other properly meant that the mist was relatively settled. This tells us that there was very little wind. That being so, it must have been extraordinarily difficult to deploy as a fighting force and manoeuvre into any position that could effectively counter an attack or, from the other side, make one. The adversaries probably did not really know each other's size and gunnery. The best commanders in these circumstances make the higher assessment. Reasonably, they each decided that the other had about the same number of ships.

Villeneuve had twenty ships of the line – that is, big ships – and seven frigates in three columns. This was not a so-called battle line. It would have been a cruising formation. Calder's fleet was slightly smaller but better equipped. At precisely noon, Calder's ship, the *Prince of Wales*, signalled to form up into battle stations. The fleet then came into two lines and, shortly after that, into a single line of battle. That manoeuvre alone took more than an hour which, given the poor conditions, was a very respectable time. Villeneuve ordered his Combined Fleet into one long line of battle, with not Villeneuve's ship, but Admiral Don Federico Gravina's *Argonauta* closest to the enemy.

Some time after three that afternoon, we would have seen two lines of ships facing each other about seven miles apart. If you stand on a beach on a hazy but not foggy day, you are unlikely to see much further than this. The British fleet was on a starboard tack. This meant that the wind was coming from the right-hand side. Therefore Villeneuve's fleet, positioned and ostensibly going the other way, would have had the wind on the port or left side. This is important when trying to appreciate how difficult it can be to manoeuvre to engage the enemy. With the rigs of these huge ships it could take hours not minutes to simply turn left, sail on for a little and then turn right to resume the line in order to get close enough to engage. In what might have been variable wind conditions, with mist coming and going, commanders and sailing masters threw all their expertise into carrying out the famous naval order: engage the enemy more closely.

When Villeneuve altered course, presumably to stop Calder attacking him at the rear, Calder had also to alter course to keep parallel to the Frenchman's fleet. The concept at that time was that a broadside of gun bombardment was the only effective way of dealing with a fleet engagement. Getting as close as possible would have made that broadside more effective. Also, we have to remember that these ships were not dead in the water. They were still sailing. The light airs meant the whole positioning exercise was taken slowly. The mist which came and went and varied between haze and fog added to the predicament of how to engage the enemy or to avoid it.

It was not until a quarter past five that afternoon that the first shots were fired. The order to fire came from Gravina, and it was his flagship, the 80-gun *Argonauta*, which blasted away at the British fleet. It took half an hour after *Argonauta* had fired on the Royal Navy's *Hero* before the British ship was able to manoeuvre into a position to return the fire. Also, because of the weather conditions, especially the mist, it was necessary to lose from the order of battle ships which could get close enough to the commander-in-chief to tell him what was happening. We can begin to see the complexities of this type of naval warfare, even before the ensuing disaster and panic when spars and rigs were shot away and men shot to pieces. By the time darkness came and the mist had settled heavily, neither commander could possibly have known the exact whereabouts of the other ships, nor of some of their own vessels.

Calder was faced with four types of fog. The first was the natural mist produced by temperature and sea. The second was the fog of all warfare, the uncertainty as to what exactly was going on. The third was created by the two fleets. Imagine the effects of dozen upon dozen of cannonballs being constantly fired, producing masses of gun smoke. Disabled, even dismasted, vessels produced a fourth fog, that of inboard chaos. If we take one example of that chaos, the big 98-gun *Windsor Castle*, we can see the confusion. The weather, the inability to manoeuvre at will and the fact of being in a position so easily seen when others were obscured, meant that all enemy gunfire was trained on her. A ship in that state could not continue under her own efforts. Therefore she had to be taken in tow. However, the *Windsor Castle* was a big ship. As a result Calder was unable to delegate one of his smaller vessels to do the job. Thus the dismasting and casualties suffered by the *Windsor Castle* meant that a vessel desperately needed in the line of battle was taken out of the offensive to look after her. The Combined Fleet suffered similar damage and at least one of the Spanish ships simply drifted into enemy lines. The British at first seemed to have come off worst. The first estimates suggested Calder had lost about eighty men. A later count suggested that about forty had been killed and somewhere in the region of 160 wounded. By the grey Atlantic dawn, the French and Spanish fleet appeared to have lost 149 men and to have almost twice that number of wounded. Interestingly, most of the casualties were Spanish. Villeneuve's flagship, the *Bucentaure*, had sustained little damage and just a handful of casualties. It is not difficult to make the assessment that it was Gravina and not Villeneuve who had done most of the fighting. They had also lost two Spanish ships and, of course, the 1,200 men who were on board. The ships were not much good and so no great prize for the British. Moreover, the capture of more than 1,000 Spanish presented a logistical headache. What was Calder expected to do with them? Also, taking two enemy vessels in tow was not an easy task. It slowed down Calder's fleet and limited its ability to manoeuvre. But those ships were worth money. Calder clung to them and in so doing lost advantage and, eventually, both his honour and his command.

With hindsight, Villeneuve had all the advantages on his side and should at least have attacked the rear of Calder's joint squadron and rescued the Spanish ships. Given the high number of British casualties, he could easily have tested Calder's will. Calder himself had taken a beating. Nevertheless, as Villeneuve did not immediately attack, Calder should have noticed the Frenchman's indecisiveness and nervousness. Equally, though we may make a judgement about Villeneuve, Calder would not have had our insight into his character. Moreover, there was certainly nothing wrong with the seamanship and tactical judgement of Gravina. On balance, Calder should have attacked as quickly as possible and Villeneuve should have taken the same decision. For once in his life, Villeneuve had naval superiority if not supremacy. Neither admiral was a Cornwallis, a Nelson, a Ganteaume, a Missiessy, a Cochrane or a Collingwood.

Villeneuve did not decide until after lunch the following day to go after Calder, who by that time was quite clearly in no fighting mood. Having made the decision, it then took Villeneuve, because of the wind condition, a further two hours to get his Combined Fleet into a battle formation. The wind and sea state were certainly not going to change because Villeneuve had made a bold decision. Calder, in the meantime, was certainly far on the horizon and occasionally disappearing in the mist or haze. He wanted to escape rather than put Villeneuve to the sword. It was a decision which was to change naval history.

At first glance, this was a naval farce. A weak French admiral apparently deciding to go in pursuit of a British fleet commanded by another admiral whose main concern is to protect his dubious prizes after receiving a bloodied nose from the enemy. Calder, it still appears, was guilty of a lack of purpose. The Combined Fleet was known by the British to be the biggest at sea. He had been given instructions by the Admiralty to engage Villeneuve. These orders were not transmitted to create a high-seas skirmish. Calder's task, even to the signal where to position himself, was either to send Villeneuve, Gravina and as many of their ships and men as possible to the bottom of the Atlantic or to take them as prisoners and prizes. In, admittedly, difficult circumstances, Calder fled from his implicit instructions. There can be no doubt that he knew the importance of this engagement. He was a vain man. Therefore he knew that success here would have given him everything he could have wanted for the rest of his career. It would even have put him above Nelson – one of his supreme ambitions. Yet he still failed to track after

Villeneuve, to wait for the right conditions to attack and then attempt to deliver the blow that would have finished the war at sea with France.

What, then, do we learn of Villeneuve who, unlike Calder, was certainly to live to fight another day? He sent his report of the battle to Decrès. Decrès must have been puzzled by the report, which made no mention of the fact that it had been Gravina and his six ships which had really fought the battle. There was no reference to Gravina's bravery and that of his men. The casualty figures were overlooked. For some reason, Villeneuve forgot to say that he had more or less kept out of the fight. Had he said so, Decrès would have had a flashback to the Battle of the Nile.

However, Decrès had a second report, from Gravina. Very calmly Gravina demonstrated that the Spanish had been in the van and that it was not until nightfall and a heavy mist that they had abandoned the engagement. It was his opinion that, by the following day, Calder had been taking evasive action and doing everything he could to avoid a further engagement. Given the lack of further evidence directly from the battle as opposed to that later presented to the inquiry, it is not possible to know the exact times that Calder broke away. Nor is it possible to know whether Gravina was instinctively – perhaps partly in the cause of his own position – trying to make the Combined Fleet's failure to get Calder look more worthy than it really was.

The consequence of Calder's action was, apart from letting Villeneuve get away, virtually the end of his career. He clearly believed that Villeneuve had been about to be joined by other French ships and that had this been true his own fleet would most certainly have been outnumbered.

Calder was not quite right on this. The engagement was broken off on 25 July. Two days later, Napoleon was told that Calder was sailing to meet Villeneuve. However, this information was old. It referred to Calder's Admiralty orders to stand 100 miles off Finisterre and intercept the Frenchman on his way from the West Indies. Napoleon immediately ordered two French squadrons to meet up at Cadiz. So, even though there were orders for French reinforcements, they were not to join Villeneuve at the battle on 22 July. Again, lapses in communication times often make tactics appear foolish. The lack of communications simply made tactics vulnerable to the silent power of intelligence-gathering, assessment and execution. Perhaps then, it is not at all odd to suppose that even a chance encounter between enemy ships could throw a strategic plan into the air. We can perhaps be a little more sympathetic towards Calder. At the same time, his fleet had been mauled and there was, so he thought at the time, an incentive to hang on to the two Spanish prizes. He could not have been much more than twenty miles from El Ferrol and so, during the nights of 23 and 24 July, it would have been only prudent of him to anticipate an attack from another angle. What he did next was to result in his court martial. On 26 July he detailed two frigates as escorts for the prize ships and the half-wrecked *Windsor Castle*. They made a course for Plymouth. Calder did not run far. On 2 August, his support squadron commanded by Stirling headed off to continue its patrol not far from Rochefort. This left Calder with fewer than ten fighting ships blockading El Ferrol. He thought he was going to meet up with Nelson's fleet. That did not happen. Calder, a complex figure and in his day a good tactician, must have believed the odds too much against him that afternoon and evening of 22 July. That is far from certain. However, his judgement about reinforcements to Villeneuve had not been far off the mark. On 9 August he received intelligence that the Franco-Spanish Combined Fleet was comfortably moored in El Ferrol and that two other squadrons had joined it. Calder was thus faced with the proposition that should Villeneuve put to sea, there was no way in which he, with his nine fighting ships could expect to take on the Frenchman's twenty-seven. So Calder, again, made a run for it and joined the safety of Admiral Cornwallis's blockade, under Lord Gardner.

Villeneuve had in fact got to El Ferrol via Vigo. From there he had written his cringing report to Decrès. The tenor of this letter reveals how close they were. Villeneuve was able to write with complete frankness. It is his openness that tells us more of his true feelings and leads inevitably to the conclusion that he was a wretched admiral. Villeneuve considered himself unlucky in having been engaged by the combined British ships of Calder and Stirling. If we remember that he had been heading for El Ferrol, how different things would have been if he had had the same good weather as Nelson's post ship, the *Curieux*. Villeneuve might have reached the approaches to El Ferrol while Calder was still blockading it with his only nine ships. He claimed to Decrès that if that had been the case, he would have beaten Calder. He was making the assumption that Nelson was far behind. Yet to some extent Villeneuve's fantasy does lend support to the idea that a mere blip in the weather can derail strategic planning. Destroying Calder's squadron would have made any other squadron locally weaker, and, with that impetus, Villeneuve was sure he could have burst through the somewhat scattered Brest blockade of Cornwallis and caused havoc off Ushant, thus freeing the French fleet.

Villeneuve believed, probably sincerely, that with this battle pennant flying from his mainmast he would have been 'the greatest man in France'. Oh but, he moaned, the weather did not understand his natural gallantry and need for success. Strong winds blew against him for nineteen days during his crossing. Two north-easterly squalls brought down topmasts and yards which were so rotten and poorly patched that even a zephyr would have taken a similar toll. Villeneuve blamed his ships, his officers and his men. He even remembered to blame *mal de mer* for his performance. Once again, the weeping admiral thought himself the 'laughing stock of Europe'.

It might also be remembered, in Villeneuve's favour, that it was true that his ships were in poor repair, that the officers were indifferent and had no battle plan other than to follow the ship in front of them. Even in the safety of Vigo and then in El Ferrol, there was a practical difficulty facing Villeneuve. Earlier we saw Nelson having to order up bullocks and onions while planning his tactics. It was the same with Villeneuve. His men were hungry, stores were low and he had more mouths to feed because he had failed to put soldiers ashore in the West Indies. More than 1,000 of his men were either wounded or too ill to carry on. Imagine, then, the scene on the dockside. Makeshift stretcher after stretcher being lowered ashore. Ragged-minded and reluctant sailors longing for a minor wound that could get them out of their ships. Local chandlers and traders with nowhere near the amount of stores needed to cope with this friendly invasion. Practical questions about storing leapt to the minds of the pursers, gunners and captains. Where was the timber to come from to repair masts and spars? Who could provide Villeneuve's 3,000 pounds of onions? Was there enough sail canvas to quickly patch and even replace that which had been lost? Finally, what about cannonballs? Someone had to supply the powder and ammunition. It was hard to come by, even in naval ports such as Vigo and El Ferrol.

Calder's information that Villeneuve was in El Ferrol was not quite accurate. The Spanish ships were in the harbour. The French were anchored just off the coast in the bay which has El Ferrol on the north side and La Coruña on the southerly coast. It was there that Villeneuve received his new orders from Napoleon. When these were put together it became clear that the emperor was still demanding that Villeneuve fight his way to the Strait of Dover and make himself master of that narrow stretch between France and England. Would Napoleon never give up, as Villeneuve so wished he would? He could, within reason, decide for himself how he achieved this ambition of Napoleon's. There were suggestions that he should link up with, as ever, the Brest and Rochefort squadrons. However he did it, Villeneuve was expected to show initiative and achieve his purpose. He was not exactly the person for this sort of task. His instinct was to do nothing. Anchored as he was in the bay rather than in the harbour, he was far more concerned about making his ships and men seaworthy and getting them into a fighting state. Equally, he had no ambition to fight. The get-out clause for Villeneuve was the one which Napoleon, perhaps realistically, had added and which suggested that if none of this could be achieved, then he, Villeneuve, should sail his fleet down to Cadiz as part of a secondary plan of a concentration of forces, ostensibly for another action altogether.

Villeneuve rather liked the idea of the safety of Cadiz. Gravina had more backbone. It was probably Gravina who convinced Villeneuve that he should at least attempt to head north. Napoleon's idea of sailing round Britain and coming down the North Sea had now been abandoned. Even Villeneuve knew that, considering the state of his fleet, he would never make it. Gravina understood that the weather, by the time that they got to the north of Scotland in mid to late August, would not be the best for an altogether ineffectual fleet. The two admirals thought the best change was to try to free up the Brest squadron and then burst up *la Manche*, probably on the north side. However, there is much in the way that Villeneuve expressed his intentions to Decrès to suggest that he believed no confrontation was ever worthwhile. Napoleon did not see any problem. In August, he had gone to Boulogne, quite ready to lead his troops into England. The Romans had done it. Duke William had succeeded, thanks to Eustace II of Boulogne.[2] He, Napoleon, would also be triumphant – from Boulogne.

Where was Napoleon's Nelson figure? Back in his flagship, hundreds of miles away, thinking up reasons why he could not possibly storm the Channel. He would try it because, in spite of all his reservations and fears, Villeneuve had always attempted to succeed. It is this characteristic that we should not forget when, three months later, instead of escaping into the Mediterranean, Villeneuve, still, inexplicably to many, turned round to face Nelson and defeat. Now, at the beginning of August, Villeneuve was already writing to Decrès with his excuses for the failure that was to come: '. . . I have found myself hampered by the most deadly adverse circumstances. Everything – even heaven – is against me'. Heaven, of course, was the adverse weather for his sailing directions. Little wonder that he was still, on 6 August, complaining to Decrès that the fleet was appalling when it came to carrying out manoeuvres. The reasons it had not improved under his command were, in his opinion, that the ships were no good and the men even worse. Equally, Villeneuve claimed that he was devoted to Napoleon and would do his best, saying, however, that if things went wrong he wanted Decrès to tell Napoleon that it was down to bad luck rather than his fault.

Three days before this letter, Napoleon was up on the north coast reviewing the seven mini invasion fleets that stretched from Ostend to Boulogne. At his insistence his commanders had built and assembled almost 3,000 boats. Some of them were gunboats, others armed transporters. Such a fantastic plan was necessary if the emperor was going to lead his army of five corps, numbering 170,000 men and 9,000 horses. The food, ammunition, spares, blacksmiths, medics, armourers, wheelwrights and shipwrights, carpenters and harness makers, soldiers and sailors, grooms and beast herds, were all assembled on that coast. It was an astonishing display of unremitting cussedness on the part of Napoleon. The infantry alone, when formed up to be reviewed by their emperor, stretched for nine miles. What a joyous occasion this would be

---

[2] Eustace II of Boulogne is known to have fought alongside William and is clearly depicted on the Bayeux Tapestry.

for Napoleon as long as two elements of war fell into place: Villeneuve and his fleets were expected to sweep up the Channel and protect this huge investment, and the Austrian, Russian and English forces that were massing to the east did not distract him. We now, of course, know very well that the rumble of alliance warfare effectively threatening Napoleon came not from the sea but from the land. He stood on the Channel coast on 3 August 1805. By the end of that month those rumblings of land artillery had risen to a crescendo.

The realization that he should attend to his enemies in the east came to Napoleon on 10 August. The previous day, Austria agreed the St Petersburg Pact: the union of England and Russia against France. Two days earlier, on 8 August, news had reached him of the confrontation between Calder and Villeneuve. It had taken that long for something as important as what the French saw as a kind of victory to reach the emperor. Much of the news that reached Napoleon he believed because it was coming not from the admirals, whom he mainly despised, but from the soldiers. We have a picture of Napoleon not trusting his admirals and Villeneuve not trusting the generals and colonels – remember, he had 12,000 troops scattered among his fleet. The soldiers saw only indecision and weakness in the fleet commander. They neither knew about nor cared much for the difficulties of commanding such a mixture of ships against an unseen but clearly feared enemy. To Villeneuve, the soldiering mentality was a simple one: the military man spotted the enemy, gave his horse a good feed of hay and his infantry and artillery as many rounds of ammunition as they could carry, and then, with a sharp blast on the bugle, was off to battle. It is very likely that Villeneuve had only one ally in his fleet, the Spanish admiral Gravina. Gravina was, in turn, an ally of Decrès and trusted by the naval minister. Whatever he thought of Villeneuve, Gravina accepted him as commander-in-chief but decided that he would, where necessary, take the initiative himself. Decrès knew Villeneuve's limitations, and it is unlikely that he would have felt anything other than reassurance in having Gravina in the Combined Fleet. Yet even the Spanish admiral's reports of what was going on in the fleet, including the detail of that engagement against the British, were not always to be trusted. Either through misunderstanding or deliberate misinformation, Gravina's letters could be as contradictory as

Villeneuve's. For now, Villeneuve had to set aside confusion and insecurity and decide whether to head for Brest or Cadiz. If he went to Brest, it would effectively mean that he was taking the challenge to support the invasion. If he went south to Cadiz, he most certainly would need to have very good reason.

He was left in no doubt that his decision would affect everyone's future, particularly his own. Decrès wrote to Villeneuve from Paris pointing out that he might make much of his escape from Calder. However, Decrès also pointed out that a bit of patchy weather and a minor engagement with the British would not impress Napoleon if it meant that Villeneuve failed to make the Brest rendezvous and then to sail onwards to Boulogne. Decrès said such a failure would cause Napoleon's grand strategy to 'miscarry' and that he could only imagine with some horror the humiliation it would cause the whole French navy. Villeneuve was rather good at humiliation. He did not need Decrès to tell him about personal liability and the consequences of being what he most disliked, a fighting admiral. Equally, the mystery of the weather did not help. Napoleon may have been, at the time, pouring over naval charts to see exactly where his ships were now deployed. The weather would make all his dispositions inevitable rather than conforming to his planning. So when Villeneuve got into port, re-victualled his ships and attended to 200 sick sailors – enough to crew a frigate – it mattered not that he was ready for sea. The wind was blowing into the harbour on the first day, 11 August. Villeneuve did not really want to leave. He was writing instead, a panicky letter to Decrès informing him that sickness and wind conditions meant he had lost almost sixteen per cent of his fleet. He might have gone to sea with thirty-four ships of the line. He would now be pushed to find twenty-eight, and could only assume that the Royal Navy had increased its fleets. What was a poor French admiral to do?

In truth, Villeneuve had already made up his mind that he was not going to go anywhere near the range of an English cannon. He told no one, certainly not Napoleon's general in the fleet, Jacques Lauriston,[3] who wrote to Napoleon from the anchorage that they were indeed going to Brest to make invasion possible. By the time his letter reached

---

[3] Jacques Alexandre Lauriston (1768–1828).

Napoleon, the emperor's only solid item of intelligence was that his fleet was anchored off La Coruña.

Lauriston had been at sea, commanding the soldiers in Villeneuve's fleet, since the previous year. He had had plenty of time to work up a soldier's bile against Villeneuve. Perhaps he was not always understanding of the true naval position. Whatever the circumstances and misconceptions – or conceptions – Lauriston was hardly the man to whom Villeneuve should have turned in search of a new career reference.

The wind shifted on 13 August. Villeneuve put to sea before a good north-easterly. Napoleon received the word that his admiral and an impressive fleet of thirty-nine vessels, twenty-nine of them ships of the line, had sailed at last. It was just as well that he had at last set sail, because Napoleon was already telling Decrès that he thought Villeneuve was wasting precious time and that he now expected him to 'advance boldly against the enemy'. In a letter to Villeneuve, the emperor said that he believed French soldiers and sailors could not be asked to shed their blood for a mightier cause. He added that everyone was ready to die 'cheerfully' for the invasion of England, the nation which had suppressed France for six centuries. There is no evidence that Villeneuve was at that point ready to die cheerfully for anyone or any cause.

Whatever the thunderings of Napoleon, he still had to deal with the axis of English, Austrian and Russian troops at his rear. His greatest hope, and one which he confided in his foreign minister, Talleyrand, was that the Austrian troops would go off and settle in Bohemia or Hungary and leave him in what he called 'peace' to batter his enemy, England. To the Austrians, directly, he pointed out that the army he had gathered for his invasion would deal first with the British and then land on Vienna like some great military thunderbolt. Although in not quite the way Napoleon had planned, that is more or less what happened before the end of the year.

Villeneuve, at sea, was having a dreadful time. His lookouts reported ships on the horizon, and so the admiral altered course to avoid them. He believed them to be under the command of either Nelson or Calder. Having altered course, he once more picked up sail on the horizon on 14 August. Again Villeneuve altered course, which was a pity for him because they were French ships waiting to join forces. These French vessels, the Rochefort squadron under their new commander, Zacharie

Allemand[4] (he had, that summer, replaced Missiessy) also saw Villeneuve, but Allemand, too, failed to identify the other ships as French. It is likely that he was just as keen as Villeneuve to avoid the British. Now the wind returned to play games with the fleet. Villeneuve had arrived in the anchorage off La Coruña on 2 August and had scraped in on a reasonable run before the wind. He was trapped until 13 August, when he headed out from El Ferrol on something of a westerly course. During that day, the wind veered to the north-west and Villeneuve headed east. Then again the wind changed and he was back on a north-westerly track. By now it was 15 August and the wind was blowing from the north-west, quite hard. Villeneuve made even more west, with the wind coming at him and his fleet on the starboard, that is, the right-hand side. As if the weather were not bad enough for Villeneuve (one of his ships lost her topmast), even worse was information picked up from a merchant ship that there was, in the area, a British squadron. Villeneuve had no way of knowing whether this information was true. Being Villeneuve, he took no chances. That evening, with the fleet still on the westerly course, he finally lost his nerve completely. Before dusk fell on 15 August, he effectively told his fleet that he was fed up with the whole business of dodging the British and saw no chance of getting to Brest and certainly not up the Channel, even if Napoleon was telling him that he only needed to be there for twenty-four hours to have an effect. Instead, the admiral ordered his whole fleet to turn south and run away to Cadiz as fast as the north-westerly wind would carry them.

Napoleon had, indeed, in some earlier order, suggested that if all else failed, Cadiz would be a rendezvous for most of his naval forces and, of course, Villeneuve's soldiery. Nevertheless, two points ought to be considered about Villeneuve's decision to head south. What if he had not gone in that direction, and was he partly justified?

If we consider the force of the British blockading Brest and off Ushant, we can probably estimate that Cornwallis had at around this time a maximum of thirty-six ships of the line. Nelson had returned to England, sailing in *Victory* with *Superb* in company. Even that fleet of Cornwallis's was reduced by 16 August, after Calder's squadron had been redeployed.

---

[3] Zacharie Jacques Allemand (1762–1826).

Therefore, on Cornwallis's weakest day, Villeneuve outgunned him. Had Ganteaume got out from Brest as was planned, he would have added at least twenty big ships to Villeneuve's fleet. This would have represented an overwhelming advantage to the Franco-Spanish Combined Fleet. It seems very unlikely that a battle would have left much of Cornwallis's Channel Fleet in service. It most certainly would have opened the way to Boulogne. It will always be argued – with some justification – that Villeneuve should have gone north. What, then, was Villeneuve's reason or excuse?

In his report to Decrès, sent on his arrival at Cadiz (ironically, at about the same time Nelson was stepping ashore in England), Villeneuve first and foremost blamed the weather. Anyone who has tried to make passage in contrary winds will be sympathetic to his claim. These ships were square-riggers. Their ability to sail close to the wind – that is, in its general direction – is necessarily abysmal. They were never designed to do so. The wind, remember, was setting from the north-west and, according to Villeneuve, hardly appeared to be letting up. However, what he could not explain and what Decrès appears not to have asked him was that, if the wind had established itself from the north-west, surely the course for Brest and then into the Channel would have brought that wind, at the very least, on to his port beam and, as he turned, abaft that beam. In other words, if Villeneuve's weather reading and forecasting were correct, there should have been a point where his aggressive intent would have had the wind in its favour, just behind him.

What is missing from this analysis is the state of his fleet. Even though he had been at sea for a long time (ignoring the restorative interlude in El Ferrol), Villeneuve and his commanders had apparently made no progress in improving their ship-handling abilities. Moreover, the previous few days had seen gales which had damaged parts of the fleet, including a dismasting, which suggests that either the vessels were badly canvassed or the spars and masts and standing rigging (the ropes that support the masts, similar to tent guys) were in a dreadful condition. So a ragged fleet, raggedly commanded and crewed and recently very bruised from an engagement with the enemy and nervous of a further fight, almost naturally, made a run. There is an additional point that Villeneuve made to Decrès, which is difficult to substantiate. Villeneuve was convinced that Napoleon's plan had already failed. It might be recalled that the imperial notion that had stuck in Villeneuve's mind was that the entire exercise of sailing to the West Indies was intended as a diversion enabling the French to deal what Villeneuve was told would be a mortal blow against the British while they were distracted. Very clearly, or so Villeneuve thought, the British had got wise to this plan and, anyway, no one seemed to know whether it still existed. Villeneuve's feeling was summed up in one phrase to Decrès: 'I am unable to envisage any possibility of success in the present circumstances . . .'

When at first light on 20 August – Nelson was now at the Admiralty – Villeneuve was making his approach into Cadiz, he was picked up by Collingwood's flotilla. To Villeneuve's credit, he detached part of his fleet to engage Collingwood. It should not be thought that all British tars would engage the enemy whatever the odds. Collingwood was not there to take on nearly forty ships. He was there to monitor the comings and goings from Cadiz. So Collingwood escaped over the horizon. He, however, returned to his station and saw the Combined Fleet enter Cadiz harbour. At least the British now knew for certain where the enemy was.

Safely tucked up in Cadiz, Villeneuve felt nervous but a little more secure. This did not much please his emperor, who was now of the opinion that Villeneuve was not fit to be given the command of a frigate, never mind a fleet. He thought the man was nothing more than a coward and a traitor. He told Decrès that he was to arrange to have Villeneuve returned to the Channel area, if necessary by force. Moreover, Ganteaume was to be given the command of the Combined Fleet. Decrès was in a difficult position. He was unquestionably loyal to Villeneuve. Also, he was not at all sure that the Combined Fleet was the best arrangement for what Napoleon had in mind. He tried to appeal to the emperor's military judgement. He inferred that Napoleon would understand how very difficult it was to operate a combined unit on land, never mind at sea. It was likely that two military formations had different operating procedures and quite different capabilities quite apart from language differences, and so loyalties within each of them would be stressed. Napoleon saw some sense in this. Decrès, ignoring the fact that the Combined Fleet had been at sea long enough to exercise joint procedures, virtually pleaded with

Napoleon not to be so harsh on Villeneuve and most certainly not to expect the joint fleet to succeed.

Decrès also realized – and had done for years – that Napoleon was unable to grasp how a navy should be employed. He more or less told the emperor that he found himself simply unable to organize what Napoleon wanted. The French did not have the equivalent structure and command system of the British admiralty. Napoleon was in complete charge. Decrès had asked Napoleon to set up such an organization. His master's response had been that too many of the admirals were wishy-washy, and that just because the occasional bowsprit snapped and a sail was torn that was no reason why they should not carry out his orders. Deep down, he must have known the limitations confronting him, which is why, instead of telling Decrès what should happen next (apart from ordering him to practically keelhaul Villeneuve all the way to the Channel), Napoleon then threw the whole issue at Decrès. If he was so smart, what would he do? The emperor did not want letters of pleading and excuses. As he told Decrès, he wanted only one thing: success. Being bad-tempered would not resolve the issues.

Napoleon had to have someone answer the simple question: was Villeneuve going to get to the Channel or not? If he did, the invasion might still be on. If he did not, Napoleon would give his full attention to Austria. No wonder Napoleon had little more than contempt for the navy. Perhaps there was a part of him that hoped Villeneuve would breeze into the Channel after all. It is difficult to see how he could really have believed that. In reality, before he had had it confirmed, he assumed Villeneuve was not coming. If the fleet had arrived in Cadiz on 20 August, it is unlikely that the report of his making fast in the Spanish harbour could have reached Napoleon in less than a week. By that time, there had been no reports from closer deployments such as Ushant and Brest. Napoleon knew that wherever Villeneuve was during that final week of August, he was not within a thousand miles of Boulogne. So he took one last look at England across the Strait of Dover and turned his back on the ambition to bring Albion to heel.

CHAPTER TWENTY

Homeward Bound

IN PARIS, DENIS DECRÈS, SENSING PERHAPS THAT THE NAVY WOULD BE forever castigated by the emperor, tried to sell Napoleon an alternative plan. Intelligence arriving in Paris from London suggested that the British knew the invasion had been abandoned. The Royal Navy felt it had been successful in preventing the support fleet from reaching the eastern channel. The standing down of tens of thousands of troops, with their logistical wings and armaments, could not be concealed. Therefore, argued Decrès, this was exactly the time to hit the British. He did not imagine an invasion. He wanted Napoleon to authorize the use of the ships that were already in that Boulogne–Flushing area, along with a force of perhaps 60,000–70,000 troops, to make a quick dash on the eastward-flowing current and the beginnings of a flood tide, ideally on a moonless night in the now approaching late autumn, that would take this force on a raid into the Medway towns. After all, years earlier, the Dutch had done rather well at this sort of operation.

Decrès had no illusions about an occupation of south-east England, but he believed that they could, in a few hours, torch the military installations and maybe, on some sort of suicide mission, do a great deal of damage in London itself. He saw them going in while the tide was still flooding, doing their work and then escaping on the ebb tide and the westerly flow of the current. Napoleon thought him mad. It needed no imperial reflection to conclude that his own navy was an utter waste of time and that a soldier would do well never to rely on even the most medal-spattered admiral. As if in confirmation of this opinion, Napoleon now heard that the one senior officer in the navy in whose judgement he found some sense, Ganteaume, was still stuck at Brest, in spite of Napoleon's orders for him to get out and fight. Furthermore, Ganteaume was moaning that he was not at all well, that his gout was giving him hell and his doctors had suggested a change of air. Napoleon suspected that admirals had between them far too much air and that the empire would be better off if they had none at all. He put his faith in his army. He now turned to his supreme commander, Soult.

Marshal Soult stood with Napoleon and surveyed his invasion force. At Napoleon's order, on 26 August, Soult commanded his corps at Bruges, Montreuil and St Omer to move east. This was the beginning of the Grande Armée. The destination was what would eventually be called the Confederation of the Rhine.

By 19 October, the Austrian allies had surrendered at Ulm. Napoleon was in Vienna by 13 November. On 2 December 1805, he slaughtered the Russians and Austrians at Austerlitz. The Holy Roman Empire was done for. What followed is not of our story. Whatever we may have thought of as possible doubts in Napoleon's mind earlier that year no longer matter.

The huge invasion force was a fulfilment of Napoleon's genius for making people do what he wished on land. He did not control the seas. The elements did that. The splendid array of that invasion force was a row of military decorations along the breast of Napoleon's ambition. Mere tinsel.

Villeneuve, of course, had no idea of any of this. While Napoleon was harking to the distant drums of another kind of warfare, Villeneuve was still desperately writing excuses. As long as he could avoid Napoleon, he would be safe. He might even rid himself of this wretched higher command and the fear of Nelson. During this period, Nelson had returned to the Mediterranean, made plans to leave again and written quite different styles of letters to those of Villeneuve.

While Villeneuve wanted a quiet life, Nelson wanted a noisy one – with Villeneuve. If only he had been in Calder's shoes on July 22.

On the morning after Calder's engagement with Villeneuve, Nelson was writing to Barham, the First Lord of the Admiralty, who had replaced Melville four months earlier. Nelson, it seemed, had had his ships restored and was now waiting for an easterly wind to carry him out of the Mediterranean. However, he bemoaned the fact that he had no idea where Villeneuve was. Still Nelson grumbled that if it had not been for Brereton then he would have fought Villeneuve on 6 June: 'The advent would have been in the hands of Providence; but we may without, I hope, vanity, believe that the Enemy would have been fit for no active service after such a Battle.'

Here Nelson's attitude was in contrast to that of Calder. Nelson, within reason, would take on any enemy whatever the odds. He had the utmost confidence that by having a proper battle plan and then making sure that each of his captains knew exactly what was expected of them and when, he would, by that very planning and consultation, have a huge advantage over any enemy fleet. He was most certainly intending to get into any kind of fight he could. He regarded Villeneuve as his personal enemy. At the same time, he understood that he could not simply clear out of the Mediterranean in search of the Combined Fleet. He weighed anchor at noon on 23 July from his haven in Tetuan Bay. One of the last letters sent ashore was to the Admiralty secretary, William Marsden. In it, he laid out his rearguard plan standing off Malta, Naples and Cartagena.

Off Malta, he left a frigate and four sloops, together with three schooners and a fast cutter. The Naples station presented his captains with a much wider task. They had to monitor French movements out of Toulon, Genoa and Leghorn, as well as standing sentry over the British anchorages off Sardinia. The guardships at Cartagena were bigger vessels, with frigates in support. They had to be ready to engage anything that came into or attempted to leave the Mediterranean, that had slipped by the Gibraltar station or escaped the Naples squadron. For example, the French were planning to launch a new 74-gun ship from Genoa. If she got through with an escort of smaller vessels, the Cartagena squadron would be the last line of defence before Gibraltar.

Once out of the Mediterranean, the first station would be off Cape St Vincent, where Collingwood was waiting. Nelson actually needed some of Collingwood's proposed squadron for his own purposes. Nelson's fleet was not his private navy, dashing over the oceans in search of glory and Villeneuve. His precise planning included a back-up scheme for anything that might go wrong anywhere in his ambit. He was, of course, equally aware that he should never be accused of leaving the Mediterranean unguarded. After all, he had been sent there as commander-in-chief. He had never really been given orders to abandon his command in search of Villeneuve. If all went wrong, Nelson would be vulnerable to a charge of dereliction. The deployment of frigates, brigs and sloops off the main ports in the Mediterranean was more than good naval planning. Those small squadrons represented Nelson's insurance policy on his career.

In his 23 July letter to Lord Barham, Nelson was once again telling the Admiralty that he was doing what he thought best and, as they had not told him what they thought best, he would continue to do it. First he needed intelligence-gathering. Not all commanders were like Orde, who had failed to pass on the information the previous April that Villeneuve and Gravina were heading for the West Indies. Commanders, including the sturdy Cuthbert Collingwood off Cape St Vincent, knew very well that any intelligence had to get to Nelson as soon as possible. Here is yet another practical example of how the late-eighteenth-century and early nineteenth-century navy operated. There was no point in people like Collingwood having information if they could not get it to Nelson. Therefore he had a series of positions where either he or other ships of his fleet would loiter as dead letter boxes. Nelson described each of these latitudes and longitudes as a 'convenient position' for receiving intelligence. Again, given the difficulties of maintaining a station, the weather could blow a frigate off position.

The navigation and seamanship required of the sailing masters of the time must never be underestimated. The chance of bad weather had always to be countered if intelligence was to be got to a commander. Even in reasonable conditions, it was so easy for even a well-organized flotilla to miss its quarry. Given the vastness of oceans and the total lack of any form of communications other than sightings, it was little wonder that enemies could sail in the same region and miss each other completely. This was very much Nelson's concern during the last week of July 1805. He believed it perfectly possible that, thanks to Brereton, Villeneuve would reach the safety of a French or Spanish port. His continual references to Brereton expressed his absolute conviction that the man had got in the way of destiny.

Towards the end of July, Nelson's physical condition had worsened.

There was a half sense that he might not be too disappointed if Villeneuve were in port. First, that would justify his prejudice against Brereton. Second, at least then a blockade of that port could be mounted and the searching would be over. Third, perhaps most importantly, Nelson could return to England. His doctor had told him at the beginning of the year that he was wrecking his health and ought to go home. Feeling at a low ebb, he agreed to do so. Presumably, while his doctor's advice should be taken, so could his heart's. He had not seen Emma in two years. Two days later, Nelson handed over his Mediterranean command to Rear Admiral Sir Richard Bickerton.[1] He told Bickerton to watch the Spanish ships based at Cartagena and to study his detailed instructions as to how he, Bickerton, should watch the different ports, deploy such resources as he had left and await his return. Enthusiastically he claimed that at last, having picked up the intelligence that Villeneuve was heading north, he, Nelson, was off to catch him. There was every sign that Nelson did not really believe that. He lived in hope and said as much in a letter dated 27 July to his friend and the most senior naval officer at sea, Cornwallis. He said that he was heading north and had eleven big-gun ships in his squadron. Believing Villeneuve to be now making for the Bay of Biscay, he wrote: 'I shall only hope, after all my long pursuit of *my* Enemy, that I may arrive at the moment they are meeting you.'

Once again, here is evidence that, five days after the event, Nelson had no way of knowing about the engagement between Calder and Villeneuve or, specifically, about Villeneuve's escape. Nelson wrote a similar letter to Admiral Gardner telling him that if he got even a whiff of a plan that Villeneuve was heading for Ireland, he would then rendezvous ('form a junction') in order to take him on. There is a small irony at this stage. The letter to Gardner was sent by Nelson in the fastest ship of his fleet, a schooner called *Pickle*. It would be this same vessel which, three months later, would be sent to England with the news of his death (see chapter 29).

Nelson was now heading north. If Villeneuve was still at sea, he, Nelson, planned to join up with Cornwallis. Somewhere along that passage he must once again have narrowly missed his adversary. Perhaps even the

---

[1] Sir Richard Hussey Bickerton (1759–1832).

distance of an horizon was all that separated them. It was now that he wrote to his friend and prize agent Alexander Davison[2] an account of his woes that included an even more damning description of Brereton and expressed his fear that he was in danger of being condemned for his failure to engage the Frenchman. He once more remembered that he had abandoned his Mediterranean command early that spring and that only success would guarantee that he remained invulnerable to the not inconsiderable spite of the Admiralty. He told Davison that had it not been for Brereton he, Nelson, would have been the greatest admiral in England's history. He had, on instinct, broken the rules. He would admit that if he followed his own instincts they usually led him to a much more correct solution than did those instructions he received from the Admiralty. On this occasion, though, he had thus far failed, and as far as the Admiralty was concerned, or certainly his enemies within, he was nothing and might well incur 'censure for misfortunes which may happen, and have happened'.

So he continued north in the hope of hearing that Villeneuve was in port. The winds were adverse to a good passage. On 3 August, he noted in his private log that this was going to be a long passage and winds came either from the north, thus making normal progress difficult, or amounted to nothing more than light airs which had the debilitating sail-flapping effect of virtually becalming. He felt every moment of what he thought of as a foul wind. He suffered. Nelson continued to feel frail from seasickness. A modern sailor who suffered from it in the way Nelson did would have been long retired from the navy. These were different times. After all, what was *mal de mer* when an arm and an eye were missing? A journey north would take him three weeks. Vice Admiral Nelson in the *Victory* flew his pennant as Vice Admiral of the White with considerable pride. Yet below, in the Great Cabin, he appears to have been even more morose than ever. *Victory* arrived off Ushant and rendezvoused under Cornwallis's command with the old admiral's Channel fleet.

---

[2] Davison, Alexander (1750–1829). Davison made his money as a government contractor, especially in Canada and during the War of American Independence. He and Nelson met in 1782. Later, Nelson appointed Davison as his prize agent, the person who negotiated payments for any prize ships. He became Nelson's lifelong confidant.

Nelson did not hear of Calder's action of 22 July until 15 August. He had received, by mail schooner, newspapers from England sent by one of his former captains, Tom Fremantle. Fremantle had commanded the *Ganges* at the Battle of Copenhagen and was both a trusted subordinate of Nelson's and a good friend of his Captain Hardy, Nelson's post captain in the *Victory*. Fremantle now had command of the big 98-gun ship, the *Neptune*. At that moment, more importantly, Fremantle had come by the London newspapers. Nelson was confused by the reports. Officially, at that stage anyway, Calder's action against Villeneuve was described as a victory. Pitt, the Admiralty and much of Britain had been longing for a famous victory. However, some of the writings pointed out that the French and Spanish fleet, although mauled, was still at large. They then went on to say that Nelson would never have let Villeneuve survive. He would have pressed home his attack at whatever cost and would have succeeded.

It might be generally assumed that Nelson would have been pleased with this almost god-like image of himself. A better insight into his character would be that he was saddened by these writings.

He was, first and foremost, a good commander. He understood that sailors at sea could not deliver victories wherever and whenever the newspapers and politicians wanted them. His view was that he, Nelson, had the best fleet in the world, hardly an egotistical viewpoint. Villeneuve would certainly have agreed. Nelson went a stage further and judged that he also had the best-trained ships' companies and the best-officered vessels afloat. This was his band of brothers. They knew his thinking and were ready, for the most part, to follow him anywhere at any time. Yet Nelson was full of sympathy for Calder. He knew that, even given the magnificence of his ships and men, one could never know what might go wrong. It was impossible to know the circumstances created by weather, action, and that much-needed tactical advantage – luck. So, instead of cursing Calder, Nelson commiserated with him.

The cynic might briefly imagine that this generosity had a little to do with the fact that, with Villeneuve still at large, Nelson himself still had the opportunity to be the greatest admiral the nation had ever known. We cannot really tell what was on his mind other than by reading what he wrote and said at the time. He wrote to Fremantle that he was sincerely grieved that the newspapers should have insinuated that Nelson would have succeeded where Calder had failed. He could only succeed on his own merits as opposed to benefiting from the unfortunate circumstances surrounding a brother officer.

It is interesting to note that, shortly before the Battle of Trafalgar, Calder was recalled to England by the Admiralty. He was to be court-martialled for his failure to press home the attack against Villeneuve and Gravina. Apart from being concerned for his career, Calder was equally nervous of his dignity. He told Nelson that instead of going back to England in a small frigate he felt he should be allowed to return to Portsmouth in his flagship in keeping with his position. Nelson desperately needed that ship for what was now to be the coming confrontation with Villeneuve. However, perhaps reflecting the sincerity of his comments to Fremantle, Nelson agreed that Calder should sail home in his three-decker flagship, the *Prince of Wales*. Nelson sent Calder, by then feeling extremely hard done by, homeward bound, with his good wishes and hopes that the inquiry would not treat him harshly (see chapter 29). All this was to come. For the moment, Nelson too was heading home.

In the evening of 15 August, Nelson's squadron rendezvoused with Cornwallis off Ushant. He never saw Cornwallis. His old admiral friend sent a letter across to the *Victory* saying that it was far too late at night for formalities and that Nelson should take advantage of the wind and continue his passage home, leaving all but HMS *Superb* with Cornwallis's fleet. Nelson left his ships in good order. There was some scurvy aboard, but nothing that a few brassicas would not fix.

Almost exactly two days later, at 10.15 on the night of 17 August, the *Victory* anchored off the south coast and Nelson had his first glimpse of England for more than two years. He had lived in the *Victory* for the whole time. He was most anxious to be ashore. Yet again, we discover the ways in which even a famous admiral was obliged to conform with bureaucracies. Two years at sea, battling gales and disappointment, the war with France in strong fever – and yet the slightly built admiral had to remain at his desk in his ship composing his request for free pratique, the declaration stating that a commander believed his ship free of contamination and so required the freedom to have contact with the shore. The modern signal for free pratique is a yellow flag. In Nelson's time, that flag was hoisted in a ship in which there was about to be an execution.

Off Spithead, Nelson was writing to the collector of customs that his fleet had left Gibraltar twenty-seven days before and that he could assure the collector that there were no contagious illnesses in Gibraltar. To endorse his belief that all his men were hale and hearty, he added that those he had left under the command of Cornwallis on 15 August were in 'the most perfect health'. Also, on his 'word of honour', none in the *Victory* or the *Superb* had anything wrong with them and there certainly were no hospital cases.

The matter of free pratique was considered a very serious business by the shoreside authorities. To get another idea of the Nelsonian navy we might remember that officials and medics ashore had in their records at least 500 years' worth of instances of sometimes devastating diseases being carried on to land by sailors. Therefore requiring Nelson himself to sign an assurance to the collector about the state of his ships is not something that would have been done lightly. Even someone of Nelson's stature was not allowed to bend the rules. In fact, he was not allowed ashore. Nelson had come home because of his health, but had to sit in the *Victory*. On 19 August, Nelson wrote to Marsden, the Admiralty secretary, saying that he and his two ships were in quarantine. He could not even invite the captain of the *Superb* to dinner or even for consultations. A customs cutter was anchored between the *Victory* and the *Superb* to make sure none should get ashore. The quarantine was lifted after a couple of days. The Admiralty needed to talk to Nelson.

There is a footnote to Nelson's assertion that none of his sailors were ill. That was not quite true. Just as Nelson was totally exhausted and not a little debilitated after two years at sea, so others were similarly worn out. Of most concern to Nelson was his old friend and the captain of the *Victory*, Hardy. Nelson wrote to Marsden to plead that Hardy should be allowed ashore. Finally, clearance was given for free pratique, and at nine that evening Nelson's pennant was hauled down. He left almost immediately for Merton, and Emma.

CHAPTER TWENTY-ONE

Farewell to Emma

N ELSON'S ARRIVAL AT PORTSMOUTH WAS A PUBLIC EVENT. THE FACT that *Victory* was stuck offshore with his flag as Vice Admiral of the White still flying only added to the excitement. Crowds began to gather to see, and hopefully be seen by, Nelson. He was, in 1805, the only public hero England had. That evening of 19 August, when he came off the *Victory* for what would be his last homecoming, was a scene of cheering, waving and banners reserved for a conquering hero. In Nelson's heart he may well have recognized that he was a hero, but deep down he knew he was not a conquering one. Like many of his breed, Nelson could display an unenviable insecurity. Perhaps to him, driven as he was by the need to succeed, failure seemed even more of a possibility. All those doubts he had had as a sickly child were in that last stepping ashore in England.

They are most clear in his recorded warnings to Emma that because of his failure to get face to face with Villeneuve he could easily find himself without a career. He had not lost sight of the fact that he had been taking a huge gamble by leaving the Mediterranean and chasing across the Atlantic. He knew there were those who would – rightly – doubt the worth of even such a celebrated commander as himself if he had indeed put his personal vendetta and ambition before his orders from the Admiralty. It was all very well writing at length to the Admiralty declaring that if they did not approve of what he was doing they should say so. However, we have seen during this two-year period, time and again, the difficulties of communications. The idea that he could get an instant response was of course nonsense. He knew this. His gamble had failed. Yes, he had been received by the people as a hero, but his insecurities warned him that there might be fewer hurrahs in the Admiralty. He told Emma to be prepared for the worst. Emma, of course – true to her big personality – was prepared for the best.

She had called all their friends and relations to Merton for Nelson's homecoming, including his brother William, who would later be the first Earl Nelson. Also brought home was Horatia, who was then not quite five years old. Horatia was certainly, she believed, Nelson's daughter. However, to the end of her days, in 1881, Horatia insisted that Emma was not her mother. It would seem that in her teens she detested Emma, whom she accused (with some justification) of drinking away the money left by Nelson for her keep. So strong were her feelings that she went so far as to point out publicly that at the time of her birth, in January 1801, Emma had still been living in London, seeing friends and being surrounded by acquaintances and servants, and that there was no record of Lady Hamilton being confined. The other side of this story is that Emma did give birth to Horatia and that the child was immediately put in the care of one Mrs Gibson who lived in Little Titchfield Street, to the north of what is now the shopping centre of Oxford Street in London. Nelson had even gone to the extraordinary lengths of contriving a baptism, using false names for the parents. In fact, he had also suggested that the child should be called Emma, which is extraordinary because Lady Hamilton already had an illegitimate daughter called Emma who was by then aged twenty-one and probably the daughter of Charles Greville.

Hamilton himself had certainly not known about the illegitimate Emma before he married her mother, who thus became Lady Hamilton, and as a wedding present was given the maintenance order by Greville. Emma Hamilton had led a colourful life. It remained too exciting for Horatia, who, however, adored Nelson as he did her. He insisted that he should see her on his journey home. There was of course the illusion – which Nelson encouraged – that Horatia was an orphan and that he and Emma were her step-parents. Hence her formal name, Horatia Thompson. All these things were, needless to say, in times past and certainly not on the minds of the family gathered that last August of Nelson's life.

It was a curious homecoming. Having been away from each other for two years meant that Nelson and his daughter had a great deal of finding out to do. When he had left, she had been two-and-a-half years old. Now, she had grown into a child who had started her schooling, was learning French and Italian and dressed the part of a young lady astride her rocking horse. She was still in the charge of Mrs Gibson and it was clear to Nelson's friends, if not to the admiral himself, that Emma continued to favour this arrangement, especially as it meant she was able to continue with her seemingly never-ending social life. She was approaching blowsy middle age, although she continued to claim the adoration and affection of her social set. She tried to make Nelson jealous by claiming that many of the gentry had chased after her comforts and some had offered her marriage. Did the insecurities of a sailor at sea for two years play on Nelson's jealousies? Perhaps, but there was no evidence of this at Merton that August. Lord Minto[1] observed that the affections ran just as deeply as before. Neighbours and officials called at Merton, and if Emma and Nelson thought they were going to have a quiet spell of leave they could hardly have been more wrong. The admiral had gone home to recuperate and recharge his energies as well as his standing in Whitehall. For him, the former would come, hopefully naturally. The only way to find out if his professional standing had suffered, especially since his April exodus into the Atlantic, was to be face to face with their lordships of the Admiralty and even with Pitt himself.

The forty-six-year-old Nelson was never allowed to lounge at Merton. He had just over three weeks' leave in front of him. Any image of him relaxing in a soft chair on the late-summer lawn to regain his health should be discarded. The assembled relatives and friends hardly saw the front of him before they saw the back. The next day he was back in a carriage and heading for London. At ten o'clock on 21 August he arrived at the Admiralty for a very formal meeting with Barham, who had only been in the job as First Lord since April. Thus his first impression of Nelson was as the commander of the Mediterranean Fleet who had, without instructions, abandoned his area, although leaving an after-guard. No wonder the admiral was a little nervous. The interview was brief and the two agreed to meet later that day. Nelson had other calls to make. He

---

[1] Sir Gilbert Elliot, first Earl of Minto (1751–1814).

needed to talk to his personal agents, mostly about money, which included settlements for Horatia and also percentages of prize money picked up by the fleet. Being a successful commander meant taking every financial advantage of warfare, including sharing in the value of a captured enemy vessel (see chapter 2). As a vice admiral, Nelson was being paid what was a considerable sum for those days: £3,000 a year, worth £154,000 today. However, that was certainly not enough to pay for the upkeep of Merton, to cover the considerable expenses of Emma, to provide for Horatia and – let us not forget – the allowance that he still paid his wife, Frances. The Viscountess Nelson, known as Fanny, was still receiving the equivalent of alimony. Emma Hamilton viewed Lady Nelson with a disagreeable venom. Nelson's wife was ill that year, 1805, and there is every indication that Emma hoped she would die. Letters from Fanny Nelson to Alexander Davison, Nelson's friend and agent, suggest very strongly how much she still adored her husband. This hardly cheered Emma Hamilton. If there was such a thing as a last laugh in this situation, it would have been bitter and heard from the throat of Fanny Nelson. Emma took even further to drink and debt. Eight years after Trafalgar, she was arrested as a debtor and absconded with a reluctant Horatia to Calais. She tried to spend grandly whatever money she could lay her hands on, but died on 15 January 1815, mainly from drink according to Horatia, and in a rather unpleasant boarding house. Fanny Nelson, however, continued to cherish the memory of her husband, and once remarked to her granddaughter, also named Frances, that maybe one day she too would have a broken heart. But she outlived Emma and died in London in May 1831, almost forty-four years to the month since she and her young first lieutenant had been married. By that time she had almost been forgotten. Nelson would never see this tragedy performed. For now, as summer turned towards autumn, he was spending the last few days of his life in London as well as at Merton. He repeatedly expressed, in one form or another, his belief in destiny and his anxiety that it should be he and not some other commander who would rid the high seas of Villeneuve and the Napoleonic navy. Napoleon saw Nelson as a rival, inasmuch as he admired the Englishman's genius and felt frustrated by its military expression. Villeneuve never saw Nelson as anything other than a superior naval tactician and – surely more frightening for himself – a fearless opponent.

Thus, Villeneuve remained afraid of Nelson and convinced for two years that the British admiral could bring about his downfall. That one admiral was able to cause such havoc in the mind of another and in the whole strategic plan of an emperor was nothing short of a psychological and military phenomenon. Nelson's total belief in himself, combined with the accompanying insecurity which made him even more determined, made him a most formidable enemy to the French. It was not as if the Royal Navy had at sea a raft of shabby admirals, both junior and senior. In spite of the events of around 22 July that year, Calder was nevertheless a good commander. Collingwood was exceptional. Keith had been a tactical wizard. Cochrane was admired by his peers. Blackwood,[2] then a self-possessed captain full of initiative, would become a vice admiral. And above them all was Admiral Sir William Cornwallis. Certainly, the Royal Navy was, as the sailors said, down by the head with fine flag officers. Only Nelson, however, challenged the gods.

It seemed Nelson had no need to concern himself with his reputation. He may well have worried that the Admiralty and even the prime minister could have wished his career at an end. After all, Nelson had spent a disagreeable part of his life as a senior officer suffering the jealousies and not always unfair criticisms of his superiors. Even his patron, St Vincent, could sometimes exercise cruelty towards Nelson's reputation. But St Vincent was an equally larger-than-life figure, able to express sour generosity as well as sweet approbation.

Nelson had been at sea with negligible pauses for two years and three months. The times, the conditions and the stress had sapped his strength. However, as every sea officer knew, the main business was duty. It was now his duty to return that Wednesday afternoon to Lord Barham to give his views and to get Barham's opinion of where the war with Napoleon stood. He was introduced to Viscount Castlereagh,[3] who had

---

[2] Sir Henry Blackwood (1770–1832).

[3] Viscount Robert Stuart Castlereagh (1769–1822). One of the more spectacular politicians of the period. He was, until 1795, of the Whig persuasion, but then crossed the floor to become a Tory. Later, he became a distinguished foreign secretary under Lord Liverpool. He was considered one of the celebrated architects of the peace that followed Wellington's defeat of Napoleon. Yet Castlereagh was disliked with enormous passion by many. He fought a duel with Canning and died by his own hand. It is said that some cheered at the sight of his coffin.

only the day before taken office as secretary for war. What could Castlereagh know? He met also the moneybags of the navy, George Canning,[*] who would one day take over from Castlereagh as foreign secretary after the latter had committed suicide. Perhaps the admiral's most significant meeting was with the prime minister, William Pitt.

The relationship between Pitt the Younger and Nelson was important inasmuch as the former recognized that it was the navy which would guarantee that there was no invasion and that Nelson held the key to how well the country's somewhat limited fleet would fare against the French. Pitt's concept of an alliance with Austria and Russia was yet to be tested. His first need was to satisfy himself that Napoleon had indeed abandoned his invasion plan. Furthermore, Pitt saw that Napoleon's expansionist policies could not get anywhere without his navy. Nelson could not win Pitt's land battles. (Wellington was not yet the formidable commander he would become, nor was he yet needed.) However, Pitt understood that through British control of the sea lanes and the virtual destruction of the Franco-Spanish naval alliance Napoleonic armies could at least be contained within the continent. How Britain coped with French elements in the colonies was not immaterial but certainly simplified by control of the high seas. For example, both Nelson and Pitt could see that the former's expedition to the West Indies that summer had not been entirely in vain.

Nelson may have missed Villeneuve, but he had effectively weakened the French possessions. Knowing that the West Indies could not be quickly reinforced by a fleet of major warships would keep the French very much on the defensive and therefore of less concern to those who had to supply the resources for the British forces in continental Europe including what would become Wellington's Iberian campaign.

Pitt trusted Nelson. They had first admired each other four years earlier. In 1801, when Nelson was bombarding, albeit not always successfully, the beginnings of the Boulogne construction, he had anchored off the Downs. It was there that Pitt had met Nelson in the *Victory*. They were not unalike. Certainly their perceptions of warfare and of Napoleon

---

[*] George Canning, (1770–1827) At the time of the Battle of Trafalgar, Canning was Treasurer of the Navy. He was briefly prime minister during the year of his death.

chimed. It was just as well for Nelson that they did get on so famously. The admiral could visit treasurers and secretaries and victuallers of the navy to his heart's content. However, when the Admiralty accountant wavered, Nelson believed he could rely on the one man who would overrule all the inhibitions of administrators. Pitt was on Nelson's side. Moreover, when it was seen how much the two admired each other, those in the Admiralty who needed to took note of this. None of this meant that Pitt was blinded by Nelson's opinions on everything. There were after all, practical elements of the naval campaign still to be resolved.

During this period the protagonists were catching their breath. Villeneuve and Gravina were contained in port and so presented no danger other than that of seeking the chance to be repaired and re-supplied for when they did emerge. Certainly there was no reason to believe these two commanders would not re-emerge and give the British guardships the slip, as they had before. Also, what if the instructions from Napoleon were carried out to the letter? By now, the British had a reasonable idea of Napoleon's plan for Villeneuve. They could see that the plan would include disrupting Cornwallis's blockade sufficiently for Ganteaume to get out of Brest. Even Nelson's determination and resolve might easily be tested by a Combined Fleet of ships commanded by the two senior French admirals and Gravina. Moreover, no one could underestimate the Spanish element of that fleet after its unquestionably gallant and efficient display against Calder. The Royal Navy had always had a respect for Gravina, his ships and his determination.

Pitt was aware also that to fight a war he needed a great deal of money. It could not all come from taxes. It most certainly could not come from excise duties if the French proved able to turn the tables and take command of the high seas. Imagine the literally millions of pounds sterling of cargoes that were at sea at any one time, sailing for England from colonies as far apart as the Indian subcontinent and the West Indian sugar islands. A single convoy or even a well laden merchantman, lost to a French squadron, would do more than reduce the profits of a London trading house. We might remember also that merchant ships at the beginning of the nineteenth century were subjected to the same weather conditions and crew-related limitations that warships were. Those civilian vessels, however, often ran on predictable lines. Whereas a warship would alter course and make detours in order to track or invade an enemy, merchant ships usually followed known tidal streams and prevailing wind directions. True, there were ships that traded from port to port, hardly ever knowing their next destination until the skipper or the agent had fixed a cargo. These were the old sailing tramp ships. The vessels that would have interested the French and Spanish men-of-war were not these. The French and Spanish were interested in the rich cargoes returning to Britain from the colonies along the established sea lanes. Even in the days before steam made cargo shipping more reliable, a company might expect the return of one of its vessels from even as far away as India to arrive in the Pool of London, say, within a relatively small period. In time of war, because enemy vessels would know full well the normal courses taken by merchant ships, they would be particularly vulnerable to attack, which is why the convoy system was introduced. This allowed, for example, the Royal Navy to have two or three guardships sail with the convoy. It was often a successful procedure. Yet there would always be stragglers, and it was really only practical for trade between the Americas and Britain.

Knowing all this, we can imagine the nervousness of ship owners whose vessels were sailing, usually one by one, from India or Africa. Imagine also the consternation in the London offices when a valuable cargo vessel was a couple of days overdue.

So we see that threat to merchant shipping and thus, by extension, to Britain's fragile wartime economy, was an aside in the campaign against Napoleon. For example, in its edition of 27 August 1805, *The Times* announced that ships about to sail from West Country harbours – the jumping-off points for North America and the Caribbean – had been told to remain at anchor. Efforts had also been made to recall recently sailed vessels. In short, until the Admiralty was certain that it had a proper estimate of the Franco-Spanish fleet and, hopefully, the intentions of its deployment, it was best for those valuable merchant ships to wait in port. The commercial loss of having a ship alongside instead of at sea was enormous. Yet it was true that the Royal Navy could not begin to offer any guarantee of safe passage to those vessels. Here, then, was an irony: the Royal Navy was bottling up the French and Spanish in their ports, and without even leaving harbour, the French and Spanish were similarly bottling up the vital commercial vessels in English ports. Such were the practical considerations that existed at even the highest level of naval warfare at that time. To be denied the sea lanes was to be denied the commercial oxygen of the life of the nation.

The consequent loss of confidence in the markets could so easily cause a run on Britain's finances and general economy, exactly at the point when Pitt needed every penny to pay for the war as it was, and for the extended war he knew was to come. He was right, and it would last another decade. No wonder the brokers and fixers, the directors and treasurers of the London business houses, saw Nelson in such a strong light. They needed to believe in a hero who could save their current account balances.

The run on the economy was hardly exclusive to Britain. Napoleon also was so strapped for cash that his entire war effort was financially in the red. Barbé-Marbois,[5] his finance minister, kept telling him there was no money to pay the troops and the sailors and, by extension, the contractors who had supplied the impressive war machine which he had built along the north French coast in the previous two-and-a-half years. Napoleon had established the most elaborate corporate sponsorship – as we might call it – arrangements. He had raised prodigious sums from the banks at home and overseas and issued promissory notes right, left and centre. Companies and individuals in France were being bankrupted by their ruler's determination to conquer Europe and – until August 1805 – especially, Britain.

French currency was no longer worth the paper it was printed on. Consequently there was a run on gold. Merchants and traders and the general public panicked. The banks were ordered to lock their grilles. If there were gold bars to be had and coins in sacks to be counted, they were most certainly not going to angry creditors. If they had, the whole of France would have come to a standstill in a week. Inflation had no politico-economic definition in 1805. That did not stop the economy from metaphorically disappearing in wheelbarrow loads. Even the handouts promised by their closest new ally, Spain, were not coming through on time. There was gold to be had. Much of it was in Mexico.

---

[5] François Barbé-Marbois (1745–1837).

The Royal Navy loitered along that trade route, waiting for the nineteenth-century galleons. The prize would be more than coinage. It would be the ruin of France.

As ever, the banks manipulated the crisis to suit themselves, and did so internationally. Consequently, the movement of gold and credit sometimes passed not merely through French and Spanish banks but also through British finance houses. Funds offshore and onshore, transactions through friendly and unfriendly nations, had always taken place. The fact that a well-respected British bank might trade cleverly with a well-respected French one in the summer of 1805 was only to be expected. The theatre that is war could easily find angels. After all, had not Pitt himself been forced to introduce income tax for the first time six years earlier, in 1799, to finance the war against France? In 1805, the Bank of England was as sorely pressed as the Banque de France. It was as if the war was being fought on two fronts: the military and the financial.

That the British were planning to build fifty new capital ships and then rig, store and man them, maintaining them as fighting vessels, meant that Pitt was not so certain of getting the money, but he believed he had no alternative. Napoleon did not believe in alternatives. He had a plan, no matter how many times he changed it, and to his mind, the banks' failure to pay for it was tantamount to treason.

No bill and account for war ever remains in the stricter columns of the treasury. Apart from the human cost, war is rarely paid for in financial terms. Napoleon and Pitt understood this. Napoleon had built his dream into a machine. The machine worked. He could not afford to pay for it. Thus the merchants of Britain and the undersecretaries of Whitehall were not alone in trying desperately to raise money while at the same time devising schemes to protect part of the system, namely the merchant fleet, that was responsible for bringing wealth to these islands. No wonder they put their faith in the quick-witted Norfolk admiral whom they sometimes criticized so harshly. What choice had they?

In fact, the whole country needed an act of heroism or, at the very least, of reassurance. We should not get the impression that the nation was either so confident or so indifferent that it hardly took notice of the threat of invasion. People really were in no doubt that the nation was threatened. Even the action of George III in agreeing to Pitt's return to power had been recognized as an indicator of the serious state of the nation. The reports of the building of the invasion force in, and either side of, Boulogne were widespread. Detailed accounts were given of the threat and its possible consequences. Many had seen for themselves the extent of the French plan, or knew those who had. Napoleon's reputation was not that of a tinpot general. He was, in the minds of the British, a powerful personality. We might laugh today at this slightly ridiculous figure and the elaborate pomp that surrounded his imperial coronation in December 1804. Yet we must remember the times. Britain had had no such hero since Marlborough. (And even he had been accused of wrongdoing and was scorned.) The British understood ceremony and circumstance more than any other European nation. They saw regal splendour as an expression of true power. The nation was rapidly entering the era of its second Empire. Its Protestant belief in its own authority and its arrogance gave its people a confidence that, on paper at least, seemed hardly justifiable. The British would therefore be the first to recognize the possibilities of Napoleonic advance across the whole of continental Europe. Napoleon, was no nineteenth-century Hitler. Yet he held, for many British people, a similar fascination. No wonder those who ruled Britannia sensed disaster. They could see the gathering forces of Napoleon. They could do the simple arithmetic that demonstrated that should the Combined Fleet put to sea with the Brest squadron, the Royal Navy would be outnumbered – perhaps hopelessly so. The Admiralty was not thinking merely in terms of a pitched battle. It had taken note, during the past two years, of the toll and effort taken to contain the French and Spanish squadrons in their ports. Cornwallis had proved himself one of the finest naval managers the service had seen or, indeed, would see. His quiet organization and persistence had truly saved Britain from disaster. It was all very well for the crowds to be delighted by Nelson's dashing around the oceans. It does not detract from Nelson's courage to say that without Cornwallis's stifling of the main French naval effort the former would have found no use for his gallantry. Now, with all their fears and fascinations, the nation watched for Nelson. He was their gladiator, their medieval champion returned, prepared to fight their corner and with their favour.

We know that it all ended two months later in the most famous victory in British naval history. During that third week in August, Pitt, Castlereagh, Canning, Barham and, of course, Nelson were not to know this. That summer, they were the people who mattered in British defence. The Admiralty's building plan for about fifty major warships would, when commissioned, bring the Royal Navy up to at least the strength of the Combined Fleet. The shipwrights and riggers were furiously busy in at least seven yards across Britain. Yet when would these ships be ready for sea? Also, where would the navy find their captains, their bosuns, their leading hands and sailing masters? None really knew the answers to these questions. Britain could not wait; it had to go with what it had.

We should also understand that in this very month, August 1805, the newspapers and coffee houses were full of accusations against Calder. This was far more than a case of officialdom saying that one of its senior admirals had fallen down on the job. He had failed effectively to lift the gloom. The British were looking for a famous victory, not to boost national pride or enhance the myth of invincibility. They sought that victory against the French fleet for a very practical reason: they were frightened of the French navy and needed it destroyed. Therefore Calder's failure represented far more than letting down the navy. He had, so it was being said, jeopardized the security of Britain. If this mood seems exaggerated, we have to remember that by that summer the British were indeed caught in the gloom of a war mentality. Here, if for no other reason, was why the nation needed a genius who could overturn the odds. Nelson had to be that genius. There was none other.

Nelson's visit to London was not a quiet affair. He was followed wherever he went. He was doorstepped by the newspapers and the gentlemen from *The Times*. Vice Admiral Calder's vilification made Nelson even more popular. Little wonder that people gathered to catch just a glimpse of Nelson's green-coated figure (he had left his admiral's garb behind) as he emerged from his lodgings at 44 Albemarle Street, off Piccadilly. They followed him through St James's to the Admiralty, to Somerset House, then down and on across Horse Guards to the sideways end of Downing Street, then to the arches of the Foreign Office, then back to the Admiralty, back to Downing Street, across Horse Guards once more, to see Barham again, then rapidly across the

Mall and back to Albemarle Street, not to hide but to sketch out his ideas on paper. Behind him, a train of admirers and well-wishers, curious and hopeful.

We might imagine that Nelson was drawing up his plans for an Atlantic battle with Villeneuve. He saw the ambition of Napoleon's navy as being control of the Mediterranean. Apart from being a Corsican, Napoleon had to believe, according to Nelson, that naval control of certainly the north Mediterranean shores would be essential for his greater scheme. Nelson had of course already written reams on the importance of safeguarding Malta, Naples and Sicily, but particularly on the subject of Sardinia and the anchorages which he had used for his squadrons.

He returned to the subject that August. At six o'clock in the morning on 29 August, Nelson wrote to the prime minister that he would not be able to rest until the importance of Sardinia was perfectly understood by Pitt and the rest of Whitehall. He also made a point of telling Pitt that he had written on this subject many times and if, as seemed likely, the bureaucracy had conveniently misplaced those warnings and entreaties, he would be very pleased to bring along copies which he had faithfully kept because of the importance of the subject.

His main warning to Pitt was that France was about to seize the island. Pitt was not going to go into any detail, and he most certainly did not want Nelson to give him chapter and verse of his anxieties. Nelson was wise to Pitt's mood and reminded him only that

> our Fleet would find a difficulty, if not impossibility, of keeping any Station off Toulon for want of that Island to supply cattle, water, and refreshments in the present state of the Mediterranean, and that we can have no certainty of commerce at any time, but what France chooses to allow us, to either Italy or the Levant.

To allow a major French naval presence to operate from Toulon and a Spanish one from Cartagena, was unthinkable to this admiral's mind. Napoleon, he believed, would have to protect his southern flank against the possible reinforcement by British troops in that southern part of the continent. Nor could Napoleon be expected to allow the British to stop supplies coming through southern ports. Also, within the greater idea of the emperor's broader plan there remained his ambition to possess Egypt and thus the land gateway to the Indian Ocean and even the overland route into Asia. When Napoleon had been asked if there were no end of his ambition, he had said, perhaps apocryphally, there was always Turkey. In other words, there was no end to imperial dreams, and no nightmares. Nelson tried to think like Napoleon in order to anticipate what he himself should be doing to bring the French emperor to heel. This is why, in a certain sense, it was Napoleon and Nelson who were the rivals, not Villeneuve and Nelson.

CHAPTER TWENTY-TWO

The Nearly New Plan

ILLENEUVE'S AIM WAS TO AVOID NELSON THE MAN. NELSON'S AIM was to destroy not Villeneuve, but his fleet. Nelson, therefore, had come to the conclusion that that fleet would want to get back to the Mediterranean. By the end of August, it was clear that Napoleon's divisions along the Channel coastline were withdrawing and reforming to advance on the Rhine. For this reason Cornwallis's effort had to be even doubled, if that were possible, to prevent the Brest squadrons from sailing. All British naval attention that was not focused by Cornwallis through his Channel flotillas emphasized their efforts to keep Villeneuve in Cadiz. They knew that he would get out. Nelson worked hard on his Mediterranean hypothesis, anticipating that day.

He also began to produce a new tactical naval doctrine – or rather, develop an older idea. This may seem unlikely, because ships had not changed shape, had no different sailing performance, firepower or any kind of squadron composition other than the one they had had in more than living memory. Why would Nelson want now to change tactical plans? The answer is threefold: his experience, his now undoubted authority and his inquisitiveness and sense of detail that set him aside from so many other commanders who had not advanced much from the days of, say, the sixteenth century, when an admiral was a general at sea. It was this concept of how to execute a naval battle against a specific enemy that would be put before all Nelson's commanders shortly before Trafalgar in the coming October.

Up until this point, naval engagements between massed fleets had taken the form of a deadly heinous pavane. Flotillas or fleets would meet in courtly state, each side in a long battle line. From this we get the term 'line of battle', and the importance and size of a ship would thus be confirmed by her whereabouts in that line. The line would be stem to stern, all going in the same direction, and the enemy fleet would be stem to stern, slowly going in the opposite direction and parallel to its adversary, usually because of wind directions. The purpose of each commander was to manoeuvre to keep the advantage of the existing wind direction. So the two lines would manoeuvre in parallel until two conditions were reached: they would be within damning broadside range of each other and near enough to quickly close on the enemy once sufficient damage had been done by the cannonballs, whose purpose was to bring down enough rigging and sails to make manoeuvring impossible and to cause as much havoc as possible on deck, as well as blasting into the sides of the enemy ships either to silence the guns or, better still, to kill enemy sailors so that they could no longer fire them. Once closed, literally alongside, the fleet which believed it had the upper hand would board the other's ships with pistol and cutlass, to shoot and slice as many sailors to death as it took to make their captains and commander strike their colours in surrender.

This tactical plan certainly had an element of brutality, but was surprisingly inefficient and therefore not always conclusive. What it failed to allow were individual manoeuvres and the initiatives of ships' captains after a state of chaos had been reached. At that point, manoeuvre was mostly impossible. This meant that a captain was always reliant on the senior commander of the fleet, usually at least a rear admiral, for directions and inevitably feared getting out of line (the origin of the expression). The very practical side of this weakness was that if the captain of a vessel was fighting under the absolute direction of his flag officer, then he, the captain, had always to be sure that he could see that officer's signals.

With sea mists and the hopeless fog of war how could a captain know what to do next? How would he know to close, or break away, or go in support of another ship if he could not see the most elementary signals from the flagship? Moreover, the flagship was not immune to this chaos.

How, then, could the admiral know in good time the state of the battle, his weak and strong points in the line of battle and be aware of the need to give or, in many cases, *not* to give further orders? Given the limitations of these fighting platforms, with their guns in fixed positions along each side, with limited elevation, together with the restrictions on movement, if only because it could take an hour to radically alter course, naval doctrine had not much changed in the lifetimes of those who fought on board ship. Nelson thought this uninteresting.

His plan was to cause chaos and then to control it. Was it not Napoleon who had said that the battlefield was a scene of constant chaos? The winner would be the one who controlled that chaos, both his own and the enemy's. Hence Nelson's new idea to develop what was possible rather than what was predictable. His thoughts had not come out of the blue, nor were they entirely his own, in spite of the obedience to the famous October Memorandum on his battle plan.

There is always a chapter in British naval histories that describes the French defeat off the Caribbean island of Dominica in 1782. The British commander had been Admiral George Rodney, who had been fighting the French for forty years and saw great sense in the notion of the flexibility of a fleet. It was all very well to form a battle line, but why would an admiral wish to give the enemy what amounted to similar advantages? The set-piece engagement did not necessarily allow for a fleet to break the enemy up into pieces. Rodney favoured the more flexible tactic of disrupting the enemy's line. Nelson took this thinking further. In London he began to sketch the ways in which his fleet would be able to cut off sections of the French, separate them from their command centre and even surround them.

Behind Nelson's thinking lay far more than a desire to break away from the ordinary. His experience told him, as it surely did every captain and flag officer, that the limitations in ship handling caused by their construction and rigging in addition to the influence of weather conditions meant that opportunities to strike mortal blows at sections of the enemy were too often lost in the need to conform to the time-consuming operation of forming a battle line. However, was there not another reason for thinking about the standard tactics?

Really, Nelson must have been thinking very carefully about Robert

Calder's failure to destroy Villeneuve's fleet. While the Admiralty and newspapers gradually stripped Calder of every ounce of dignity and professional reputation, Nelson spent much time writing letters to the establishment and telling friends that Calder had been in a difficult position and that it was very wrong indeed for hero worshippers to say that he, Nelson, would not have let Villeneuve get away.

Villeneuve had got away from Calder partly because the latter had wanted to protect the prizes of two Spanish vessels he had taken, or rather, which had drifted into his possession. He had also let him get away because the weather conditions had not allowed Calder to form up into another battle line in an instant, when the opportunity was there. The third reason is connected with the first two: he had believed reinforcements might arrive for Villeneuve and had therefore been unable to form the British fleet into a line to cope with the Frenchman before those reinforcements arrived. Nelson knew all of this.

Senior officers in the Admiralty, who must have known professionally the difficulties of Calder before they criticized him, were naturally under pressure from the politicians and also from the public mood to obtain a victory. Those who witnessed the same pressures on the navy in 1916 when Britain wanted another Trafalgar and got Jutland instead, or in 1982 when the then prime minister Margaret Thatcher[1] needed the famous victory at Goose Green to keep the public on side during the Falklands conflict would easily appreciate the reason why Calder was so criticized in London. Nelson was always aware of the hell of personal criticism. He had suffered from it. He could also see the inevitability of the limited tactical engagement plan producing yet another stalemate or – worse – defeat.

Nelson had a generous nature when dealing with most of his fellow officers, particularly his subordinates. It was well within his personality to defend Calder. Having at long last the opportunity, whether by prompting or experience, to rethink battle plans, Nelson refused to capitalize on Calder's discomfiture and stuck sensibly to his principle of 'There but for the Grace of God etc.' So it was that Calder's degradation,

---

[1] Margaret Thatcher (1925–), prime minister 1979–1990, became Baroness Thatcher of Kesteven in 1992.

and the circumstances surrounding it, concentrated the effort Nelson put into thinking through a 'new' battle plan.

The concepts of fighting ships had to be revised. Waiting for what he thought to be the inevitable call to battle made Nelson sit down with paper and draw diagrams, planning to ensure that when the moment came he would destroy Villeneuve. Nothing less was acceptable than the French admiral's complete and utter removal from the ocean. Nelson knew there would be no more opportunities. It is therefore worth studying the years of experience and understanding that went to make up Nelson's naval career to appreciate what followed or was supposed to have followed. He had spent the best part of four decades either fighting at sea or waiting to do so. Those thirty-odd years went into preparing for what he sensed would be his final and greatest battle.

As we have seen, if naval tactics had not changed much in decades, it was partly because ships had not. Moreover, the complexities of a full engagement meant that every captain had to follow the commander and, in a big battle, the commander-in-chief. However, this did not mean that the captain of even a smaller ship might be considered to lack initiative. Far from it. A successful captain was one who had very likely made his name in single engagements with just one enemy ship. We should not get the idea that the oceans were full of cannon-firing, cutlass-wielding matelots. In fact, the number of contacts that led to a naval engagement – what the army would call a skirmish – were very few. Yet when a British frigate met a French one and they did fight, the result for the successful captain in question would nearly always be almost as great as for a large-scale fleet action.

The captain of a Royal Navy frigate, a relatively small vessel, would not necessarily subscribe to the purist naval doctrine that a superior fleet was one which confined the enemy to port, anchorage or home waters enabling the British to have sea superiority if not supremacy. Sea superiority meant that the Royal Navy was able to counter any French moves against British shipping (both commercial and naval) and British possessions. Sea supremacy, on the other hand, meant that British shipping could sail and British settlements could go about their business knowing that there was no question of a French attack. A superior navy was one capable of countering an attack; a supreme navy was one that dominated to such an extent that an attack would never be contemplated.

This refinement of maritime doctrine did not serve much purpose for an ambitious Royal Naval officer. He needed a victory, however small, to make money, to enhance his reputation and therefore to further his career. Consequently, a frigate's captain, spying a French vessel, would want to attack. If successful, he might do reasonably well by taking the French frigate as a prize. This would depend on the degree of military energy expended in taking that ship. If the Royal Naval officer had shot it to pieces, the amount of prize money would not be significant. For example, the two Spanish vessels taken by Calder on 22 July, and protected so carefully by him that their presence was cited as one reason for his failure to re-engage Villeneuve, proved almost worthless financially. Also, they did nothing for his reputation. The frigate captain reporting even a single success could, in those tense days of the Napoleonic wars, expect many honours. There were occasions when a captain successfully overcame a French frigate and, as a result, was given a knighthood and, equally important, enough recognition to, at the very least, maintain his foothold on the slippery promotion ladder in the Royal Navy. The author has a drawing of the Royal Navy frigate *Nymph* taking the *Cléopatre* in 1793. The *Nymph's* captain, Edward Pellew,[2] was knighted. Pellew was quickly promoted, commanded Cornwallis's Cape Finisterre squadron between 1803 and 1804 and was later gazetted as Admiral Viscount Exmouth. Pellew, incidentally, was not at Trafalgar because in 1804 he had become commander-in-chief of the Royal Navy in India. A few years later he took command of what by then had become the late Viscount Nelson's fleet in the Mediterranean. Pellew would have succeeded in almost any circumstances, but it was that single action against the *Cléopatre* that gave his career the impetus that was to earn him a commander-in-chief's pennant.

The rewards were ample. Nelson was created a viscount after the Battle of the Nile. Jervis became an earl after the Battle of St Vincent, from whence he took his title. Commercial companies, cities and colonial

---

[2] Sir Edward Pellew (1757–1833).

settlements would honour even minor captains after a victory with silver, money and civic handouts.

If, however, a captain of a frigate or ship of the line failed to win in an engagement, it would inevitably mean that his ship had been taken as a prize by the enemy. In other words, he had struck his colours and surrendered. If this unfortunate commanding officer ever returned, he would be court-martialled. The court martial did not necessarily assume that the captain was in utter disgrace.

The court martial was there to determine the circumstances that had caused such a dishonour as surrender. There were many cases where a captain had fought his ship brilliantly but had been overwhelmed. He could perhaps expect sympathy, but no gallantry awards, whatever his conduct. At the least, he might suppose that he would go to the bottom of the pile from which promotions were selected. An officer did not even have to surrender to face a court martial. He may merely have abandoned an engagement. No one would necessarily expect a frigate's captain to hazard his ship by taking on a 100-gun ship of the line. But only a court martial could decide whether the circumstances of avoiding a fight had been honourable or otherwise. If the incident became a matter for public discussion, there was even more reason to examine the conditions surrounding the event. So it was with the court martial of Calder. He had engaged the enemy. He had, however, failed to return to the fight. That, with public feeling running high, was enough for 'swords and medals' – the Royal Navy's euphemism for a court martial.

Calder's had been a large-scale confrontation. Some, because he had two prize ships, would have called it a victory of sorts, and, indeed, Nelson himself did so, although not for long. But a single action could and did inspire as much feeling. A captain who had surrendered his ship would be examined just as closely as one who had not. The latter was, in sporting parlance, the goal scorer of the day.

We ought not to be surprised at the scale of recognition that might arise from a single action. A nation at war needs heroes. The majesty of a single action in a huge sea is a forceful image, especially when the people are hungry for success. Also, that single incident has the further advantage of being conclusive. An army victory may easily be reversed the following day or week, when a particular area is retaken by the enemy.

Mostly, the victorious vessel leaves little debris and only an impassive witness – the sea.

The action of one frigate against another was not unlike the battle plan of two major flotillas. The tactic was, on the whole, to sail parallel to the enemy, fire as many broadsides as possible into her and then grapple alongside to take the surrender. Also, the single action had much in common with the fleet action, because the first task was to overcome the disadvantage of manoeuvring against an enemy when relying only on the sea state and the wind direction. Paintings of ship in full sail engaged in battle can be quite misleading. To better manoeuvre a ships her sailing masters would hand in most of, if not all, the lower sails. It was easier to manoeuvre using only the top sails. This was certainly the case with a frigate when playing catch-as-catch-can with an enemy ship. It was even more important to have such a simple rig when a whole fleet had to be kept in order. There was the added advantage that once action had started not only were the huge main sails unnecessary and the process of bringing them in a lengthy one, but they could cause havoc below, not to mention appalling ship-handling if struck by enemy shot.

Thus the topgallants and staysails were furled and the main courses hauled in (see chapter 3). The triangular sail at the front of the ship, the jib, and the main and fore topsails, were used to manoeuvre. The mizen, the sail at the stern of the ship, would be used as a sort of brake (see chapter 3). A further advantage of having the sails further up the mast to manoeuvre by was that the bosun would not need so many ratings to handle the ship. Once the vessel was more manoeuvrable, advantage could be taken and disadvantage avoided by the single vessel, and the whole fleet order could be quickly followed.

The range of the first engagement of a vessel depended upon the sea state, the position of the two fleets or the single vessel and, necessarily, the distance over which a ship's guns could be fired accurately. However, this was not over-the-horizon fighting. Typically, sailors in both ships would have seen the enemy quite clearly as they waited to fire. A common engagement for that first broadside into the upper decks and hull would have been fifty yards or even less. It was not uncommon for a ship to come right alongside, even touching, and then blast away at the other vessel and its crew at, literally, point-blank range. Nelson's navy had a rule of thumb for engaging to fire the initial broadside. A captain had only to leave as much room as he needed to manoeuvre his vessel. Once he was that close, he was expected to be firing. The same tactic would have been used by the whole fleet. Having got into position, and assuming that no attempt was being made to rake the opponent's vulnerable stern (probably the weakest above-water part of the vessel), the tactic of the broadside had to be quite clear in the minds of all the commanders.

Some engagements have shown that the French saw a great advantage in firing into the enemy rigging and spars, on the assumption that the vessel would then be out of control and the crashing timbers would create chaos below. The British were inclined to favour firing into the enemy hulls. This had the advantage of killing more people and thus disabling more guns. Whatever the target, the broadside itself had to be a carefully controlled firing exercise. Again, the vision of cannon being run out and all firing at the same time should be treated with some caution. The shock effect of firing all at once in broadside would tip a vessel in the opposite direction and make it the most unstable platform, as well as rattling and dislodging essential equipment. If we imagine the effect of an emergency stop at high speed on a family car, its contents and passengers, we can begin to see the result of a single broadside-firing of all guns in a ship of the line. Therefore the most effective broadsides would come from a consecutive firing from the line of gun ports. To fire into the quarters (the rear sections of a ship) could have an equally devastating effect. Apart from the steering gear, here would be the command and control centre. The overall British purpose, however, was to dye the decks of the enemy ships with the blood of any sailor who could fight. There was even a notion that it was better to wound an enemy sailor severely than to kill him. His wretched screaming would fill those about him with fear, making them therefore less efficient and thus less threatening. An extension of this hypothesis was to keep the surgeon busy on his lower deck.

For the engagement to work properly Nelson believed that it was no longer possible to use predictable, traditional tactics. He, more than most commanders, understood that lining up two opposing forces and blasting away until one side had no more blood to shed was a reasonable style of naval warfare only as long as his own navy was the one taking and not giving a surrender. The Royal Navy had had enormous success in sea battles, and so it could have been argued that the old system was working. Yet Nelson knew that naval warfare had to move on. If nothing else, Calder's experience, made very public, had proved this. Nelson saw the weakness in the line-of-battle campaign as being the fact that everything could so easily come to a standstill or even fail if individual captains happened to be either following apparently inflexible orders or were unable to see, in the confusion of war, signals that changed the direction of the conflict.

Instead of having one line of battle sailing parallel to the enemy, Nelson literally turned his fleet (in planning terms anyway) ninety degrees. Imagine, then, the two traditional lines: on the left, the enemy moving south and, on the right, the line of the Royal Navy moving north. The normal way of attacking, as we have seen, would have been for the Royal Navy to wait for the other side to line up opposite. Assuming they were close enough, both would then fire. In its simplest terms, we can still keep the image of two lines of ships, one facing south, the other north, parallel and opposite and ready to fire. However, the Nelsonian plan meant that the line on the right, that is, the Royal Navy, would suddenly turn to the left and point at the enemy line.

Nelson's fleet would now break into three columns. Two of those columns would be the main ships of the line. Each column would have sixteen ships. The third column would be an advance squadron. This would be half the size, faster and smaller. This third group would have flexible tactics. If one of the columns of big ships needed reinforcing, that extra help would come from the third column. Therefore, instead of having one long broadside of vessels hoping to outgun a similarly long broadside of French and Spanish vessels, Nelson had changed naval warfare on one piece of paper.

He had created three columns of naval knights who would, on their 74-gun chargers, pierce the enemy's lines, split them into at least three groups and then, because the front of the column could be through before the enemy knew what was happening, the French ships would be fired upon from both sides. Of course, this meant, when we remember the firing range we saw earlier, that with Royal Navy ships on both sides of the enemy, it was inevitable that they would hit one another as well as the enemy. Nelson recognized this. In theory, the Royal Naval tactic of firing into the hull of the enemy and not into the rigging (where a cannonball would go straight through) reduced the chances of 'blue on blue', that is, being hit by friendly fire.

Nelson had said it was impossible to control a line of forty ships without first being able to control the weather, something even he knew to be impossible. The line of thinking he adopted was not entirely new. It is simply a puzzle why no one at fleet level had thought of it before and had the confidence to put it into action.

At squadron level, with perhaps six or seven ships, there was always the flexibility to split an enemy. Yet again, a scattered fleet was harder to fight than one gathered together. Both enemies were subject to the same conditions.

Nelson did not produce his diagrammatic battle plan without giving explicit instructions as to who was to do what on the day. Three lines of British warships, piercing and separating the one line of the Combined Fleet, and thus surrounding pockets of that fleet, was difficult enough. What was equally important was that Nelson knew exactly which ship should be in which column and, even more importantly, would gather all his captains and commanders together, explain his plan, telling them individually exactly what was expected of them so that each of his senior officers would be inspired and part of his thinking. These were not the days of fleet exercises. There were no weekly mock battles to bring fleets, individual ships, captains and ratings up to speed. Here was a piece of paper upon which was Nelson's plan to wipe the French and Spanish navies from the maritime list. Britain had, in spite of the nervousness in Whitehall, naval superiority. The stress on the Royal Navy was growing and that superiority could not be guaranteed. Nelson, with his new thinking, believed that after the battle which he knew must come Britain would have achieved the ultimate victory, naval supremacy.

Nelson was at Merton. Villeneuve was in Cadiz. Barham and Pitt knew that the inspirational figure at Merton was the man to take command of the whole fleet that waited for Villeneuve to emerge. Napoleon had by then turned his attentions to the Danube. Yet he had not lost sight of the outrageous military felony of Villeneuve. Decrès had made excuses. Napoleon had taken so much. He would take no more. He ordered Decrès to get rid of Villeneuve. Napoleon instructed Decrès to send Admiral Rosily to take over as soon as possible.

That order for his going and the disgrace likely to follow once he had been replaced might just have been the reason why Villeneuve instructed the combined squadron to sail from Cadiz. He was disgraced and had nothing to lose, unless it was his life. That would come later.

At Merton, Emma waited for Nelson's return. He was lodging at Gordon's Hotel, 44 Albemarle Street[3] virtually next door to Byron's publisher, John Murray.[4] Incidentally, Byron's grandfather was Foulweather Jack, more formally Admiral John Byron,[5] whose adventures off the coast of Chile became the inspiration for the poet's *Don Juan*. Murray would have liked to receive something from Nelson or poetry about Nelson. There was, in London, an eagerness to record the sayings and the likeness of the admiral. He was a personality as big as Pitt himself. Henry Edridge,[6] the portraitist who had recently painted a full-length picture of William Pitt the Younger, was finding it necessary to use the prime minister's office as a conduit to present his case for getting Nelson to agree to sit for him. Nelson had become such an important figure that an artist could expect a handsome commission or sale from such a picture. Emma would have loved him to sit again. There were portraits that would become famous, by fine artists including John Hoppner[7] who had also painted Pitt. Also, Johann Heinrich Schmidt[8], Sir William Beechey[9] and Lemuel Francis Abbot.[10] These paintings were quite apart from the illustrations and scenes that included Nelson. A. D. McCormack's[11] painting showing Admiral Jervis (as then he was)

---

[3] The site is now occupied by a modern building, one of the few in that thoroughfare.
[4] John Murray (1745–1793) set up his publishing house in 1768.
[5] Admiral John Byron (1723–1786).
[6] Henry Edridge, ARA (1769–1821).
[7] John Hoppner (1758–1810) had court connections and painted many distinguished people of the time.
[8] Johann Heinrich Schmidt.
[9] Sir William Beechey (1753–1839) was knighted having become portrait painter to the queen.
[10] Lemuel Francis Abbot (1760–1803) specialised in naval portraits.
[11] A. D. McCormack.

greeting Nelson after the Battle of St Vincent became one of the more memorable scenes in British maritime painting. The caricatures were even greater marks of distinction. James Gillray's[12] vision, after the Battle of the Nile, shows the one-armed Nelson wielding a rough cricket bat, entitled *British Oak*, as he wades through and conquers treacherous crocodiles, supposedly representing the French. Here was the opportunity for the common people to glimpse their hero, although, in pure Gillray style, he produced another caricature entitled *Hero of the Nile*. But instead of the correct insignia on his cap, the cynical Gillray gave a rather bleary-looking Nelson a purse which entitled him to a pension of £2,000 a year (worth £102,000 today). This artistic adoration did not come with an admiral's flag. One of the earliest paintings of Nelson was commissioned in 1777 from the artist John Francis Rigaud.[13] Pitt's close advisor and sometime paymaster general and treasurer of the navy, George Rose,[14] was encouraged to ask Nelson to sit for his portrait. Nelson had no time, although in normal circumstances there was nothing in his vanity that would have led him to turn down such a request, especially as Rose had enormous influence with Pitt.

In spite of his public popularity, Nelson was still not certain that Pitt would order that he should be sent south. One reason for his uncertainty was his expectation that Villeneuve would reappear from Cadiz at any moment and that of all people Calder, who had command of the flotilla (he was not brought back for the inquiry until shortly before the battle – a remarkably stupid decision on the part of the Admiralty, for surely Nelson needed him and his ship and Calder would have fought like a tiger to redeem himself) would once again take on the French admiral and this time deal with him as he should have done earlier. Having been at his writing pad since before six that morning, Nelson left Gordon's Hotel by noon of 29 August. By carriage it was not much more than an hour from Merton. By afternoon, rather than dallying with Emma, the admiral was back at his writing desk.

---

[12] James Gillray (1756–1815), the extremely popular satirist of George III's court.
[13] John Francis Rigaud (1742–1810).
[14] The Honorable George Rose (1744–1818).

Yet again, we find Nelson not at his charts and schemes, but engaged in writing a lengthy dissertation concerning the entitlement of the Mediterranean flag officer (namely himself) to a percentage of the prize money from an enemy ship. This aggravation of Nelson's had gone all the way to the Admiralty solicitor and was now down to an argument over phraseology. Clauses, sub-clauses and pre-clauses occupied the whole afternoon before he was ready to send his case to Marsden, the Admiralty secretary. This is about more than Nelson's attention to detail. He continued, like every other senior officer, to be desperately worried that he was not getting his just deserts. There was always an assumption that the navy would find a way of avoiding having to pay for anything. Here was a case where a captain in the Mediterranean had taken into his small squadron a few ships from the fleet. He had then taken a prize. Nelson argued, against the Admiralty solicitor, that because that captain had assumed control over even one vessel in the Mediterranean fleet, that officer had put himself under the command of the commander-in-chief of the Mediterranean fleet. Hence Nelson argued that the captain could not have exclusive rights to the prize money. If this seems mean-mindedness, then we should consider that Nelson was always campaigning for not only his rights but those of even the most junior rating in his fleet. On this occasion, a great deal of money was involved, so there was an added incentive to take on the Admiralty's legal department. Being an admiral was an expensive business. Being an admiral with Emma Hamilton in convoy was an *extremely* expensive business.

August was coming to a close. Nelson had, at this point, seven weeks to live, and it is perhaps our instinct to get on with the battle. Yet it could not happen that way. He had much to do. Every signal, each order and all the letters that ran between Whitehall and Merton were to be dealt with as if they were vital pieces in the jigsaw that Nelson had before him. He had no final picture to crib. So, gradually, he put the matching information and colours together as he attempted to work out for himself an idea of what the Combined Fleet would be doing and an opportunity for him to take command in time to commit himself to what he implicitly saw as his destiny.

The letters to Cornwallis, Rose and Marsden had all stated his humble acceptance that it might be another's role to take on and destroy Villeneuve.

No one who read those letters believed anything other than that Nelson was saying that it was his – almost divine – right to put an end to the French and, by extension, the Franco-Spanish navies. So he waited.

On 31 August, Nelson was writing apologies from Merton that he could not accept any invitations for social events. Every ship was on standby. Most had gone south. Nelson was surrounded by those family members who were able to cram themselves into Merton. True, none had seen him for more than two years, and so affections were high and there was much to talk about. However, there was a sense of anticipation and, within that feeling, one of danger. *Victory* had been ordered to sea. Perhaps it is only our hindsight that gives the impression that the family were gathering because they sensed this was to be the last time they would see him alive. How can we know? Yet we cannot ignore the tensions of the whole nation. We certainly cannot dismiss the atmosphere that must have existed at Merton as, almost on the hour, messengers arrived day after day. There were private conversations and sealed documents. This was no time for a family to relax.

On 2 September 1805, at five o'clock in the morning, Nelson was officially told that the Combined Fleet was in Cadiz. It may seem surprising that this was the first hard intelligence that he had had of Villeneuve's whereabouts, but again, news travelled slowly. When the envoy, Captain The Honourable Henry Blackwood, arrived at Merton at daybreak, he found Nelson fully dressed and anticipating, as he had every single hour, news of Villeneuve. The coincidence of Blackwood's arrival at Merton to give Nelson news is that it was the same officer who would, seven weeks later, as commander of the inshore squadron in his ship the *Euryalus* standing off Cadiz, bring Nelson, then in HMS *Victory*, the news that Villeneuve had sailed.

The two men then went to London. Blackwood was to report officially. Nelson was to offer his services off Cadiz. There is another version of what happened.

Nelson was not seen at the Admiralty, and it was not until the next day that he returned to see Barham, the First Lord. It was at this point that the Admiralty told Nelson he was to proceed south and take over the whole command from Calder. Calder was miffed. He had little reason to be. Nelson was, after all, resuming the command that he had left when he made his way to England, supposedly for rest and recuperation. On 5 September, Nelson's sea chest was sent from Merton to Portsmouth.

The excitement was beginning to spread among the dockyards and ships in and around Portsmouth. To use a modern expression, Nelson was back. It was also a very thoughtful admiral who wondered whether he would have sufficient numbers of ships under his command to give, as he was supposed to have said, Mister Villeneuve a drubbing. He thought the fleet small compared to that of Villeneuve. As he wrote to Alexander Davison the next morning, 6 September, whilst still at Merton, he would do his best and he hoped 'God Almighty will go with me. I have much to lose, but little to gain; and I go because it's right, and I will serve the Country faithfully.'

For a man preoccupied with destiny, Nelson was out of sorts with his personal arrangements. He was still broke and continued to blame Admiral Sir John Orde for hijacking prizes that were rightfully his and, worse still, for having failed to tell him when Villeneuve had sailed across the Atlantic. He was even paying his extended family's bills, or at least attempting to. Emma had made life less easy financially by studiously avoiding the cost of running Merton and the house in Clarges Street in London. Baubles and accounts had a magnetic effect on the lady.

Barham is often credited with being the inspiration for returning Nelson to the command of the Mediterranean squadron off Cadiz. Certainly, as First Lord, he would have had a formal position. The two men hardly knew each other, Barham having only been appointed that year, long before Nelson's return. It is said also that Barham told Nelson that he could have whichever officers and ships he wanted. Nelson is said to have replied that he, Barham, could choose anyone he wished, because the same spirit existed throughout the navy; meaning that it certainly did under Nelson's command. There is little doubt that the sheer imagination, reputation and persistent personality of this slightly built officer impressed Pitt sufficiently for him to understand the fine line between being self-opinionated and uncompromisingly professional.

Nelson had not yet left England, but he had immediately started to reshape his command. One of the first letters he wrote was to his sturdy friend, Cuthbert Collingwood. On 7 September, he scribbled a quick note to be taken by dispatch and then fast sloop, to reach Collingwood in the area off Cadiz. Collingwood was deputy to Calder. Nelson wanted to keep Collingwood. Now that he was resuming his command, he could make sure that happened.

> you will change the *Dreadnought* for the *Royal Sovereign* [which was still undergoing repairs in England] which I hope you will like. Ever, my dear Collingwood, most faithfully yours,
> Nelson and Brontë.

Collingwood was delighted. Philip Durham, the captain of HMS *Defiance*, was sent similar instructions. At a time of gathering the fleet and either of the resumption of a command or a new command being assumed by a flag officer, the admiral sends a letter to each of his captains. On 11 September 1805, Nelson's text was common to all.

> Pursuant to instructions from the Lords Commissioners of the Admiralty, you are hereby required and directed to put yourself under my command, and follow and obey all such orders as you shall from time to time receive from me for His Majesty's Service. Nelson and Brontë.

CHAPTER TWENTY-THREE

Southward Bound

NELSON WAS READY FOR WAR. ON THURSDAY EVENING, 12 SEPTEMBER, he began making his first farewells and putting in order his most recent papers, including one from Prince Edward, the Duke of Kent.[1] Edward wrote that his 'best and most fervent wishes will ever attend you, and it will be a subject of real pride for me to be considered one of your warmest friends and admirers.' There is no doubting the royal duke's affection and admiration, but he was also hoping to have some of Nelson's success and popularity rub off on him. He longed to have command of any army in the land campaign, but had been stood aside.

For Nelson to be successful the campaign against Napoleon would take a different direction, and the duke was anticipating that the need for more soldiers would mean he would get his command. Victory against Villeneuve would give Nelson unparalleled influence. It seems that the duke was inverting an axiom that it was always good to have friends at court. It was hardly any time at all since Nelson, forced to be ashore on half pay, had had similar anxieties and wrote similar letters of affection and admiration in the hope of once more getting a command.

He spent most of the next day with Emma. By nightfall, there was nothing to keep him at their house except one final duty. He went into the room of the sleeping Horatia shortly before ten o'clock, knelt and said his evening prayers by her cot. That done, he left the house and climbed

---

[1] Prince Edward, Duke of Kent (1767–1820). Died a few months after the birth of his daughter, Princess Alexandria Victoria – the future Queen Victoria.

into his chaise, which trotted out of the gates of Merton and south to Portsmouth for the final time. The date was Friday 13 September 1805.

Most have thought Nelson had a singular premonition of his death. Possibly. It is certainly true that commanders facing such a hideously glorious event as a battle would be likely to contemplate mortality. Just a few days earlier, Nelson had visited a workshop in London where the proprietor looked after his upholstery. He had gone to see his coffin. He confided in the foreman that he should engrave the lid carefully because he felt he might soon have need of it.

It is probably in his diary, a very private book, that Nelson tells as much as we can expect to know of his personal thoughts that night, after leaving Emma and Horatia. He writes of his sadness of leaving 'dear, dear' Merton. We should not underestimate the power of that house in his thinking. He had fought hard to afford it, although he never really could. Merton represented happiness when ashore and, most of all, the security he wanted for Emma. Nelson was no fool when it came to understanding the frailty of public recognition. He had little money to support his and Emma's style. He knew also that however loud the huzzahs of the crowds, it would be the clerks and treasurers who would have the final word on Emma's future should he die. He could plead for pensions and assurances. Once an enemy ball had rid him from the treasurer's books, Emma, he knew, would be reliant on the generosity of one or two friends. Therefore his feelings on leaving Merton were really those of a man who could not be certain of the future and of all he held dear, as he went to serve 'my King and Country'.

> May the Great God whom I adore enable me to fulfil the expectations of my Country; and if it is His good pleasure that I should return, my thanks will never cease being offered up to the Throne of His mercy. If it is His good providence to cut short my days upon earth, I bow with the greatest submission, relying that He will protect those so dear to me, that I may leave behind. – His Will be done; Amen, Amen, Amen.

HMS *Victory* was anchored off Southsea, at St Helens. Robert Southey described, not long after the event, Nelson's embarkation. At around lunchtime on that Saturday, 14 September, Nelson, accompanied by George Rose and George Canning, who had travelled from London to see him off, avoided the Portsmouth steps where the coxswain of the admiral's barge would normally have expected to have taken on board his flag officer. Instead, they went to the beach by the bathing machines in the hope that the crowd waiting by the steps might be fooled.

but a crowd collected in his train, pressing forward to obtain sight of his face: many were in tears, and many knelt down before him, and blessed him as he passed. England has had many heroes, but never one who so entirely possessed the love of his fellow-countrymen as Nelson. All men knew that his heart was as humane as it was fearless: that there was not in his nature the slightest alloy of selfishness or cupidity; but that, with perfect and entire devotion, he served his Country with all his heart, and with all his soul, and with all his strength; and therefore they loved him as truly and as fervently as he loved England. They pressed upon the parapet to gaze after him when his barge pushed off, and he was returning their cheers by waving his hat. The sentinels, who endeavoured to prevent them from trespassing upon this ground, were wedged among the crowd; and an Officer, who not very prudently upon such an occasion, ordered them to drive the people down with their bayonets, was compelled speedily to retreat; for the people would not be debarred from gazing till the last moment upon the hero – the darling hero of England!

At 11.30 in the morning of 14 September, Nelson hoisted his flag in the *Victory*. That night, he dined with Canning and Rose in the Great Cabin. Blackwood stood by in the *Euryalus*. By the Sunday forenoon, there was nothing to keep them, and *Victory*, with *Euryalus* in company, weighed anchor and made for the Channel, sailing not through the Solent but off the eastern seaboard of the Isle of Wight, the traditional deep-water route to and from Portsmouth. As *Victory* weighed, the mail gig pulled for the shore with yet more letters of instruction. Most importantly, Nelson needed orders issued to all captains on where they should meet up with *Victory*. He did not know where all his ships were. Very few people did. An officer commanding a squadron, standing off, say, El Ferrol or Cadiz, may have known the whereabouts of his own vessels, but he would have been uncertain of the location of the main fleet. Some ships were in port in England, undergoing repairs. Squadron commanders and even the commander-in-chief would probably not have known how far those repairs had got. He most certainly would not have known if even an assisted maintenance vessel had been ready for sea. In one of Nelson's letters sent ashore to Southsea before he sailed, he told the naval secretary, William Marsden, that there were ten of his ships whose positions he did not know. One of those was the *Pickle*. Another was the *Amazon*. She was delivered instructions to dock and refit. Yet Nelson did not know when she would arrive to do so.

Significantly, this huge communications delay in 1805 meant that the Royal Navy at sea did not even know that their admiral had embarked in his flagship and was heading in their direction. If they had known, they could have made only a reasonable estimate of his expected time of arrival. There were, of course, devices, including the rendezvous system and that of sending a frigate on ahead, to bring some order to this chaos of silence.

Before sailing, Nelson had agreed a secret latitude and longitude rendezvous. So a captain at anchor or alongside or even on a station offshore would receive either the rendezvous number or the latitude or longitude, with instructions from Nelson that the captain should make every possible speed to get his ship to sea with six months of stores and provisions on board. Furthermore, he had instructed that a frigate should be stationed off Cape St Vincent. That ship would have the secret rendezvous point of the *Victory*. Therefore the captain sailing south or from the Mediterranean would know that he had to make for that cape. However, what would happen if the frigate were not there? This was quite possible. An easterly storm, for example, the previous day could easily have blown the frigate way off station. An enemy squadron might have been sighted, causing the frigate to make a good run over the horizon. To cover this, the Royal Naval captain searching for the frigate would have standing orders to cruise the area off Cape St Vincent in, weather permitting, a diagonal, which would allow the maximum radius of horizon to be maintained within sight of the Cape. He would continue his search for twenty-four hours. That frigate would then tell the searching captain where Nelson and his, by then, gathering fleet, was to be found. If the frigate did not appear during that day, the captain was to sail for Cape St Mary's and Cadiz, where he would find the standing squadron.

However, this could be a dangerous task. These were enemy waters. A lone Royal Naval ship would have to get quite close to other vessels before they could be positively identified as friend or foe. Today's captain can tell from the shape the general nationality of another ship. In Nelson's navy, there were captured French and Spanish ships. Identification was always a close-up business. It is not easy to exaggerate the importance of these schemes to bring the fighting fleet together. Nelson insisted that the gathering should happen quickly and smartly. He had to have a full fleet under his command, with each captain fully briefed on his new plan of attack as soon as was possible because, as experience had shown that previous spring, Villeneuve could be out of Cadiz and gone in just one night's darkness and over the horizon before any action against him could be contemplated.

The weather off the south coast of England as the new week dawned was foul. Twenty-four hours after sailing, Nelson's flagship was banging into a west-south-west wind and they got no further than Portland Bill. The *Victory* altered course slightly to port, but it was still a tough beat into that same westerly. By nightfall of the sixteenth *Victory* had Torbay on her leeward side and managed to get mail ashore. Along the south coast, a series of boatmen plied their dangerous trade. They would go out to fetch mail from passing ships. Nelson wrote one of his last and more cheerful letters to Emma, for the Torbay boatman to take ashore. He wrote to her of his discomfort but, more importantly, of his hopes for them both. He knew how much she needed cheering. In spite of her frequent teasing about being chased by other men, and her self-indulgences, she was as insecure as he. He promised that their future would be happy and long together, surrounded by their children's children. His heart and soul, he wrote, was with her and Horatia. Nelson hoped for their future, all the time more deeply contemplating mortality. That night, with *Victory* and *Euryalus* thumped by the unceasing half gale, the Torbay boatman made it alongside and took Nelson's letters.

The conditions were so bad that Nelson doubted very much that the ships that were supposed to join him from Plymouth, just around the corner from Torbay, would ever be able to put to sea in what would be for them an impossible headwind. Twenty-four hours later, the westerly had blown through. *Victory* was off the Lizard in a debilitating Atlantic swell and, ironically, hardly any wind to encourage the passage. Such was the impossibility of pinpoint planning without the weather's consent. Final letters were written. Blackwood, in the *Euryalus*, would now carry the mail to pass on to any homeward-bound vessel he sighted. Nelson could write to Emma, 'Once more, heavens bless you! Ever, forever, your Nelson and Brontë'. But his mind was now very much with matters further south. Blackwood had been ordered to use his greater speed to pile on sail from a southerly direction, to inform Nelson's subordinate commanders that he was on his way. Here also, was a further example of Nelson's deeper thoughtfulness about battle and how it should be set up. Blackwood was carrying instructions to captains and commanders, especially Collingwood, that when they sighted the *Victory* they should not carry out the normal signalling honours of the navy. They should not fire a gun salute. A snooping enemy sloop would take the intelligence that salute would give, that Nelson had arrived in the area. He wanted to maintain every advantage, including surprise and continuing uncertainty.

Villeneuve had no sure intelligence of what was going on at sea. His personality was such that every bump in the night could have been made by a one-eyed, one-armed English admiral. Nelson, of course, had no idea what Villeneuve was doing. The French vice admiral was, that late August, full of self-pity yet again, moaning to Denis Decrès in Paris by letter and hopelessly inadequate in the role of fleet commander. Napoleon still thought him a coward. Decrès, after a quarter of a century as a brother naval officer, still tried to convince Napoleon that this was not cowardice. Napoleon wanted to know what Decrès called it. His naval minister hopefully offered the thought that Villeneuve had simply lost his head. Napoleon wished that he had. He thought Villeneuve the worst possible wretch who would 'sacrifice anyone and anything in order to save his own hide'. The emperor made it known that he did not want Villeneuve's name mentioned, ever again, in his presence. It was on 17 September that, in theory, Villeneuve's appointment came to an end when Rosily was ordered by Decrès to Cadiz. It says something of the state of the French Navy that Rosily's reputation among his peers was even lower than that of Villeneuve's.

On 20 September, Decrès reluctantly wrote to his friend Villeneuve, telling him of the change of command and stating, ominously, that he, Villeneuve, was to return to Paris to give the emperor in person a report on his actions. If communications in 1805 had been just a little quicker, there probably would have been no Battle of Trafalgar. It took a month for that letter to get to Cadiz. If the replacement order, plus Rosily, had been there in normal travelling time – let us say, two, or even three weeks – Villeneuve would have been relieved of his command and his tactics at sea would not have led to the battle. A speedier Rosily to Cadiz could so easily have restored Nelson to Merton.

Villeneuve had new orders to proceed into the Mediterranean with his Combined Fleet and head for the French naval headquarters at Toulon as well as Genoa and Naples. However, Napoleon had no faith that the fleet would ever arrive. Moreover, although Villeneuve made preparations to put to sea, he found very real difficulties in doing so. Earlier we saw how, in the middle of detailed preparations for engagements and voyages, Nelson was to be found ordering bullocks and onions as well as canvas and spars for his ships. Villeneuve and Gravina would necessarily have had to do exactly the same thing. After the voyage across the Atlantic and back, plus the 22 July fight with Calder's squadron and, the considerable storm damage and normal wear and tear in ships daily at sea and among the men sailing them, the Combined Fleet needed an urgent maintenance period alongside. This meant cordage had to be bought, timber found and purchased, shipwrights and coppersmiths engaged and chandlers ready to re-store these fighting ships. Villeneuve also needed men, because he was at least 2,000 short through illness and desertion. All this took a great deal of money, organization and the authorization of French and Spanish admiralities ashore. However, there was no money, there was no chandler and there were no authorizations forthcoming. Paris had cut off its wayward son without a sou.

Villeneuve's officers found that their admiral's credit was nil in Cadiz. Traders and suppliers along the coast were approached. They certainly knew the miserable conditions of the fleet, and they agreed to help, showing their generosity by only doubling rather than trebling their prices. Even then, Villeneuve was able to store his ships for just three months. The norm for any captain in either navy would have been twice that much. Word spread round the dockyards that Gravina and Villeneuve were being starved of funds, food and supplies. Collingwood, and probably Nelson, had assumed from the intelligence picked up ashore that the Combined Fleet would have to put to sea in order to store elsewhere. After all, it was hardly a difficult sail from Cadiz into the Mediterranean and to Cartagena or even Toulon.

Instead of sailing, Villeneuve ordered the fleet to remain in harbour. Instead of issuing maintenance orders, he wrote more moaning letters to Decrès. He complained about a lack of credit and activity from the French and Spanish agents that Paris supposedly controlled. He also found time to accuse the rest of the navy of having little character. If it had more, he suggested, his new mission would be a brilliant success. It would seem that Decrès did not pass this observation to Napoleon. Denis Decrès had huge difficulty in locating resources for Villeneuve. By now, Decrès was not working simply on behalf of his navy. He sensed that his own position was suspect in Napoleon's eyes. However, the French system was chaotic, and, once more, the lack of on-the-spot direction and the time it took for a communication to travel from France through often hostile Spanish territory, together with a certain disdain for those communications on the part of the shore-based officials, made Decrès' job almost impossible. The exception was probably Le Roy, who was the equivalent of a commercial attaché working with the French fleet at Cadiz.

Between Le Roy and Decrès, every effort was made to get the reluctant Villeneuve to sea. Yet every trader, and especially Spanish officials able to authorize credit, knew that the banking arrangements were less than encouraging. We might remember that at that time a great deal of business at this level was paid for by letters of credit. It would soon become apparent if the French were not honouring those letters; by the middle of September, it was apparent they were not. Supplies of equipment and food were not nearly as plentiful as the French imagined, and the reason was not only doubts about French creditworthiness. The Spanish, too, were at war, so their resources were quite limited. It took until the middle of October, seven weeks after the fleet of thirty-three ships had arrived at Cadiz, for officials, ministers, ambassadors, bankers and even a member of the royal family of Spain to reach some financial agreement that would be able to satisfy the suppliers that they were going to get paid to repair and store the Combined Fleet. We can imagine the despondency that spread throughout Villeneuve's fleet. Men had jumped ship, never to be seen again in a forecastle. Captains, who had to anticipate that they could be ordered to put to sea within hours, looked about their upper decks and saw nothing but disrepair and – most importantly – an inability to fight. Gravina, who just a year earlier had had all the self-assurance of an ambassador and celebrated naval officer, now found himself almost helpless in the middle of this Franco-Spanish pickle of bureaucracy and unseamanlike behaviour. Villeneuve, a most unbalanced personality to command a quarterdeck, saw everyone else as a fool and presented a figure of anxiety as the news buzzed about Cadiz that *Victory* had slipped her Portsmouth moorings and Nelson was heading south from England. Here was hardly an atmosphere to encourage the men in the mess decks who would soon, they knew, be going into battle.

Two weeks earlier, on 28 September, Villeneuve had been in quite a different mood. It was then that he had received Decrès' orders to sail for the Mediterranean, just around the corner from Cadiz. At that stage, he had not heard that Nelson was on his way and was of the opinion that Calder's fleet, standing off Cadiz, was in just as bad a state as his own and quite unable, by any naval standards, to remain on station for much longer. Maybe also, remembering the way in which it had been easy to slip through the blockade the previous April, Villeneuve had been in reasonably high spirits about the possibility of escaping any confrontation and, better still, of making haste to a sensible haven, Toulon. He would be able to pick up the Cartagena squadron and be safely tucked up in his French headquarters. The news of Nelson's approach at first gave him even more impetus to escape Cadiz. Perhaps Villeneuve was a slow thinker. It seems to have taken him some time to realize that even with its long time at sea, the force building off Cadiz was hardly the addled-minded fleet that he commanded. The Royal Navy had deployed twenty-seven ships of the line; seven of which were big three-deckers. Villeneuve looked once more at his own vessels at the end of the first week in October and wrote, once more alarmingly, to Decrès.

He reported that the ships of his Combined Fleet were dreadfully manned and in poor condition. In fact, some of the newly commissioned Spanish vessels, after a refit, had neither crews nor guns. In spite of apparently at first welcoming the orders from Denis Decrès that he should sail immediately for the Mediterranean, Villeneuve now rapidly backtracked. He insisted his fleet should stay in port until both men and ships were in a fit state.

We should have some sympathy with Villeneuve at this stage. To understand the naval situation, we have only to consider three points. First, the French admiral was seeing, outside Cadiz, one of the most successful navies the world had ever seen or would ever see. The British believed they could beat anyone. Their ships were well commanded, properly trained and reasonably equipped. They were about to welcome Nelson, the admiral for whom they would unquestionably give everything, including their lives. Villeneuve understood this perfectly. Second, Villeneuve was at a disadvantage because his own fleet was in exactly the opposite condition. Although, when it came to a fight, the Spanish and French soldiers would give a brave and sometimes brilliant account of themselves. Villeneuve never quite understood this last point. Third – and this is not to be overlooked – Villeneuve had to face every disadvantage just as he was leaving harbour. As he cleared his moorings he would be without sea room to manoeuvre. The Royal Navy at sea had the further advantage of being able to manoeuvre, exercise their guns, change station and, in athletic terms, warm up. They had all the sea space they needed to do this. Remembering again the limitations of controlling a single vessel through winds, sea states and tides and then multiplying that by the difficulties it takes to manoeuvre a whole fleet into a single formation, and adding to that the fact that Villeneuve's fleet might well have been sailing straight out of port into conflict, we can see that he would have had little or no time to shake down his ships' companies and manoeuvre into his own positions of advantage.

In practical naval terms, the odds were stacked against Villeneuve, unless he succeeded in slipping out almost unnoticed at a time when the wind was in his favour to carry his fleet swiftly south and east and into the Mediterranean before the Royal Navy could catch his wind. The reality of fighting his way out of Cadiz could have held no attractions for him. The sand-boxed tacticians would always have a solution. Ships having to come together quickly in circumstances of another's choosing were always going to be in need of all the luck that weather conditions could offer. Even then, it would take a good commander to exploit that fortune. Villeneuve was not best placed to do so.

There is another aspect of the case against Villeneuve's competence which will be explained. At Gravina's suggestion, he had called together the captains, both Spanish and French, of the Combined Fleet. This was an unusual meeting. It came about because Gravina, by far the more intelligent and professional of the two admirals, felt the fleet had reached a point of considerable crisis. It was being ordered to sea and to make all speed to Naples. It would have, so it appeared inevitably, to fight its way out of local waters to get into the Mediterranean. The fleet was in no condition to sail under those circumstances. Villeneuve was clearly overwhelmed by the situation. Gravina was not, but he wanted the senior commanders brought together to have everything explained, to discuss the options and then to make sure that the Combined Fleet was speaking with one voice.

That meeting on 8 October was the nearest Villeneuve came to facing mutiny. One of his own commanders would later show his contempt for him by virtually deserting the battle, taking his much-needed squadron with him (see chapter 28). The result of the gathering was a collective agreement not to obey the order from Paris to sail *immediately* for Naples. The commanders said they were ready to fight almost anyone in the name of Napoleon. However, it would be foolhardy for them to attempt to do so then. Remember, it would be another week before the financial arrangements were completed that would allow them to refit and re-store their ships. Therefore there was certainly good, practical reason for the entire Franco-Spanish fleet to disobey orders. Gravina at least, and Villeneuve most certainly, had to accept the possibility of another form of naval warfare occurring. We began our story of Villeneuve by reminding ourselves of his failure to push home his rearguard squadron to help save the French fleet at the Battle of the Nile. Thus Villeneuve knew that Nelson was quite capable of ordering a repeat performance of the earlier battle by sailing into Cadiz and attacking the Combined Fleet. After all, the British had a rather famous history of attacking ships at Cadiz. On balance, Villeneuve might well have thought that if he could not be certain of slipping out virtually unnoticed, he would have a better chance of success by positioning his vessels and preparing them to defend themselves in harbour – Latouche-Tréville had proved that possible, albeit in different circumstances, in Boulogne.

Some have seen the decision to stay in port as a suggestion that the Franco-Spanish fleet was close to mutiny or had, even by their decision, already mutinied. Villeneuve, as ever, presented Decrès with his version of the story. In this case it appeared a unanimous decision of the Tuesday-morning meeting. Some of the captains had been insistent that their role was to follow Napoleon's orders to their best ability and that they should therefore ready themselves for sea in whatever numbers they could muster. There was a schism between the French and the Spanish and it is easy to understand, especially in the twenty-first century when coalitions become fractious, why many of the Spanish officers began to wonder why they would be fighting an unpopular war against a seemingly invincible enemy in order to satisfy the megalomania of the leader of another country. As we shall see, the open suspicion – even resentment – was not expressed only by the Spanish. Whatever the reasoning, the fleet would for the moment stay in port. Outside, the Royal Navy was not without its own disappointments, especially as seen through the eyes of Calder.

It was not until the last week in September that Calder realized that public opinion in London was so against him. It was not through any formal channel that Calder learned of the feelings stacking against him but through the newspapers. He had thought himself in a reasonably good position. He had been given a command by Cornwallis that should potentially have made him as famous as Nelson. Here again, we have a glimpse of Cornwallis's dedication and unselfishness – not a universal assessment of his character.

The previous month – August – Cornwallis had been forced to rethink his whole campaign strategy and also his personal objectives. When he had learned of the scrap between Villeneuve and Calder, he had two immediate questions: why had not Calder sent Villeneuve to the bottom, and what did Villeneuve's return to European waters mean for his, Cornwallis's, blockade of Brest and the defence of the Channel?

The first question was best answered by an inquiry, even a court martial – and it would be. Cornwallis had, for almost three years, stuck assiduously to his prime objective, which was to stop French ships from being at liberty to attack British shipping in the Channel and to discourage them from even thinking that they could freely either bombard south-coast towns or, worse, put landing parties ashore. Significantly, he did not consult Nelson on what should be done next. The decision was taken while Nelson was still in the area on his homeward voyage. Cornwallis was not jealous of his junior flag officer. It was simply a matter of dealing with a situation as the conditions existed. Nelson was heading home and was out of the fight. Cornwallis had to assume that he would not be back for some time, if at all, especially as his main reason for returning to England was ill health. Nelson himself would have conceded that possibility. Cornwallis needed to strengthen his Channel defences and, most importantly, to reinforce what had until a few days earlier been Nelson's command, standing off the Spanish coast close by Cadiz. Calder had not been under Nelson's command. He was one of Cornwallis's flag officers. So he was called aboard Cornwallis's flagship, the *Ville de Paris*, for new instructions and deployment south.

Throughout this campaign Cornwallis had hoped that it would be he who would lead the final assault against the French navy. That confrontation would have been a glorious swansong for the sixty-one-year-old admiral. He knew that with Villeneuve taking the Combined Fleet into Cadiz he had two options: to create space for him to come north to the Channel where Cornwallis would be able to get at him or to position a large squadron within sight of Cadiz and take on the Combined Fleet immediately it emerged as, he judged, it would inevitably do. The problem in his first assumption was that there was no guarantee Villeneuve would come north. He might easily go south and east into the Mediterranean, or even back across the Atlantic. This Cornwallis understood, and so, in mid-August, with Nelson entering the Channel on his way home, Cornwallis took a professional deep breath and ignored his personal ambition to sink the French navy. He issued orders that irrefutably weakened his own position but would strengthen that of the British Navy as a whole. He detached twenty of the thirty-five biggest ships, the ships of the line, of his Channel squadron and sent them south to join the gathering eight major warships of the Mediterranean fleet to the south. This, he knew, would put Ganteaume at an enormous advantage should he now try to break out from Brest. With that order for redeployment, he then placed the reinforced Mediterranean fleet, until recently Nelson's, under the command of Calder. This was no great tactical decision, nor any judgement on Calder's action on 22 July. It was simply that, with Nelson going home, Calder was the senior admiral in Cornwallis's command and therefore the man who should have his flag flying in the southern squadron. In fact, at that stage, Cornwallis thought that the Combined Fleet was still at El Ferrol, but assumed that if it went south, as seemed likely, it would head for Cadiz. Calder was in an excellent mood. His instructions were clear. He was, as the formal order quoted,

> required and directed to proceed off that port [El Ferrol] immediately . . . you are to endeavour, as soon as possible, to get information of the enemy's force and situation, and to use your utmost exertion to prevent their sailing, or to intercept them should they attempt it.

On 19 August, Captain Thomas Dundas's frigate, *Naiad*, reached Collingwood with the news that Villeneuve had sailed from El Ferrol.[2] *Naiad* was turned around to search for Calder. There was nothing Cornwallis could do to help. Even though he hoped to get reinforcements for his depleted fleet, the French in the area were able to pick off ships one at a time and even capture two of them. Ganteaume had been told that Cornwallis was, at last, weakened. Accordingly, on 22 August, he decided to put to sea with a fleet that was at least half as large again as Cornwallis's and, of course, not scattered, as Ganteaume thought the British commander's to be.

However, Cornwallis was not dispersed as Ganteaume started to emerge. Napoleon's most trusted admiral took one look at the British squadron, apparently under full sail searching for French blood, and ducked back in under the protection of the shore batteries, which did more damage than the French ships managed. Not long after, Ganteaume wrote to Decrès saying he was not feeling very well and needed some shore leave.

---

[2] Captain Thomas Dundas (?–1841).

Calder had no need to know any of this. He was heading south to command what he thought was to be the most triumphal squadron in the king's navy. All looked rather well until the latter part of September, when newspapers were brought from the reinforcements sailing ahead of Nelson. Calder was incensed. He had thought himself – certainly after Cornwallis's expression of faith in him – cleared of all suspicion that he had acted wrongly during the hours after that engagement on 22 and 23 July.

The newspapers were no less scurrilous in 1805 than they are today. Also, although the news was old in those pages, it was new to Calder, and he was just as sensitive as any other public figure. Even after his first reaction, he had no intention of dismissing the reports as tittle-tattle. Instead, he penned a demand that the Admiralty should set up an inquiry, not into the actions of the newspapers (there was no Press Complaints Commission in those days) but into his own conduct on 22 and 23 July. Back in London, Barham had already thought of that, but not for any reason that would please Calder. The Admiralty remained less than satisfied with Calder. Again, we cannot guess the reason for such shoddy thinking on the part of the Admiralty. Just when Nelson most needed Calder, the Admiralty was about to remove him for an inquiry that would prove very little.

When Nelson met Calder, he warned him that in his, Nelson's, opinion, a fair inquiry was all but impossible. Barham insisted on one, and Barham was First Lord of the Admiralty. Cornwallis's orders were thus tacitly countermanded. Anyway, Nelson had been placed in command of the reinforced fleet. Calder's grand moment had passed. Even worse, there was no possibility of him assuming the role of deputy to Nelson. That admiral chose his own team and there was never a doubt in his mind as to who should be deputy commander-in-chief: the admiral he trusted more than any other, Cuthbert Collingwood.

Calder was now told to pack his chest, strike his flag in his own ship, *Prince of Wales*, and make ready for the long plod home and the ignominy of an inquiry. Nelson was not trying to belittle the admiral. Losing his command had done that. Nelson needed Calder's flagship. It was a large three-deck vessel which sailed well and was a good ship to handle in the battle that was to come. She was a better fighting ship than the *Victory*.

Here is an aside into the characters of both officers. Calder knew the exact value of the *Prince of Wales*. He was, however, more concerned about his dignity and appealed to Nelson's sense of honour that he should be allowed to sail home with his flag flying defiantly in the big ship. Nelson also knew how extremely important the *Prince of Wales* was to his order of battle. Yet he was not insensitive to Calder's position and so allowed him to go north in her with an escort. There was a footnote to this. How could Nelson possibly be demanding more ships to be sent from England if he could afford to send back the *Prince of Wales* and her ninety big guns? Calder sailed with proper salutes and the best dignity he could muster, on 14 October 1805 – the anniversary of the Battle of Hastings, an event full of symbolism for the British, who had imagined a second invasion from northern France. The *Wales*'s cannons, which might have dealt bloodily with the French, were tied down and muffled. Exactly one week later, Nelson was dead. Would the *Prince of Wales* have made a difference at Trafalgar? Most definitely.

On 27 September 1805, the *Victory* was off Cape St Vincent. Nelson did not want Villeneuve to know he had arrived off Cadiz, because he feared the Frenchman would simply stay in port and not come out and fight. However, Collingwood, having had the instructions that there should be no telltale gun salutes when Nelson joined the fleet, was planning a surprise for him. There would be a party. The celebration was not in advance of the battle, but on 29 September for Horatio Nelson's forty-seventh birthday. Not all admirals got surprise birthday parties from their subordinates.

The following day, after some indifferent airs, the breeze freshened from the north-north-west but died away again by the time of the noonday sights. Frustratingly for the admiral, he had not quite joined up with the fleet. And then, instead of the usual evening calm, the wind again freshened and, thirteen days after weighing anchor in Southsea roads, Nelson rejoined his fleet. Within a week, he knew that battle was imminent. The sense of war freshened as did the west wind in his instincts.

CHAPTER TWENTY-FOUR

About Face

NELSON, WHEN HE EVENTUALLY ARRIVED SOUTH, FOUND THE FLEET IN fair condition, although he was shortly to lose six of his twenty-nine big ships. Keeping vessels at sea for long periods was a continuous difficulty for the bosuns, carpenters, sailing masters and the equivalents of first lieutenants. Only certain things could be done at sea and only certain supplies could be brought into the fleet. Half a dozen of those vessels were due to rotate to Gibraltar for re-storing and quick repairs before turning round to rejoin the rest. So Nelson had to assume that at any time until reinforcements arrived, he would have no more than about twenty-one ships of the line at battle stations. Moreover, returning ships to Gibraltar would not necessarily resolve immediate victualling concerns for the pursers. The longer Villeneuve remained tucked up in port, the more pressures there were on Nelson's captains to maintain seagoing and fighting efficiency. Every single day meant a reduction in the amounts of food and water on board, increased wear and tear on canvas, standing and running rigging, and also a lowering of the strengths of the ships' companies. These were not inconsiderable logistical conundrums.

Furthermore, Nelson had to make certain in his own mind that his tactical plan, which his commanders thought so revolutionary in battle terms, could be put into operation when Villeneuve appeared. This could not be just a matter of hoping that the Combined Fleet came out in a straight line, expecting a broadside confrontation, only to shorten sail in horror as Nelson, with the wind and sea state to his advantage, tacked sharply to port, formed three columns and charged. It would work on a mess-deck table, with knives, forks, spoons and pepper pots representing fleet positions. In practice, there had to be far more planning, and a desperate trusting to luck.

For example, where would Nelson be if and when Villeneuve appeared? Should he sail up and down outside Cadiz, metaphorically yelling to the Frenchman to come out and fight? Should his fleet remain all together? A compact group could perform the cumbersome manoeuvres that had to be executed, with all the deftness of a dancing display. Nelson chose to position the bulk of his fleet out of sight of Cadiz. He stood off the shoreline by about fifty miles. We should picture what this meant in sailing terms and times.

Fifty miles offshore could well mean that wind conditions were quite different from those inshore at certain times of day when differences in land and sea temperatures create wind movements. So-called sea breezes, for example, can create a freshness in the wind that might not exist fifty miles away. What would that matter? If Villeneuve came out by surprise, those stiffened inshore breezes might just have him away to the south with enough of a head start to ensure that Nelson would be unable to catch him. Furthermore, standing off fifty miles away, the land mass would offer no shelter from the Atlantic sea state and wind conditions for as long as the westerlies and even north-westerlies persisted. So Nelson had to guarantee that his alarm system would work in any conditions. There was no point in having a vessel which could sail in ideal conditions and at express speeds, with intelligence for their admiral, if that same vessel was finding it impossible to beat into a strong westerly coming from the direction in which Nelson was waiting. As we have seen, the answer was to position vessels between Nelson and Cadiz in the hope that a simple signalling system would be able to relay the news he wanted to hear. This relay of frigates had at its front line the *Euryalus* under the command of Henry Blackwood, who had escorted Nelson from Portsmouth. Blackwood was as close as three miles off the Cadiz shoreline. He could, at times, see almost everything that was going on in the harbour, from the reports of his topmast lookouts as well as of his own glass from the quarterdeck. His small squadron of similar frigates at different positions could report similarly or confirm intelligence. There was, of course, another hope in this ploy. If, day after day, Villeneuve saw only a squadron of relatively powerless frigates cruising Spanish waters, there was just a possibility that he would be fooled into thinking that was all the British had in the area. He just might decide to put to sea and run what he could easily judge to be an ineffectual blockade, and perhaps take the risk that if there were other ships in the region it would take too long to alert them to his intentions. What Nelson could not know was that Villeneuve had discovered an incentive to sail that he had not before imagined.

Villeneuve had been told that he should move the whole fleet as quickly as possible into the Mediterranean. Decrès had sent that instruction on 16 September. By now, Villeneuve was feeling cheered up no end with this news. Furthermore, he was particularly happy because the general commanding the French soldiers in his fleet, Jacques Lauriston, had been recalled to Paris. Villeneuve could immediately relax. For most of the year, certainly that spring and summer, Lauriston had been utterly critical of Villeneuve's capabilities. Even though Villeneuve assumed the general would hardly sing his praises in Paris, he was very relieved to see the back of him. Lauriston had already given his full report – not, of course, to Decrès, minister for the navy, but directly to Napoleon. Lauriston had written that Villeneuve was haughty and indecisive. This did not much stir Napoleon, who knew all that anyway. So at the beginning of October, Villeneuve was more like his old self, haughty and indecisive. At one moment he was reporting to Decrès that the ships were ready to sail, only to send word later that they were not. The council of war of Villeneuve and his commanders on 8 October confused matters even more. In spite of the apparently unanimous declaration, some wanted to sail and some did not – with Villeneuve, once again, at the end of that meeting, in the latter camp. Two days later, Villeneuve ordered his commanders to make ready for sea. Hardly had captains relayed his instructions when he issued a countermand. Fortunately for Villeneuve, a belt of dirty Atlantic weather stormed in from the west. They could not have sailed anyway. So they sat out the gales in Cadiz harbour and Nelson's fleet hoved to and rode them.

Had Villeneuve been serious about sailing? No one really knows, but eight days later he most certainly was. What changed his mind? On that

day, 18 October 1805, Villeneuve was given the news that Vice Admiral
Rosily had left Paris and was now in Madrid. Villeneuve had had no
formal notification of Rosily's pending arrival. However, even Villeneuve
– or perhaps he especially – would have been quick to recognize that
French vice admirals do not appear without notice in the Spanish capital
without a distinct purpose. Madrid was not a place for a fifty-three-year-
old vice admiral to take the waters. Moreover, Villeneuve was hearing
that Rosily was being promoted to full admiral.

The one person who could have told Villeneuve why Rosily was there
was Pierre Beurnonville,[1] one of Napoleon's trusted generals who was,
at the time, French ambassador to Madrid. Beurnonville knew that
Villeneuve was to be replaced, on Napoleon's instructions. However, he
had absolutely no regard for Villeneuve and, indeed, had a soldier's proper
suspicion of all sailors. Moreover, Beurnonville had been dragged into
the rantings and ravings of Villeneuve when the latter had been trying
to procure extra crew, food and provisions as well as dockyard facilities
and tradesmen to get the Combined Fleet into a seaworthy state. General
Beurnonville had had quite enough of Villeneuve's mood swings and
ravings in his direction. Villeneuve, on hearing rumours of Rosily's arrival
at the Spanish capital, wrote immediately to Decrès. He pointed out that
if he was about to be replaced as commander, he would naturally have to
accept that instruction, although it would have been nice for someone to
have told him. Then, in full support of Lauriston's opinion, Villeneuve
declared haughtily to Decrès that he expected to be given an appointment
as second-in-command rather than be confined to the bin of failed naval
officers. Here was a crazy combination: an individual who loves the
uniform, pomp and position but lacks the exceptional talent and courage
necessary in a fleet commander. Everything about him tells us that he
was, deep down, pleased at the opportunity to be rid of this responsibility.
Yet he could not help, even at this late moment, telling Decrès and
therefore, presumably, Napoleon, that it would be quite wrong of them to
deny him a place of some distinction at the inevitable battle, where he
intended to show them exactly what a superb naval commander they had
in him.

---

[1] Pierre de Ruel Beurnonville (1752–1821).

Rosily knew exactly what sort of man Villeneuve was. The whole fleet knew, and, anyway, Rosily was not much better. He was already feeling out of sorts because it had taken him three weeks to get from Paris to Madrid and he was now delayed in that city because his coach was broken. Rosily had arrived in the Spanish capital on 10 October. Normally, a coach would expect to take between eight and ten days to travel at top speed from Madrid to Cadiz. These were not normal times. Rosily would, just like a modern motorist, have to be assured that his vehicle was in a condition to make the final leg of his trip. These were not smooth tarmacadam roads. In 1805, the track between Madrid and Cadiz was difficult, potholed and rutted. Moreover, murderous robber gangs who knew no law, and disregarded any that might be rumoured, loitered along the route. Consequently, Rosily would need a fully fit coach with a schedule for horse changes or rests plus, most importantly, a squadron of heavily armed mounted guards. It was a disagreeable journey and a hazardous one. Villeneuve could expect Rosily to take anything up to two weeks to reach him and seize his command. This being so, Villeneuve, even allowing for a good speed and fortune on Rosily's part, had to take a decision on whether to stay calmly for the handover or to escape, his admiral's flag flying, into the Atlantic. He had Rosily behind him and Nelson in front of him, and he was not sure which of the two evils it was better to face. He knew, however, that at best estimate he had until 22 October to make up his mind.

Villeneuve sat in his flagship, the *Bucentaure*, and watched the weather. As so often, the gales having blown through, there came a calm. There came also reasonably good intelligence that a squadron of perhaps six of Nelson's fleet had detached itself from the main body and was further south in the area of Gibraltar. Villeneuve was enough of a sailor to know how difficult it would have been for Nelson's ships to have kept station with one another during the bad weather of the previous few days. He assumed that it would take some time before Nelson could once more bring all his vessels together in order to be ready to manoeuvre into a line of battle. In fact, what Villeneuve could not know was that the six ships seen off Gibraltar had not scattered from the main fleet but were those ordered to the Rock for supplies.

It is tempting also to believe that a further miscalculation of

Villeneuve's was his ignorance of Nelson's new tactic of a three-pronged attack, not that this would come to matter very much, as we shall see. However, this popular conception might prove misleading. In spite of Villeneuve's obvious shortcomings as a commander, he was not unintelligent. Moreover, he had spent at least the past seven years convincing himself that Nelson was invincible. He had personally fought in actions, from the Battle of the Nile onwards. The Frenchman was so caught up in Nelson's reputation as a tactician of enormous daring and, above all, original thinking that he probably understood his enemy better than Nelson's own fellow commanders. It is as if Villeneuve had, in his sleeping moments, studied the genius of the British admiral to the extent that he knew he could never beat Nelson on equal terms. If that is correct, Villeneuve would even have reached the same calculations in tactical thinking that Nelson had done. Even if it were only to convince himself, and perhaps Decrès, how vulnerable the Combined Fleet was it is almost inevitable that Villeneuve would have come to the conclusion, as Nelson had, that the line-of-battle concept was outdated. He had by then become absorbed in studying Nelson's way of thinking. He would have seen that there were limited tactical changes that could be made by cumbersome vessels relying entirely on the weather as well as on seamanship.

Villeneuve, too, understood that instead of lining up to blast the enemy an exceptional tactical advantage would be gained by forming the traditional battle line and then suddenly turning ninety degrees to form a trident of warships through the enemy line before surrounding and destroying it. The difference between Nelson and Villeneuve is that the former saw this as a perfect line of attack, had the confidence of knowing that he was right and the knowledge that his British fleet captains were good enough to make it work. Villeneuve saw it as a possibility, looked at his own fleet and knew that he would never be able to exercise this surprise manoeuvre. The adage 'Know thine enemy' was perfectly understood and practised by Villeneuve. His shortcoming was that despite having studied Nelson so closely he was convinced he could do nothing with the knowledge he had gained.

With Rosily on his heels, the time for tactical appreciation was almost done. He would, of course, write the battle orders for his captains and his version of 'France and Spain Expect Every Man To Do His Duty'. There was not much left to be done, apart from convincing his officers that he was in command and should be.

Villeneuve was hastily finishing his sailing instructions. He wrote to his captains that he would do everything he could to avoid Nelson. Considering that the British fleet, albeit a small part of it, was in sight (including the *Agamemnon*, clinging to an American prize ship which was far too valuable to abandon), this may have seemed a little odd to the Combined Fleet's captains. Villeneuve now assumed all the character that had belied many of his previous actions and his reputation. Although he made it clear that he wanted to avoid Nelson, there was little doubt that he believed he could not skulk away. He sat at his desk and produced rousing pages of exaltation. Thin booklets were broken out from the store and sent to each of his captains, with the good advice that they should read and digest the content during the hours of darkness before they put to sea first thing in the morning. The captains read pages of naval signals, procedures, regulations and even lines of encouragement. It does seem odd that those officers were not already perfectly familiar with these publications. Villeneuve wanted them to become inspired by his words to do great things in the name of France (and also, presumably, of Spain). They should pass on this enthusiasm to their ships' companies. They should make each and every soul aware that the time had come to be counted.

Moreover, if any captain was not in the thick of the fighting when the cannons roared and a signal came from Villeneuve's flagship that this had been observed, that captain would surely know, as would the fleet, that his career and character were stained dark for ever. Coming from Villeneuve, with his reputation, this was a bit rich. It seems, however, that the Spanish at least took his words to heart. Again, judging by their experiences in July against Calder, they had no need of advice from the French admiral.

Villeneuve, exactly as Nelson would do before the battle, now dressed in his best uniform, gold-laced and stuck with medals and decorations. The idea that he was thinking like Nelson – even to the point of accurately guessing that admiral's new battle plan – behaving like him in the way he wrote in good cheer to all his officers prior to the battle, and even in the way he desired, just like Nelson, to stand out in order to be seen by every one of the sailors under his command tends to contradict every impression he had given before. It could not all be put down to the approaching ignominy of Rosily relieving him of his command. There had to be something else. Perhaps it was merely a form of martial ritual that had survived since the Greeks and before. Death wish? Impossible to say. Yet at that moment in Cadiz, and two days later when it seemed quite possible for him to escape the fight, there was something in his behaviour that was quite contrary to his reputation. It was reported from the decks in Cadiz harbour that when the admiral appeared in full fig, the huzzahs from the mess decks to the yards, to the gallery on the wharves, were as loud and as genuine as any that Nelson might have inspired. If only Villeneuve's tailor had had the opportunity and talent to cut the jib of his client's character, France might have had an admiral to remember instead of one it would have rather forgotten.

So the Combined Fleet, with at least a 400-gun advantage over Nelson's, was given orders on 18 October to prepare for sea. Stores ashore, scheduled to be brought on board over a period of days, were now destined for immediate embarkation. Running rigging was prepared, sails were checked to ensure that they were bent on properly, gun decks were ready for clearing. Having taken the decision and apparently convinced that he would not again change his mind, Villeneuve was ready to make a run for it. In theory, the wind direction he needed to clear Cadiz and make a course for the Mediterranean would not necessarily be the one that would give Nelson an advantage to attack. Villeneuve was looking for a land breeze that Friday night. Light winds persisted from the west-north-west. He seems to have forecast that the wind would change. These ships could not be towed from their anchorage to any advantage. They would rely on the good seamanship necessary to sail off a mooring – an important manoeuvre and one that the celebrated Spanish had, literally, fouled up the previous April. How that Atlantic run the previous spring must have seemed an age away. When the west-north-west breeze slackened, Villeneuve ordered his fleet to stand fast but be prepared to weigh and put to sea at first light, at about five on the following morning. Here, once more, was what at first sight appears to be inept command. There was absolutely no sign at that point, nor during the night, of a freshening wind. Consequently, only a few of the smaller vessels managed to weigh and begin to clear harbour.

This bad seamanship on Villeneuve's part, presumably the result of listening to the advice of his flag captain and sailing master, failed to get his fleet to sea and – worse – signalled conclusively his intention to the enemy that he was trying to escape from Cadiz.

Nelson's faithful watchdog, Blackwood, in his frigate the *Euryalus*, was standing just offshore. He had kept station, even through the gales. Now his vigilance paid off. Blackwood saw what he had longed for. When a big ship sailed off her anchorage – remembering that they had no engines – we can imagine how difficult a manoeuvre this would be in a confined space. A vessel lying at anchor or tied to a buoy swings naturally to face the direction of the oncoming tide. So in a harbour it is usually possible to tell whether the tide is coming in or out by looking at the way a vessel is facing. If she is facing towards the land, the tide is going out or ebbing. If she is facing the harbour entrance, the tide is coming in or flooding. A big ship at anchor would therefore be facing the flow of the tide and, as the anchor would be hauled in, might swing perhaps across that tide. Then, if no other action were to be taken, when the anchor was free of the bottom and the ship had no grip she would swing away and be swept along with the tide. In addition to this factor the big-ship sailing master had to consider the wind direction. Even without sails, the wind would have an effect on the ship because the hull above the water was effectively a wooden sail. Now imagine a combination of these factors, plus the fact that there were twenty other ships at the anchorage. We can then see the complicated procedures involved in getting a fleet to sea.

Each captain had to make sure that his vessel cleared the anchorage without fouling other lines (which is what Gravina's squadron had done in Cadiz harbour the previous April and why he had continued to sail long after Villeneuve). Each vessel handled differently. Certainly, a frigate or sloop would be easier to come off and gather way than a big three-decker. To manoeuvre under sail more easily in a relatively confined space, the way to control the ship was not to bend on every sail in the locker but to use the ones which could most easily be tacked and backed for quick course-changing. It would take so long to hand the big sails that a vessel could be aground within minutes of weighing anchor. So the smaller sails on the yards towards the top of the mast were used (and still are in square-riggers).

Now we come back to Blackwood, loitering three miles off Cadiz harbour. What was the first thing he saw through his spyglass to tell him Villeneuve was preparing to leave harbour? Activity in the topsail yards and their changing position. Those sails being so high up made it easier for him to see them, which is why when he saw so much going on he made the simple signal that the Combined Fleet had their topsail yards hoisted. He could then hove to and wait. Which is what he did. Having warned his fleet, fifty miles off, that there was movement that suggested a departure, he now waited to see whether it continued. He also ordered his yeoman to stand by with signal number 370. The yeoman was the rating who hoisted the cloth signal flags, which is why he later became known as the bunting tosser.

To make signalling as simple as possible a system of flag numbers had been devised according to which flags hoisted in a certain order would form a sentence (see chapter 27).

It took sixty minutes for the Combined Fleet to sort itself, not into good order, but some kind of order Those topsails started showing towards the mouth of Cadiz as they reached the sandbar, and Blackwood gave the order to his yeoman to hoist signal 370 – Enemy Putting To Sea.

Villeneuve was on the move. Blackwood gave two orders. The first was to begin the relay of signals to the *Victory*, some fifty miles away. Second, he sent the fastest ship in his small squadron towards the fixed rendezvous off Gibraltar where Rear Admiral Thomas Louis[2] was in command of the six vessels that had been reported as off station to Villeneuve. As it turned out, by the time Louis was located, it was too late for him to rejoin the fleet for the Battle of Trafalgar.

At first sighting, Nelson was going to have all the time in the world to engage the enemy. Furthermore, Villeneuve was hardly having the best of it. For ten days there had been open questioning of his worthiness to command. Many of the captains had refused to hide their feelings towards the senior officer at the council of war. It is likely that had it not been for

---

[2] Thomas Louis (1759–1807).

the Spanish admiral Gravina, who was a seasoned and loyal campaigner, there would have been an open mutiny against Villeneuve. Some wanted to go to sea. Others said the whole notion was crass and made neither tactical nor maritime sense. The ships were not ready. The wind was in the wrong direction. The wind was not strong enough. Nelson was sitting there waiting. Once outside – if it ever got there – the Combined Fleet could too easily find itself on a lee shore, with a wind coming from the sea that could blow the vessels towards the beach. That was a tidy list of reasons for staying in port until ships and conditions were in their favour. Moreover, not a few of them had caught the rumour that Rosily was on his way. That was enough to send Villeneuve to sea. It was enough to keep some of the sailors in port.

It could even be that Villeneuve was risking a mutiny directed at his sailing orders. Why should so many of those officers risk their ships and their lives for this commander-in-chief whose days were numbered anyway? Little wonder that some of the Spanish continued to express the feeling that there was no good reason after all to die in someone else's war.

One consequence of this dissension was that instead of a united and confident fleet emerging from Cadiz – or, in those conditions, attempting to – some of the Spanish vessels did not weigh until the very last moment, and even some of the French ignored their commander's orders, and so Villeneuve's fleet straggled to sea. In fact the order had been to sail at about five. Blackwood had seen the topsail yard activity at six, but by seven only two French frigates had cleared harbour. This was probably routine. Those frigates would have been sent out first to see how many British ships were at hand. Villeneuve's own people had, of course, been ashore and sent on reconnaissance to scan the horizon for Nelson. However, they would not have seen very much in that October light early in the morning. Nor would Villeneuve's officers have been able to rely on what had been there the previous day. Let us suppose that Nelson had decided to close the shore in darkness. Even at six knots, he could have arrived by daybreak or be well in sight. So the role of the two frigates, joined at about lunchtime by the rest of the observation squadron, was more than forward scouting. They might well have been engaged by the British, who might at any point have had the wind advantage and even cut them off, preventing them from getting back into port. There was also, in Villeneuve's mind, the real possibility that Nelson would be daring enough to sail into Cadiz and take them on in the harbour. Precedence is a forthright reminder to those of a nervous disposition.

Villeneuve, no matter how many uniforms, stars and garters he tried on, could not change the fact that his command had never really inspired his officers. There seems every evidence to suggest that although Gravina and a couple of other senior officers were willing to do what he said, there were too many ships' captains, both French and Spanish, who were following his orders under protest. We may allow for inopportune wind conditions and indifferent seamanship, but disgruntled officers affect their ships' companies. By one o'clock that Saturday the effect of lack of training and inspiration may have got the Combined Fleet to sea after a fashion but not in good condition. Villeneuve had issued his orders that the fleet should exit the harbour and immediately form up at battle stations. It did not. So anxious were Gravina and Villeneuve that, instead of presenting the Combined Fleet as two allied units, Spanish and French, their concern about loyalties among their own captains led them to mix up the fleet in the hope that one lot would not break away. There were three consequences of this action. First, the resentment, where it existed, increased. Second, the mixed squadrons found it difficult to work together. Third, Villeneuve was held in such contempt that in some cases his orders were disobeyed.

Once the fleet was clear of the harbour, which did not happen till well into that afternoon, Villeneuve ordered it – preposterously, it would seem – to anchor overnight. Admiral Magon, who had been one of Napoleon's naval commanders at Boulogne, thought this a stupid order and one that confirmed him in the opinion that his commander-in-chief had no right to his appointment. So, in the circumstances quite rightly, he refused to anchor. Why on earth would he want to be a sitting duck for any of Nelson's ships, especially as Blackwood's forward observation squadron was clearly to be seen? Sensibly he kept his ship, the *Algésiras*, at action stations. (Magon would be killed in battle the next day.)

At shortly before seven on the Sunday forenoon, Magon turned his squadron on Blackwood's, ready to engage them. He could see they were smaller ships than his and, also, the *Agamemnon* had refused Blackwood's orders to release their lucrative prize, the American merchantman. When Magon turned, Blackwood gave the order to withdraw. It was no duty of his to engage in a fight at that stage, and the wind direction was not entirely in his favour. He was able to turn and run before the wind and outrun Magon, which is what he did. Blackwood himself, seeing that *Agamemnon* could herself be in deep trouble, was at last induced to abandon the merchantman.

Even with the possibility of a minor action or victory, many of Villeneuve's ships had not left the harbour. Some of them were having difficulty in doing so, the light airs being to no one's advantage, and some of the newly signed ratings were in an odd environment and next to useless because they had only recently been signed on from the backstreets and villages. They were better at hoeing than at handing sails. That afternoon, the already bedraggled fleet of French and Spanish vessels ran into another hazard. The wind freshened, west-north-west, then it rained and, later, fog began to roll in. Given the wind direction, this could have been to Villeneuve's advantage. He had anchored partly in the hope of gathering his fleet, although he did not succeed in doing so until mid-afternoon on the Sunday. If he could now use the slightly freshening winds and the wind-drifted fog as cover, he might be able to escape towards Gibraltar.

Villeneuve now did exactly what Nelson had not bargained for. He formed his ships into three columns. Nelson had imagined that a fool like Villeneuve would have kept in one line, thus making him vulnerable to the British admiral's new tactic. This should not have worried Nelson's forward observers. Villeneuve was merely consolidating his force to gather it into a single direction and in such a way that when he went to battle stations he could then have them turn in formation and so be in one line of battle. His ships remained for that afternoon and early evening in three squadrons or divisions: the first his own, in which he flew his flag in the *Bucentaure*, the second that commanded by Admiral Ignacio Álava[3] and the third, leading the combined squadrons, that of Gravina. For the moment, the wind fetched them a good course for Gibraltar. Gravina's squadron was slightly ahead and to the right, on the starboard side, that

---

[3] Admiral Ignacio Álava (1750–1817).

is, of Villeneuve. This meant Gravina's ships were acting as pickets, keeping a lookout for vessels that might be ahead and capable of cutting them off and also on the Atlantic side where they knew Nelson's main body was sailing, by now, to windward of them.

The observation squadron was doing its work. On the evening of 20 October, Gravina's picket spotted what it counted as a British flotilla of eighteen ships coming up on the horizon to the north-west. This would have meant that Villeneuve's fleet was not being intercepted but followed. Villeneuve was no more than a horizon's distance south-west of Cadiz, probably nine or ten miles. The three columns of Villeneuve's which confounded Nelson's battle plan now, as midnight approached, altered formation to confirm Nelson's prediction. Although Villeneuve had, just twenty-four hours earlier, suggested how he believed Nelson would fight, he clearly did not have confidence in his own tactical ability. Instead of maintaining his own three columns, with Gravina, much the better tactician, remaining on point duty, Villeneuve at some time after eleven at night on 20 October ordered his fleet to form up in that traditional – and now vulnerable – line of battle. It can only be assumed that he did so while communications were good and time was at hand because if Nelson had caught up during the night the Frenchman would have had no chance to form the defensive line.

We might suppose that at least the order to re-form ready for battle showed a discipline and a level of seamanship in the Combined Fleet thus far sadly lacking under Villeneuve's command. That would be a generous assumption. Moreover, during the night, as can so often be the case in those latitudes at that time of year, the daytime breeze had disappeared and the best that could be recorded in a French log was that the wind consisted of nothing more than light airs. To maintain, in the dark, a strict battle line of ships of quite different rigs and handling abilities and manned by seamen of varying capabilities was a very difficult task. Consequently by morning the battle line was more like an amiable amble of Sunday strollers.

When there was enough light for Villeneuve to take stock, he saw his ships in an indifferent line straggling over nine miles of sea which was showing all the signs of a calm before the storm. However, he was still ahead of Nelson, and he was not that far from Gibraltar. A look at the map, or a chart, of the area would show that if Villeneuve was ten or so miles off Cape Trafalgar, there was only one more headland to make before turning east through the Strait of Gibraltar. Much has been made of the close-run thing of Nelson's chase after Villeneuve at this point. It is often assumed that, once through the Strait, Villeneuve would have been, at the very least, safer. From the point of view of seamanship and tactics there would be something in this hypothesis if it were assumed that Villeneuve would then have had a good following wind, a high level of seamanship and an unopposed run to Toulon, followed, perhaps, by the luxury of being met by reinforcements of the Spanish squadron off Cartagena and whatever French ships were cruising off Toulon, the French Mediterranean naval headquarters. However, a sloop, say, detached from Villeneuve's fleet, would not have had the speed to sail ahead for reinforcements. Equally, Nelson could not have warned the vessels that had remained in the Mediterranean under his own command that the French were coming.

Villeneuve may also have believed that the British would attack him once he was in the Mediterranean. But would that have been so? One of Jane Austen's[+] brothers, Francis', was an officer in the revictualling squadron that had been sent by Nelson to Morocco and Gibraltar for supplies. This was one group of ships Villeneuve would have expected to take on. Yet let us look at it from the British squadron's position. Austen, who was in the *Canopus*, had written home that they knew Villeneuve had left Cadiz. His admiral, Louis, had been forced to take the decision that if Villeneuve gave Nelson the slip and got into the Mediterranean, the British would *not* have attacked. There were two reasons for this decision: first, six ships could hardly expect to do much against Villeneuve's fleet; and second, the *Camopus* and other vessels had gone to re-store, and what they had on board was for the rest of the fleet. So Villeneuve would not have been so threatened once he had passed through the Strait of Gibraltar. He was hardly to know that.

However, the British squadron off Gibraltar, Cartagena and Toulon

---

[+] Jane Austen (1775–1870). At this time, Jane Austen was unpublished, even though she had written many of her books during the closing years of the eighteenth century. *Sense and Sensibility*, the first novel to be published, appeared in 1811; Sir Francis Austen (1774–1865).

would have been on the lookout. Moreover, there is nothing in the weather plot over those two or three crucial days to suggest that Villeneuve had any chance of picking up a strong wind to blow him quickly through any British squadrons he might have surprised and into the safety of Toulon. Villeneuve's orders from Napoleon via Decrès were that if he failed to clear harbour and make for Brest, he should go to Naples. Villeneuve was very likely in no doubt that if he saw the safety of Toulon on his port bow along the way, that is where he would seek safe haven.

So, early in the morning of the battle of 21 October, we have Villeneuve showing signs of panic, although maintaining a course for Gibraltar, and Nelson trailing him just about on the horizon, between ten and twelve miles away.

When Villeneuve saw the state of his fleet first thing that morning, he very sensibly and immediately gave the order to re-form into three squadrons. He was in the middle, in his flagship *Bucentaure*, with Álava on his port side and Gravina's picket squadron once more on his starboard hand. The fleet started to drop back into these positions which, as we have seen so often, was a very time-consuming manoeuvre under sail. But within the hour Villeneuve, who by then had received intelligence reports that Nelson had perhaps as many as thirty ships under his command, changed his mind. Signals were run up that a line of battle should once more be formed with between 160 and 190 yards between each vessel and that all vessels should go to action stations with decks cleared and guns run out and manned. Villeneuve's fleet was simply not up to this change of instructions.

Whatever the failings of his fleet, Villeneuve tested not their seamanship but his own personality. For an hour, between giving the command to form the line of battle at seven in the morning and watching the jumbled manoeuvre, he was at least able to see that by the time some semblance of order had been created from his instructions, they were closing quickly on the Strait of Gibraltar. The distance from Gibraltar to Toulon to Naples would take days to sail, not hours. Villeneuve could certainly have been in no doubt that in turning into the Mediterranean he remained vulnerable to Nelson's persistence and proven genius. This, again, contradicts the notion that had he been able to turn east he would have been, if not safe, then safer.

There is another possible reason for Villeneuve's reversing course to meet Nelson. Again, we look at weather conditions, visibility and the accuracy of the reports coming from the combined observation vessels, the pickets. Some of the French and Spanish logs suggest that the whole of Nelson's fleet was not sighted at first light on 21 October. It may have been that until a detailed assessment of the strength of the British force – including, crucially, the number of vessels in that force – reached Villeneuve, he believed Nelson to have fewer ships than he actually did and also – importantly – fewer big ones. Therefore one of the factors in deciding to turn and fight might have been a miscalculation on the part of the Frenchman and his pickets, aware that in terms of big fighting ships their fleet far outnumbered Nelson's.

None has satisfactorily explained Villeneuve's personality, nor the reason for his doing what he now did. Two points were obvious to Villeneuve. His instructions were to go to Naples. Those instructions had come from Napoleon and therefore had to be obeyed. Villeneuve believed that if Nelson caught him, the British admiral would win. So, logically, if Villeneuve was to fulfil Napoleon's instructions a battle with Nelson had to be avoided at all cost. That was good tactical logic as well as a very good reason – excuse – to keep running. However, there was a second plague eating away at his decision-making process.

Villeneuve knew that he had a reputation for not being brave enough and not committing himself, which dated at least from the Battle of the Nile seven years earlier. He was aware that for this reason Napoleon spat on his very name and that probably even now, on the quay at Cadiz, stood the fuming and not very distinguished admiral who was to replace him as commander-in-chief. Even if he, Villeneuve, managed to bring the fleet unmolested into Naples – and he could not have thought that very likely – he would not remain there in triumph. His orders would be to travel immediately to Paris and explain his miserable actions since assuming command of the Toulon fleet.

Therefore Villeneuve's options were few. He could either continue to run, in the hope that Nelson would not catch him, and then go to Paris where Napoleon would certainly catch him and then contradict every opinion (but his own) of himself – or he could turn and fight. It was not in Villeneuve's nature to put himself at risk. He was a whining and unstable figure with an accompanying erratic temperament. There is no reason to look for a logical explanation, therefore, of what he next did at shortly after eight o'clock on the morning of 21 October 1805.

In an Atlantic sliding swell, the most atrocious kind of sea for battle manoeuvres, and with unpredictable wind conditions, Villeneuve gave the order to about turn. In any situation this would have taken some time to achieve. Within sight of Gibraltar and not far offshore from Trafalgar, which makes freak wind directions even more likely and certainly unpredictable, the whole Combined Fleet, in its gaggle of a battle line, attempted to face the other way. The wind was all wrong, the timing ineptly chosen and the element of surprise to his own people, who could almost smell the Mediterranean, was bewildering.

We might just imagine what, in the seconds before the order came to reverse course, Villeneuve's battle line would have looked like. Gravina, the best tactical admiral in the Combined Fleet, was at the head of the column. The weaker ships were more or less at its stern. Villeneuve was somewhere in the middle. In theory, by reversing, the weaker ships were now at the sharp end. Gravina was at the stern. It took about two hours for the course change to come into effect. In those two hours, Nelson's fleet was gaining on the Franco-Spanish line. So by, let us say, ten o'clock that morning, when Villeneuve and his captains had more or less sorted themselves out, Nelson was easily within spyglass distance. Even if Villeneuve had experienced another mood change, he would not have been able to put it into operation. After months and months of telling Decrès that Nelson was unbeatable, he was now on a collision course with HMS *Victory*. He could not avoid battle.

The wind directions sometimes dropped to variable. What persisted was the Atlantic swell. Especially in south-westerlies, conditions in that area are rarely without the swell. When the swell is long and slow and the air conditions are muggy with light winds, there is usually a south-westerly storm approaching across the Atlantic. Ironically, if Villeneuve had tried to leave Cadiz twelve hours later than he had done, there might well never have been a battle. By mid-morning on 21 October, a martial storm was certainly brewing. By late evening, shortly after the battle was done, an Atlantic gale swept the debris of the conflict before it.

CHAPTER TWENTY-FIVE

The Weather Factor

WE OFTEN FORGET THE ROLE PLAYED BY WEATHER CONDITIONS at the Battle of Trafalgar. It is too easy to imagine that the daring and expertise of the Nelsonian sailors should be the centre of our attention. Yet the weather was an enormously important element in the outcome and, even the cause, of Trafalgar. As we have reminded ourselves, the big ships of the line were not nearly as fleet as the smaller vessels such as the frigates. There was, too, the distinction between those vessels which were magnificent when sailing downwind, that is, with the wind behind them, and some of the smaller craft with fore and aft rig which could sail closer to the direction from which the wind was coming. So we have to remember that at Trafalgar, with a mixed and – at this stage – deliberately widely deployed fleet, the sea state and wind played an important part.

In fact, had there been during the forty-eight hours leading up to the battle a wind from a different direction with a slightly increased strength, Trafalgar might not have taken place. Villeneuve's fleet could easily have escaped into the Mediterranean. Thanks to work done by the Meteorological Office, Oliver and Kington and, particularly Dennis A. Wheeler, we are able to put together a weather pattern for that period and show how it affected and to some extent determined both its outcome and immediate aftermath.

If we imagine where the various squadrons and fleets were we can see immediately why the weather would have mattered. When Nelson lost Villeneuve in the West Indies, the French admiral's fleet had crossed the

Atlantic and most of it had gone into Cadiz. Vice Admiral Cuthbert Collingwood had followed Villeneuve's ships. He now deployed frigates to keep a close eye on the port and withdrew to an easy distance keeping not so much guard as a lookout.

Nelson, as we have seen, reached Collingwood on 28 September after two weeks' vigorous sailing from Portsmouth. It is at this point that Nelson's fleet had taken up its positions, not for battle but for what modern sailors would call C3 – command, control and communications. Nelson was about fifty miles offshore with his main force. Close to Cadiz he had frigates which were fast and relatively well armed, but not there to fight the Combined Fleet. The frigates were the intelligence-gatherers. They could tell Nelson, fifty miles away, what Villeneuve was doing. Between those frigates and Nelson was a line of three other ships, the *Mars*, the *Colossus* and the *Defence*. These were the signal stations. The frigates would signal to the *Mars* and the *Mars* to the *Colossus*, which in turn would signal to the *Defence*, and that ship would signal to the *Victory*. If Villeneuve so much as put a nose outside Cadiz, Nelson would know about it in well under two hours. What is this to do with the weather? The weather offshore fifty miles away would be quite different from that where the frigates were. Nelson needed to know that weather. So did Villeneuve. If he were to make an escape from Cadiz, he wanted to know exactly the prevailing wind because he could not afford to shift anchorage until he had the right wind to set in a good speed, not to the west where Nelson was, not to the north where other British ships were, but round the corner from Cadiz down to Gibraltar, into the Mediterranean and the sure safety of Toulon. So Villeneuve needed a wind to take him to the south-east and then a westerly to blow him through the Strait of Gibraltar and home for tea.

Nelson also wanted winds enough to encourage Villeneuve to think that he could escape. In practical terms there was no point in Nelson praying for a westerly that would make sure Villeneuve was stuck in harbour.

There was what is generally described as an anticyclone from the Azores. Anyone sailing as far north as British waters understands the effects of the Azores anticyclone. If we look at the weather records for three weeks before the battle, we see the constraints on the British fleet, and, more importantly, what was keeping Villeneuve bottled up in Cadiz.

For example, land records as well as the logs of ships as far apart as the *Foudroyant* standing off Ushant and the *Africa* off Corunna give a good idea of the effects of a low-pressure area a fortnight before the battle. The high-pressure area, moving from the Azores, would in the main affect the sea state and weather further to the south. The two pressure areas were of course linked. From here comes the so-called weather pattern. From these records we can see that during those first three weeks of October 1805, wind forces were at a maximum of a fresh breeze; what the meteorologist would call force five. But what about wind directions? These were more confusing for the sailing masters. They followed no pattern. The naval meteorologists' dictum that the only predictable element of the weather is the wind, which tends mostly to be variable, applied during those three weeks leading to the battle. Standing off Cadiz, Collingwood and Nelson would have had four days of westerlies followed by a couple of days of north easterlies which then veered to the south-east, then – and here we are getting towards the time of the battle – for a week leading up to 18 October, a north-westerly. That north-westerly could have been favourable to Villeneuve. If Villeneuve wanted to sneak out, to get downwind from a north-westerly and round the corner through the Gibraltar Strait would have been nigh on perfect weather for him.

The possibility of an Azores anticyclone to the south-west of Cadiz is borne out by the reports of weather conditions, certainly between 11 and 18 October. On 18 October, the wind lost strength. From the logs it would seem that the almost variable conditions between south-south-east veering to south-south-west were no more than force two.

Anyone who has waited for a change in the weather before going out has experienced the dilemma that there comes a point when it is best to make a run for it. This was Villeneuve's dilemma, was it not? He knew that he was about to lose his command. The longer he loitered in Cadiz, the closer that moment would be. Sometime during the night of 18 October, the weather looked as good as it was going to get, and by the morning of the 19th it was clear to the British frigates standing offshore that there was enough activity in Cadiz to suggest that the Franco-Spanish fleet was to put to sea. The weather did not conform to Villeneuve's plan. The wind was south-east veering to south-west. Twelve of Villeneuve's ships put to sea. They were heading for Gibraltar. The wind dropped. The squadron was becalmed. The next day, 20 October, the wind strengthened between the south and south-west. The remainder of the fleet put to sea. The wind directions and strengths may have been to some extent to Villeneuve's disadvantage. They were not directly helpful to Nelson. He began to move his fleet in the hope of cutting off Villeneuve before Gibraltar. By the morning of the 20th, it was clear he would not catch them even though the south westerlies meant that Villeneuve's inability to sail in a direction close to the wind was limited and therefore, so was his progress.

It is inevitable that the French and British sailors, once at sea, would have had a reasonable sense of what was to come from the weather. Anyone who has sailed in those waters understands the meaning of the long calm before the storm and, most importantly, knows the first telltale sign: the increasingly long Atlantic swell. The ships did have barometers. Put this rather basic instrument alongside the Atlantic experience of the sailing masters – Nelson was an exceptional weather forecaster – then what was to follow the light and variable breezes was simply a matter of time.

Nelson's fleet had an enormous advantage over Villeneuve's. In spite of the discipline and good seamanship in Gravina's Spanish vessels, the French were ill-trained. Handling a big vessel in variable wind conditions is a difficult task. Even a vessel by itself is hard work. It can take forty-five minutes to make a major course change. Imagine the effort needed when the commander of an entire fleet of some thirty vessels has to issue manoeuvre orders to all his ships, which often have variable degrees of competence and, because of their construction, react in different ways. A multinational force will also have to deal with the issue of ensuring its men work together. The Franco-Spanish fleet was still not good enough to beat the weather conditions, which were never on their side as they ran for Gibraltar.

On the afternoon of 20 October, the wind strengths had increased and a couple of squalls blew through. Those squalls were sighted by Wheeler as 'speculation, for it can be no more, that this general disturbance is associated with a leading front on an advancing low pressure system'. The local weather had changed completely. Villeneuve was struggling through some of the poorest conditions for weeks, with captains and sailing masters of no great distinction. His south-south-east course throughout the night meant that by daybreak (probably as early as 5.30 even though this was October), he was sailing about ten miles off Cape Trafalgar. Nelson's fleet, altogether more disciplined, had taken advantage of the wind rather than struggled against it. His ships had picked up on the south-westerly and so could easily see Villeneuve against the rising sun – which suggests that the weather had not completely closed in at that point. Moreover, according to the log of Collingwood's *Royal Sovereign*, the wind had dropped to somewhere around a force three. This was a perfectly manageable breeze unless, of course, you were heading straight into it. Again, from Collingwood's log, the general direction suggests a south-westerly still. We should always remember the variation in directions at any one moment and the effects on vessels of different rigs.

At first sight these conditions seemed good for Nelson. However, let us not forget what the drop in wind conditions, together with the increased swell, suggested to the sailing masters. There was heading in their direction, that is from the south-west, at least a gale. The captain of *Euryalus* was later to describe the weather after the battle as a hurricane. A hurricane force has certain well-defined conditions. However, what followed would certainly have felt like one if you had happened to be in a frigate in the middle of it.

At breakfast on that morning of the battle, Villeneuve took a decision which has baffled many naval historians. He was more or less making progress to Gibraltar. His goal was not so far away. Nelson's fleet was standing off about ten miles to the west of him. Therefore, once round on the Gibraltar course, Villeneuve must have considered that Nelson would have had certain difficulty in catching him – after all, they were all in the same weather together. Through the night the weather pattern shifted. It could take nothing more than a wind change to decide the fate of a whole fleet, perhaps the fortunes of a nation. A good admiral planned ahead. An even better admiral was a good weather forecaster.

At 8.30 in the morning Villeneuve decided to make a U-turn in his planning: to go back and hide in Cadiz. Or that is how it seems. As we shall see below, it could have been that he had finally plucked up the courage to have it out with Nelson. The weather pattern was not much interested in this moment of history. To head north and head back to Cadiz meant turning his whole fleet in one movement in the other direction. There are two ways to move a big ship on to another course. A vessel can tack, which means swinging the head of the vessel through the direction of the wind and then setting the sail once the wind is on the opposite bow. The other way is what in smaller sailing vessels is called a gybe and, in larger ones, to wear ship. To gybe or wear ship the vessel veers away from the wind until it turns right round so that once more the wind is on the same side but sending the ship in approximately the opposite direction. The bigger the ship, the better it is to wear. This is a most complex movement of timing, ropes and sheets (the ropes which control the sails and the sails themselves). Imagine a vessel sailing, let us say, with the wind at about two o'clock on its starboard bow – roughly forty-five degrees. As the order is given to wear ship, the bow moves away from the wind. As it continues to swing away, the wind is now at four o'clock – on the beam – and eventually at six o'clock abaft (or behind) the port, not the starboard beam. That vessel handles and sails quite differently from how it did when the wind was at forty-five degrees. The task of the sailing master is to go even further round. We can see how complicated this is for a vessel. Imagine the effort to get a fleet of some thirty ships to do it all at once. This is the most hazardous form of ocean formation dancing ever conceived.

When Villeneuve ordered his fleet to wear ship, the swell was heavy. Anyone who has been rocked by a small wave when swimming off the beach understands that dynamic. So imagine the effect on the beam of a ship as she moves round. The winds remained light and variable, so sails would not easily fill as the vessel turned. The whole operation to get his ships travelling in the different direction – hopefully, for him, towards Cadiz – took Villeneuve at least one and a half hours, merely to turn the ship round. Anyone who imagines that all it takes is an order from a romantic master-and-commander figure to have a ship of the line, especially thirty of them, whizzing off in the other direction, might consider all these difficulties. We may like to think that this was simply a problem for the useless French. Not so. Nelson's fleet, many of whose captains the admiral had never worked with before, had similar difficulties in such conditions, even though it was generally accepted that the British ships were better drilled. So Nelson, even though he had ordered full sail, was not making much progress towards Villeneuve.

The fleets turned at 8.30 that morning. It seems unlikely that even the *Royal Sovereign* and the flagship, the *Victory*, could have made much more than two knots in those conditions. Two knots is a slow walking pace. Little wonder, then, that it was lunchtime, closing in on one o'clock, before the two fleets engaged. Meanwhile, the gathering gale was rumbling up from the south-west. It would be nip and tuck whether or not Nelson could be done with the battle before the terrible storms hit the fleet.

CHAPTER TWENTY-SIX

Hands to Breakfast

$\sim$

SINCE EIGHT O'CLOCK, VILLENEUVE'S FLEET HAD BEEN TRYING TO GET into some semblance of a battle line. It had failed, for reasons of seamanship, ship handling and the weather. Vessels would come into line and then drop back. They would stand in line and then, because of the sea state and winds, find themselves at best parallel to the main fleet. From a distance, as Nelson would have seen it, there was no line of battle. He would have seen what could almost be described as a two-tier arc of ships. This did not at all conform with Nelson's preconception of what he would attack.

Nelson had been on the chase since the previous Saturday. Early in the morning, Blackwood's signal had been relayed to the *Victory*. The intelligence assessment was accurate. Blackwood had sent a fast ship to warn Louis, who was still in the Strait of Gibraltar. Nelson bent on every sail his considerable fleet could carry, not to trail Villeneuve but to get to the approaches to the Mediterranean before the Combined Fleet and thus cut off its chances of getting through the gap between southern Europe and Saharan Africa. Nelson could not see the French in the dark. First thing in the morning on 20 October, Nelson was back off Gibraltar. It was now clear that Villeneuve, with all the difficulties of controlling his ships, was still in the north. There was a reasonable southerly veering to south-westerly blowing and Nelson headed north again. He was too far to the west, and this was confirmed when one of his picket ships, the *Phoebe*, sighted Villeneuve's fleet sailing south from Cadiz and lying at about forty-five degrees; that is, roughly north-east from where Nelson was. By the afternoon of 20 October, Blackwood, who had been trailing the fleet, signalled that Villeneuve was making a more westerly course than imagined. In spite of painters' images, not much fighting was done in the dark, ever. And so by mid afternoon on 20 October, Villeneuve had the advantage, because by the time, even with enormous luck, Nelson found him, formed into battle attack and then got into range, it would be, at the very least, dusk. Nelson knew that if there were to be a battle it would not be on 20 October. That did not mean the British fleet would simply sit there and see what would happen by the morning.

Nelson could not have had, in spite of Blackwood and other small-ship captains, a complete picture of where Villeneuve was and the state of readiness of the Franco-Spanish fleet. There was an obvious position for him to get into: first and foremost, he needed to manoeuvre his fleet so that when he saw the French and Spanish ships, he did so with the wind behind him. Remember the tactical advantage of a square-rigged sailing ship, running before the wind. In general terms, she is more easily handled and, most importantly, while she has speed, the enemy will have the wind against her and her manoeuvrability reduced to not much above zero. To create this advantage, there was no point in Nelson turning his fleet, in whatever formation, to run before the wind. After all, in the middle of the night he might have a superb run and go whizzing past an unseen Villeneuve and Gravina, then have to turn and have the wind against him.

Shortly after dusk on 20 October, Nelson manoeuvred his fleet on a south-westerly course to begin the moderately paced advance. He had to judge the direction Villeneuve was sailing, seek the following wind and, under controlled conditions, point somewhere ahead of where he expected Villeneuve to be when they sighted. This was a complicated manoeuvre, to gain the same sort of advantage that a sportsman might seek when aiming off the head of a partridge. At dawn, Nelson moved from the parallel course to one not quite to the south-east. Shortly before 6 a.m. on 21 October, the *Victory* hoisted signal seventy-two. This was the order for Nelson's battle fleet of twenty-seven ships of the line and four frigates to move into the two columns that he had now decided should be used to pierce and then surround Villeneuve's fleet. In his original plan, there had been a third column, but that would have been led by Rear Admiral Louis and his six ships which were still, as we have seen, in the Gibraltar

Strait region and had only just been contacted. (Which is why Nelson had only four frigates and not five, the fifth having been used to run the message to Louis.) This loss of the third, the advance squadron, hampered Nelson's planning only slightly.

Nelson would have overall command, of course, and immediate command of one column. Collingwood, in the *Royal Sovereign*, would have the column on Nelson's starboard side. For the first time in this plan, Collingwood would have command of his own battle line and could – and did – expect to have the authority to make his own judgement and adapt his tactics to whatever situation he found himself in. This, he would later that day do, even to the extent of not following a direct order from Nelson.

At 6 a.m., *Victory* hoisted signal thirteen: Prepare For Battle.

At 7.40 that morning, the four frigate captains went aboard *Victory* for their final orders where they should lie in the battle.

At 8.30, the hands were to breakfast. The ships were ready for battle. All live animals had been thrown overboard, although in the *Neptune* the captain's ducks and geese were battened down in their coops to take their chances with the rest of the hands. Anything that got in the way of hurrying seamen was lashed and stowed. The seawater pumps were used to soak large canvases which were then draped in the deck spaces and kept wet to act as firebreaks once the ships were in action. The decks were swabbed and then covered in sand so that sailors did not slip on the blood of their shipmates. The shot racks were opened, the powder hatches slipped and made fast on the deckhead and the pistols and cutlasses distributed. The surgeons set out their saws, knives, scalpels and probes, bandages and tourniquets. The sailors knew the routine. Any wounded would be taken below to the surgeon and treated, not according to their wounds but in order of their arrival at the surgeon's table. There would be no screaming. Any on deck who were dead, or looked as if they were dead, would be tossed over the side out of the way. There would be memorial enough for them at some other time.

It was while the hands, having readied the ship, were eating their bread and meat, washed down with wine or rum, that the word came through to Nelson that the chase south (remember, Nelson was now on a south-easterly course) was about to alter. Villeneuve had turned back from the approaches to the Strait and was heading their way. Any speculation that

Villeneuve had once again lost his nerve and was trying to regain Cadiz mattered nothing. If he wanted Cadiz, he would have to fight through Nelson's columns. In fact shortly before noon, when the battle had started, Nelson signalled to Collingwood that he intended to pierce the last section of Villeneuve's ships in order to stop the Frenchman escaping to Cadiz. So here is, if not proof, at least a hint that Nelson was never certain of why Villeneuve had altered course to face him and that he had always thought the French admiral would make a run for it if he got the chance.

The admiral had now manoeuvred his fleet into the two columns. Collingwood would not accept that he had to follow Nelson's orders to the letter. We might remember that Nelson's squadron was to windward and Collingwood's to leeward. The effects of the winds and sea states on both were similar. How they faced the enemy was not so similar. Moreover, not all the ships were of a standard that allowed them to slip in and out of line at their flag officer's will, as if they had been some kind of demonstration squadron compared with Villeneuve's fleet with its often inefficient manoeuvrings. Nelson was very clear as to what he expected Collingwood to do. Collingwood was very clear that he was in command of his own squadron and that to keep station he might need to follow different sailing instructions from those Nelson would have liked. Moreover, Collingwood had different expectations of some of his captains. He signalled changes in position in his squadron, considering that he knew exactly where he wanted his ships to be once they broke into the enemy. This is why, for example, Hargood[1] was ordered to bring his 74-gun *Belleisle* into second place of the squadron immediately astern of Collingwood's flagship, the 100-gun *Royal Sovereign*. Nelson did not approve. Collingwood, though, had his way.

Unlike ships with engines or soldiers ashore, Nelsonian vessels have found it difficult in those conditions to be hove to while waiting for the enemy. The momentum had to be maintained. To do that, Nelson and Collingwood had to do exactly what Villeneuve and Gravina were doing. Individual ships were ordered to make more speed, or to change station, or to close up or fall away, in order that the two tight lines should be maintained.

---

[1] William Hargood (1762–1839). Performed heroically at Trafalgar and was later awarded the sword of honour.

There was, too, perhaps from our perspective, an unexpected element of competition in the two British squadrons. Collingwood, with the wind to his advantage (*Royal Sovereign* was a more easily handled ship than the often ungainly *Victory*), appeared determined that it should be he himself who would lead the British into this battle. He would be the first to crash through the expected barrage. When the breeze stiffened slightly, it was Collingwood who gave the order for his squadron to tighten sheets and alter course a little, to take advantage of that wind and pick up speed. Nelson's only response was to give a similar order. We should not make the mistake of picturing, as an artist might, two taut. and disciplined lances of British vessels speeding into the French crescent. The British may have frightened Villeneuve, but some of their own captains thoroughly annoyed Nelson and Collingwood. Not all had the skill or the reputation sometimes given to the post captain. In light and variable airs, waiting for a gale and slithering in the Atlantic swell, some of those vessels were tubs to handle. If a ship could not keep up close to the flagship at the head of a squadron, it slowed down the entire squadron because the other vessels were following in line behind it. Therefore those slow vessels in, say, Collingwood's line of fifteen ships, had to drop back. The skill of the flag officer was to decide when a vessel should drop back, where it should go in the line and which vessel should replace it, all the time keeping the momentum of the advance. This, for example, was why Collingwood had ordered the *Belleisle* up from the rear marker – that is, the fifteenth vessel – to be the second vessel. It was also one of the reasons that Nelson disapproved of Collingwood's order, because he would have put a different vessel there. The other reason Nelson probably disapproved was that he was not keen on Collingwood asserting his authority at that stage. He would never say so publicly, and nor did he.

If this sounds as if the sometimes expressionless Collingwood was caught in the grip of warfare and that Nelson would have preferred the fleet, including its admirals, to remember that he, Nelson, was the hero and not them, we should see the consequences of Collingwood's keenness and self-assertion. Nelson's reputation is that of the imaginative, dashing and often unconventional naval tactician. Cuthbert Collingwood, had he been born a little to the north of his native Northumberland, might have been labelled dour and unimaginative. In the line of battle, approaching an enemy, an admiral needs (apart from luck) three talents: clear-sightedness, utmost tactical appreciation and an unqualified ability to make sure that everyone in the squadron knows exactly what to do, has been positioned according to his capability and is aware that, when the fighting starts, he has the confidence of his flag officer.

Collingwood led his squadron in the heat of battle. Nelson never felt the effects of that heat and had no need to issue unnecessary commands. By the time the two squadrons reached the curve of the Combined Fleet's muddled position, Collingwood's team was not in disciplined order. Nelson's, in defiance of the weather conditions and the limitations within the squadron, was as sharp as it might have been at a fleet review before the monarch off Spithead – in spite of the irregular positioning and behaviours of the captains of the *Africa*, the *Orion* and the *Britannia*.

In fact the *Britannia*, the flagship of Rear Admiral the Earl of Northesk,[2] was supposed to have been leading one of the flotillas. The *Britannia* somehow dislodged herself from the battle line, was hardly seen during the fighting, and most certainly was not where she should have been, alongside *Victory*, when Nelson's flagship was fought almost to a standstill.

If there was a sense of adventure in Nelson's squadron, it was probably expressed by Eliab Harvey,[3] captain of the *Téméraire*. Harvey wanted to lead Nelson's squadron into the battle. He was not looking for promotion. Nor was he alone in wishing to be first into the fray. Blackwood had gone so far as to submit to Nelson that the *Victory* was not the best place for him to direct operations. He suggested that Nelson might wish to transfer to his smaller vessel, the *Euryalus*, so that he could stand off and better direct operations of both squadrons once they clashed with the Combined Fleet. Harvey and Blackwood had two concerns: they thought it wrong that the flagship should be in the middle of the fight because, in the fog of gunfire, masts and dismantled and crashing spars, the flag officer – that is, Nelson – would not be able to see the whole battle and his captains would not be able to see their admiral's signal. Second, they feared that Nelson would be, at the very least, badly wounded and that it would be wrong militarily for the author of the battle plan to be

[2] William Carnegie, Earl of Northesk (1758–1831).
[3] Captain Eliab Harvey (1758–1830).

incapacitated. As we know, Nelson chose to remain in the *Victory*, in the middle of the battle and, in spite of Blackwood's expressed concern, dressed in his vice admiral's uniform. He was not about to hide from a Frenchman. As he found to his cost, nor did he.

Nelson had not slept during the night before the battle. Blackwood, in his usual role of tracking the enemy, had ranged his frigates in order to communicate in daylight and darkness with the *Victory*. The line of signals would be simple. Blackwood, in the *Euryalus*, would watch Villeneuve's fleet. If there should be movement to report, he would signal to the first frigate he had between himself and Nelson's fleet. That frigate would then signal to its sister ship. The signals would be relayed through HMS *Defence*, then to the *Colossus* and, finally, to HMS *Mars*. *Mars* would send on the signal to *Victory*.

During the night, the signalling system had to be even simpler. If Villeneuve (who, remember, appeared to be sailing towards Cadiz) altered course to the south or more directly to Gibraltar, Blackwood would signal his change by burning two blue lights together every hour. If Villeneuve altered course completely and started to head in a westerly direction (no one had forgotten his slipping away to the Caribbean) during the night, Blackwood would show this by burning white lights and, if the Frenchman took a westward track, by firing three guns very quickly on the hour.

On the Sunday, there were south-south-westerly breezes which had increased by lunchtime until they sometimes approached gale force. Those southerly winds increased speculation that Villeneuve might not have reached Gibraltar. By the afternoon Blackwood was signalling that Villeneuve was trying to get to the west – his track dictated by wind directions and not tactical design. Throughout the night, the system of blazing lights and rapid triple gunfire told Nelson all he needed to know of Villeneuve's directions.

By four in the morning, Nelson's fleet had a good north-westerly and was making an easy sail to the east. Cape Trafalgar was a little over twenty miles away and slightly to the south of east, so bearing approximately 110 degrees.

Nelson appeared on deck shortly after daybreak. He was in a good mood. He must have had some concerns about the manning of his fleet. He believed his captains, with few exceptions (the Earl of Northesk in the *Britannia* being the obvious one), to be pretty good and the men under their command the best that could be got to sea. Today, the navy complains of manpower shortages. Exactly 200 years ago, Nelson's sentiments were similar. Some of his ships had no more than two-thirds the number of men they needed. It was common enough for gun crews to fire from one side and then run across and fire from the other. Nevertheless, Nelson told Hardy that he was, as ever, confident of victory and expected his ships to take at least twenty of the enemy as prizes. He could also have wished that he had his six extra ships that were still loitering about Gibraltar and Calder's flagship, but he spent little time wondering what might be. That date held a certain significance for Nelson's family, who celebrated 21 October as the anniversary of a minor battle in which his uncle, Maurice Suckling (who had got him into the navy in the first place), had been victorious.

The Sunday's strong winds had abated and there was not much more than a westerly breeze, but still those big swells, which meant that a ship unable to find enough wind to stretch her canvases to the full unless she kept the breeze astern, could slither and wallow at a crucial moment in the approach to the fight. The broad-beamed big ships would tend to veer anyway, when the wind was right astern. Nelson watched the weather. He knew those Atlantic swells suggested the gales that would be with them by nightfall. Moreover, because of the wind direction Nelson was having to be on the landward side of the enemy and being pushed towards that Cape. In sailing terms, he was in the most dangerous position for an engineless vessel, on what is known as a lee shore.

So in the morning, anticipating how the day might go with the wind and also the certainty that every ship would suffer a great amount of wreckage from collapsed and shot-away spars and masts, Nelson ordered, before the battle, that immediately it had ended, ships should anchor. Nelson knew that even in a light breeze the fleet would be in no state to operate together. Surviving captains and crews would need absolute calm in order to jury rig their ships, clear up the decks and dispose of as much of the damage as possible. To attempt to do this in a storm was difficult enough. To do it in weather that would push them towards that lee shore when, remember, they would probably not have a serviceable sail to manoeuvre by, was courting disaster. Nelson was right. After Nelson's death Collingwood, who assumed command, ignored the dead admiral's order. The British fleet did not anchor. The consequences of this were terrible. Not only were prize ships lost, but also men from both sides drowned. In spite of the navy's later respect for him, Collingwood, an old friend of Nelson, might not always be admired.

Blackwood's impression of Nelson, hours before the battle commenced, was of a man supremely confident and determined to annihilate as many French and Spanish and their vessels as possible. To Nelson there were no half measures. The only certain way to demonstrate victory was to kill whatever stood in the way of that occasion. So, at 6.40 in the morning, Nelson ordered his fleet to split into their two battle columns. His own squadron would be to windward, that is, on the weather side of Collingwood's. The ties were undone on the steering sails, the royals and the topsails. The enemy was still some way off, but the columns were closing in on Villeneuve.

There were two important things left for Nelson to do. When a ship clears for action, all fixtures and fittings have to be removed, lashed and stowed. These included the admiral's personal belongings. The last possession but one to be taken from the Great Cabin was a portrait that hung on the bulkhead. This was what Nelson called a picture of his guardian angel, Emma Hamilton. The cabin was quite bare except for his writing table and his sword. Nelson now sat to write the final entry in his diary, dated that Monday morning, 21 October.

At daylight saw the Enemy's Combined Fleet from East to E.S.E.; bore away; made the signal for Order of Sailing, and to Prepare for Battle; the Enemy with their heads to the Southward: at even the enemy wearing in succession. May the Great God, whom I worship, grant to my Country, and for the benefit of Europe in general, a great and glorious Victory; and may no misconduct in any one tarnish it; and may humanity after Victory be the predominant feature in the British Fleet. For myself, individually, I commit my life to Him who made me, and may his blessing light upon my endeavours for serving my Country faithfully. To Him I resign myself and the just cause which is entrusted to me to defend. Amen. Amen. Amen.

CHAPTER TWENTY-SEVEN

The Battle – Part I

NELSON NOW ROSE AND WENT TO THE QUARTERDECK. LEFT BEHIND ON his table were his diary, now closed – and his sword. For the first time, he did not wear it in battle. There was a procedure that when a ship strikes – that is, hauls down – her flag, it is a sign that she is ready to surrender. The surrender is actually taken when the defeated commander symbolically hands over his sword to the victor. It is perhaps fanciful, but only just, to think that Nelson did not forget to wear his sword, as some have suggested, but left it off to show that he had no intention of surrendering to any Frenchman, particularly Villeneuve.

Now we come to the battle itself. We might remember, as we go through the events of that long afternoon of 21 October 1805, a few points that will make them more significant and easier to understand. First, contrary to general opinion, the majority of French and Spanish captains and crews fought ferociously, bravely and at huge cost. Second, Villeneuve in battle was not nearly as useless as his previous statements and actions might have suggested. When he hesitated, it was often because it was unclear how the battle was going. Equally, some of his captains metaphorically spat on him. Third, Pierre Dumanoir,[1] Villeneuve's deputy commander of the Mediterranean fleet, removed his squadron from the battle and abandoned his superior to Nelson. Had he stayed and fought, it is perfectly possible that Villeneuve would have been victorious at Trafalgar.

Fourth, Nelson was foolish when he exposed himself to French

---

[1] Pierre Dumanoir Le Pelley (1770–1829).

marksmen. Blackwood was correct when he observed that it was wrong for his admiral, who was there to direct operations, to risk his life so easily and therefore potentially leave the British fleet leaderless when he was most needed. Fifth, Nelson's new tactic did not work as he had said it would. Sixth, Collingwood should not have outpaced the rest of his squadron and made himself so vulnerable to French gunfire. This determination to be first into the fight – and, most importantly, before Nelson – did not help the British fleet.

Lastly, the battle was not between two forces in close formation blasting away at each other. It was a ferocious engagement between individual ships which arrived early, others which arrived late, some locked together by their spars and lashed bowsprits and individual ships fighting, being surrounded and yet somehow surviving as burning, charred and bloody hulks well away from the main group.

This last point sets the scene. The French waited in a disorganized group and the British charged in two columns. Shortly after the first guns were fired, the waiting group and the two columns were virtually indistinguishable from each other. It was, as the expression at the time would have it, a pell-mell affair. We must begin, therefore, by seeing which ships were where at the beginning and then, rather than offering a naval debriefing of the tactics of the battle, follow the fortunes of some of those ships and men as they fought their individual actions. In that way we shall not become confused as to the state of the battle at any one time. Moreover, by looking at some of the experiences of individual ships – for example, the *Belleisle*, which looked like a mastless abattoir and should have surrendered but did not – we can get a better sense of the remarkable action executed on both sides among Spanish, French and British.

Therefore we begin by showing which ships were where shortly after eleven o'clock in the morning. The combined French and Spanish ships were supposed to be in a straight line of battle. Because of the circumstances and their lack of seamanship and the difficulties of ship handling in the Atlantic swell, which was increasing as the distant gale-force westerlies pushed big seas before them, the Combined Fleet was arranged as an irregular crescent with some vessels slightly behind the main arc. In all, there were forty ships. Thirty-three of those were ships of the line, that is, big vessels, the smallest having 74 guns and the biggest, the *Santisima Trinidad,* 136. There were also five frigates, four of which had 40 guns each and the fifth, 32. There were also two small vessels, brigs, the *Argus* and *Furet.* The important vessels in the battle were the thirty-three ships of the line. They now sailed in that jumbled crescent. (For a full list of all the ships at the Battle of Trafalgar, see page 366.)

Twelve commanders died at Trafalgar: Beaudouin[2], Churruca[3], Cooke[4], Denieport[5], Duff[6], Filhol-Camas[7], Galiano[8], Gourrège[9], Le Tourneur, Admiral Magon, Vice Admiral Nelson and Poulain[10]. Admirals Álava and Gravina later died of their wounds.

Aboard his flagship, Villeneuve watched the approaching British. At 8.30 in the morning, he gave the order to form the line that did not quite make the formation he wanted. He did not realize it, but he was creating an arc that would be imitated in late twentieth- and early twenty-first-century warfare. Because his ships had been unable to get into a straight line they had inadvertently produced a double-hedged cup. Any enemy going into this curve would therefore risk being in range, on both port and starboard sides, of more than one defender. Also, Villeneuve had brought his fleet on to the port tack, that is, with the wind blowing on the port side. Therefore he had the land on his starboard bow and imagined that if all else failed he could escape into Cadiz. This meant that Nelson had to put part of his formation in a position to block that escape. This diverted part of his effort, which was already frustrated by the irregular formation of the Franco-Spanish fleet, even though Villeneuve's command had not realized that that was the consequence of indifferent seamanship in trying weather conditions.

In some ways, the difficult Atlantic swell, the light airs and probably, at that time of the year also, the sea breezes off the land (see chapter 25) which made life difficult for Villeneuve actually gave him an advantage

---

[2] Louis Alexis Beaudouin, Captain of the *Fougueux.*
[3] Cosmé Damián Churruca (1761–1805), captain of the *San Juan Nepomuceno.*
[4] John Cooke (1763–1805), captain of the *Bellerophon.*
[5] Gabriel Denieport (1765–1805) commanded the *Achille.*
[6] George Duff (1764–1805), captain of the *Mars.*
[7] Jean Gilles Filhol-Camas (1760–1805) commanded the *Berwick.*
[8] Dionisio Alcalá Galiano commanded the *Bahama.*
[9] Pierre-Paul Gourrège, captain of the *Aigle.*
[10] Jean Baptiste Poulain (1767–1805), captain of the *Héros.*

over Nelson. In places where, instead of being a single line of ships, French and Spanish vessels were three deep, Nelson's plan to lance through a conventional line of battle and thus surround that single column of ships was near impossible. It was yet another plan that looked good on paper but not at sea. Moreover, because of the light airs and irregular breezes Nelson's charge in two columns was hardly that. It would appear that even the best of the vessels found it hard to make more than four knots – that is, roughly walking pace. As they drew closer to the Combined Fleet, this lack of speed made them easier targets for the French and Spanish gunners, especially as the leading British ships in both squadrons arrived without their backup vessels.

To get some idea of the slow-motion build-up to the actual point of contact, it is interesting to see that as Nelson's two squadrons headed for the enemy he called on board the captains of his frigates for final discussions. We might imagine that there was nothing more to be said and that when the ships were running straight for the enemy the difficulty of transferring from the frigates to the *Victory* and back again was an almost impossible task. It was not. Naval seamanship (as opposed to merchant navy seamanship) was quite used to doing quick transfers from small, fast boats, and this three- or four-knot advance was hardly likely to outstrip the communication boats.

What did Nelson see as he approached the Combined Fleet? The crescent and its jumbled form was apparent and frustrating, for the British anyway. He himself was looking for Villeneuve but could not see him. The French and Spanish flagships were not flying their pennants. It had to be assumed that they were deliberately trying to confuse Nelson. Why, after all, should Villeneuve advertise his own position when he knew that Nelson would come looking for him? He had misgivings enough and sensibly saw no reason to make life easier for the British admiral. Nelson also saw that the irregular formation complicated his plan of attack but might have been a deliberate tactic on the part of Villeneuve. Furthermore, Nelson and Collingwood saw that the French and Spanish were very close together, which suggested that they were determined to put an end to their poor reputation. This was not a fleet that huddled together in fear but one which saw the bunching as a good tactic to further complicate Nelson's approach. Remember, although we have no proper evidence of Villeneuve's tactics, we do know that long before the battle he had anticipated Nelson's.

Aboard the *Victory*, there appears to have been an enormous confidence. The surgeon and Blackwood, as we have seen, were more concerned for Nelson's safety than for their own. Nelson was too busy to take seriously what they had to say. As they closed towards the French line, he left the quarterdeck and went below among the gun decks and his sailors. He wanted each one of them to see and hear him and for them to know that he had the most enormous confidence in their capabilities. He had, also, a single instruction: whatever the enemy did, they, *Victory*'s gunners, should not fire until they knew that each round would count.

As the enemy waited for the British to approach, Captain Jean Lucas[11] in the *Redoutable* made similar rounds. It was a more elaborate affair than Nelson's walk through the mess and gun decks of *Victory*. Lucas was preceded by drummers and fifers. When, at 11.30, the *Redoutable* hoisted her flags (Villeneuve had failed to hoist his in his own ship), the ceremony was accompanied by soldiers presenting arms and rolls being beaten on side drums, while the French ship's company called for not three but seven cheers for Napoleon.

The log of HMS *Naiad* gives the sequence of events from *Victory* that morning: At 6.40 am, Victory hoisted signal number 13: prepare for battle. At 6.50 am, signal 76: sail on the same course steered by the admiral. 10 am, signal 92: shorten sail and carry as little sail as possible. 11.05: make all sail possible with safety to the masts [this was made to the Africa which was clearly lagging]. At 11.35, *Victory* hoisted from its mizzen (the rear mast) the most famous signal in British naval history, Signals 253 [England], 269 [expects], 863 [that], 261 [every], 471 [man], 958 [will], 220 [do], 374 [his], 4 [D], 21 [U], 19 [T] and 24 [Y].

That was not the signal Nelson had originally intended. We can see that there was no single signal number for 'DUTY'. Therefore four flags had

---

[11] Captain Jean-Jacques Étienne Lucas (1764–1819). The commander Napoleon most admired in the Combined Fleet.

to be hoisted to spell out the word. Nelson had wanted, according to his flag lieutenant, John Pasco, to send the signal, 'England *confides* that every man will do his duty', but as with the word 'duty', there was no single flag for 'confides'.[12] Therefore Pasco, in a later letter to Sir Nicholas Harris Nicolas, who was editing the dispatches and letters of Nelson, said that it was he, Pasco, who had pointed out that it would take quite a long time and space to hoist single letters, and therefore, if Nelson did not object, it would be much simpler to substitute 'expects' for 'confides'. So signal 269 was hoisted instead of eight separate flags, a certain tribute to Sir Home Popham, who had invented the telegraphic code of flags.[13]

At noon, signal 63 was sent: prepare to anchor, followed by signal 8: the above signal to take place immediately after the close of day. This was Nelson's last instruction and the only one to be ignored and then countermanded by Collingwood.

Blackwood stayed on board *Victory* until the very last moment. Gunfire could be heard – at this stage, ineffectual. The French and Spanish were ranging their guns. It was really Blackwood who came closest to persuading Nelson against leading the charge of his squadron. Not long before ten o'clock Nelson agreed with Blackwood's submission that *Leviathan* and *Téméraire* should be ordered to go ahead of the *Victory*. Nelson may have agreed, but there was no way in which he was going to let the other two ships get ahead. Nelson himself, using the voice horn, called across to the *Téméraire*. His instruction was simple: that she and the *Leviathan* should proceed ahead. However, he knew very well that his voice would be carried away on the wind and that neither ship would hear him. He then went through the motions of sending a message by boat. This took time. During that time, Nelson ordered Hardy to pile on as much sail as he could in the *Victory*. By the time the *Téméraire* and the *Leviathan* received their instructions there was no way in which they could possibly have got in front of *Victory*. Blackwood saw exactly what his commander-in-chief was doing and wanted Hardy to shorten sail to let them overtake.

James, in his naval history of the time, said that Nelson openly agreed with Blackwood and is supposed to have said, 'Oh yes, let her [the

---

[12] John Pasco (1774–1853).
[13] Sir Home Riggs Popham (1762–1820).

Téméraire] go ahead.' Meaning, if she could. Blackwood's account is slightly different and might be explained partly by the circumstances under which he wrote it, after the death of his admiral. Blackwood, having had his suggestion turned down that Nelson should transfer to the *Euryalus*, remembers asking him to allow not only *Téméraire* and *Leviathan* but also *Neptune* to lead the squadron into action. Hardy was brought into the conversation and apparently supported Blackwood. It was apparently Blackwood himself who was sent across to the *Téméraire* to 'communicate his wishes, which I did'. At 12.15, *Téméraire* looked like getting ahead. According to the log of HMS *Conqueror*, *Victory* signalled 269: take your station astern of *Victory*. Whichever version is exactly right hardly matters. What we have is a determination on the part of senior officers to protect Nelson's life. From a personal point of view, Blackwood and Hardy could not bear the thought that a hair of his head would be grazed. From a tactical one, Blackwood and Hardy thought it essential to have the one man who had the battle plan in his head and was able to adjust it according to circumstances stay on his feet. Whether the course of the battle would have been different had Nelson transferred to the *Euryalus* is impossible to say.

Before we examine our version of what happened during the next four hours or so, we might read Collingwood's report. On Nelson's death Collingwood became the senior flag officer. Moreover, it was his post-battle report that was sent to the Admiralty and appeared a little more than two weeks later in the official public record of the day, *The London Gazette*. Collingwood, now in command of the Mediterranean fleet, had maintained the blockade of Cadiz, where some ships of the Combined Fleet had taken haven. So he wrote his report whilst still at sea off Cadiz and sent it in the fastest of his ships back to England.

The London Gazette Extraordinary

Wednesday, Nov. 6, 1805.

Admiralty Office, Nov. 6.

Dispatches, of which the following are Copies, were received at the Admiralty this day, at one o'clock. A.M. from Vice Admiral

Collingwood, Commander in Chief of his Majesty's ships and vessels off Cadiz:-

Admiral

SIR, *Euryalus,* off Cape Trafalgar, Oct. 22, 1805.

The ever-to-be-lamented death of Vice Admiral Lord Viscount Nelson, who, in the late conflict with the enemy, fell in the hour of victory, leaves to me the duty of informing my Lords Commissioners of the Admiralty, that on the 19th instant, it was communicated to the Commander in Chief, from the ships watching the motions of the enemy in Cadiz, that the Combined Fleet had put to sea; as they sailed with light winds westerly, his Lordship concluded their destination was the Mediterranean, and immediately made all sail for the Streights' [sic] entrance, with the British Squadron, consisting of twenty-seven ships, three of them sixty-fours, where his Lordship was informed, by Captain Blackwood (whose vigilance in watching, and giving notice of the enemy's movements, has been highly meritorious), that they had not yet passed the Streights.

On Monday the 21st instant, at day-light, when Cape Trafalgar bore E. by S. about seven leagues, the enemy was discovered six or seven miles to the Eastwards, the wind about West, and very light; the Commander in Chief immediately made the signal for the fleet to bear up in two columns, as they are formed in order of sailing; a mode of attack his Lordship had previously directed, to avoid the inconvenience and delay in forming a line of battle in the usual manner. The enemy's line consisted of thirty-three ships (of which eighteen were French, and fifteen Spanish, commanded in Chief by Admiral Villeneuve; the Spaniards, under the direction of Gravina, wore, with their heads to the Northward, and formed their line of battle with great closeness and correctness; but as the mode of attack was unusual, so the structure of their line was new; it formed a crescent, convexing to leeward, so that, in leading down to their centre, I had both their van and rear abaft the beam; before the fire opened, every alternate ship was about a cable's length to windward of her second a-head and a-stern, forming a kind of double line, and appeared, when on their beam, to leave a very little interval between them; and this without crowding their ships. Admiral Villeneuve was in the *Bucentaure*, in the centre, and the *Prince of Asturias* bore Gravina's flag in the rear, but the French and Spanish ships were mixed without any apparent regard to order of national squadron.

As the mode of our attack had been previously determined on, and communicated to the Flag-Officers, and Captains, few signals were necessary, and none were made, except to direct close order as the lines bore down.

The Commander in Chief, in the *Victory*, led the weather column, and the *Royal Sovereign*, which bore my flag, the lee.

The action began at twelve o'clock; by the leading ships of the column breaking through the enemy's line, the Commander in Chief about the tenth ship from the van, the Second in Command about the twelfth from the rear, leaving the van of the enemy unoccupied; the succeeding ships breaking through, in all parts, astern of their leaders, and engaging the enemy at the muzzles of their guns; the conflict was severe; the enemy's ships were fought with a gallantry highly honourable to their Officers; but the attack on them was irresistible, and it pleased the Almighty Disposer of all events to grant his Majesty's arms a complete and glorious victory. About three P.M. many of the enemy's ships having struck their colours, their line gave way; Admiral Gravina, with ten ships joining their frigates to leeward, stood towards Cadiz. The five headmost ships in their van tacked, and standing to the Southward, to windward of the British line, were engaged, and the sternmost of them taken; the others went off, leaving to his Majesty's squadron nineteen ships of the line (of which two are first rates, the *Santissima Trinidad* [sic] and the *Santa Anna*,) with three Flag Officers, viz. Admiral Villeneuve, the Commander in Chief; Don Ignatio Maria D'Alivà, Vice Admiral; and the Spanish Rear-Admiral, Don Baltazar Hidalgo Cisperos.

After such a Victory, it may appear unnecessary to enter into encomiums on the particular parts taken by the several Commanders; the conclusion says more on the subject than I have language to express; the spirit which animated all was the same: when all exert themselves zealously in their country's service, all deserve that their high merits should stand recorded; and never was high merit more conspicuous than in the battle I have described.

The *Achille* (A French 74), after having surrendered, by some mis-management of the Frenchmen, took fire and blew up; two hundred of her men were saved by the Tenders.

A circumstance occurred during the action, which so strongly marks the invincible sprit of British seamen, when engaging the enemies of their country, that I cannot resist the pleasure I have in making it known to their Lordships; the *Temeraire* was boarded by accident, or design, by a French ship on one side, and a Spaniard on the other; the contest was vigorous, but, in the end, the Combined Ensigns were torn from the poop, and the British hoisted in their places.

Such a battle could not be fought without sustaining a great loss of men. I have not only to lament, in common with the British Navy, and the British Nation, in the Fall of the Commander in Chief, the loss of a Hero, whose name will be immortal, and his memory ever dear to his country; but my heart is rent with the most poignant grief for the death of a friend, to whom, by many years intimacy, and a perfect knowledge of the virtues of his mind, which inspired ideas superior to the common race of men, I was bound by the strongest ties of affection; a grief to which even the glorious occasion in which he fell, does not bring the consolation which, perhaps, it ought; his Lordship received a musket ball in his left breast, about the middle of the action, and sent an Officer to me immediately with his last farewell; and soon after expired.

I have also to lament the loss of those excellent Officers, Captains Duff, of the *Mars*, and Cooke, of the *Bellerophon*; I have yet heard of none others.

I fear the numbers that have fallen will be found very great, when the returns come to me; but it having blown a gale of wind ever since the action, I have not yet had it in my power to collect any reports from the ships.

The *Royal Sovereign* having lost her masts, except the tottering foremast, I called the *Euryalus* to me, while the action continued, which ship lying within hail, made my signals – a service Captain Blackwood performed with great attention; after the action, I shifted my flag to her, that I might more easily communicate any orders to, and collect the ships, and towed the *Royal Sovereign* out to Seaward. The whole fleet were now in a very perilous situation, many dismasted, all shattered, in thirteen fathom water, off the shoals of Trafalgar; and when I made the signal to prepare to anchor, few of the ships had an anchor to let go, their cables being shot; but the same good Providence which aided us through such a day preserved us in the night, by the wind shifting a few points, and drifting the ships off the land, except four of the captured dismasted ships, which are now at anchor off Trafalgar, and I hope will ride safe until those gales are over.

Having thus detailed the proceedings of the fleet on this occasion, I beg to congratulate their Lordships on a victory which, I hope, will add a ray to the glory of his Majesty's crown, and be attended with public benefit to our country. I am, & c.

(Signed) C. COLLINGWOOD.

Collingwood gives here what we might call a sanitized version of the battle. Official reporting requires no more than essential facts, delivered with restraint. Moreover, until the individual logs of the British vessels could be consulted, Cuthbert Collingwood was perhaps in no position to expand. Of course, those logs would have been difficult to keep by the deck officers once the engagement started. There would be discrepancies between one ship and another. Not every vessel would agree on times of events and even records of wind directions might vary. The pell-mell was no benign atmosphere for the ship's writer. Multiply these discrepancies by about thirty ships' logs, introduce the fact that all but one British ship sustained heavy casualties and add the detail that the log was not completed until after the engagement and the ship had been made safe, and we can see that the later records were, like even those of modern-day battles, a subject best left to an analyst coming to the event ten or even a hundred years later. We can regard Collingwood's report as an outline of what happened. We might also take bits and pieces from the logs of some of the ships that took part, including those of the Combined Fleet, and try to get a sense of what took place in that dreadful conflict of 21 October.

CHAPTER TWENTY-EIGHT

The Battle – Part II

A T NOON THAT DAY, CAPE TRAFALGAR WAS ABOUT TWENTY MILES AWAY. We know no more than that, because the logs that have survived from the various vessels do not entirely agree. In the circumstances, approximately twenty miles was good enough for the battle to be known as that of Trafalgar. It was at about this time, however, that the British fleet, now led into battle by Collingwood in the *Royal Sovereign*, came under fire. Within an hour and a half, Nelson would be shot. In the *Victory*, he ordered his white ensign to be flown. Union flags were flown from the main topmast stays. Also flown from the *Victory*, at its highest point, was Nelson's personal signal to his fleet or squadron, signal 16: Engage the enemy more closely. With the exception of Villeneuve, the Combined Fleet also hoisted their ensigns, and the Spanish vessels swung at the end of the after boom (the boom that came from the mizen mast) a large wooden cross.

Collingwood made the first kill. He had been fired upon by the *Fougueux*, but it was a few minutes after noon that he drove the *Royal Sovereign* astern of the *Santa Ana* and fired. One record, supposedly supported by the Spanish, suggests that that broadside alone killed almost 400 Spaniards. Collingwood was in full flow and is said to have remarked to his captain, Rotheram[1] (with whom he was normally hardly on speaking terms) 'What would Nelson give to be here?' Nelson was most certainly watching, with Pasco at his side confirming the initial fire.

---

[1] Captain Edward Rotheram (1753–1830).

The difficulty for Collingwood was that in his determination to beat Nelson into battle he was on his own. The *Santa Ana* was not finished by any means. That ship and the *Royal Sovereign* were now so close that they were nearly touching, and they murderously fired round after round into each other. Moreover, the *Santa Ana* was not alone. The *Fougueux* now attacked Collingwood's stern, and from a few yards ahead of *Royal Sovereign* the *San Leandro* began firing into Collingwood's bow. Also bearing down on his bow and his quarter came the *San Justo* and the *Indomptable*. One report from the logs suggests that Collingwood was being attacked from so many angles that sometimes the criss-crossing of the cannonballs meant that many of them were colliding.

During fifteen minutes of furious action, the *Royal Sovereign* was in a dreadful state and the only British ship in the battle. Rescue came from the *Belleisle*. Her approach, with others following, caused all but the *Santa Ana* to haul away from the *Royal Sovereign*. The *Belleisle* sent a broadside into the quarter of the Spanish ship. The *Belleisle* would herself later suffer terrible damage and losses.

The 74-gun *Belleisle* and her sister ship, the *Mars*, along with a slightly bigger vessel, the 80-gun *Tonnant*, had not been able to keep up with Collingwood when he sent the *Royal Sovereign* full tilt into the enemy lines. The *Belleisle* was the first to catch up and come to the rescue of Collingwood, who by this time had at least taken an awful toll aboard Álava's flagship, the *Santa Ana*. Álava himself was hit and would later die of those wounds. The *Royal Sovereign* was by this time a complete mess herself. More than 140 were dead or wounded in the British admiral's ship, a sad but perhaps remarkably low figure considering the action. The only worthwhile mast left was the foremast, and that was next to useless once the weather got up. *Belleisle*, having fired into the *Santa Ana*, chased off the *San Justo*. The *Belleisle* was now taking on the *Indomptable* and the *Fougueux*, which had done so much damage to the *Royal Sovereign*. Then on *Belleisle*'s starboard side appeared Captain Cosmé Churruca with his 74-gun Spanish ship of the line *San Juan Nepomuceno*. *Belleisle* and her youngish captain, William Hargood, were in deep trouble. The *Mars* was coming up for the rescue. But by the end of the afternoon, two of those captains would be killed, George Duff in the *Mars* and Cosmé Churruca in the *San Juan Nepomuceno*. Now the latter's ship, firing into *Belleisle*'s starboard side, shot away her main topmast. It was 12.45 in the afternoon. *Belleisle* carried on firing. Fifteen minutes on, with *Belleisle* tottering or appearing to, she was now attacked by the *Fougueux*, who also came up on the starboard side. Hargood was not giving up, and nor were his crew. *Belleisle*'s gunners blasted into the French rigging, and by 12.30 *Fougueux*'s mizen mast was hanging over the side. She could now manoeuvre with difficulty. At this stage, Duff's *Mars* arrived to help out *Belleisle*. For sixty minutes the three crippled ships blasted away. The British vessels should have had the legs of the French and Spanish, and so it seemed when the *Fougueux* escaped. *Belleisle* was now on her own, but still not done with the Spanish and French. The 74-gun ship of the line, the French *Achille*, arrived, rapidly firing into *Belleisle*'s stern. Yet another French 74, the *Aigle*, took up on her starboard side, firing into Hargood. As if that were not enough, the *San Justo* and *San Leandro* returned and began a systematic bombardment of *Belleisle*'s bows. Seeing the opportunity to finish off the British ship and what was left of the crew, Gravina's flagship, the *Príncipe de Asturias*, ran astern of the *Belleisle* and fired a broadside into her.

This action had started shortly after midday. It was now creeping towards 2.30 in the afternoon. *Belleisle*'s mainmast had crashed to the deck. Rigging, spars, slashed canvas and ropes and blocks and tackle covered the deck, making passage round them, at least for those who were capable of it, well-nigh impossible. Meanwhile the Spanish and French fired round after round into the British ship and, as if this had become a sport, up sailed the French *Neptune* (there was also a *Neptune* in Nelson's squadron) which now attacked *Belleisle*'s starboard bow, toppled the foremast (the only one left standing) and the bowsprit, which was useless anyway with the masts gone. Hargood, apparently, thought the whole thing rather difficult, but not a disaster. He had a cannonade left and some, but by no means all, starboard guns. He had very little ammunition and many casualties. Later, it appears that he had seemed to think that being surrounded by French and Spanish ships was about the right odds for the Royal Navy and so carried on firing whenever the gunners who were left were able to stand. In the army, there would be hope of the cavalry arriving. It turned up for Hargood, but not for another three-quarters of an hour. By now it was 3.15 in the afternoon. *Belleisle* had been under attack for close on three hours non-stop. The cavalry appeared in the form of the 64-gun *Polyphemus*, followed first by the even bigger

Defiance and then shortly afterwards by the *Swiftsure*. (The French had the *Swift-sure*.) *Polyphemus* ran between *Belleisle* and the deadly fire of the French navy's *Neptune*. *Defiance* took on the *Aigle*. *Swiftsure* pumped broadsides into the *Achille*. At 3.30 in the afternoon, *Belleisle* and her captain and crew were true heroes of that afternoon's battle – if any single ship could be so called. The hull was just about hanging together, with seawater coming in. Her anchors had gone and there was not even a stump of a mast to which rigging could be attached. She looked what she was, a ship that had been blasted to maritime hell. What remains astonishing is that she had suffered only 126 casualties. If one were looking for an anecdote to illustrate Royal Naval phlegm, it would be the entry at 3.30 in *Belleisle*'s log: 'Ceased firing, and turned the hands to clear the wreck.'

But even then, Hargood was not done with the enemy. Just a few hundred yards away, the big Spanish ship, the 80-gun *Argonauta*, had also had enough and was showing signs of surrendering. Hargood had one small boat that looked about seaworthy among the wreckage. He lowered her into the water and sent a small band of his survivors over to the *Argonauta* and claimed her surrender.

One of the French ships which had attacked the *Belleisle* was the *Aigle*. She experienced just as damnable a time as had the *Belleisle*. Much of the damage to the *Aigle* was done by the British ship *Bellerophon*, known throughout the navy as *Billy Ruff'n*. The *Bellerophon*'s reputation was that of the hardest ship in the fleet, whose ratings wrote along their guns 'Victory or Death'. None took cover in the *Bellerophon*. She and the *Aigle* ran so closely together that the yards, the horizontal spars on the masts, locked. Each ship poured round after round into the other. The *Aigle* fought fiercely. *Bellerophon* took the assault in her stride and, on the other side of the vessel, proceeded to fire at three other French ships, while engaging the *Aigle*. The *Bellerophon*'s gunners completely destroyed the French lower decks and, having done that, elevated their guns to such an angle as to destroy the bulwarks and accommodation in the Frenchman. Almost wrecked but still fighting, the *Aigle* managed to break away from *Bellerophon*. Her captain, Pierre Gourrège, ordered his soldiers into the shrouds and on to the upper decks. He was losing the cannon fight with *Bellerophon* and thought the only way out from disaster was with muskets and hand grenades.

For a moment, a very long one, this suited *Bellerophon*, who had easier range to continue the destruction and slaughter. Instead of limping to the safety of clear water, Gourrège saw the *Revenge* attempting to close in on Admiral Gravina. The *Aigle* tried to intervene, and for her pains received from the *Revenge*, a double broadside. The French ship was now assaulted by the *Defiance*. The British ship, firing into the defenceless *Aigle*, went alongside and sent a boarding party. The French had hardly a man standing, and within minutes the British boarding party had hauled down the tricolour and was flying the English ensign. This final humiliation was simply too much for the French who were still able to stand. Every musket and pistol that could be found was primed, aimed and then fired at the rejoicing British sailors on the French quarterdeck. The British ratings and officers escaped back to the *Defiance* quicker than they had arrived. Yet the *Aigle*'s defiance was the flicker of a dying candle. The British ship stood off the French one and fired round after round after round into the sitting duck. When the *Aigle* had gone to action stations, she had had more than 600 men on board. When the *Defiance* ceased firing at her, some 270 were dead or wounded, including Captain Gourrège, who shortly died of his wounds. There was barely a Frenchman left standing. Certainly, the determined and proud heroes were not all sailing under the Union flag. French and Spanish sailors talked of limbs and entrails in the scuppers and of blood running so thickly that no gritting of sand could ever make the gunners' job easier.

Captain Pierre Servaux,[2] a French marine, was the master-at-arms in the *Fougueux*. Servaux, in his memoir, wrote about the superior and heavy guns of the English ships which 'decimated our men in a fearful manner'. Towards the end, *Fougueux* was in such a terrible state that the only thing visible above decks was the French flag. None had thought to strike their colours, yet they were about to be done for by a British ship with a French name, *Téméraire*. With her 100 guns and three decks, she literally overwhelmed the Frenchman. The *Fougueux* was in the way. The swell carried the British ship down on to the Frenchman. She sent a broadside down into the *Fougueux*. By this time the French were arming themselves with swords, but the *Téméraire*, from her great height, picked off the

---

[2] Captain Pierre Servaux (?–1823).

French ratings at will: 'From two to three hundred of them . . . rushed on board . . . our captain fell dead, shot through the heart . . . the few men who were left could make no resistance.'

The *Fougueux* had, for four hours, fought literally to the bitter end. When it came, it did so because they had no ammunition left, hardly a man standing and more than half the ratings killed. Yet, even at this stage, none would strike the French colours. It was left to the British to snatch it as a prize.

The tricolour still stood and flew forlornly in another French ship, the *Achille*. She had taken a terrible beating. She had not entered the battle until two o'clock that afternoon. Alone, she fought with four British ships, the *Polyphemus*, the *Defiance*, the *Swiftsure* and the *Prince*. Within an hour and a half, 400 men in the *Achille* were either dead or wounded. We can only imagine the carnage in one ship and the effects of that number of bodies, either still or bleeding. The captain was dead and so were his senior officers of the quarterdeck. The most dramatic and awful event was still to come in that ship. She was on fire in her forward arms chest. The *Prince* shot her main mast. The sails and ropes were on fire as they fell to the main deck. The fire then spread throughout the vessel. The French could do nothing, and many of her ratings leapt overboard. The *Prince* and the *Pickle* rescued as many as they could. Yet they could not get too close to the *Achille*. She was burning terribly and magazines and cannon were exploding. There was a moment of sheer agony when it was realized that no attempt at rescue could be continued. Then the hull exploded.

There is an unidentified witness, a British officer, who later wrote, 'A column of vivid flame shot up to an enormous height . . . and terminated . . . into an immense globe . . . speckled with many dark spots, which the pieces of timber and bodies of men occasioned while they were suspended in the clouds'.

In the middle of this disaster there came Jeannette. We speak of the British fighting the French and Spanish. Yet there were all nationalities in those ships. That was the way of recruiting. There were, too, some oddities. For example, there was an actor, still dressed as Harlequin, having been pressed from the shoreside of Cadiz. The story of Jeannette, outdoes all the rest. Some of the prisoners, the survivors of the *Achille*, were taken aboard the *Revenge*. Jeannette was not unusual in that ships often had women on board. Her husband was one of the French ratings and her job during the battle had been that of powder monkey, running from the forward magazine with the gunpowder. When the firing stopped, she tried to get on to the main deck to see if her husband had survived, but she was trapped. There were no ladders surviving and the wreckage blocked the alleyways. The ship was in such a blazing state that the decks had cracked open and guns were falling down to the lower decks where she was crouched. She said that she had wished for death. There was one stage, where the molten lead from the fire was dripping on her and all about her, when she saw a chance of getting out through a gaping hole. There she was, clinging to wreckage, when she was picked up, naked, by a boat's crew. She was said to be more dead than alive and terribly burned. And yet there was, for Jeannette, a happier ending and a curious commentary on the etiquette of early nineteenth-century warfare. Four days after being rescued, she discovered her husband was a prisoner of war. During those four days she had been cared for by the officers and made a temporary member of the wardroom. After all, she was a lady. But once her husband was found, she left the wardroom because she knew that he, as a prisoner and a rating, would never be allowed in.

The explosion in the *Achille* was the last terrible event before the storms came. Yet there could hardly have been a vessel that afternoon in October which could have escaped its own spectacular and horrifying fate. For example, one of the British ships that had been driven fast and straight to *Belleisle*'s rescue was the *Mars*. She had not hesitated to take the brunt of the firing. Even more devastatingly, she had dropped away from the *Belleisle* and been set upon by two Spanish ships. One of them was the *San Juan Nepomuceno*, which had sent barrage after barrage into the *Belleisle*. Now she, together with another Spanish ship, the *Monarca*, and two Frenchmen, the *Pluton* and Rear Admiral Magon's flagship, the 74-gun *Algésiras*, sent ball after ball into the *Mars*. The *Tonnant* attempted to come to the rescue of *Mars*. Her captain, George Duff, on the quarterdeck, had his head blown to pieces. Close by him was his son, then a young midshipman. It was he and a sailor who had carried what was left of his father below. *Mars* would easily have become a French prize if the enemy had sent a boarding party, but with other British ships in the area and looking as if they might come to her rescue, *Mars* was left alone with her approximately 100 casualties. The *Tonnant* was also in a difficult state. She had gone to the rescue of *Mars*. Her captain, Charles Tyler,[3] had judged that the best way of doing this was to head straight for Admiral Magon's flagship, the *Algésiras*. She fired on the bigger ship and then attacked the ship on her port side, the *Monarca*, with such venom that the *Monarca* made a show of surrendering to the *Tonnant*. This in itself was a remarkable state of affairs. We should not imagine the dashing *Tonnant* as some white charger of the seas. She was a hard vessel to handle and just as vulnerable as any ship caught in a crossfire, which indeed she was, being between the *Algésiras* and the *Monarca*. Moreover, the odds were beginning to overwhelm the British vessel.

Captain Tyler, in some desperation, with many of her yards shot away, decided to ram Magon's flagship. Tyler was literally at point-blank range and fired furiously into Magon's ship. Tyler had not forgotten the *Mars*. He could see that the *Mars* was on his port side and that beyond her was one of the original French attackers and the ship which had accounted for the life of Duff. The Frenchman was in a poor state but still threatening. Tyler could not know if the *Pluton* might recover and had to assume that she could. After all, the *Monarca*, which had surrendered, had then changed her mind, had re-hoisted her colours and was ready for battle again. Worst of all, back came the *San Juan Nepomuceno*. Tyler, by now slipping in his own blood, with his ship entangled in the *Algésiras*, behaved in an unconventional manner. In theory, and according to the odds of battle, he should have surrendered. Instead, he pumped rounds into the *Algésiras* next door, took a bearing on the *Pluton* across the other side of his sister ship, the *Mars*, elevated his guns on the port side as far as they would go and fired over the top of the *Mars* and into the *Pluton*. He still had on his port side guns that could be fired forward. Not wanting to waste them, Tyler, still clinging to his bloodstained quarterdeck, but only just, ordered the guns to be trained on the *San Juan Nepomuceno*. The casualties alone tell us that this was no gradual shoot-out with pot shots and trick firing at the *Pluton*. This gunnery went on without a break for over one-and-a-half hours.

---

[3] Charles Tyler (1760–1835).

Although this is just a small part of the overall battle, once again, just as with the *Belleisle*, we have to imagine the intensity, the destruction and, above all, the carnage. Cannonballs and shot were coming into Tyler's ship seemingly non-stop. When a man fell at his side, there was no ceremony; he was tossed into the sea. When the mizen mast crashed to the deck, the axes cut away at the rigging so that the firing could go on. Somewhere between one-thirty and two o'clock, Tyler was so badly wounded – he had been standing boldly on his quarterdeck throughout the engagement – that he could no longer keep command. He was taken below, but his ship was not done for.

John Bedford,[+] who was not much more than thirty, was Tyler's first lieutenant. Tyler's orders were quite specific. Whatever the 1805 naval version of 'Keep at them' was, then those were his orders. So he did. At 2.30, the mighty *Algésiras*, with her admiral, Magon, dead, had had enough. Bedford was following in the style of his captain and also the amazing Hargood aboard the *Belleisle*. The *Tonnant* may have been in a state suitable for the knacker's yard, but in such a terrible battle her surviving ship's company did not see it that way. Bedford sent a boarding party over to the *Algésiras* and claimed her. Then the *San Juan Nepomuceno* also surrendered.

Just across the water from where all this was going on, HMS *Bellerophon* had followed *Tonnant* into battle. *Monarca*, having surrendered and then changed her mind, now engaged the British ship. So did the *Aigle* on one side and the *Montañes* on the port side. The *Aigle* was in the better position and dropped shot after shot into the British ship's rigging and main decks. Here, then, was the *Aigle*, firing into the starboard of *Bellerophon*, the two Spaniards, *Monarca* and *Montañes*, firing into the port side and, as if that were not enough, another Spanish ship, the *Bahama*, appeared to fire into *Bellerophon*'s stern with the French *Swift-sure* sending a broadside into her starboard side.

So, what had happened to Nelson's exquisite plan that British ships following his unique insight would burst through the Franco-Spanish lines, surround the enemy and set about destroying them? The answer: the British ships had followed Nelson's plan as best they could and had indeed burst through, but into an odd, defensive double-strength crescent

---

[+] John Bedford (*c.*1773–1814).

and had then themselves been surrounded and given a terrible pasting by an enemy that was supposed to be inexpert and cowardly.

The French and Spanish commanders and crew had proved to be, in battle conditions, far from inexpert and most certainly not cowardly. Magon's flagship had demonstrated a tenacity and bravery which, for all the later jingoism of the British, could only be solemnly admired.

The *Bellerophon*, having swept in via the Nelsonian plan, was undergoing the treatment that had earlier been handed out to the *Belleisle* and then to the *Mars* and the *Tonnant*. She was hemmed inside the crossfire of the *Montañes*, the *Monarca*, the *Bahama* and the *Swift-sure*. Her main and mizen topmasts had gone. Her sails were on fire, her sailing master lay dead, and so did John Cooke, her captain. As *Belleisle* had looked for the cavalry, so now did *Bellerophon*. It came in the form of the 74-gun *Colossus*. The *Montañes* laid astern and the *Bahama* was beginning to feel the heat, but then turned with *Swift-sure* on the *Colossus*. A French boarding party had nearly gained the *Bellerophon*'s decks, which were covered with dead and wounded. There was not even time to drop the bodies over the side. At about a quarter to one, HMS *Revenge* joined in. It does seem remarkable that the *Bellerophon*, a shredded wreck, was still able to fire some of her port guns into the *Monarca*, which had started the whole action. Even more astonishingly, the *Monarca* now surrendered to the smouldering British hulk. The *Bellerophon* had 150 casualties. Lieutenant William Cumby,[5] who had taken command when Captain Cooke was killed, was wearied in spirit but rallied his ship's company and sent a crew on to the *Monarca*. Her captain, Teodoro de Argumosa,[6] was barely standing, so wounded was he among more than 240 of his officers and men, dead, dying or wounded.

These stories of three ships in just one part of the battle give us some idea of the unremitting intensity of that afternoon. Well-thought-through and even famous battle plans were rolled up during those hours and lay in the bloodied scuppers of British, Spanish and French ships. And this was but one part of the battle. It cannot be claimed that captains like Cooke or Hargood had not followed the plans and had therefore got themselves

---

[5] William Cumby (1771–1837).
[6] Don Teodoro de Argumosa (1743–?).

surrounded, with terrible consequences. *Belleisle* and the others were in Collingwood's squadron. What had happened to him? He, after all, was Nelson's deputy. Surely he had made the plan work? No, he had not.

We shall remember that Collingwood wanted to be first into battle. He had charged on (which is why the *Belleisle* had gone to his rescue). Then what about Nelson? He could hardly blame Villeneuve for not cooperating with his supreme tactical plan. What had happened to the *Victory?*

The two squadrons had made for the jumbled crescent. Nelson was to windward so, looking at the Franco-Spanish line, Nelson was on the left. Collingwood's squadron was on his right. Collingwood went ahead, straight into the battle line, in chaos. Nelson's officers had pleaded with him to allow two other ships to go ahead but, as we have seen, he agreed to this with absolutely no intention of letting them do so.

Nelson's ships attacked in this order. *Victory* at the front with *Téméraire* sweeping round on the starboard quarter and *Neptune* on the port quarter. So both *Neptune* and *Téméraire* were slightly behind. In a curved line of six ships, *Neptune* was followed by *Leviathan, Conqueror, Spartiate, Minotaur, Ajax* and then *Agamemnon.* This squadron line formed almost a question mark. In the hook of the question mark was the *Britannia,* which never really got into the battle, and the *Orion,* a valuable 74-gun ship commanded by the thirty-five-year-old Edward Codrington.[7] He had a long life.

Way off to the left-hand side, also out of formation, was Henry Digby's[8] 64-gun *Africa.* Unlike the *Britannia, Africa* was most certainly not avoiding the conflict. She was simply off station and desperately trying to get back, but she was so far away she had actually dropped into the killing zone by herself and was being bombarded by Dumanoir's squadron, led by his flagship, the 80-gun *Formidable.* This was before Dumanoir deserted Villeneuve.

By this time the enemy was bunched into three vague formations. Nelson was charging the centre, the van of the fleet. He was looking for Villeneuve in the *Bucentaure.* She was not recognizable from *Victory's* quarterdeck.

---

[7] Captain Edward Codrington, later Admiral Sir Edward and commander-in-chief, Portsmouth (1770–1851). Father of Henry Codrington, 1808–1877. The son was wounded when under his father's command in 1827 at the Battle of Navarino. Shortly before his death, he was promoted to Admiral of the Fleet.

[8] Captain Henry Digby (1770–1842).

Nelson knew that Villeneuve's flagship was the *Bucentaure*. However, he did not know if Villeneuve was in his flagship. Just as Blackwood had tried to persuade Nelson to transfer to his frigate, there was at this stage no telling if Villeneuve had moved ship. There is some evidence that Collingwood, in the *Royal Sovereign*, thought this to have been the case. Collingwood and his squadron were about three quarters of a mile off Nelson's starboard side. Thus, according to Nelson's plan, he would lead his squadron in, cut through, as they all would, with some left facing the Franco-Spanish line on the port side and the others on the starboard side, engage them in a vicious crossfire, and that would be that. As we saw from Collingwood's squadron, that it would not be. Shortly after noon, *Victory* reached the huddle of Villeneuve's *Bucentaure*, with the huge 136-gun Spaniard, the *Santisima Trinidad*, ahead of the flagship, Captain Jean Lucas's 74-gun *Redoutable* close astern of the *Bucentaure* and five more ships, the *Héros, San Agustín, San Justo, Neptune* and *San Leandro* close by astern. The last three were therefore in a position, as we have seen, to turn on the *Royal Sovereign*, and they did so.

So, in a somewhat shaky condition, the *Victory* led the way into the very mouth of the French and Spanish cannon of the *Héros*, the *Santisima*, the *Redoutable* and, of course, the *Bucentaure*. They were almost touching. *Victory* could not and would not stop. However, she could not get astern of Villeneuve's flagship. Villeneuve was too well protected by the *Redoutable*. Nelson and Hardy had to make a quick decision. *Victory* could either ram Villeneuve's stern, which would have the effect of damaging both vessels and probably also risk locking *Victory* between *Redoutable* and *Bucentaure*, or Hardy could alter course. He did so. He came round *Redoutable*'s stern. At 12.15, as this was happening, French guns, including accurate marksmen lodged in the yards among the rigging and sails, fired away with great effect at *Victory*. These were not static actions. Even the light breeze had its effect. Perhaps more importantly, so did the swell which had increased rather than abated. Nelson was determined to push through and cut the line. In fact, under those conditions, there was nothing else he could do now. If he tried to stand off and form a traditional line, his squadron would have been cut to pieces in the slow and elaborate manoeuvre to do so. It was now every ship for herself. *Neptune* did get in astern of *Bucentaure* and she was followed by the

Leviathan. The cost was enormous. A thousand yards away, Collingwood, for all his enthusiasm, had still failed to pierce the Combined Fleet and was being pasted. Nelson, in the *Victory*, was not faring much better. His paper plan had not accounted for the disposition of the French ships and, most of all, for the gun deck layout of the *Victory*. Whereas, for example, *Redoutable* could fire a virtual broadside into the *Victory* as well as shoot from the masts, *Victory*'s gun arrangement would not let her fire much forward of the beam. The more she turned towards another ship, the less vulnerable that vessel would be to *Victory*'s gunfire.

Hardy understood that the French and Spanish resistance was far greater than the British had imagined it would be. It was as if Nelson had led his squadron, and Collingwood his, into a fleet quite different from the one they had expected. All their readings and observations, together with their quite correct assessments of at least the French abilities during the past year, had been misleading. Here was the distinction between ability and capability. There had, too, been an overestimate of the fleet's ability on Nelson's part.

Most students of Trafalgar and of Nelson have grown up with this image of a seemingly invincible figure ready to defeat any Frenchman if only the idiots of the British Admiralty would step aside. Those same students would certainly refuse to believe that the ranging of forces at Trafalgar could ever have led to an instant, easy victory. Sea battles do not work that way. As we have seen, weather and sea conditions do not take sides. Moreover, once committed to the fight, men expend an astonishing amount of effort in attacking the enemy, not simply for patriotic reasons but usually because this is the surest way of staying alive for longer. Hardy and Nelson now saw, for example, the way that Lucas and his men in the *Redoutable* and Commodore Maistral[9] in the French *Neptune* (as opposed to the British *Neptune* commanded by Fremantle in Nelson's squadron) fought like fury and with enormous professionalism to block what was the essential thrust of the *Victory* and her closest British vessels.

It was the *Redoutable* and the French *Neptune* that began the continuous bombardment of *Victory*, locking the British flagship into a position which Nelson had not anticipated. It was in this exchange that a not-quite-

---

[9] Esprit Tranquille Maistral (1763–1815).

passing cannonball literally sliced John Scott, Nelson's secretary, in two. He had been standing just a few yards from the admiral. At about the same time, the main steering wheel aboard *Victory* was smashed into splinters and the flagship could now only be steered from the tiller-flat down below in the gun room. The next casualties were Nelson's minders, the Royal Marines, on the quarterdeck. They were killed and shovelled over the side. It was not yet lunchtime.

The French *Neptune* and *Redoutable* were also getting in the way of Nelson's target, Villeneuve's flagship. It was exactly what Lucas had intended. The French captain and his sailing master displayed fine seamanship in keeping up the pounding from their guns, as well as manoeuvring under dreadful conditions. *Victory* could not close up on Villeneuve's *Bucentaure*. However, *Bucentaure*'s gunners were able to get a clear shot at *Victory*'s spars and rigging. With the first round, and without *Victory* being able to retaliate, *Bucentaure* brought down Nelson's mizen topmast and damaged almost every other mast and crosstree. *Victory* had never been a ship to handle easily. She was now less so, and still not alongside the French flagship.

It was not until one o'clock that *Victory* could begin to defend herself, such was her unenviable tactical position. She had been under constant fire for over half an hour. More than fifty British sailors aboard Nelson's ship had been either killed or wounded. It was only now that Nelson was close enough to take revenge on Villeneuve. The *Bucentaure* now came under the maritime cosh. It was said that Villeneuve may have regained some prestige through valour at this point, but he gained nothing from his apparent inability to assess the tactical situation and do something about it. Only the *Redoutable* and the *Neptune* remained at his elbow. Some French and Spanish captains were later criticized for not coming to his aid. Yet they were having all their work cut out trying to maintain their own ships and positions in the confusion of the battle. *Victory* was in a near, but not quite, hopeless, state. There was not an area of her rigging that had not been damaged or made useless. Below, her casualties were increasing by every round that was blasted into her side, especially by the *Redoutable*.

Captain Eliab Harvey's *Téméraire* now brought relief to *Victory* by drawing fire from the French *Neptune* and the *Redoutable* on their starboard side, although this did not help *Victory*'s port side. Hardy,

Nelson's captain, now, at ten past one, executed what in terms of ship handling and battle tactics management was an exquisite move. However, his skill may have been the death of Nelson.

Hardy backed shredded top sails and, using the Atlantic swell, brought *Victory* right alongside *Redoutable*'s port side. The action locked the two ships together.

As they did so, *Victory*'s gunners on her starboard side fired at literally point-blank range into the *Redoutable*. *Redoutable* was a lesser-gunned ship anyway. She was now in a terrible position of disadvantage. *Victory*, meanwhile, continued to fire into her hull and also, from the other side, at the nearest French ships, including Villeneuve's already battered *Bucentaure*. Lucas was not about to give up, and he still had valuable weapons. In the rigging, he had men with what we would now call hand grenades. These were being tossed on to *Victory*'s main deck, causing a great deal more than havoc. Also in the topmasts of *Redoutable* were her surviving sharpshooters.

One of them saw Nelson on the quarterdeck. At 1.25, it is said, precisely, on 21 October 1805, the musketeer fired at Nelson. Nelson was standing where Scott had died. The musketeer's round went through Nelson's left shoulder, through the gold epaulette, through his lung and stuck in his spine. As three men carried their dying admiral to the orlop deck below, the surgeon's cockpit, forty of his marines also fell about *Victory*'s decks. Her main deck guns were all but silent, having been put out of action under fire from *Redoutable*. For another fifteen minutes, until about 1.40 that afternoon, *Redoutable*, under the most deadly fire from *Victory*'s lower deck guns and especially from *Téméraire*, refused to capitulate. She had more dead and wounded than active. Lucas himself was so wounded that he was barely conscious and his ship had just crashed into *Téméraire*. He still tried to hold out. Then, seeing the hopelessness of his position and the wretched carnage all about him, Lucas struck his colours and surrendered, after all this fighting, to two young British midshipmen and a platoon of Royal Marines.

Hardy, looking about him, with his admiral below, had no time to drop down to the orlop deck to see the state of Nelson. The pandemonium of sea battle would not cease. The French *Neptune* thought nothing of *Téméraire*'s brave and brilliant actions that had saved *Victory* from even worse destruction. By now *Téméraire* had two French prizes strapped to her, the *Redoutable* and the *Fougueux*. *Neptune* fired round after round into the British ship and, of course, hit her own French vessels that were lashed alongside *Téméraire*. When one salvo from *Neptune* brought down *Redoutable*'s main mast, it landed not on deck but on *Téméraire*, reducing the mizen stump and poop deck to matchwood and doing for many sailors caught beneath the falling wreckage. Had it not been for the *Leviathan* closing in on the French *Neptune*, it is quite possible that the *Téméraire* would have been finished off, prizes or no prizes. *Neptune*, in no great state herself, prudently cleared the area as *Leviathan* approached.

With such wounding and killing all about, it is hardly surprising that a number of gory tales and descriptions – mostly true – should have emerged from that dreadful event to stir the emotions. Decks were literally running with blood, as if some butcher had thrown buckets of abattoir swill across the main and gun decks. Men did not simply keel over cleanly with a polite moan.

William Robinson, the purser's steward in the *Revenge*, was by some accounts an ugly fellow, so much so that the officers and warrant officers nicknamed him Jack Nasty-face. It was under that nom de plume that he wrote his often scathing recollections of serving in the Nelsonian navy.

As we were closely engaged throughout the battle, and the shots were playing their pranks pretty freely, grape as well as canister, with single and double headed thunderers all joining in the frolic; what was termed a *slaughtering one*, came in at one of the lower deck ports, which killed and wounded nearly all at the gun, and amongst them, a very merry little fellow, who was the very life of the ship's company, for he was ever the mirth of his mess, and on whatever duty he might be ordered, his spirits made light the labour. He was the ship's cobbler, and withall a very good dancer; so that when any of his messmates would *sarve* us out a tune, he was sure to trip it on light fantastic toe, and find a step to it. He happened to be stationed at the gun where this messenger of death and destruction entered, and the poor fellow was so completely stunned by the head of another man being knocked against his, that no one doubted but that he was dead. As it is customary to throw overboard those, who, in an engagement are killed outright, the poor cobbler, amongst the rest, was taken to the port-hole to be committed to the deep, without any other ceremony than shoving him through the port; but, just as they were about to let him slip from their hands into the water, the blood began to circulate, and he commenced kicking. Upon this sign of returning life, his shipmates soon hauled the poor snob in again, and, though wonderful to relate, he recovered so speedily, that he actually fought the battle out; and, when, he was afterwards joked about it, he would say, 'it was well that I learned to dance: for if I had not shown you some of my steps, when you were about to throw me overboard, I should not be here now . . .

We had a midshipman on board our ship of a wickedly mischievous disposition, whose sole delight was to insult the feelings of the seamen, and furnish pretexts to get them punished. His conduct made every man's life miserable that happened to be under his orders. He was a youth not more than twelve or thirteen years of age; but I have often seen him get on the carriage of a gun, call a man to him and kick him about the thighs and body, and with his fist would beat him about the head; and these, although prime seamen, at the same time dared not murmur. It was ordained however, by Providence, that his reign of terror and severity should not last; for during the engagement, he was killed on the quarter-deck by a grape-shot, his body greatly mutilated, his entrails being driven and scattered against the larboard side; nor were there any lamentations for his fate! No! for when it was known that he was killed, the general exclamation was, '*Thank God, we are rid of the young tyrant!*'

Robinson's view was that too many of the officers were overly harsh and without an ounce of charity for their men. This does not always match other writings, but certainly in the case of Robinson's captain, Sir Charles Paget[10] there was a man who few wished to serve under.

There are, too, amazing stories of how men with terrible wounds either carried on as usual as best they could or showed a virtual

---

[10] Sir Charles Paget (1778–1839) later became an MP.

indifference to pain. Iron men in wooden ships, perhaps born of hardships. This explanation, however it is offered, is not enough for our soft twenty-first-century sensitivities. For example, the captain of the *Leviathan*, Henry Bayntun, wrote about that part of the action against the Spanish four-decker, the *Santisima Trinidad*, and the *San Agustín*, describing how a shot, probably from *San Agustín*, 'took off the arm of Thomas Main'. A couple of so far unscathed ratings offered to take him down to the surgeon's cockpit. Instead, Main gripped the rail with his good hand (the other arm lying in the scuppers) and made his way down to the surgeon, standing respectfully in the queue of wounded, waiting his turn. The surgeon had to cut off what was left of the arm, right to the shoulder. Bayntun insists that through this whole operation, with no anaesthetics, Thomas Main[11] distracted himself with a steady clear, voice singing the whole of 'Rule Britannia'.

Above and beyond the surgeon's cockpit, the battle carried on until after four o'clock. However, about an hour after Nelson was hit, the flagship he had steered so resolutely and confidently against an enemy he had underrated was knocked out of the battle. Her mizen topmast was shot over the side. The rest of her masts, all their yards, her bowsprit and booms, were mangled. Yet *Victory* had a big, strong oak hull. This might in some way account for the fact that in spite of the ceaseless pounding there were only 107 wounded aboard *Victory* and 57 dead. At 2.30, *Victory* drifted. She was no longer in the war against Napoleon. Nelson was able to hang on, as if unable to let go until Hardy brought the news his admiral craved.

William Beatty,[12] the ship's surgeon, had instructions to treat others that might be saved. Nelson said that he had felt the musket ball break his back. From the waist down, his body was numb, the spinal nerve crushed. The lung pierced, the internal bleeding flowed at its will.

Beatty left a record that said Nelson had been shot at 1.15. Hardy could not get below, so fierce was the battle, for more than an hour after that. He stayed but ten minutes. At 3.25, Hardy reappeared and saw Nelson for

---

[11] Main died in Gibraltar, not, it is said, of his wound but of a fever caught while he was in hospital.

[12] William Beatty (1773–1842).

the last time alive. By about ten to four, the admiral could no longer speak. It was his steward named, perhaps ironically, Chevalier, who called Beatty at 3.53, fearful that his master was now close to dying. According to Beatty's record, Nelson died at three minutes after four o'clock. That record is probably poorly written and should have read 4.30.

Hardy had gone below at 3.30. He had served with Nelson at the battles of the Nile and Copenhagen. He, perhaps, along with Blackwood, was one of the two post captains Nelson most trusted and admired. This was to be their last meeting. Hardy gave Nelson the news that fifteen of the Combined Fleet had already struck their colours. Others would follow. By now, Nelson was fading and his voice no more than a whisper. He had a wish and an order. The wish was that he had never left the quarterdeck. The order was a reminder to Hardy that when the battle was over the British fleet should anchor. Even at the moment of death, or perhaps because it was so close, everything was clear. Nelson knew the storm was coming. He knew ships could not safely ride out on that lee shore, other than at anchor. Perhaps he knew also – or feared – that Collingwood would ignore his instruction. Hardy returned to the quarterdeck and the battle.

What was to be done with the information that the commander-in-chief was dead? There seems to be some confusion as to exactly when Collingwood was told. In his official report, Collingwood said he had at first been told that Nelson was seriously wounded, but that he had been able to tell from the face of the young officer that the admiral was either close to death or had died. How did that information get to Collingwood? By an officer in a small boat. Also, another boat arrived alongside *Victory*. Here again was Blackwood, wanting to know the state of Nelson. Hardy and Blackwood, as soon as it was safe to do so, cast off from the *Victory* in a small boat to find the *Royal Sovereign* and tell Collingwood that he should assume the role of commander-in-chief.

Hardy emphasized Nelson's last order to anchor – it was a waste of the admiral's last breath. From all the accounts, it does seem that Collingwood first knew that Nelson was dead when a ship's punt set off from the *Victory* to the *Royal Sovereign* with young Lieutenant Hills aboard. This would have been almost immediately after Hardy's second and final visit, when he was in no doubt of Nelson's impending death.

Much has been made of Cuthbert Collingwood's decision not to anchor as Nelson had ordered him to. Nelson had anticipated the chaos following the battle and the need to consolidate forces and assess damage. He knew also that the approaching storm meant that many damaged ships could not ride out that storm because their rigs had been carried away and their reduced companies were exhausted. Heaving-to, the sailing action of keeping a ship safe while not sailing in any direction was a good practice in such vessels. But it demanded great skills and resources, especially with little sea room in which to manoeuvre. So was Collingwood ignoring good seamanship all for the opportunity of showing that it was he, and not Nelson, who was in command? Or was the urge to take prizes overwhelming?

Collingwood was above all, a fine sailor. He would have made his own judgement based on three factors. Firstly the wind and sea state, which may have easily made it difficult to keep an anchored vessel safe, especially in a huge swell. Second, the depth of water where the ships were gathered meant anchoring would be difficult and extra long anchor cables would have been needed – which most of the ships did not have. There were about thirteen fathoms of water off Trafalgar – nearly eighty feet. A ship would need anchor cables in those conditions of five times that length. Third, and above all, many of the ships were by then in no state to anchor. Their capstains were either damaged, dislodged or destroyed and many ships no longer had anchors. Both *Victory*'s anchors, for example, had long been lost overboard. It was not until much later that Collingwood, who according to his own log had prepared the signal to anchor, had his fleet secure in the shallows off Trafalgar.

So as a footnote to this story, we should give Collingwood far more credit than is often handed to him. After all, the surviving French and Spanish sailors recorded their true admiration for Collingwood and his officers as they watched them command and handle their ships in the atrocious weather that followed the battle.

Villeneuve had not a hair of his head harmed. There was not another deck officer either alive or capable of being on deck. The British *Neptune* and the *Leviathan*, followed by the *Conqueror*, fired round after round after round into Villeneuve's ship, reducing it to a useless hulk. Yet, but for the action of a single French junior admiral, all might have been different. Villeneuve's second-in-command, Rear Admiral Pierre

Dumanoir Le Pelley, had deserted. He had flown his flag in the 80-gun *Formidable*, with ten ships under his command. Shortly after the action had started, Dumanoir quit the battle line and headed north.

At ten minutes before two, Villeneuve signalled the fleet. Dumanoir had covered himself by signalling that his squadron had no enemy ships about it. Instead of directly signalling his deputy that he should then find some enemy ships to have about him, Villeneuve weakly made a general signal.

> L'armée navale Française, combattant au vent ou sous le vent, ordre aux vasseaux qui, par leur position actuelle, ne combattent pas, d'en prendre une quelconque, qui les reporte le plus promptement possible au feu.

A ready translation would be that all ships which were not in the action should get into it! It was a version of Nelson's 'Engage The Enemy More Closely'. Given the wind conditions that were, at best, light airs, it was far from easy for any of his ships to manoeuvre. This would have meant Dumanoir's squadron coming about in another direction so that the wind was blowing onto the sails from the starboard side, the starboard tack. It may have been that to haul round, Dumanoir's squadron would have had to lower boats, put men to the oars and tow the great vessels onto the other tack. Villeneuve was still not satisfied and so ordered his deputy to join the battle. It is true that some vessels in Dumanoir's squadron joined the engagement. The *Formidable* appeared to keep well clear. Dumanoir's squadron had fired some shots, most of them ineffectual except for a horrid coincidence. One cannonball was fired at the *Conqueror*. A junior lieutenant was apparently congratulating a senior lieutenant on his pending promotion to commander. The cannonball took off the head of the junior, carried on and killed the senior lieutenant. This, from the log of the *Conqueror*. Still Dumanoir pressed on. Villeneuve sent a direct signal (that is, he named Dumanoir's flagship) to tell him to return to the battle. Dumanoir did not, although two of his ten-ship squadron, the *Intrépide* and *San Agustin*, did break away.

It is a reflection on Villeneuve's ability as commander and his history as a naval officer that any flag officer under him should have abandoned his commander and his fellow sailors, in such a situation. Considering the size and state of Dumanoir's squadron there can be no doubt that if he had stayed in the vanguard of Villeneuve's battle line as he was supposed to have done he and his squadron would, at the very least, have had a major effect on the outcome.

There is a certain ambiguity in some of the accounts of Dumanoir's action. For example, according to British ships, shortly after three o'clock the *Minotaur* and the *Spartiate* did engage four Frenchmen, including Dumanoir's *Formidable*. There was also an account that Dumanoir fired on a British ship that was strapped to two of her Combined Fleet prizes. It is difficult to see how, in the few months immediately after the conflict, anything other than negative could have been said about Dumanoir. He later denied that he had fired at the French and Spanish prizes and had been aiming at *Téméraire*. However, no one really believed him. The French naval ministry set up a series of inquiries into his action (or inaction). A measure of the seriousness of his leaving the battle was that those inquiries continued for five years. By that time all interest had been lost and the French could see no value in making any more of his refusal to fight. After all, the more they inquired, the more they remembered the outcome of the battle. So Dumanoir was exonerated and given a command, the first since Trafalgar. The impression at the naval ministry persisted that he might well – with a little more ingenuity and perhaps determination – have changed the course of the battle.

As it was, at 4.15 Villeneuve surrendered. At 4.30, Nelson died. The Battle of Trafalgar was done.

The clearing up of the ships included the disposal of the dead and wounded. Collingwood gave a further report to be carried by the ubiquitous Captain Blackwood, who delivered it late at night to the Admiralty on 26 November. In it Collingwood observed that while his men had been clearing captured ships of prisoners they had come across so many wounded sailors that, as Collingwood put it,

to alleviate human misery as much as was in my power, I sent to the Marquis de Solana, Governor General of Andalusia, to offer him the wounded to the care of their Country, on receipts being given;- a proposal which was received with the greatest thankfulness, not

only by the Governor, but the whole Country resounds with
expressions of gratitude ... I have ordered most of the Spanish
prisoners to be released; the Officers on parole; the men for receipts
given, and a condition that they do not serve in war, by sea or land,
until exchanged

Until this period, prisoners taken in warfare were quite often sent back.
Ransoms were paid, but guarantees were sought that officers particularly
would take no further part in the confrontations. There were, as many as
100,000 French prisoners of war in Britain. Famously, Dartmoor Prison
was built partly for them and by them. In France, there were 16,000
British prisoners.

Of the thirty-three ships in the Franco-Spanish fleet, sixteen were
destroyed and nine had got into Cadiz, although six of those were thought
to be wrecked. There were four in Gibraltar, and the four surviving ships
in Jean Dumanoir's squadron escaped to the south. On 4 November they
surrendered to a British squadron. Of the six Combined Fleet flag officers,
Villeneuve and Cisneros surrendered, Dumanoir did so later, while
Gravina got away in Cadiz but was so badly wounded that he died, Álava
was also wounded and died later and Magon was killed at the battle.

In the British fleet, according to *The London Gazette* of 27 November
and 3 December, twenty-one officers, including Nelson, were killed. So
were, sixteen petty officers, 299 seamen and 113 marines – a total of 469
dead. Forty-three officers, fifty-nine petty officers, 900 seamen and 212
marines were wounded. In the Spanish ships during and after the battle,
1,025 died and 1,383 were wounded of a total of 11,817. It might be
remembered that many of the Spaniards were not sailors but soldiers.
For example, in Gravina's flagship, only 609 of those 1,163 aboard were
sailors. The French casualty list was horrendous: 3,370 killed or drowned
and 1,160 wounded.

The British navy would know other battles, but none in its entire
history would ever be remembered as this one would be. Nelson's portrait
became that of the only instantly recognizable military hero in British
history. He had challenged the gods.

CHAPTER TWENTY-NINE

Epilogue

THE NEWS OF THE BATTLE AND – MOST IMPORTANTLY – NELSON'S death arrived in Falmouth late on the night of 5 November 1805. It had been brought under full canvas in the schooner *Pickle* by Lieutenant John Lapenotière.[1] A coach was found and Lapenotière carried the news to London. The coach, after more than a dozen change of horses, arrived in Whitehall after midnight. The First Sea Lord, Lord Barham, was roused at one in the morning. Pitt was woken at three.

We should understand that the news was not only of Nelson's death but of the victory over the French. That the vice admiral had perished would eventually cast some gloom across the nation. The sea victory was everything. Britain was at war. This was no huge adventure story with a theatrical dying moment of a hero. Two hundred years on, we may ponder whether Nelson had said 'Kiss me, Hardy' or 'Kismet, Hardy' or, indeed, nothing at all. At three in the morning of 6 November 1805, Pitt was not sleepless, worrying about Nelson. He was anxious and depressed about the still-echoing news from Ulm where, almost three weeks earlier, Britain's ally, Austria, had surrendered three divisions to Napoleon's army. For Pitt, Trafalgar was proof that Britain, by her example, could save Europe from Napoleon.

Pitt, of course, saw the broader picture, and victory at Trafalgar was a large part of it. Nelson's death was terribly sad, but a minor detail.

---

[1] John Richards Lapenotière (1770–1834).

Moreover, if the first assessments were correct and the Franco-Spanish naval alliance all but destroyed, there was no longer a need for Nelson.

He was a heroic loss, but not a strategic one. In the country as a whole, of course, such a cynical view was not widely held. George III is supposed to have said, 'We have lost more than we have gained' and remained silent for close on five minutes. The king, who was used to losing great men and who, anyway, as a monarch never mourned anyone other than a member of royalty, immediately diverted his regrets by expressing his praise for Cuthbert Collingwood. That admiral, he thought, was an officer of consummate valour. Indeed, Collingwood's dispatch was impressive in the way it heaped praise on the officers and ratings under his command while saying nothing of its author's own efforts. Pitt, disturbed in his sleep so early in the morning, got up and went to his study. This may seem an obvious thing to have done, but the prime minister, who was very ill and had but three months to live, might have been expected to follow his normal pattern when being given dramatic news in the middle of the night: turn over, go back to sleep to wait for the agitations that daylight would bring. Yet on such an occasion no prime minister would have slept. The two great newspapers, the *Morning Post* and *The Times*, were inspired by the occasion. The *Morning Post* saw Nelson's victory (it was that, rather than Britain's) as the marker buoy for his immortality. *The Times* thought it the greatest victory in British naval history but one so dearly purchased:

> The official account of the late Naval Action, which terminated in the most decisive victory that has ever been atchieved [sic] by British skill and gallantry, will be found in our Paper of this day. That the triumph, great and glorious as it is, has been dearly bought, and that such was the general opinion, was powerfully evinced in the deep and universal affliction with which the news of Lord NELSON'S death was received. The victory created none of those enthusiastic emotions in the public mind, which the success of our naval arms have in every former instance produced. There was not a man who did not think that the life of the hero of the Nile was too great a price for the capture and destruction of twenty sail of French and Spanish men of war. No ebullitions of popular

transport, no demonstrations of public joy, marked this great and important event. The honest and manly feeling of the people appeared as it should have done: they felt an inward satisfaction at the triumph of their favourite arms; they mourned with all the sincerity and poignancy of domestic great, their HERO slain

George III, on 7 November, issued a royal proclamation. Almighty God was thanked for His 'signal interposition of his good Providence'. The British are not alone in always thanking God for victory and quickly following it, as did the Proclamation, by giving full credit to the man on the ground, or, in this case, on the sea. Vice Admiral Lord Viscount Nelson had achieved a truly great victory, and therefore the king commanded that a 'general thanksgiving to Almighty God for his (sic) mercies to be observed throughout those parts of our United Kingdom called England and Ireland, on Thursday the fifth day of December next'.

The thanksgiving that December was celebrated in all churches with a common prayer of thanksgiving. Two days before the services, the Committee of the Patriotic Fund met at Lloyd's coffee house in London. Shortly before the battle, Nelson had fully anticipated the consequences in terms of mortalities and wounded. He had written requesting that the wounded, widowed and the orphaned should be provided for by the Fund.

The Committee observed Nelson's wishes. They resolved that the collections contributed on the day of thanksgiving, 5 December, would be used entirely for the relief of wounded sailors, soldiers, marines and other volunteers and for the families of those killed at Trafalgar. Every sailor or marine disabled after the battle would receive £40. A severely wounded though not necessarily disabled rating or marine would be given £20 and even the slightly wounded would receive £10 each.

The night before the thanksgiving services, appropriately, HMS *Victory* arrived off Portsmouth. The ship, surely only just seaworthy, had brought home the body of Nelson. This was wrapped in cotton and bandaged from head to foot in the style of Egyptian embalming. His remains had then been lowered into a leaden coffin which was then filled with brandy, camphor and myrrh. The lead coffin was then placed inside a wooden one. It would remain there in Nelson's Great Cabin until 21 December. The *Victory* left Portsmouth, and on 22 December the coffin was transferred in what had been his flagship to a Royal Commission yacht, the *Chatham*. Mourning guns, with 'subdued' charges, fired as the *Chatham* made its way upriver on the flooding tide. She made fast off Greenwich, and Nelson's body was removed to the Greenwich Hospital. Quietly, an autopsy took place. It was not until the New Year, 5 January, that the body, now in a new coffin made from the main mast of *L'Orient*, was taken to the Painted Hall at Greenwich to lie in state for two days. January is not a good month for parade marshals to plan a state funeral. Almost on cue, south-westerly gales, the likes of which had immediately followed the battle, swept the south-east of England.

On Wednesday 8 January, the admiral's barge, with its solemn and single cargo, was rowed in treacherous waters from Greenwich to Whitehall Stairs. In the early hours of 9 January, the corps of drummers beat to arms. Every regiment was represented in London that day. By eight o'clock it was hardly light, and coaches were arriving at the Admiralty as the procession assembled. Even the Prince of Wales and his brothers were there. (It was not then customary for royalty to attend a non-royal funeral.) At noon, the biggest mourning procession the capital had seen moved off, headed by General Sir David Dundas[2] and Lieutenant General Harry Burrard.[3] The army led the way with light dragoons, Highland regiments, grenadiers, cavalry and the horse artillery. The navy had gathered around their hero and were led by Admiral of the Fleet, Sir Peter Parker,[4] then well into his eighties. The coffin was on an open hearse drawn by six horses. The hearse was a mock ship with the name *Victory* inscribed. The late admiral's heraldry decorated the sides and, at the stern, a Union flag drooped at half-mast. Above the Union flag in large black letters was the word 'Trafalgar'. There could not have been, apart from the king, more than four of the grandest people and high-office holders of England missing from the

---

[1] John Richards Lapenotière (1770–1834).
[2] General Sir David Dundas (1758–1820).
[3] Lieutenant General Harry Burrard (1789–1809).
[4] Sir Peter Parker, Admiral of the Fleet (1721–1811).

funeral procession as it moved towards Nelson's final resting place, St Paul's Cathedral.

Emma Hamilton was not there. No women were. William Pitt was in Bath, desperately ill, and would die on 23 January. Nelson's old patron, the Earl St Vincent, that 'great sea officer', chose not to attend. Finally, there was one missing to whom the nation owed a debt equal to that it owed Nelson. Billy Cornwallis, who had demonstrated his mastery of naval tactics and remained at his post at sea, blockading the entire French fleet in Brest and had thus done more to foil any invasion plans of Napoleon, was not invited. It is said that all flag officers were asked to attend. Not Cornwallis. Why he should have been ignored and thought unimportant is a puzzle. Instead, still on guard as commander-in-chief Channel, Cornwallis was standing off the East Devon coast in Torbay, sheltering from that same sou'westerly that had blown through London. John Jervis, Admiral Earl St Vincent, probably thought it best he stayed there. He, after all, fancied holding a sea command once again, and the Channel was the most prestigious. After Pitt's death that month, Cornwallis was called ashore and St Vincent had his flagship for himself. The rest of the story is one of the dispersal of various characters and an attention which swung instead to Napoleon's march through Europe for the next ten years.

Collingwood became Baron Collingwood of Caldburne and Hethpoole. He did nothing after Trafalgar other than remain for four years as commander-in-chief Mediterranean, an appointment given him after Nelson's death. A year later, in 1810, he died of stomach cancer. William Beatty, the ship's surgeon in *Victory*, made something of a name for himself when he published in 1807 the *Authentic Narrative of the Death of Lord Nelson*. He spent much of the rest of his life until his death in 1842 as the physician at Greenwich Hospital. As for Robert Calder, who had missed the Battle of Trafalgar and returned to England and his court martial in his much-needed flagship, he was severely reprimanded, became an admiral and died in 1818. Hardy became a baronet and a rear admiral and, in 1830, First Sea Lord. The ever loyal Henry Blackwood also became a baronet and, later, commander-in-chief in the West Indies and, more importantly, at the Nore. As for Emma Hamilton, she simply went through the money that Nelson had arranged for her. Merton was sold off, as was the small but smart house in Clarges Street. She lodged with other people or in their houses, and by the age of forty-six she was something of a hag. In 1813, she was arrested for not paying her bills and the following year, drinking more and growing stouter, she fled with Horatia to Calais. On 15 January 1815, she died.

Finally, what of Nelson? Supposing he had not died at Trafalgar? There would have been nothing left for him to do other than to be First Lord and build a fleet in his image. Might he have gone into politics? He was certainly more popular among the people than Wellington would ever become – and Wellington was to become prime minister one day.

We should not imagine that Nelson was a simple sailor with no grasp of the greater picture. In this sense, the duel with Napoleon had not been military, but strategic. Both saw the larger tapestry of power politics supported by military capability. Wellington met Nelson but once. It was in an ante-room in the War Office of Robert Castlereagh, shortly before Nelson sailed for that last time. Wellington judged Nelson to be shrewd with a well-informed and intelligent understanding of the wider political and strategic world. So maybe, after all, Nelson did have the qualifications to become a foreign minister, but a prime minister? His attention to detail may have helped, but not his temperament.

Perhaps the answer lies in his title, Duke of Brontë, named after a district of Sicily. Nelson's long-term happiness with Emma would probably have been guaranteed not in England but in Brontë. There, the couple would have remained hero and heroine. Even today, Nelson is still remembered in that place. Would he have been a lasting hero had he survived Trafalgar?

Nelson was a hero because he challenged the gods. Within that challenge lies hubris, from which comes nemesis. He made his challenge within his own rules as if there had been none in authority over him other than his Creator. His judgement was often found wanting. Critics might say no more so than in his infatuation with Emma Hamilton. Does this suggest an admiral who would have become a great First Lord of the Admiralty? Perhaps not. Is it not more likely that he would have found enormous difficulty and frustration without the constant possibility of naval engagement? Being a hero might have been enough for him. It is very possible that his memory would not have been immortal. Instead, he could have gone from England, forgotten at his estate on Sicily at Brontë.

Apart from anything else, Nelson was probably going blind, even by Trafalgar. The right eye had gone, but the left eye had such impaired vision that surgery would have been the only possibility of saving it. Nelson, blind and all but alone in Sicily, is not the image of a hero.

Glossary

Able Seaman	Senior of the three lowest ratings.
Aft	Back section of ship. So, to lay aft would be to go to the back.
Amidships	The middle of the vessel. A piece of kit in the middle part of the ship would be lying amidships. Also, when the steering wheel was centred – that is, being turned neither to starboard nor to port – it was called wheel amidships. An order to centre the wheel, would be 'Wheel amidships.'
Belaying pins	Wooden carrot-shaped pins used to jam or hold ropes, particularly running rigging.
Boatswain	Or bosun, the senior non-commissioned officer.
Bosun	See boatswain.
Bosun's mate	A 'deputy' bosun.
Bumkin	Short wooden boom sticking out from either bow in order to pull down a foresail so that the ship can better go to windward. Also, a similar boom pointing from the stern to better set the mizen sail.
Bunting tosser	Yeoman signaller who sent signal flags up the mast.
Cat-beam	The broadest beam in the ship, often made from two tied, pegged or bolted together.
Course	The direction going towards. A ship taking a westerly course would be heading in a westerly direction.

Courses (sails)	The sails hanging from the lower yards (spars) of a ship usually the mainsail (mains'l), foresail (fores'l) mizen. These names indicated which mast they're on. When a sailing ship was sailing with only these three sails set, she was said to be under her courses.
Draft	The depth of hull beneath the waterline, so restricting sailing in shallow waters.
Fore and aft sails	Usually triangular or distorted square and set on a stem to stern line as in a modern yacht but in Nelson's time, and even today in Tall Ships, all those sails other than the 'galleon looking' square sails (see square sails, below). The fore and aft sails include jibs, staysails, tri-sails, boom mainsails, boom foresails, gaff topsails and the spanker, which is the aftermost sail in a ship and still seen as a steadying sail at the stern of fishing vessels.
Forecastle	Or fo'c'sle. Forward part of ship.
Foremast	Front mast.
Freeboard	The distance between the sea or river and the deck line.
Gallants	Flags flown on the mizen (the after) mast.
Halyard	Ropes used to haul up and lower spars and sails.
Jaunty	Regulating petty officer, the ship's policeman, probably the sailor's version of 'gendarme'.
Landsman	Or Landman. A recruited or pressed rating who had never been to sea.
Lay	Go, as in lay aft – go to the stern of the vessel or, as in laying or lying indicating the position of an object in the ship.
Main course	The lowest square sail on the mainmast (see below)
Mainmast	Middle and tallest mast in three-masted ship and tallest in two-masted vessel.
Midshipman	A cadet officer.
Mizen	The shortest and furthest back mast in any vessel with two or more masts.
Ordinary Seaman	Middle of the three lowest ratings.

Orlop deck	The lowest deck in a ship, below the water line and often simply planks laid over beams and used for storage. From over lop. In battle, the deck was cleared for the surgeon's table. Nelson died on the *Victory*'s orlop deck. From over lop.
Pompey	Later, naval slang for Portsmouth.
Poop	The furthest aft and highest part of a ship.
Pooped	When a wave comes over the stern and over the poop deck.
Port	Left side of ship facing forward. Used to be larboard the abbreviation of Italian term for left side, *quella borda* ('that side').
Quarterdeck	The part of the main or upper deck directly abaft (behind) the mainmast. The most respected deck in the ship. All sailors would salute the quarter deck when coming on to it. Officers commanded the ship from the quarterdeck.
Rating	Non-commissioned and junior sailor.
Royal	Sometimes known as the topgallant royal. A very light sail set above the topgallant. Used in very light airs when all sail is needed.
Running rigging	As opposed to standing rigging, ropes or wires that are hauled or slacked and therefore run through blocks.
Sail burton	The rope-and-blocks arrangement (block-and-tackle) for sending up sails from the main deck to be bent on to yards, etc.
Sea officer	A naval officer, usually senior, with a regular seagoing appointment and commission.
Sheets	Ropes on the corners of sails used to tension or slack them away.
Shrouds	Supporting ropes or wires of masts running down to the side decks.
Sin bosun	Naval slang for chaplain.
Square sails	Square-shaped sails usually set across the ship – courses, topsails, topgallants, royals, skysails.

Standing rigging	Ropes or wires that are fixed – for example, a shroud
Starboard	Right side of ship facing forward. Abbreviation of Italian term for right side, *questa borda*, 'this side'.
Stays	Wires or ropes to support masts, particularly the forestay running from the top of the mast to the bow and bowsprit.
Stern	Back of ship.
Topgallants	The third row of sails, that is above the topsails.
Topsails	Not the uppermost sails, but the second row of sails above deck level, so above the courses (see above).
Trucks	Circular mini-platforms through which ropes are led through holes to prevent them from tangling.
Waisters	Usually older sailors with neither the skills nor the physical capability of going aloft who remained in the ship's waist, the main deck, where they were used to haul on ropes, swab decks, etc.
Warrant Officer	A junior officer without a commission holding a warrant – for example a gunnery officer, chaplain or surgeon.

French, Spanish and British Ships at Trafalgar

The Combined Fleet of French and Spanish ships at the Battle of Trafalgar in order of sailing, with their nationality, number of guns and captain's names.

1. *Neptuno* (Spanish, 80-gun, Commodore Cayetano Valdés)
2. *Scipion* (French, 74-gun, Captain Charles Bérenger)
3. *Intrépide* (French, 74-gun, Captain Louis-Antoine-Cyprien Infernet)
4. *Formidable* (French, 80-gun, Rear Admiral Pierre-Etienne-René-Marie Dumanoir Le Pelley, Captain Jean-Marie Letellier)
5. *Duguay-Trouin* (French, 74-gun, Captain Claude Touffet)
6. *Mont-Blanc* (French, 74-gun, Commodore Guillaume-Jean-Noël Lavillegris)
7. *Rayo* (Spanish, 100-gun, Commodore Enrique MacDonnell)
8. *San Francisco de Asís* (Spanish, 74-gun, Captain Luis de Flores)
9. *Héros* (French, 74-gun, Captain Jean-Baptiste-Joseph-René Poulain)
10. *San Agustín* (Spanish, 74-gun, Captain Felipe Jado Cajigal)
11. *Santísima Trinidad* (Spanish, 136-gun, Rear Admiral Baltasar Hidalgo de Cisneros, Commodore Francisco de Uriarte y Borja)
12. *Bucentaure* (French, 80-gun, Vice Admiral Pierre-Charles-Jean-Baptiste-Silvestre de Villeneuve, Captain Jean-Jacques Magendie)
13. *Redoutable* (French, 74-gun, Captain Jean-Jacques-Etienne Lucas)
14. *San Justo* (Spanish, 74-gun, Captain Miguel Gastón)

15. *Neptune* (French, 80-gun, Commodore Esprit-Tranquille Maistral)
16. *San Leandro* (Spanish, 64-gun, Captain José Quevedo y Cheza)
17. *Santa Ana* (Spanish, 112-gun, Vice Admiral Ignacio María de Álava y Navarrete, Captain José Gardoquí)
18. *Indomptable* (French, 80-gun, Commodore Jean-Joseph Hubert)
19. *Fougueux* (French, 74-gun, Captain Louis-Alexis Beaudouin)
20. *Pluton* (French, 74-gun, Commodore Julien-Marie Cosmao-Kerjulien)
21. *Monarca* (Spanish, 74-gun, Captain Teodoro de Argumosa)
22. *Algésiras* (French, 74-gun, Rear Admiral Charles-René Magon, Captain Gabriel-Auguste Brouard)
23. *Bahama* (Spanish, 74-gun, Commodore Dionisio Alcalá Galiano)
24. *Aigle* (French, 74-gun, Captain Pierre-Paul Gourrège)
25. *Montañes* (Spanish, 74-gun, Captain Francisco Alcedo)
26. *Swift-sure* (French, 74-gun, Captain C. E. L'Hospitalier-Villemadrin)
27. *Argonaute* (French, 74-gun, Captain Jacques Epron)
28. *Argonauta* (Spanish, 80-gun, Captain Antonio Pareja)
29. *San Ildefonso* (Spanish, 74-gun, Captain José de Vargas)
30. *Achille* (French, 74-gun, Captain Gabriel Denieport)
31. *Principe de Asturias* (Spanish, 112-gun, Admiral Federico Carlos Gravina, Rear-Admiral Antonio de Escaño, Captain Rafael de Hore)
32. *Berwick* (French, 74-gun, Captain Jean-Gilles Filhol-Camas)
33. *San Juan Nepomuceno* (Spanish, 74-gun, Captain Cosmé Damian Churruca)

There were five frigates attached to the Combined Fleet: *Cornélie*, *Hermione*, *Hortense*, *Rhin* (all 40-gun) and *Thémis* (32-gun); and two brigs, *Argus* and *Furet*.

The Royal Navy at Trafalgar

The Windward (Nelson's) Flotilla
1. *Victory* (100-gun, Vice Admiral Lord Nelson, Captain Thomas Masterman Hardy)
2. *Téméraire* (98-gun, Captain Eliab Harvey)
3. *Neptune* (98-gun, Captain Thomas Francis Fremantle)

4. *Leviathan* (74-gun, Captain Henry William Bayntun)
5. *Conqueror* (74-gun, Captain Israel Pellew)
6. *Britannia* (100-gun, Rear Admiral the Earl of Northesk, Captain Charles Bullen)
7. *Spartiate* (74-gun, Captain Sir Francis Laforey)
8. *Minotaur* (74-gun, Captain Charles John Moore Mansfield)
9. *Ajax* (74-gun, Lieutenant John Pilford, acting captain)
10. *Agamemnon* (64-gun, Captain Sir Edward Berry)
11. *Orion* (74-gun, Captain Edward Codrington, out of formation)
12. *Africa* (64-gun, Captain Henry Digby, out of formation)

The Leeward (Collingwood's) Flotilla
1. *Royal Sovereign* (100-gun, Vice Admiral Cuthbert Collingwood, Captain Edward Rotheram)
2. *Belleisle* (74-gun, Captain William Hargood)
3. *Mars* (74-gun, Captain George Duff)
4. *Tonnant* (80-gun, Captain Charles Tyler)
5. *Bellerophon* (74-gun, Captain John Cooke)
6. *Colossus* (74-gun, Captain James Nicoll Morris)
7. *Achilles* (74-gun, Captain Richard King)
8. *Defence* (74-gun, Captain George Hope)
9. *Defiance* (74-gun, Captain Philip Charles Durham)
10. *Prince* (98-gun, Captain Richard Grindall)
11. *Dreadnought* (98-gun, Captain John Conn)
12. *Revenge* (74-gun, Captain Robert Moorsom)
13. *Swiftsure* (74-gun, Captain William George Rutherford)
14. *Thunderer* (74-gun, Lieutenant John Stockham, acting captain)
15. *Polyphemus* (64-gun, Captain Robert Redmill)

The British frigates included *Euryalus* (Captain the Hon. Henry Blackwood), *Naiad* (Captain Thomas Dundas), *Phoebe* (Captain the Hon. Thomas Bladen Capel), *Sirius* (Captain William Prowse) and *Juno* (which was not present at the battle). Lieutenant John Lapenotière commanded the schooner *Pickle* and Lieutenant Robert Benjamin Young the cutter *Entreprenante*.

The Main Characters

ADDINGTON, Henry, first Viscount Sidmouth (1757–1844) Unsuccessful prime minister 1801–1804.

ALLEMAND, Zacharie Jacques Théodore (1762–1826) French squadron commander at Rochefort.

ARGUMOSA, Teodoro de (1743–?) Captain of the *Monarca*, wounded at Trafalgar.

AUGEREAU, Pierre François Charles (1757–1816) French commander in charge of invasion preparations.

BARBÉ-MARBOIS, François (1745–1837) Head of virtually bankrupt French treasury.

BARHAM, Lord, Sir Charles Middleton (1726–1813) First Lord of the Admiralty at the time of Trafalgar.

BAYNTUN, Henry William (1766–1840) Captain of the *Leviathan* at Trafalgar.

BEDFORD, John (*c.*1764–1827) Assumed command of the *Tonnant* when Captain Tyler was serious wounded.

BERTHIER, Louis Alexandre (1753–1815) Overall commander of the French invasion plan.

BEURNONVILLE, Pierre de Ruel (1752–1821) French ambassador to Madrid who did not tell Villeneuve that he was to be replaced.

BLACKWOOD, Sir Henry (1770–1832) Excellent and faithful captain trusted by Nelson.

BONAPARTE, Napoleon (1769–1821) First Consul and later Emperor of France.

BRERETON Robert (?–1818) British military commander in the West Indies, detested by Nelson.

BRUIX, Eustace de (1759–1805) Commander in Chief of the French invasion flotilla until death in March 1805.

CAJIGAL, Felipe Jado Captain of the *San Agustín*, wounded at Trafalgar.

CALDER, Sir Robert (1745–1818) Should have defeated the Combined Fleet when he had the chance in July 1805 – there would then have been no Trafalgar.

CANNING, George (1770–1827) Follower of Pitt and future prime minister.

CASTLEREAGH, Robert Steward, Viscount (1769–1822) War secretary 1805–1806 and eventually foreign secretary. Committed suicide.

CISNEROS, Báltasar Hidalgo de (1770–?) Spanish squadron commander wounded at Trafalgar.

CLARENCE, Duke of (1765–1837) Sailor patron of Nelson and later King William IV.

COCHRANE, Sir Alexander (1758–1832) Squadron commander off El Ferrol.

CODRINGTON, Edward (1770–1851) Captain of the *Orion* at Trafalgar.

COLLINGWOOD, Cuthbert (1750–1810) Nelson's deputy at Trafalgar.

COOKE, John (1763–1805). Captain of the *Bellerophon*, killed at Trafalgar.

CORNWALLIS, Sir William (1744–1819) Commander-in-chief Channel Fleet who masterfully conducted blockade of Brest which did more than any other naval operation to frustrate Napoleon's attempt to invade England.

COTTON, Sir Charles (1753–1812) Cornwallis's deputy.

CUMBY, William Pryce (1771–1837) Assumed command of the *Bellerophon* when Captain Cooke was killed at Trafalgar.

DECRÈS, Denis (1761–1820) French naval minister, champion of Villeneuve.

DIGBY, Henry (1770–1842) Captain of the *Africa* at Trafalgar.

DUFF, George (1764–1805) Captain of the *Mars*, killed at Trafalgar.

DUMANOIR LE PELLEY, Pierre (1770–1829) Villeneuve's deputy who, defying his commander's orders, sailed away with his squadron, so making the Combined Fleet even more vulnerable.

DUNDAS, Sir David (1735–1820) Land commander in south-east England.

DUNDAS, Henry, First Viscount Melville (1742–1811) First Lord of Admiralty who was forced to resign following charges of corruption.

DURHAM, Philip Charles (1763–1845) Captain of the *Defiance*, wounded at Trafalgar.

ELPHINSTONE, George Keith, Viscount Keith (1746–1823) Noted commander of the Downs squadron in the English Channel facing the French.

FORFAIT, Pierre Alexandre Laurent (1752–1807) Designer of flat-bottomed vessels for the French invasion fleet.

FOX, Charles James (1749–1806) British MP who opposed the war.

FREMANTLE, Thomas Francis (1765–1819) Captain of the *Neptune* at Trafalgar.

FULTON, Robert (1765–1815) American inventor of the submarine, which he demonstrated to the French and British with no success.

GANTEAUME, Honoré Joseph Antoine (1755–1818) Succeeded Admiral Truguet as Fleet Commander at Brest, 1804–1805.

GARDNER, Alan, Lord (1742–1809) Commander of the Channel Fleet while Cornwallis was ashore.

GEORGE III (1738–1820) King of England at the time of Trafalgar.

GOURDON, Adrien Louis (1765–1805) Captain of the *Aigle*, killed at Trafalgar.

GRAVES, Sir Thomas (1747–1814) Subordinate commander to Cornwallis.

GRAVINA, Federico Carlos (1758–1806) Judged to be an excellent admiral and deputy to Villeneuve. Died of his Trafalgar wounds.

HAMILTON, Lady Emma Lyon (*c.*1765–1815) Nelson's common-law wife by whom he had a daughter, Horatia.

HARDY, Thomas Masterman (1769–1839) Captain of the *Victory* at Trafalgar.

HARGOOD, William (1762–1839) Captain of the *Belleisle* at Trafalgar.

HARVEY, Eliab (1758–1830) Captain of the *Téméraire* at Trafalgar.

LACROSSE, Jean-Baptiste Raymond (1765–1829) From March 1805 Commander-in-chief of the French invasion fleet.

LAPENOTIÈRE, John Richards (1770–1834) Captain of the *Pickle*, which carried the news of Trafalgar and Nelson's death to England.

LATOUCHE-TRÉVILLE, Louis Levassor de (1745–1804) Sometime inspired naval tactician whose death in August 1804 led to the luckless Villeneuve being made commander of the Toulon fleet.

LAURISTON, Jacques (1768–1828) Troops commander in Villeneuve's fleet and the admiral's severest critic.

LE ROY, Commissaire Général des Relations Commerciales at Cadiz in 1805.

LUCAS, Jean Jacques Étienne (1764–1819) Captain of *Redoutable*. Wounded at Trafalgar and much admired by the British as well as by Napoleon.

MAGON DE MÉDICINE, Charles René (1763–1805) Admiral killed aboard the *Algésiras*.

MAISTRAL, Esprit-Tranquille (1763–1815) Captain of the *Neptune*.

MARSDEN, William (1754–1836) Naval secretary at the time of Trafalgar.

MISSIESSY, Edouard Thomas de Burgues (1756–1837) First-class French admiral, little recognized by Napoleon.

MOORE, Graham (1764–1843) Captain of the *Indefatigable*.

NELSON, Horatio, Viscount (1758–1805).

NEY, Michel (1769–1815) French army commander.

NORTHESK, Earl of, William Carnegie (1758–1831) Commander at Trafalgar who saw little action.

ORDE, Sir John (1751–1824) British admiral who was jealous of Nelson and omitted to give him the information that Villeneuve and Gravina had escaped to West Indies.

PAREJA, Antonio (?–1813) Captain of *Argonauta* who survived his dreadful wounds at Trafalgar.

PELLEW, Sir Edward (1757–1833) Captain of *Conqueror*, in which he fought with distinction at Trafalgar.

PELLEW, Israel (1758–1832) one of Cornwallis's commodores off Finisterre.

PITT, William (1759–1806) Prime minister of Britain at the time of Trafalgar.

PIUS VII (1742–1823) Pope, 1800–1823.

REDMILL, Robert (?–1819) Captain of the *Polyphemus* at Trafalgar.

ROSILY, François (1748–1832) Appointed to take Villeneuve's command.

ROTHERAM, Edward (1753–1830) Captain of the *Royal Sovereign* at Trafalgar.

ST VINCENT, Earl, John Jervis (1735–1823) First Lord of the Admiralty.

SOULT, Nicolas Jean De Dieu (1769–1851) Had command of the French invasion army 1803–1805.

STIRLING, Charles (1760–1833) Subordinate commander to Cornwallis.

TALLEYRAND-PÉRIGORD, Charles de, Prince (1754–1838) Napoleon's foreign minister until 1814.

TYLER, Charles (1760–1835) Captain of the *Tonnant*. Wounded at Trafalgar.

VARGAS, José De (1769–?) Captain of the *San Ildefonso*, wounded at Trafalgar.

VILLENEUVE, Pierre Charles (1763–1806) Commanded the Combined Fleet at Trafalgar and later either committed suicide or was murdered ashore.

Bibliography

Albion, R. G., *Forests and Sea Power, The Timber Problem of the Royal Navy, 1652–1862*. Hamden, Connecticut, 1965.

Allen, Joseph, *The Life of Viscount Nelson*. G. Routledge & Co., London, 1853.

Annual Register (The) or a View of the History of Politics and Literature for the year 1805. Printed for W. Otridge & Son & Others, London, 1807.

Ayling, Stanley, *George The Third*. Collins, London, 1972.

Baker, Norman, *Government and Contractors: The British Treasury and War Supplies, 1775–1783*. Athlone Press, London, 1971.

Beatty, Sir William, *The Authentic Narrative of the Death of Lord Nelson*. T. Cadell, London, 1807.

Beresford, Lord Charles, and Wilson, H. W., *Nelson and His Times*. 12 parts. Harmsworth Brothers, London, 1897–8.

Berthaut, Jules, *Manuel du Chef: Maximes Napoléoniennes*. Payot, Paris, 1919.

Bingham, D.A., *A Selection from the Letters of the First Napoleon*. Vol. 2, Chapman & Hall, London, 1884.

Black, J., and Woodfine, P., (eds.), *The British Navy and the Use of Naval Power in the 18th Century*. Leicester University Press, Leicester, 1988.

Bowen, Marjorie, *Patriotic Lady: A Study of Emma, Lady Hamilton and the Neapolitan Revolution of 1799*. John Lane, London, 1935.

Bradford, Ernie, *Nelson: The Essential Hero*. Macmillan, London, 1977.

Broadley, A. M., and Bartelot, R. G., *Nelson's Hardy: His Life, Letters and Friends*. John Murray, London, 1909.

Bruce, H.A. (ed.), *Life of General Sir William Napier.* John Murray, London, 1864.

Castelot, André, *Napoleon.* Harper & Row, London, 1971

Charnock, John, *Biographical Memoirs of Lord Viscount Nelson.* H. D. Symonds, London, 1806.

Chevalier, E., *Histoire de la Marine Française sous le Consulat et l'Empire.* Paris, 1886.

Clarke, James Stanier, and M'Arthur, John, *The Life of Admiral Lord Nelson K. B. from his Lordship's Manuscripts.* 2 Vols. T. Cadell & W. Davies, London, 1809.

Cleveland, Duchess of, *The Life and Letters of Lady Hester Stanhope.* John Murray, London, 1914.

Colley, Linda, *Britons: Forging the Nation, 1707–1837.* Yale University Press, New Haven, Connecticut, 1992.

Collingwood, Cuthbert, Lord, *The Private Correspondence of Admiral Lord Collingwood.*, ed. Edward Hughes. Vol. XCVIII. Navy Records Society, London, 1957.

Constant, Louis, *Mémoires de Constant, premier valet de chambre de l'Empereur sur la vie privée de Napoléon, sa famille et sa cour.* Vol. 2. Lavocat, Paris, 1830.

Corbett, Sir Julian, *The Campaign of Trafalgar.* Longmans, London, 1910.

Cornwallis, Marquis, *The Correspondence of Charles First Marquis Cornwallis.* Vols 2 & 3, John Murray, London, 1859.

Cornwallis-West, G., *The Life and Letters of Admiral Cornwallis.* Robert Holden & Co. Ltd, London, 1927.

Courtney, Nicholas, *Gale Force 10.* Review, London, 2002.

Desbrière, Edouard, *The Naval Campaign of 1805*, trans. Constance Eastwick. 2 Vols. Clarendon Press, Oxford, 1933.

Earle, Peter, *Sailors, English Merchant Seamen 1650–1775.* Methuen & Co., London, 1998.

Fauvelet de Bourrienne, *Mémoires.* Translation, Vol. 1, Hutchinson, London, 1885.

Forder, Charles, *A History of the Paston School.* Paston Grammar School, North Walsham, 1975.

Fraser, Edward, *The Sailors Whom Nelson Led: Their Doings Described by Themselves.* Methuen & Co., London, 1913.

Fraser, Flora, *Beloved Emma: The Life of Emma, Lady Hamilton*. Weidenfeld & Nicolson, London, 1986.

Gagnon, *France since 1789*. Harper & Row, 1972.

Gentleman's Magazine, 1804, 1805.

Haig, William, *William Pitt the Younger: A Biography*. HarperCollins, London, 2004.

Harbron, John, *Trafalgar and the Spanish Navy*. Conway, London, 1988.

Harcourt, Levenson Vernon (ed.), *The Diaries and Correspondence of the Right Honourable George Rose, containing original letters of the most distinguished statesman of his day*. Bentley, London, 1860.

Harrison, James, *The Life of the Right Honourable Horatio, Lord Viscount Nelson*. 2 vols. London, 1806.

Hattersley, Roy, *Nelson*. Weidenfeld & Nicolson, London, 1974.

Hill, Richard, *The Prizes of War*. Sutton, Stroud, 1998.

Horne, Alistair, *How Far From Austerlitz?* Macmillan, London, 1886.

Hough, Richard, *Nelson*. Park Lane Press, 506, London, 1980.

Howarth, David, *Trafalgar: The Nelson Touch*. Collins, London, 1969.

Howarth, David and Stephen, *Nelson: The Immortal Memory*. Dent, London, 1988.

James, William, *The Naval History of Great Britain from the Declaration of War by France in 1793, to the Accession of George IV*. Vols. 3 and 4. Bentley, London, 1837.

James, William, *Old Oak, The Life of John Jervis, Earl of St. Vincent*. Longmans, Green & Co., London, 1950.

Keate, E. M., *Nelson's Wife*. Cassell & Co., London, 1939.

Keevil, John Joyce, *Medicine and the Navy*. 4 Vols. E. & S. Livingstone, Edinburgh and London, 1957–63.

Laughton, Sir John Knox, *Letters and Despatches of Horatio, Viscount Nelson*. Longmans, Green & Co., London, 1886.

Laughton, Sir John Knox (ed.), *Letters and Papers of Charles, Lord Barham 1758–1813*. 3 Vols. London, 1907.

Laughton, Sir John Knox, (ed.),*The Naval Miscellany*. Vols. 1 & 2. Vols. XX and XL, Navy Records Society, London, 1901.

Laughton, Sir John Knox, *The Nelson Memorial: Nelson and His Companions in Arms*. George Allen, London, 1896.

Lavery, Brian, *Nelson's Navy, The Ships, Men and Organisation, 1793–1815*. Conway, London, 1989.

Lavery, Brian, *The Arming and Fitting of English Ships of War, 1600–1815*. Conway, London, 1987.

Lee, Christopher, *This Sceptred Isle: The Empire*. BBC Books, London, 2005.

Legg, Stuart (ed.), *Trafalgar: An Eye-witness Account of a Great Battle*. Hart-Davis, London, 1966.

Leyland, John (ed.) *Dispatches and Letters Relating to the Blockade of Brest, 1803–1805*, 2 vols. Navy Records Society, London, 1899, 1902.

Mahan, A. T., *The Life of Nelson, the Embodiment of the Sea Power of Great Britain*. 2 vols. Sampson, Low & Co., London, 1897.

Maine, René, *Trafalgar, Napoleon's Naval Waterloo*, trans. Rita Eldon and B. W. Robinson. Thames & Hudson, London, 1957.

Malmesbury, 3rd Earl of, *Diaries and Correspondence of James Harris, First Earl of Malmesbury*. 4 vols. Bentley, London, 1844.

Mark, William, *At Sea with Nelson, being the Life of William Mark, a Purser who Served under Admiral Lord Nelson*. Sampson, Low & Co., London, 1929.

Markham, Clements (ed.), *Selections from the Correspondence of Admiral John Markham*. Navy Records Society, London, 1904.

Marsden, William, *A Brief Memoir of the Life and Writings of William Marsden*. Privately printed, London, 1838.

Masson, Philippe, *Les Sépulcres Flottants Prisonniers français en Angleterre sous l'Empire*. Rennes, 1987.

Matheson, Cyril, *The Life of Henry Dundas, First Viscount Melville 1742–1811*. Constable, London, 1933.

Mowat, R. B., *The Diplomacy of Napoleon*. Arnold, London, 1924.

Murray, Geoffrey, *The Life of Admiral Collingwood*. Hutchinson, London, 1936.

Nicolas, Sir Harris (ed.), *Dispatches and Letters of Vice-Admiral Lord Viscount Nelson*. 7 vols. Henry Colburn, London, 1844–6. Republished by Chatham Publishing, London, 1990.

Oliver, J. and Kington, J. A., 'The Usefulness of Ships' Log-Books in the Symoptic Analysis of Past Climates' in *Weather Journal*, 1970.

Pocock, Tom, *Horatio Nelson*. Headline, London, 1987.

Pope, Dudley, *England Expects*. London, 1960.

Pope, Dudley, *Life in Nelson's Navy*. Naval Institute Press, Md., 1981.

Popham, Sir Home, *Telegraphic Signals or Marine Vocabulary*. London, 1803.

Public Record Office, Foreign Relations, Kew: France FO 27; Spain FO 72, 185, 186; Portugal FO 63; Miscellaneous FO 148.

Raigersfeld, Jeffrey, Baron de, *The Life of a Sea Officer*. Kent Arms Press, c. 1830.

Robinson, William, 'Jack Nastyface', *Nautical Economy or Forecastle Recollections of Events during the last War, dedicated to the Brave Tars of Old England, by a Sailor politicely called by the Officers of the Nacy, Jack Nasty-face*. London, 1836.

Rose, J. Holland, and Broadley, A.M. *Dumouriez and the Defence of England against Napoleon*. John Lane, London, 1904.

Russell, Jack, *Nelson and the Hamiltons*. Anthony Blond, London, 1969.

Schom, Alan, *Trafalgar*. Michael Joseph, London, 1990.

Southey, Robert, *The Life of Horatio Lord Nelson*. 2 vols. John Murray, London, 1813.

Southey, Robert, *Southey's Life of Nelson*, ed. Sir Geoffrey Callender. J. M. Dent & Sons, London, 1922.

Stanhope, Lady Hester, *Memoirs of the Lady Hester Stanhope, as related by Herself in conversations with her Physician*. Vol. 2. Colburn, London, 1845.

Syrett, David, and others, *The Commissioned Sea Officers of the Royal Navy 1660–1815*. Navy Records Society, London, 1994.

Terraine, John, *Trafalgar*. Sidgwick & Jackson, London, 1975.

The Times newspaper 1804–1805.

Tucker, J. S., *Memoirs of the Earl St Vincent*. Vol. 1, p. 297. R. Bentley, London, 1884.

Walder, David, *Nelson*. Hamish Hamilton, London, 1978.

Wardropper, John, *Kings, Lords and Wicked Libellers, Satire and Protest 1760–1837*. John Murray, London, 1973.

Warner, Oliver, *The Battle of the Nile*. B. T. Batsford, London, 1960.

Warner, Oliver, *Trafalgar*. B. T. Batsford, London, 1959.

Watson, J. Steven, *The Reign of George III, 1760–1815*. Clarendon Press, Oxford, 1985.

Wheeler, Dennis A., 'The Weather at the Battle of Trafalgar, 21 October 1805: A forecast reconstruction' in the *Journal of Meterology*, Vol. 23, no. 232, October 1998.

Wheeler, H. F. B., and Broadley, A. M., *Napoleon and the Invasion of England, the Story of the Great Terror*. Vol. 2. John Lane, London, 1908.

Winton, John, *Hurrah for the Life of a Sailor*, Michael Joseph, London, 1977.

Index

Note: 'HN' denotes Horatio Nelson. Page numbers in *italic* indicate references outside of the main text. A subscript number appended to a page number indicates a footnote, a subscript 'c' indicates a chart. The following ship prefixes have been used: HMS (British ships), FS (French ships), SPS (Spanish ships).